Overland In 1846

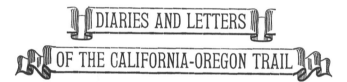

DIARIES AND LETTERS
OF THE CALIFORNIA-OREGON TRAIL

Overland In 1846

DIARIES AND LETTERS
OF THE CALIFORNIA-OREGON TRAIL

Volume II

EDITED BY
DALE MORGAN

University of Nebraska Press
Lincoln and London

© 1963 by Dale Morgan
Manufactured in the United States of America

First Bison Book printing: 1993
Most recent printing indicated by the last digit below:
10   9   8   7   6   5   4   3   2   1

Library of Congress Cataloging-in-Publication Data
Overland in 1846: dieraies and letters of the California-Oregon
trail / edited by Dale Morgan.
p.   cm.
Originally published: Georgetown, CA: Talisman Press, 1963.
ISBN 0-8032-3176-8 (cloth: v. 1). — ISBN 0-8032-8200-1 (pbk.: v. 1). —
ISBN 0-8032-3178-4 (cloth: set). — ISBN 0-8032-3177-6 (cloth: v. 2). —
ISBN 0-8032-8201-X (pbk.: v. 2). — ISBN 0-8032-8202-8 (pbk.: set)
1. West (U.S.)—Description and travel—To 1848.   2. Pioneers—West
(U.S.)—Diaries.   3. Oregon Trail.   4. California Trail.   5. Overland
journeys to the Pacific.   I. Morgan, Dale Lowell, 1914–1971.
F592.094   1994
978'.02—dc20
93-8247   CIP

Reprinted from the original edition published by the Talisman Press,
Georgetown, California, in 1963.

∞

Contents

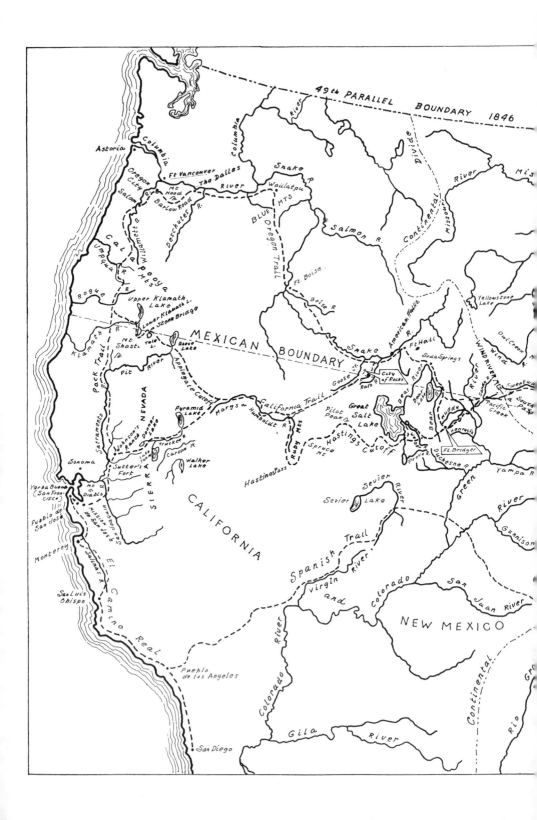

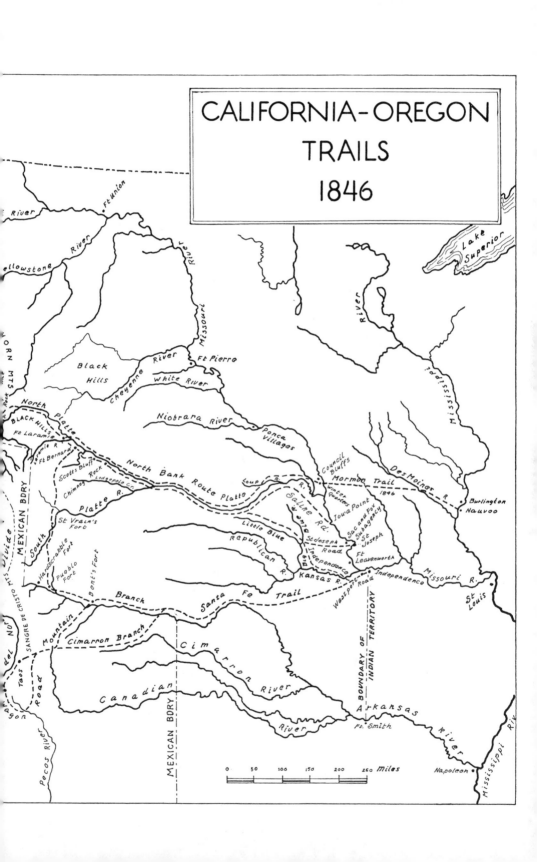

CALIFORNIA-OREGON
TRAILS
1846

"The Overland Route"

Introduction

The overland emigration of 1846 to Oregon and California was self-willed, contentious, and cantankerous. It was also large, sprawling, energetic, confused, and confusing, and these characteristics will doubtless make the strongest initial impression upon readers who by this volume are carried back to the year 1846. Since the emigration describes itself, the viewpoint continually shifts and changes. Now the newspapers speak up; now the emigrants have their say, and from different places at different times. Underneath the surface flow of event, however, is the iron discipline of time, and very quickly, I believe, readers will begin to see pattern and progression.

Our story begins at an unlikely point, the mouth of the Arkansas River, with D. G. W. Leavitt making what can fairly be called Napoleonic pronouncements preliminary to starting off to California. Where Leavitt came from, and what became of him finally, is for the future to disclose. In the history of 1846 he is a truly eccentric figure, for Arkansas was his base, and he proposed to reach California not via South Pass but by way of Santa Fe. He intended to travel the Spanish Trail, and with a following which at one time was expected to approximate a thousand souls. That Leavitt intended to take a good-sized company to California from Arkansas, because mentioned in *Niles' Register,* attracted attention from H. H. Bancroft, almost alone among historians of California and the overland trails. But only now may it be seen that Leavitt actually succeeded in getting off—if with a party which in the end numbered no more than 11 men—and what is more, that he reached Santa Fe so as to write a letter from there, and that he started on from Santa Fe. After that? Perhaps we can compel Leavitt to account for himself by beginning a record. Even if he and his men disappeared without trace in the upset occasioned by the Mexican War, that fact will yet be established.

From Leavitt in Arkansas, our attention shifts to James M. Maxey, advising James Frazier Reed from Independence, Missouri, one of the key localities in the history of 1846; and after that the scene rapidly broadens, as one Missouri personality or community after another is seen to address the shaping emigration. On the frontier, contention was for primacy in leading companies or as outfitting points. St. Louis, sufficiently removed to have a certain detachment, yet stirred by the same emotions that were creating the emigration, benignly contemplated and reported the spectacle as it developed.

Much else was in the air in 1846; above all the war with Mexico that came on after a late-April clash on the Rio Grande. Since Colonel (soon Brigadier General) Stephen W. Kearny at Fort Leavenworth was ordered to march upon New Mexico even as the last emigrants were leaving Independence and St. Joseph, the Santa Fe Trail staged a full-blown spectacle of its own. The Missouri newspapers had an enthralling time reporting war and rumors of war in Texas and New Mexico. Considering the demands upon their space by the war, it is surprising how much was printed concerning the emigration.

Very early the overland emigrants began to speak for themselves, and as our narrative gets under way, we develop a kinship with particular correspondents. Since it has seemed best in this volume to develop the story on an essentially chronological basis, the various letters are printed according to their date. The advantages of so organizing the record are obvious, but it becomes desirable to say something here, concerning the principal letter-writers. Those interested in various correspondents may read their letters consecutively by referring to their dates.

Biographical notes should begin with the original commander of the best-known company to take the trail in 1846. William Henry Russell, sometimes confused with William Hepburn Russell of Pony Express fame, was born in Nicholas County, Kentucky, on October 9, 1802. According to the sketch by W. J. Ghent in *Dictionary of American Biography,* he practised law in Nicholas County and in 1830 represented it in the legislature, at about that time marrying Zanette Freeland of Baltimore. "He early came to the attention of Henry Clay, who befriended him, and it is said that for a time he was Clay's secretary. . . . He was a large man, expansive in manner, boastful and bombastic in speech. His egotism sometimes made him the sport of his companions. In a story often told about him, he is said to have mistaken the chorus of 'tu-whoo's' from a flock of owls for a challenge of 'Who are you?' and to have thundered back, 'Col. William H. Russell, of Kentucky—a bosom friend of Henry Clay!' Ever after he was known as 'Owl' Russell. He was, however, a man of many substantial and endearing qualities, and was widely popular."

Ghent relates further that in 1831 Russell emigrated to Callaway County, Missouri. Next year he served in the Black Hawk War. In 1841 Russell was appointed U. S. Marshal for the District of Missouri, which included the Indian country, serving until 1845. Sometime during these years he acquired the courtesy title of "Colonel." In these pages, we follow him to California. After reaching Monterey, Russell served in Fremont's California Battalion with the rank of major. He helped to frame the treaty of Cahuenga on January 13, 1847, and afterward Fremont as Acting Governor appointed him Secretary of State. Upon the demise of the Fremont administration, Russell set out for home via the southern route, reaching Missouri in July, 1847, then going on to Washington. He was a principal witness for Fremont in the celebrated court-martial next winter. Returning to California overland in 1849, Russell practised law at San Jose and elsewhere. In 1861 he was appointed U. S. consul at Trinidad, Cuba, and in 1867 sought to be named consul-general at Havana. He died in Washington, D. C., October 13, 1873.

Six letters by Russell, characteristically addressed to newspapers, are printed in this volume. Five were written along the trail, on May 10, May 18-19, May 19, June 13, and July 12. Only the last was composed after he resigned as captain of the company. A letter of January 26, 1847, describes in general terms his experiences to that time. These letters exhibit his nature — his energy, his vanity, his politician's arts, his qualities of leadership— and add much to the trail chronicle of 1846.

A companion of Russell's as far as Fort Bridger was George Law Curry, represented in this volume with a dozen letters addressed to the St. Louis *Reveille,* mostly over his pseudonym "Laon." Born at Philadelphia on July 2, 1820, at the age of 11 Curry was apprenticed to the printer's trade. Robert C. Clark remarks in

Dictionary of American Biography that Curry attended school only three months, but his writings attest "that he became a well-educated man through reading and study. When eighteen he was elected and served two terms as president of the Mechanic Apprentices' Library Association of Boston." Another biographical sketch printed in Oregon Pioneer Association *Transactions,* 1878, says: "In 1843, he became a resident of St. Louis, where he became acquainted with Joseph M. Field, the actor and manager (father of Miss Kate Field), and connected himself with him in the publication of the *Reveille,* which publication also had as inaugurators at that time, Col. Charles Keemle and Mat., brother of Joseph Field ('Straws' and 'Phazma' of the *N. O. Picayune.*)"

Considerations of health induced Curry to go West in 1846. The *Reveille* was very Western-minded, as our pages make abundantly clear, but Curry may have got nothing out of his letters other than the satisfaction of having them printed. These letters consist of two on April 23, others on April 28, 29, May 6, 11, 15, 19, June 12, 16, 25-26—these carrying him as far west as Fort Laramie—and one of July 12 written (like Russell's of the same date) from the upper Sweetwater. Curry was then traveling in the Russell pack party, in which he continued as far as Fort Bridger. Although the *Reveille* was sanguine that Curry would go on to California even if he had to go alone, at Fort Bridger he altered his mind. Edwin Bryant relates the circumstances on July 18, two days after reaching the fort:

"We determined, this morning, to take the new route [Hastings Cutoff], via the south end of the great Salt Lake. Mr. Hudspeth—who with a small party, on Monday, will start in advance of the emigrant companies which intend travelling by this route, for the purpose of making some further explorations—has volunteered to guide us as far as the Salt Plain, a day's journey west of the Lake. Although such was my own determination, I wrote several letters to my friends among the emigrant parties in the rear, advising them *not* to take this route, but to keep on the old trail, via Fort Hall. Our situation was different from theirs. We were mounted on mules, had no families, and could afford to hazard experiments, and make explorations. They could not. . . . Messrs. Curry and [R. H.] Holder left us to-day, having determined to go to Oregon instead of California."

Other emigrants sent back letters from Fort Bridger, including the unknown correspondent whose communication of July 23 mentioning Curry's continuing bad health is printed herein. But whether from physical weakness or some malaise of the spirit, Curry wrote no more letters, not from Fort Bridger or Fort Hall, nor from Oregon City after reaching the Willamette Valley. On arrival via the new Barlow Road, Curry was installed as editor of the *Oregon Spectator,* which may have afforded him a sufficient literary outlet. In this capacity Curry occasionally appears in the latter part of this volume, but in the *Spectator* he had little to say about his personal experiences, beyond an overly "literary" contribution about his last camp in the Cascade Mountains, one which I have not thought fit to reprint.

We see on a later page how Curry, as editor of the *Spectator,* first became embroiled in the controversies relating to J. Quinn Thornton. Eventually, in January, 1848, Curry was dismissed from the editorial post. Two months later he founded his own *Oregon Free Press*; and in that same month married Chloe Donnelly Boone, daughter of Alphonso Boone. The *Free Press* died with the California Gold Rush, and for the rest of his life Curry was a farmer. But he also continued active in public life.

Concerning his later years, Clark writes: "After serving as a member of the legislature of the provisional government (1848-49), as chief clerk of the Territorial Council (1850-51), and as member of the lower house of the legislature (1851-52), he was appointed secretary of the territory in 1853. He acted as governor from May to

December 1853, until the arrival of Gov. John W. Davis, and was appointed governor when the latter retired in August 1854. Curry's appointment gave great satisfaction because he was a resident of the territory. Besides, he was *persona grata* with the 'Salem Clique' a group of Democratic leaders, who . . . dominated affairs and directed governmental policies. He is best remembered for his part in vigorously defending the settlers against the Indians in 1855." After serving as Oregon's last territorial governor, Curry came within one vote of being elected U. S. Senator in 1860. He died at his farm home near Oregon City on July 28, 1878. That Curry contributed a notable series of letters to the *Reveille* from the California-Oregon Trail in 1846 was long forgotten. The present volume, by reprinting these letters, restores a lost chapter to his life.

Next among our principal correspondents are the brothers Nathan J. and Charles F. Putnam. The elder brother did not long survive the journey. An obituary by W. J. Bailey in the *Oregon Spectator,* June 10, 1847, says in part:

"DIED—suddenly, at my residence near the Willamette, on the 30th of May, of disease of the heart, Mr. NATHAN JAMES PUTNAM, aged 25 years—son of JOSEPH PUTNAM, of Lexington, Kentucky. He left his home in the Spring of '46, principally for the benefit of his health, and arrived in this country last November, by the Southern route. On account of great sufferings and exposures which befell him on the road, his disease became so confirmed that it was not in the power of medicine nor art to restore him. Mr. Putnam was a gentleman of rare worth—possessing uncommon strength of mind and mental capacity, and he greatly endeared himself to us by his social embellishments—his moral rectitude—his intelligence—his gentlemanly deportment and the propriety of his manners, all of which he maintained to the last moment of his existence. During life he had been doubtful of the truth of divine revelation, but in his last illness he began to perceive his error on reading 'Incidents of travel in the Holy Land,' and pursuing a search for truth, he was led to acknowledge himself a 'believer in the Scriptures—in God—in Jesus Christ and in the Holy Ghost,' and often spoke of the comfort he experienced in having the Bible and religious books read to him. He was anxious to make a public profession of religion by being baptised and partaking of the Lord's Supper, but he was prevented by his sudden removal. . . ."

Commenting on this "touching tribute to the memory of an esteemed friend," Editor Curry remarked, "We traveled in company with the deceased, a great portion of the journey from the Missouri settlements to this country, and shall ever bear in remembrance the many virtues of our deceased friend. . . ."

The younger brother was born in Lexington, Kentucky, July 7, 1824. George Himes, writing in the Oregon Historical Society *Quarterly* for September, 1902, at a time when Charles F. Putnam was still alive though in feeble health, residing near the town of Drain, says that Charles learned the printer's trade in New York City. After coming to Oregon in 1846 he settled in Polk County, marrying Jesse Applegate's daughter, Rozelle. In 1848 he began printing the short-lived *Oregon American and Evangelical Unionist* for John Griffin, one of the earliest Oregon periodicals. In the fall of 1849 he removed to the Umpqua Valley, settling near Mount Yoncalla. A number of letters written by his wife to her family and her husband's parents from that locality, 1849-1852, have been printed in Oregon Historical Society *Quarterly,* September, 1928.

The letters of 1846, preserved in the Oregon Historical Society Library, were printed in part, edited by Sheba Hargreaves, in *The Frontier,* November, 1928, pp. 56-62. These nine communications are dated April 11, May 6, 11 (two), June 10, 17, July 11 (two), and August 8. The correspondence breaks off at Fort Hall, in time to mention the appearance of Jesse Applegate from the

Willamette Valley, but too early to report that Charles decided to accompany Applegate's party back to the settlements.

Many references to the Putnam brothers occur in the trail records of 1846—in Bryant's journal, McKinstry's diary, and Thornton's journal, among others. In this volume the brothers tell their own tale, first in the Russell company as part of the California emigration, subsequently as emigrants who had made the decision for Oregon. Neither returned home to bring out their parents, but Joseph and Susan Putnam eventually joined Charles in Oregon. Not written for publication, as were the letters of Russell and Curry, the correspondence of Nathan and Charles Putnam has a quality all its own.

In some ways like the Putnam brothers was Charles Tyler Stanton, who traveled with them in the Russell company for some time after leaving Independence. Stanton is one of the best remembered figures in the history of the Donner Party, the bachelor who reached California in safety and had no family ties to draw him back across the Sierra, but with supplies recrossed the mountains accompanied by two of Sutter's Indian vaqueros, and died honorably in the snow in January, 1847.

After his death, George McKinstry wrote Philip V. R. Stanton, who replied in a letter dated "Brooklyn (Long Island) Feby 14, 1848," now preserved in the McKinstry papers in the Bancroft Library. This document must be quoted as an introduction to the trail letters:

"My Dear Sir,

"To delay any longer writing to you, who have shown so much attention to every thing that concerned the terrible death of my dear brother, would be in the highest degree criminal. My negligence in writing has not been from any want of a due appreciation of your kind and truly generous services, but a disinclination to attempt to put my thoughts upon paper. Had the bereavement been a less severe one, I think I should not have felt thus; but that brother, Charles T. Stanton, was indeed a favorite brother, not only of mine, but I may say of our whole family.

He was always noble and generous, even to a fault — always ready and willing to share his last cent with his less fortunate brothers and sisters. This characteristic he bore from his earliest childhood. He was ever ready to sacrifice his own interest and means to the welfare of others, and hence it is not so surprising that he should be found willing to yield up his life in endeavoring to relieve his perishing companions. His was indeed a sad and terrible fate; yet it is a consolation, mournful though it be, that the last acts of his life were devoted in the laudable effort in endeavoring to assist others.

"About the year 1835, Charles went to Chicago and engaged extensively in mercantile business, which in the end proved unfortunate, and he failed some two or three years prior to setting out on the fatal expedition to California. During those two or three years, he appears not to have done scarcely anything. The active business energies which he before possessed seemed to have deserted him. I endeavored in my letters to him to re-awaken his ambition and to induce him again to engage in some sort of business; but all my efforts were apparently unsuccessful until within a few months prior to his setting out on his western journey. He then seemed to revive and to determine to do something, although he did not impart his plans to me, if indeed he had formed any. The first inteligence therefore, I received that he had left Chicago, was a letter written by him from St. Louis, and almost upon the heels of that, was received another letter from him from Independence, announcing the astounding and overwhelming inteligence, that he should leave the very next morning for California— This letter was dated May 12, 1846, in which he requested me to write him by ship to California. This request I complied with by writing him several very lengthy letters, giving him as full details as I could of every thing that had transpired since he left, as also my views of the course he had taken, hoping that it would prove beneficial to him. But alas, those letters he was never destined to see.

"After Charles left Independence, he wrote long and interesting letters to us by every opportunity, until the company had passed the Rocky Mountains and had reached the Bear river valley, the 3d of August, and in the whole forming a complete journal of the incidents. All of these letters were duly and promptly, to an astonishing degree, received. His last letter was received I think in October 1846. From this time no further inteligence was received. Time passed on; and occasionally I became extremely anxious about him, but was quieted by the last words of his last letter, viz. that the company took a new route down the Bear river valley, not traveled before that season, and he might not write to us again until he got to California.

"From the time my brother left Independence, I had a map lying before me on my table, and whenever I received a letter from him, I would trace out his course on the map, and his letters being full in detail, I was enabled to travel along with him. So much attention did I pay to this, that the whole route became perfectly familiar to me, and I was in mind and spirit with my dear brother in all his long and tedious journey—

"The month of February 1847 came, and with it I observed by the news papers, that dispatches were received by the Government at Washington from California, of a then recent date, but without any tidings of Charles. I was again very anxious and much troubled, but business drove the subject from my mind in a measure. I fancied many excuses, hoping always for the best, and that I should hear of the safety and well to do of my brother. The month of July came. The arrival of a ship at Boston with California news papers, was announced in the New York papers. The next morning upon awaking, the first thought that I had was that during the day I should hear from Charles. The first thing I did was to look through the N. Y. Herald which contained extracts from the California papers, but found nothing in reference to Charles. About noon a friend came in with the Tribune and pointed out to me an extract from the California Star containing the crushing account of my brothers sufferings and death.

"I went immediately over to the Herald office, and obtained through the kindness of the editor, the number of the C. Star, I think of March 13th, containing the account. This account, together with the subsequent accounts published in the California papers, so kindly prepared and sent by you, were published in the Syracuse papers and also in the papers of this City.

"You will I trust excuse me from attempting to picture to you my feelings. The whole scene of the terrible sufferings of my brother, and the others of the company has become indelibly impressed upon my mind. I found Trucky's lake on the map. I saw my brother, in imagination, engaged in making snow shoes the day prior to setting out with a view to cross the mountains. I followed him, with the other fifteen, poorly clad and almost destitute of provisions, up into those mountains, —and then my poor brother becoming snow blind,—lying down, with no friend or relative to soothe his last moments or receive his last counsels, to die. But you must excuse me—I cannot write further upon this topic.

"I fear that I have already trespassed too much upon your patience by this long letter; but you who have taken so deep an interest, and to whom we are all under so deep a debt of gratitude, will I trust excuse me. We are also under the greatest obligations to Captn Sutter for the great kindness shewn my brother, while there—To Captn Fallon for and others for their attention, and kindness—It is hardly necessary I think for me to say to you, that when you return, I shall be pleased to see you I hope you will make it convenient by all means to call on me—

"The vest and pin were received about the middle of November. I then intended writing immediately to you. I made inquiries in New York and ascertained that a vessel would sail for California in January or first part of February — I wrote to my brother at Syracuse to that effect and he forwarded letters to me to send, but I delayed until the 2^d inst., when, upon inquiry, I found that the vessel had sailed that very day. I am now informed that a government vessel is to sail in a day or two from this port, and I hasten my letter to send by this conveyance.

"Please therefore in conclusion to accept my sincerest thanks for the great interest you took in my dear departed brother, and the great services you have rendered his surviving relatives and friends in promptly and faithfully communicating every thing of interest concerning him.

"With the highest regard and esteem, I remain yours
Very truly
Philip V. R. Stanton
N° 3 Front St—"

When, almost thirty years later, C. F. McGlashan became interested in the history of the Donner Party, he entered into correspondence with Sidney Stanton, who recalled letters and keepsakes received from McKinstry. Charles was born, Sidney said, in Pompey, Onondaga County, New York, March 11, 1811. "He was 5 feet and 5 in. high. He had brown eyes and brown hair. He had a strong constitution. He was rather slender in his youth, but at the age of 15 he became strong and could endure as much hardship as any of his brothers. He had five brothers and four sisters. He was the seventh child."

In one letter Sidney recalled, "My brother wrote me regular till he got to dividing point where the water decended to the Pacific. Many of his letters were published in the New York papers at the time." Again: "In my last, I sent you two original letters of my brother in his own hand writing. One written when he had made up his mind to leave the States with the emigrant train and his last letter dated at the south pass where the party had resolved to take a new route when you get through with them you [will] please return them to me. His discription of his travels . . . from Chicago to the South pass would make quite a good sized book and would be quite interesting to the general reading public. His description of the Mormans at that time is quite interesting. You can have them to copy such parts as you may think best, for the benefit of your book. . . ."

Sidney also sent McGlashan the original of Charles T. Stanton's letter to Sutter, of October 20, 1846, printed in Volume I. These letters McGlashan copied and returned. Unfortunately the originals have since disappeared, and some can be printed only by recourse to the McGlashan transcripts. But another source exists for Stanton letters, as indicated by Sidney's remarks. Pursuing a clue afforded by McKinstry's copy of John Bidwell's journal, into which is pasted an 1846 letter, unsigned but identified as from the *Herald,* I found that a whole series had been published, mostly signed "S. T.C." It was apparent that Stanton was the author; and before the McGlashan papers were opened to research, I found confirmation in McGlashan's book, where extracts from letters are quoted. Unfortunately, the *Herald* did not print all of the letters Stanton wrote after leaving Independence. It may be that some were never received, despite Philip's speaking to McKinstry of "a complete journal of the incidents." What has survived is nevertheless a remarkable addition to the literature of 1846. The Stanton letters now available consist of three written on May 12, and single letters dated June 12 and 28 and July 5, 12, and 19 (this last with a postscript dated August 3). Two mere notes written later, one probably from Johnson's Ranch on October 20 and the other from the lake cabins on December 9, are printed in Volume I.

Most of the letters so far mentioned relate to the fortunes of the Donner Party, which is necessarily true of two letters by Tamsen Donner, dated May 11 and June 16, and one by George Donner written from Fort Bernard on June 27. Edwin Bryant was still the Donners' fellow traveler when he wrote his letter of June 16; and kindred records are the letters by Virginia E. B. Reed and James Frazier Reed printed in Volume I.

This rather narrow concentration upon one segment of the emigration of 1846 is counterbalanced somewhat by single letters from other emigrants, notably B. F. E. Kellogg, T. Pope Long, Daniel Toole, William J. J. Scott, William Edgington, Peter Quivey, and some of particular Oregon interest, including those written by Jesse Applegate from Fort Hall on August 9 and 10, 1846.

The latter part of this volume is dominated by stories from the *Oregon Spectator,* the *California Star,* and the *Californian,* illustrating how the public was first informed concerning those whose hard lot it was to cross the Sierra belatedly or to cope with the Applegate Cutoff after the rains set in. There is a grisly fascination to the details, and he will be a hardened reader who can lay down this volume, unshaken by the recital.

Even as today, in 1847, death and disaster compelled the imagination, and the history of the 1846 overland emigration will always be colored by these chronicles of hardship and suffering. But rightfully the newspapers of the Pacific Coast, numbering no more than three in 1847, reminded the world that the large majority of the year's overland travelers had come safely to their destination, satisfied with what they found. Virginia E. B. Reed, who in her 13-year-old innocence had no axes to grind, truly spoke for the emigration, Oregon as well as California, in the letter printed in Volume I, "We are all very well pleased with California. . . . it is a beautiful Country it is mostley in vallies it aut to be a beautiful Country to pay us for our trubel geting there."

"Emigrant Family"

Ho! For California and Oregon

Arkansas Gazette, Little Rock, October 27, 1845

CALIFORNIA AGAIN!

In accordance with a resolution passed at a called meeting held at Napoleon, on Monday the 6th October, 1845, notice is hereby given, that the Arkansas Californians will rendezvous at Fort Smith, Arkansas, on the first Monday in April next, preparatory to taking up the line of march for the Pacific coast. Every person starting is expected to be well armed with a rifle or heavy shot gun, 16 lbs. of shot or lead, 4 lbs. of powder, caps, &c., two horses or mules for each person, or a wagon and 8 cattle for every 5 persons, tents, &c.

Deeply imbued with the absolute necessity for positive and immediate action on this subject, the committee

think proper to give this timely notice to all those energetic men, who are willing, and anxious to carve out a
new home for themselves and families. This trip, it is
true, has been ridiculed and treated with levity by many,
whose intelligence and reading should have made them
act differently. California to us is no further now, than
Arkansas or Louisiana was to our fathers, and if they
possessed the nerve and spirit of enterprise sufficient,
then, to settle where nothing civilized dwelt, surrounded
by savages, more numerous and warlike by far, than the
California Indians, why should we faulter? Distance is
little but imagination, an idle spectre, whose friendship
(to speak in all charity) is stronger than their judgment. What next? The danger? Alas! That is pure
fancy, arising from a diseased and morbid tempera-
ment.— Were men to be deterred from great actions
through the fond anxieties of others, or the possible fear
of failure, then would the world remain stationary; aye,
would retrograde. It is a matter of deep regret that this
contemplated movement to the extreme West, should
be received with such cold indifference from some, and
violent opposition from others. And why is this? The
Pilgrim Fathers when they first landed on Plymouth
Rock, had not a more laudable object in view when they
left the mother country, with the ostensible purpose of
worshipping God under their own vine and figtree, and
letting others do likewise.

We will go out as peaceful citizens—we have no ambition, and have no sinister purpose to subserve. — We
will "in our right hand carry gentle peace to silence en-
vious tongues," and if we fall, "in great attempts 'tis
glorious e'en to fall."

The day of discussion with us is past—the morn of
action and determination has dawned upon us, giving
us the promise of a glorious day, and we will enjoy it.—
With our knapsack and rifle on our shoulders, we will
silently and steadily move on to our future homes; and
we do this after calm reflection and mature delibera-

tion—not coming to this conclusion hastily, or in a moment of heat; not as wild enthusiasts, but as intelligent men, after a long and mature study and examination of the whole subject.

And now we ask all those who wish to accompany us to be ready at Napoleon on the 20th of March, or at Fort Smith on the first Monday in next April. It is expected that arrangements will be made by which those with families that prefer a trip by sea can go by water.

D. G. W. LEAVITT, CH'N

OF COMMITTEE OF ARRANGEMENTS.

Napoleon, Oct. 9th, 1845.

JAMES M. MAXEY TO JAMES FRAZIER REED, AT SPRINGFIELD, ILLINOIS, INDEPENDENCE, MISSOURI, NOVEMBER 10, 1845 [1]

Dear Sir

It is with great pleasure that I embrace this opportunity to answer your Kind Note and It will do me great pleasure to give you all the information on the subject that I can, and I would of done it before this time but I have been waiting to learn some few things— and it is very hard for me to give you a correct answer unless I new what way you intend to go wheather you intend to go by Sante Fee or wheather you intend to travel the Oragon rout—if you intend to go by Sante-fee—you had better in the first place get you a large waggon made about 3 inches on the tread and will beare about 6 thousand pounds and have you 5 yoke of first-rate Cattle & the goods you take must be Blch^a & Bron Muslins and Calico of high colars very distect but if you take them in the Spanish County you will have to pay about from 5 & 750 hundred Dollars on the waggon without you can Smuggle them in and then if they find it out they will take them from you and imprison you they are very strict but their is a great many Good Smugled in, but I would be afraid to try it with my

family with me you can trade a good may Bron mus-
lin on the rode at the little Spannish towns on the rode
between here and Santefee you Spoke something about
your expeces you will be at no expence after you leave
here untel you git to the Spanish Settlements but if you
go the Oragon route you will be at no expence for you
will see no person to sell goods to until you get to Some
of the Forts their you can trade Brown or Blch^a Muslins or Calico or any thing of that kind for comon Bacon but you had better take with you about 2 or 3 years
Supply with you of all kinds of goods Shuch as Shoes
and Bron Muslins up reflection the advise I gave you
in regard to the waggon is not rite without you intend
to take with you a good may goods it will be to large
you Cattle cannot stand to go to Calafornia you had
better get you a good family ox waggon their is a good
prospect for a large Company for Oragon next Spring
and you had better Get here the first of April if you
can or by the middle at farthest you can Get all Sorts
of Suplies here if you dont want to hawl them Bacon
Flower Meal &c Cheapter than you can get them at
home You will have a long and teadous jurney before
you and you had better make good preperation get good
large oxen and if you take any horses atal take mules
one good fleet horse for a Bofalo horse a mule will not
do to kill Bofalo on they are not fleet enough Get you
Good Gun with about an ounce Ball and a Good flint
lock I believe I have nothing else of importance to
write I wish you all the luck in the world dont be puny
[?] get a good Out fit and the Journey is nothing in
Comparison to what our forefathers went thru but dont
for get to take plenty to eat and all the mony you
can money is good any wheere in the World you mite
trade a good deal with the Indians if you well take Blue
Calico and Beeds in little narrow Red Blue & Green
Ribbon Give my best Respects to all my friends and
that will be every body in Sangamon County let the
old men know that you got a letter from me and that I

am well pleased there has been agreat deal of sickness in this part of the county but the town is very healthy Give my respects to Doct Mc [Neil?] and tel him I would like to hear from him if he can open his heart enough to write

You must excuse this letter for it was writen in a great Hurre

I remain your friend & Brother
JAMES M. MAXEY

WILLIAM J. MARTIN TO THE ST. JOSEPH *Gazette,* PLATTE CITY, MISSOURI, JANUARY 5, 1846 [2]

Mr. Editor:

For the benefit of those who intend to emigrate in the spring, I beg the use of your columns for a few suggestions which they will find useful and important. I give them as briefly as possible, and without regard to style—matter is of more moment to such as wish to embark in this long trip.

First, the wagons should be sufficiently strong to carry from 2000 to 2500 lbs—they should be made with falling tongues.

Each wagon to have good double covers.

Each wagon to have at least three good yoke of oxen from 4 to 7 years old—the oxen should be well broken—yokes and bows to be all good and complete.

Two hundred pounds of flour to each person over ten years old—100 pounds to each child over three and under ten.

Fifteen pounds of coffee, and the same of sugar to each person.

100 pounds of bacon to each person over ten years old—50 pounds to all over three and under ten.

50 pounds of salt to each mess.

50 pounds of rice to each mess.

5 pounds of pepper to each mess.

50 pounds of dried fruit, apples and peaches.

Each mess to have a good tent of sufficient size to contain from five to eight persons.

Each man to be armed with a good rifle or heavy shot gun, with 5 pounds of powder and twelve pounds of lead or fifteen pounds of shot to each man.

Emigrants should have all things completed and in readiness to start by the 10th of April at farthest. A great deal depends on starting early in the spring, so as to reach Oregon early in the fall, and have time to erect cabins for the winter, and put in wheat crops in time to be able to raise their own bread stuffs.

☞ I would advise all persons who intend emigrating to Oregon from the Platte purchase or elsewhere, to cross the Missouri river AT ST. JOSEPH, AS THAT IS BY FAR THE BEST ROUTE.

Let me repeat and urge it upon all who intend emigrating in the spring, to have all things ready to start from the west bank of the Missouri by the 10th of April.

WM. J. MARTIN

D. G. W. LEAVITT TO A GENTLEMAN IN MEMPHIS
NAPOLEON, ARKANSAS, JANUARY 24, 1846 [3]

The Memphis *Enquirer* says:—We have been requested to publish the following letter to a gentleman of this city for the information of those who may contemplate joining the projected expedition to California. Here is a fine field held open for that daring spirit of enterprise so characteristic of the pioneers of the west:

"Napoleon, January 24th, 1846.

* * * "Yours of the 17th inst. came duly to hand. I am in the receipt, daily, of similar letters from different parts of the Union. That our company will be large I am confident, although many may disappoint us; but with those who lack the energy to lay hold of the many advantages which an early emigration to California holds out we can dispense. Ours is a peaceful migration, still energy of character is requisite to the undertaking of the journey; this alone will give the country the very best citizens of the world. The country is unsettled and unoccupied, and we believe the earth was made for man and for his occupancy and use.—We wish not to aggress, nor do we intend to suffer aggression, come it from what quarter it may (ever excepting Uncle Sam.) My impression is that our company at the rendezvous at Fort Smith will number 1000—perhaps more, perhaps less; but 5 or 5000, we start, and for Americans of Anglo Saxon blood to start, is to go. We shall rendezvous 1st Monday in April, and probably start by the 10th. Those passing here should be at this point by the 15th or 20th of March at the latest. The expense of outfit will be about $125 to $150, including every thing. Every man should have two horses or mules to ride and carry his baggage, or for baggage every five men can unite and obtain a wagon and eight cattle or four horses or mules. Every five men must have a tent and camp equipage sufficient for comfort, but not burdensome. Also, every man must have a good rifle or heavy double barrelled shot gun, 16 lbs. lead, 4 lbs. powder, caps, &c. &c. Those going from Tennessee had better go across from Memphis by land and meet at Fort Smith.—There will be many little necessaries which we shall want to take along that are not enumerated, but they can be obtained at Van Buren or Fort Smith. Many families are expected along. Those having teams should take a few necessary farming utensils, such as the iron work of ploughs, hoes, axes, &c. &c. I am negotiating for one or two field pieces, but whether I shall succeed in getting them is somewhat doubtful. I should like to see you soon—call when you pass this way. I expect to leave here about the 20th of March." * * *

Arkansas State Gazette, LITTLE ROCK,
FEBRUARY 9, 1846

HO! FOR CALIFORNIA! — We had a conversation—, a few days ago, with *D. G. W. Leavitt,* Esq., whose contemplated trip to California, when Spring opens, has been published far and wide. We never saw any person more sanguine of the success of an enterprise, than he is of the difficult one, in which he is about to embark. He showed us several letters from intelligent men in different parts of the Union, written in behalf of many neighbors and friends who were eager to join in planting an American colony on the shores of the distant Pacific. He pointed out to us on the map the harbor of San Diego—the next best to that of San Francisco—as the destination he had in view for the company. He informed us that he had received nearly two hundred letters of inquiry, in behalf of the writer and many others, and expressed his belief that between 500 and 1000 would rendezvous at Fort Smith by the first Monday in April, ready for the journey.—He expects to remain at Napoleon, at the mouth of the Arkansas until the 20th of March, when he will start for Fort Smith.

The Gazette, ST. JOSEPH, FEBRUARY 20, 1846

OREGON & CALIFORNIA

ALL PERSONS intending to emigrate to the country west of the Rocky Mountains the ensuing spring, are requested to assemble at St. Joseph, on Saturday the 14th of March next, for the purpose of making such arrangements as may be necessary in relation thereto.

Feb. 20, 1846.—tdm.

[*This advertisement again appeared on February 27 and March 13.*]

Missouri Reporter, St. Louis, Feb. 21, 1846

We learn from the Columbus (Ohio.) *Statesman* that Col. Wm. H. Russell, of Missouri, delivered a lecture at Columbus, on the 13th inst., for the purpose of encouraging emigration to California.

Weekly Reveille, St. Louis, February 23, 1846.

EXPEDITION TO CALIFORNIA.—We refer our readers to the announcement, in another column, of a proposed expedition to California. Mr. A. J. Grayson, an esteemed friend, will take charge of the emigration, subject to the pleasure of the company when it shall have assembled at Independence, previous to its departure. He is eminently qualified for such a responsible station, being a young man of enterprise, courage and determination— one who has not been accustomed to the "soft lap of luxury," but who has rather courted, from his youth up, the excitement and dangers of an adventurous life in the extensive wilds of the South-west — a gentleman whose rifle is as true to its aim, as his heart is true to the principles of honor.[4]

— — —

HO FOR CALIFORNIA!

At the suggestion and desire of a number of my friends, who propose emigrating with me to California, and deeming it actually necessary that some one should take the lead, whereby we may be able to organize an expedition and preserve good order while on the route, I have consented to take the charge upon myself, and pledge my life to the safe conduct of those who are disposed to join us in our journey to that country. Should any one of the company however, be considered more efficient than myself, by a majority at the *rendezvous,* I shall be most happy to resign him the duties of the command.

As it is my intention to take my family with me, which is quite young, I sincerely hope that we may have an orderly and well organized company. Those who design going should be at Independence, on the Missouri river, by the 15th of April next, as that will be the time of our departure from that place.

Emigrants should be well provided with arms and amunition, good teams of mules or oxen, and provisions for at least six months. It is better not to be burdened with any heavy and unnecessary articles of house furniture, but good assortments of farming implements, useful tools, garden-seeds, and such things only as will be serviceable in a new country, and not easily to be had in California.

A good interpreter and pilot will be wanted for the expedition.

A. J. GRAYSON.

St. Louis, Feb. 20th, 1846.

The Gazette, ST. JOSEPH, FEBRUARY 27, 1846

☞ The Oregon emigrants from the Platte purchase will rendezvous opposite this place on the 15th of April next, preparatory to their departure for the land of promise. We give this notice in due time, in order that others from the adjoining counties, or other States, who have resolved upon going to Oregon may know at what point to assemble. Emigrants can be supplied in this place with all necessary outfits.

Sangamo Journal, SPRINGFIELD, ILLINOIS,
MARCH 5, 1846

OREGON EMIGRATION.

Emigrants are now rapidly collecting in the Western part of Missouri, preparatory to a move for Oregon. The St. Louis *Republican* notes a meeting recently held in Platte city of Emigrants, and says, they appointed Elizabethtown,[5] near St. Joseph, on the opposite side of the Missouri, as the place of meeting, on the fifteenth day of April next, to make preparation for taking up the line of march. They say that it is not expedient for any emigrant to take stock with him for the purpose of speculation, but only such as are intended and necessary for the use of the person taking them; and all persons, intending to go, are requested to observe this recommendation. They further advise, that each emigrant should equip himself with a wagon sufficiently strong to carry from two thousand to two thousand five hundred pounds—to have good double covers—at least three yoke of oxen, from four to seven years old, well broke, and one hundred pounds for those under that age; fifteen pounds of coffee, and the same quantity of sugar, for each person; one hundred pounds of bacon for persons over ten, and half that quantity for those under that age; fifty pounds, each, of salt and rice, for every mess; five pounds of pepper, and from three to five bushels of corn meal, for each mess; fifty pounds of fruit, dried apples and peaches; a good tent, to accommodate five to eight persons; and last, yet most important a good rifle or heavy shot gun, with five pounds of powder and twelve pounds of lead, or fifteen pounds of shot, to each man.

The Gazette, ST. JOSEPH, MARCH 6, 1846

HO! FOR OREGON OR CALIFORNIA!

The season of the year is approaching when all those who are desirous of emigrating to Oregon or California, will naturally turn their attention to the western boundary of Missouri, to select some favorable point at which to rendezvous, and where all their necessary outfits can be procured, at the least possible expense. Feeling a deep interest in the settlement of those countries, and consequently a solicitude in promoting the welfare of those hardy spirits, that are desirous of emigrating there. I would suggest to them the propriety of selecting *St. Joseph* as the place to which they should all direct their course, possessing as it does, all the facilities for furnishing such necessaries, as may be required for the journey.

ST. JOSEPH, is situated on the bank of the Missouri river, in Buchanan county, contains a population of about 1000 persons, has 13 large mercantile establishments, which are capable of furnishing every article in the *Grocery* and *Dry Good* line that may be required for an outfit, at prices as cheap as the emigrant can bring them from St. Louis.

There is a large Flour Mill, within the limits of the town, besides several others in the neighborhood, that can furnish all the flour and meal requisite, at prices, far below what such articles can be brought there.

There is a large Beef and Pork packing establishment there, the enterprising proprietors of which have slaughtered about 250 Beef cattle, and 5000 Hogs this winter, and are prepared to furnish such articles, either cured in Bacon, or otherwise, as may be needed, at prices, cheaper than can be procured, in any other town in the West.

There are a sufficient number of Black-smiths, Wagon Makers, Saddlers, and other mechanics, who are always prepared with plenty of stock on hand, to make or repair any article in their line, in a manner that will bear a successful comparison, with similar establishments in the West, and at prices that will give satisfaction.

There is a *Ferry* kept at the town, furnishing every facility to cross the Missouri River to the Indian country, (opposite) where the emigrants can pitch their tents and have plenty of grazing for their stock, &c. and a sufficiency of timber for necessary purposes.

The route thence is a *direct course* to the South Pass of the Rocky Mountains, and is upwards of ONE HUNDRED MILES nearer than *any other point,* on the western frontier.

Two emigrating companies, the first consisting of about 100, and the last about 300 wagons, averaging six persons to each wagon, having procured all their out-fits at St. Joseph, left there for Oregon within the last two years.[6] Intelligent gentlemen—members of said companies — have written from there, advising their friends, and those desirous of profiting by *their experience,* to make St. Joseph the point, whence to take their departure for Oregon, being much the *nearest* and *best* route, and where all necessary supplies can be furnished.

Mr. Clarke, a gentleman (who has been engaged in the Mountain trade for the last 10 years, and who is perfectly well acquainted with the country between St. Joseph and Ft. Larime,) acted in the capacity of Pilot for the last Oregon company, that left St. Joseph, and pronounces it to be the best and nearest route, having an abundance of *grass, timber* and *water,* for the use of the emigrants, and at regular intervals for camping.[7]

Emigrants from Illinois and the Northern States, wishing to travel by land, can cross the Mississippi river at Hannibal, Mo., or Burlington, Iowa, and can travel across the territory of Iowa, or the northern part of the State of Missouri, where they will find good roads, plenty of grass, and abundance of water, for their stock, until they arrive at St. Joseph.

Emigrants wishing to travel by water, can find plenty of steamboats at St. Louis, for the Missouri river, on which they can procure a passage to St. Joseph, at as cheap a rate, as to Independence, or any intermediate point.

In view of all these statements, I would honestly ask every emigrant, desirous of saving either *money, time,* or *hardship,* to view calmly the above *facts,* and give them such weight in their minds as their *interests* may require, and should they be found serviceable—as I believe they will—all the wishes will be realized of a

FRIEND TO THE CAUSE.

[*This communication was reprinted on March 13.*]

Missouri Reporter, St. Louis, March 9, 1846

The Independence (Mo.) *Expositor* recommends Mr. [William] Fowler, of that place, as pilot to the proposed California expedition. He is well acquainted with the route, having accompanied the first party that ever crossed the mountains with wagons into that Territory.[8]

James M. Maxey to James Frazier Reed, at Springfield, Illinois, Independence, Missouri, March 9, 1846[9]

Dear Brother

I received You letter of the 26 of Feby which informed me the you wanted Some more information which I take great pleasure in giving — You can get all the artickles here that you want on the trip and after you get their—now for the artickles

Superfine Flour—from $2 to $2 25 pr 100—

Bacon Hoground—5c   Beens $1.50 pr Bushel

Coffee & Sugar 10c   Tea from 75c to $1.50 pr lb

Crackers $3 pr Barrel

Their is a great many things that you will want that I cannot think of at this time I could tel you better if I was with you for a Short time—I will try a give you about the quanity of each artickle you want 10 lb Sugar for each person over the age of 10 years or by the by it is not worth while for me to write you any thing about that matter for you cant make your outfit out until you get here for the vey good reason that you do not know whot you want for there is a great may things that you want on the trip that I cannot ascribe to you Shuch as a camp kettle and a number of things and you can get them just as cheap here as you can any place for their is a great deal of competition here and we have to sell things low put up with a small profiet I would advise you to bring with you as many of them U S Yawgers as you can get the[re] youst to be a great many of

them about Springfield and you can get them low. and
you can sell them here if you do not want to take them
with you I would advise you also if you want to take
any dry good with to get a large lot of cotton Hdkfs
Some Blue calico and lots of small beeds and all Shuch
little Trinkets but for you own use get Shoes & Boots
enought to last you at least two years & lots of Satten-
etts or Home made Jeanes but all these artickles if
you have the money you can get them here cheapter
than you can in Springfield for the reason the merchants here keep all Shuch things expresly for the eme-
grants and they do not sell well to any body else you
will want 3 or 4 peaces of Blue Drilling you will have
to take all you flour & meal in Sacks these you can get
here also in fact you can get all you want here and as
cheap as any place—Gov Boggs talks of Going but I
have not had a chance to see him Since i got your letter
but I can tel you that you need not fear about him for
you can get lots of Company here and that good the
Methodist Preacher [James Dunleavy] that we have
had here this year is going & his family and what is better he is a good Bro Mason as well as Methodist & also
an Irishmn I told him about you and he told me to
tel you to come in that there was som 8 or 10 family
from below here that ware going that ware all Meth-
odit and we put a gentleman [William Fowler?] through
the first degree of Masonry on Saturday night that lives
in Califª who has his mother & family here waiting for
the Compay to Starte he will be the *Pilot* I have no
dout but that Ex Gov Boggs will go but he is not at
the head of any company they will meet here and then
elect their captain there will be a large compay leave
here now about the time I consulted Sum of the compay on that Subject they tel me that you had better be
here about the fist of April or by the 15ᵗʰ any how I
think he told me that they would leave here abt the 15
of May you had better get here as [*torn*: early?] as
you can to let you Stock Rest a while I beleave that

is all that I can give you on that Subject—I will say to you that it made me feel good when I opened your letter and saw that you said Bro for since you seen me I have become a member of the E M Chuch and I think a Christian—I can tel you mor when I see you write to me again if you can before you Start

I remain Your Obt Bro

JAS M MAXEY

Weekly Reveille, ST. LOUIS, MARCH 9, 1846

CALIFORNIA AND EMIGRATION.

The tide of emigration is still flowing westward. Newer countries, with healthier climates and even richer soils, alone constitute the golden future of the emigrant, and is the only necromancy that lures him to leave his home and friends, in the eastern or middle States, to try his fortunes in a country that is Daguerreotyped, as it were, upon his fancy as the *beau ideal* of farming interests. He is not troubled with visions of Elysian bowers, and a life of luxury. He owns no estates in Utopia. His imagination entertains no sound

"Of dulcet symphonies and voices sweet."

to cheat him in a false belief. He knows that there will be hard labor and plenty of it in his new home, but he knows also that this is the source of all wealth — that there is no enjoyment without it — that labor is as necessary to a healthy existence as food itself. He has not determined to endure the privations of emigration unreflectingly; he has thought deeply, and weighed carefully, and his resolution, consequently, is unshaken.

There is no country holding forth such great inducements to emigrants as California. Its natural advantages are of the most important character—a most salubrious climate, a perpetual spring, as it were, without the sultriness of summer or the chilling winds of winter—a soil unsurpassed for richness and productiveness, some of the principal articles of agriculture growing in a wild, uncultivated state, and in excessive abundance—immense herds of wild cattle, whose hides, tallow, meat, &c., would be most profitable articles of traffic—the wealth of the woodland and rare water privileges—a prize for industry and enterprise—the gold, silver and precious gems that the earth is holding in its flinty bosom, and which, in some cases, nature has so exposed as to render them available without the cost of labor and expense—the position of the country, a lap for the wealth of the Pacific and Indian Oceans, possessing some of the best harbors in the world. This is California as nature has made it, and this is the point towards which that extensive emigration which will shortly invade the solitude of the western prairies, directs its course.

We already know of three expeditions that are being organized, and which will take up the line of march, in a few weeks, for California. One from Fort Smith, on the Arkansas, numbering one thousand souls, under charge of Mr. Leavitt, as we understand, intends starting on the 15th proximo. Major Russell, of Missouri, with a party embracing many friends from Kentucky, we are informed, is likewise making active preparations for departure. Our friend, Mr. Grayson, as we stated a few days since, is busily engaged in getting ready with his company, to leave Independence for the valley of the Sacramento on the 15th of next month. This expedition will be the best appointed in every way, probably, of any going out; it is composed of numerous influential and respectable families, who intend permanent locations, and do not trust to chance for the means of prosperity. One who has been connected with this paper since its commencement [George L. Curry], will it is altogether likely, take a twelve-month's tramp with this latter company, and may, perhaps, give an etching or so of California life, for the benefit of our readers.

STEPHEN COOPER OPEN LETTER, ATCHISON COUNTY, MISSOURI, MARCH 4, 1846[10]

TO CALIFORNIA EMIGRANTS.

The undersigned, as he is going to that country himself, and professes to be as well acquainted as any person, with all the routes from this state to that country, would suggest to the emigrants the propriety of crossing the Missouri river at Council Bluffs. There is now ready a company organized to cross at that place, knowing that the above route is the most practicable.—There are no streams or water courses, but what loaded wagons can be drove across with perfect safety, at ordinary stages of water. This route in a word, is one cut out by nature for the benefit of all who may think proper to emigrate to California or Oregon. The company to which I belong has a first rate Blacksmith, with a good set of tools, which he will take with him.—Should any accident happen we will be prepared to make any repairs that may be necessary. We are informed that there is a company of fifty families, now under way for this point from Dubuke [Dubuque, Iowa], under the command of Capt. Craig, for California.[11] There is also ready a good boat to ferry emigrants across the river, and arrangements made with the ferrymen, to this effect—one dollar for each wagon, and nothing for persons or stock of any description.

I would suggest to all those who may wish to emigrate to California by this route, to meet at Council Bluffs by the 1st day of May, in order that we may get through in the early part of the season. All those who have not laid in their provisions for the route, can be supplied in Atchison county, upon as good terms, as any county in the State of Missouri.

STEPHEN COOPER

Atchison county, March 4, 1846.

Oregon Spectator, OREGON CITY, MARCH 19, 1846

PUBLIC MEETING

— — —

To the Editor of the Oregon Spectator:

SIR—I am requested to forward to you for publication the proceedings of a public meeting, which was held at Salem mills on Saturday the 14th inst.—said meeting being convened for the purpose of devising means to explore and open a wagon road from the waters of the upper Willamette to Snake river.

The meeting was organized by the appointment of Hon. J. M. GARRISON to the chair, and JNO. B. McCLANE secretary, when the following items of business were transacted: A subscription which had previously been circulated, was presented to the meeting, the aggregate of which amounted to one thousand dollars; whereupon it was

Resolved, That a committee of six be chosen to still further circulate said subscription.

The following persons were selected as said committee, viz: Jno. B. McClane, Thos. Holt, Jas. P. Martin, J. W. Boyle, A. C. R. Shaw, and Moses Harris.

The aforesaid committee were instructed to circulate the subscription as extensively as possible, and to call a meeting of the subscribers whenever they shall judge proper; also to inquire who are willing to go on the expedition, and are competent to go as pilots, and to report the result of their inquiries to the aforesaid meeting, which is to convene at the call of said committee.

J. M. GARRISON, CH'MN.

JNO. B. McCLANE, SEC'Y.

FEBRUARY 14, 1846.

GEORGE DONNER, ET AL, ADVERTISEMENT,
SPRINGFIELD, ILLINOIS, MARCH 18, 1846[12]

WESTWARD, HO!
FOR OREGON AND CALIFORNIA!

Who wants to go to California without costing them anything? As many as eight young men, of good character, who can drive an ox team, will be accommodated by gentlemen who will leave this vicinity about the first of April. Come, boys! You can have as much land as you want without costing you any thing. The government of California gives large tracts of land to persons who have to move there.—The first suitable persons who apply, will be engaged.

The emigrants who intend moving to Oregon or California this spring, from the adjoining countries, would do well to be in this place about the first of next month. Are there not a number from Decatur, Macon county, going?

G. DONNER AND OTHERS.

Springfield, March 18, 1846.

Missouri Reporter, ST. LOUIS, MARCH 20, 1846

The Independence (Mo.) *Expositor* says:

"In the Company forming for California, some of our best citizens will be among the number. Our Methodist minister, Mr. Dunleavy, we understood, will take up his line of march; he is at present in feeble health, and thinks the climate is of such a character as to restore it.

[On March 31 the *Reporter* advised: "It is said that Ex. Gov. Boggs will head one of the emigrating companies for Oregon which will leave St. Joseph in a few weeks."]

Weekly Reveille, ST. LOUIS, MARCH 31, 1846

FOR CALIFORNIA.—The preparations are going on briskly for an early start. The chief of the Arkansas company, Leavitt, thus writes:

It is desirable that we should be completely organized, ready to leave the frontier as early as the 10th of April next. I shall be at the place of rendezvous by the 5th of April, at which time and place I hope to meet many hundreds ready and ripe for the enterprise. The prospect for a large company is flattering. I am receiving letters upon the subject of the California movement from every State in the Union. Many, however, may disappoint us—many may have the will, but lack the nerve. Such, however, will be no loss—with such we can dispense. Ours is a peaceful migration; still much energy and determination of character are requisite to the undertaking of the journey. We apprehend no danger, yet we should be prepared to meet aggression, come from what source it may. I have made arrangements, which I think will not fail, for competent guides to conduct us the most direct route, which will be many hundred miles nearer than *via* South Pass.

Arkansas State Gazette, LITTLE ROCK, MARCH 30, 1846

The note of our friend *Leavitt,* which appears in to-day's *Gazette,* was written with the haste of a Commander of an Army, dictating Despatches. It will be seen that he has "taken up the line of march" for the shores of the Pacific. We [Benjamin J. and J. B. Borden] hope that he will manage to keep us advised of his progress, and also, let us hear from him when he reaches his destination.

— — —

Camp California, Opposite Little Rock
March 28, 1846

Dear Borden: I am now *en route* to California. We shall rendezvous at Fort Smith, on Monday the 6th of April, and probably take up the line of march about the 10th of April. Tell our friends who are bound for the Pacific to delay no time in meeting us. Our company may be smaller than we anticipate, but they will

be of the right kind, and we anticipate no danger.
Yours, ever,
D. G. W. LEAVITT

Weekly Reveille, ST. LOUIS, MARCH 31, 1846

OREGON EMIGRATION.—We have received a letter from
Detroit, desiring information in regard to the emigration to Oregon. We can only say in brief, that we do
not know, nor have we any means of forming an idea
as to the amount of the expeditions thither this spring.
Most of those emigrating this season depart for another
point of *destination, California;* yet we understand that
there are some already assembled at Independence who
are bound for Oregon, and will probably start about the
25th or 20th [*sic*] of April, or as soon as the grass is sufficiently advanced to admit of it. The general point of
rendezvous, either for the California, Oregon or Santa
Fe companies, is Independence; although we believe that
Westport would be found a much better point. Our correspondent enquires "what are the requisite articles to
be provided for the journey?" Emigrants with families
chiefly travel with wagons drawn by oxen. Each man
should furnish himself with a good rifle or shot gun, six
pounds of powder, and from twenty to twenty-five
pounds of lead. Every grown person, likewise, should
be provided with at least two hundred pounds of provisions, as no *dependence* is to be placed upon the procuring of food on the route by hunting.

NATHANIEL FORD, ADVERTISEMENT, MARCH 30, 1846

OVER THE MOUNTAINS.

The company to examine for a practicable wagon route
from the Willamette valley to Snake river, will rendezvous at the residence of Nat. Ford, on the Rickreall, so
as to be ready to start on the trip on the first day of
next May. The contemplated route will be up the Willamette valley, crossing the Cascade mountains south of

the three snowy butes. A portion of the company will
return after crossing the Cascade mountains. It is hoped
that several young men will be prepared to go on to
meet the emigration. Those agreed to start at the time
above mentioned, are Solomon Tetherow, Nathaniel Ford,
Gen. C[ornelius] Gilliam, Stephen H. L. Meek, and
Moses Harris, and many others, it is expected, will be
ready by the time above specified.

    March 30, 1846—3tf   Nath. Ford.

[This advertisement appeared in the Oregon *Spectator*
April 2, 16, and 30, 1846.]

Daily Morning Missourian, St. Louis, April 3, 1846

OREGON, HO! — We find the following announcement
in the last Burlington (Iowa) *Gazette*:

We learn that a company of some dozen families contemplate leaving this county in April next, for the promised land — Oregon. May success attend them in their
laudable enterprise.

Weekly Reveille, St. Louis, April 6, 1846

CALIFORNIA EMIGRATION. — *Room on the Prairies.*—
The tide of emigration appears to be setting in stronger
and stronger towards California—the valley of the Sacramento. Oregon, for this season at least, seems to have
lost much of its attraction. The enthusiasm seems to
pervade all classes, old and young, rich and poor, and
to have reached remote sections of the Union. A party
from Pennsylvania, excellently well equipped, passed
through our city yesterday for Independence. We hear
of small companies having started from various parts
of Illinois, Indiana and Kentucky. Those from this
city are chiefly young men, and we have become acquainted with a good many of the same stamp from
other sections of our country.

    As Congress has refused to give protection to the
emigration about to take up its line of march across the

mountains, these young men will be an excellent substitute for mounted riflemen, and will afford such defence and security, we doubt not, as will make the trip safe and comfortable for women and children, rather than dangerous or unpleasant.[13]

A party of English gentlemen are now in our city, preparing for a tramp in the mountains and through the countries on the Pacific.[14]

Mr. Grayson, who has been delayed by a slight indisposition, will be at Westport with the remainder of his company by the 15th inst. Westport has been recommended as the best point of rendezvous, as it is much more convenient to good pasturage than Independence. We are informed by experienced gentlemen, that it would not be prudent for any expedition to leave the settlements until about the 1st of May.

The emigration promises to be a very large one, and "the cry is still they come." There is plenty of room on the prairies, however, and we "reckon" the emigrants will be able to make room for themselves on the Pacific either in California or Oregon.

Since writing the above, a party of young gentlemen arrived from Kentucky, bound to California. We are rejoiced to see that men of sterling worth are thus casting their fortunes in a land destined to fill no insignificant portion of the world's history.

The Gazette, ST. JOSEPH, APRIL 10, 1846

CALIFORNIA AND OREGON.

Mr. Editor:

At a meeting in the town of St. Joseph on the 28th ult., the following preamble and resolutions were offered and accepted by the unanimous vote of those who entered [*i. e.,* intend?], to emigrate to the shores of the Pacific this spring.

Whereas, we believe it necessary that some point, on the Missouri river, in the Platte Purchase, for the emigrants to start from should be selected; that those who may come from other States and Territories may know where to rendezvous.

Therefore, be it resolved, That we believe St. Joseph possesses the most advantages as a starting point, and the emigrant can procure all the necessaries for his outfit. The ferrys being regulated by law, and the keeper of the ferry offers to take all companies at half price, provided they will furnish sufficient help to work the boats.

ONE OF THE CO.

CHARLES F. PUTNAM TO JOSEPH PUTNAM AT LEXINGTON, KENTUCKY. INDEPENDENCE, MISSOURI, APRIL 11, 1846.[15]

Dear Father & Mother

We have all arrived at Independence except Nathan [Putnam], who we left at St. Louis to come on with the baggage that we could not get on the boat we came on; it being already too heavy loaded. Nathan was in good health, Will be here tomorrow. We are all in excellent health & fine spirits & hope this may find you & all enjoying the same. Do not give yourselves any uneasiness about us, for we are well provided with every thing that is necessary for such an expedition, both as it regards our equipment & the number & respectibility of the persons that are going to California. Many of the most respectable farmers in this County have sold their farms, and made all the necessary arrangements for such a trip. There will be several companies of single gentlemen who will start in a few days, with only two Mules, for each person, one of them to ride & the other to carry their provisions. But we intend to wait until the main body start, as we think it will be more expedient & much safer to go with those who have families.

Among those who intend to remove their families,

are Gov. Boggs, Dr. McDowell of St. Louis & Col.
Russell, together with *many* others who have already assembled on the plains. The three gentlemen named have
not arrived yet, but will be here next week. The number of persons that have arrived already to go with us
I have not ascertained, but I have seen twenty myself
& there are a number in town whom I have not seen.
Those who live near will not come in until we appoint
a day for the election of officers, & this will not be until after the 15ᵗʰ of April, it was put off on account
of the unfavorable season, which has prevented many
from arriving who supposed that we would not start
until the grass on the pararies would sustain their animals, and who did not wish to be here on expense. We
expect to commence our journey about the 10ᵗʰ of May,
the people here are all for California & many who can
not get off this season will start next.

I sent you a paper that was printed at this place, containing a letter from Capt. Sutter, and if you will go to
Mr Wickliffe you can see another letter that was published previous to that, also written by Capt. Sutter, I
could obtain but one of the first letters or I should have
sent you both.[16] I sent them both to Mr Wickliffe hoping
that he would publish them. Tell Mr. Toury Beard to tell
Mason Brown that his brother is in a Mess with a gentleman from [*deleted*: St. Louis] Boston, Mass., who has a
wife & one or two children, he was recommended to Mr
[John C.] Buchanan & he has every appearance of a gentleman. We have not obtained our Oxen yet but intend
to go & see Mrs. Dale, on Monday, the gentleman you
wrote to, Who says he has three yoke that we can have
& will show us where we can obtain more if we desire
it. Oxen are plenty, and not as high as we expected
from reports. as you will see from an article in the paper I sent you.

This is a business place at this season of the year on
account of the great number of emigrants that make
this their starting point There are a great number of

San Te Fee trapers here & there will be a great many more, they intend leaving next month for San Te Fee. Three Wagons arrived from there yesterday bringing with them a great many furs, three Spaniards & 17 Indians, the Indians are going on to Washington City, the Spaniard intend returning with the traders. There is an Orregon company also here, but some of them have changed their notion and are going with us to California. The California fever rages high here. I will tell you what a preacher said who had been there he said this to Mr Webb the editor of the paper here. "That he saw a gentleman in California who said he had died & been to heaven & that he rapped at the door & Father Gabriel came out, and asked him where he was from? he said from California, well said Father Gabriel, you had better go back, California is a heap better country than this! Webb reports it for the truth, but most persons think he is jesting.[17]

The weather is very cold. It has taken up more room than I anticipated to express what little I have, but I am in hopes that I can be able to give you a more definite state of things in my next. Tell Virginia that there are a number of young Ladies going along & that she must endeavor to obtain her accomplishments soon & be ready to start with the next emigrating company. Board is $2.50 per week. We intend to move to the plains as soon as possible. Our passage was $21.25 for each person from Lexington to Independence. Mr. Buchanan sends his thanks for the bagg of camphor. Messrs. Bosworth, Brown & Buchanan sends their respects to all enquiring friends & do likewise for me. Send me Observer papers or tell some of the hands in the office.

Write soon. Give my love to sister Bell & Joseph & all. From your son

C. F. P.

Missouri Republican, St. Louis, April 14, 1846

EMIGRANTS TO CALIFORNIA.—

There are now in this city a number of gentlemen on their way to Independence or Weston, to join a company which is going out this spring to California. They will leave the city during the week, and it is expected, if the grass on the plains is sufficient for the subsistence of their horses and stock, that they will commence their march between the 1st and 15th of May. The cold and wet weather of the spring has delayed them some weeks. It is expected that this company, which is composed entirely of men, will consist of from one hundred and fifty to two hundred—some say three hundred. A number go out merely to see the country and enjoy the sport of the trip, now a fashionable excursion with many of our western young men. Of those going for this purpose, there are several English gentlemen. A few take this trip to improve their health, but the largest number go with the purpose of remaining in the country.

So far as we have been able to acquire information on the subject, we are led to believe that the larger number of the emigrants, going out this year, will make California the place of their destination. It is decidedly in the ascendant in popular favor, as compared with Oregon. Nevertheless, there will be a large number of emigrants for Oregon; and, counting the women and children, few of whom go to California, it is probable that the difference will be small.

The companies for California will follow the Oregon route until they reach Fort Hull [Hall], when they will diverge in the direction of the Great Salt Lake, and thence to the place of their destination. We wish them every success in their enterprise.

Missouri Republican, ST. LOUIS, APRIL 16, 1846

Emigrants are beginning to gather at Independence. The Hennepin *Herald* notices the departure from that county [Putnam County, Illinois] of a party of sixteen males, seven females, six wagons, twenty yoke of oxen and a large lot of provisions, headed by John Robinson.

— — —

D. G. W. Leavitt, who has been gathering up a company for California, writes from Little Rock, that he would rendezvous at Fort Smith, Ark., on the 6th of April, and probably take up the line of March about the 10th of the month. The company may be smaller, he says, than was anticipated, but it will be of the right kind.

Some of our citizens leave today on a similar expedition. They congregate at some one of the towns on the Missouri, and thence commence their wandering.

Missouri Reporter, ST. LOUIS, APRIL 20, 1846

FOR OREGON. — The Burlington, (Iowa,) *Hawkeye* of Thursday last [April 16] says: "Quite a number of staunch built wagons and good teams crossed the Mississippi at this place on Monday evening, on their way to Oregon. They were from Michigan. They were followed by others on Tuesday, from Benton township in this county. A large company will meet in a few days at Keosauqua, at which place they intend to organize and then take up their line of march. Iowa will be well represented in that far off region."

Weekly Reveille, ST. LOUIS, APRIL 20, 1846

[*From the daily of Thursday, April 16:*]

☞ We understand that a bearer of despatches to the Pacific squadron [Selim E. Woodworth] is in our city, making preparations for an immediate start to Monterey. He contemplates performing the journey in less than ninety days, pursuing the accustomed route across the mountains to Fort Hall, and branching off at that point direct for Monterey.[18]

— — —

[*From the daily of Saturday, April 18:*]

FOR CALIFORNIA. — A portion of Mr. Grayson's company started up last evening, on board the *Nimrod,* on their way to Weston, the rendezvous of the emigrants for California. They expect to take up their line of march, *en masse,* about the 10th of next month.

— — —

☞ We are informed that Col. Russel, of this State, arrived in town on Thursday evening, and leaves in a few days on his contemplated trip to California. The Col. heads an expedition to the new *El Dorado.*

Weekly Reveille, ST. LOUIS, APRIL 20, 1846

UPPER CALIFORNIA.

THE SPRING EMIGRATION. — Mr. George L. Curry, who has been connected with this paper since its commencement, is now on his way to Independence, to join the California company there collecting. Mr. C. is a gentleman of intelligence and enterprise; his object is to obtain a full acquaintance with a region which, more than any other upon the Pacific coast, is destined to be the seat of commerce, wealth and political importance; and his letters, (to be published in the *Reveille*) replete as they will be with shrewd observation, intelligent calculation, and dashed, moreover, with the spice of novelty and adventure, may be fairly looked for with interest. He will write us by every opportunity, and no point, whether connected with the present welfare of the emigrants, or the prospective charges of the country, will be neglected by him . . . .[19]

Sangamo Journal, Springfield, Illinois,
April 23, 1846

HO! FOR OREGON AND CALIFORNIA.

The company which left here last week for California, embraced 15 men, 8 women and 16 children. They had nine waggons. They were in good spirits, and we trust will safely reach their anticipated home.[20]

A company have left Putnam county, consisting of 16 males and 7 females, for Oregon. John Robinson, one of the first settlers of Madison County, was one of their number.

A Chicago paper states that some forty persons will leave Rockford this spring for the same destination.

Conneaut Reporter, Conneaut, Ohio, April 23, 1846

HO! FOR OREGON! — About forty families are getting ready, at Rockford, Ill., and will take up their line of march for the fertile and healthy plains of Oregon, on the 5th of May. They are, we believe, principally, hardy sons of the soil, and will take with them strong arms to subdue the wilderness, and cause it to blossom as the rose, and stout hearts to defend it. Possessing all the essential materials for husbandry, and intending to settle contiguous to each other, for mutual support, they cannot be otherwise than prosperous and happy.

Young men, or families, who desire to unite themselves with an emigrating company, for Oregon, this spring, can have a favorable opportunity of doing so by uniting with the Rockford company. For information, address Jacob Spoor, Rockford, Illinois. — *Gem of the Prairies.*

Weekly Reveille, St. Louis, April 27, 1846

THE CALIFORNIA PARTY. — A note from our correspondent [George L. Curry], on his way up on the steamer *Nimrod,* states, that they got aground about twelve miles above St. Louis, on last Friday evening

[April 17], and remained fast until Sunday morning about 10 o'clock. In a postscript he adds that one of their steam pipes had bursted, slightly injuring an engineer.

[GEORGE L. CURRY] TO THE ST. LOUIS *Reveille*,
MISSOURI RIVER, APRIL 23, 1846[21]

We have reached Glasgow, on our trip up the Missouri to Independence. The truth is, the good steamer *Nimrod* (and there is not a stronger or better boat in the Missouri trade) has had a "heap" of right down bad luck, and under no other commander than her present enterprising and indefatigable one, Capt. Thomas Dennis, would she have continued on her trip. On a sand bar in the Mississippi two days;—about getting off, and the steam pipe burst with the sound of a young cannon, and with the most miraculous escape from injury on the part of passengers and crew. The pipe was sent down to St. Louis and repaired, and on Monday evening [April 20], after "lighting off," the *Nimrod* was in the Missouri river. Everything has been pleasant and favorable since—most delightful weather, and the very excellent accommodations of the *Nimrod,* with her sociable and agreeable officers, have added greatly to the enjoyment of the trip.

Our California company of emigrants was most agreeably enlarged this morning, at Rocheport, by the presence of Col. William H. Russell. He is large of stature, commanding in appearance, and of very pleasant address. We now number over twenty, out of the *Nimrod's* many passengers, who are bound for "the El Dorado of the West."

It is altogether probable that the emigration to Upper California alone will amount to about five hundred souls, and that it will be divided into two companies, which, it is altogether likely, will be commanded by Captain A. J. Grayson and Col. Russell. It will be extremely gratifying to you of the *Reveille,* for you have interested yourselves to some considerable extent in this emigration, to know that the character of those who are taking up their line of march for the valley of the Sacramento is of the right stamp—men who are well informed—who are accustomed to the use of the rifle, and at the same time are true to their enlightened ideas of freedom and personal right. Whilst they are going to the Pacific with the intention of improving their own worldly welfare, they will spread the "stars and stripes" to the winds of the Pacific. I have never, in all my travels, fallen in with a better class of people than those whom I have made my companions.

We presume that the young men of the party—meaning the *unmarried* ones,—the *disconsolate* ones, perhaps— will number from fifty to eighty, and will make the best possible kind of a substitute for Government's "Riflemen" that were to be. *We* don't need them and don't ask for them; but the time may come when they will be extremely effective upon the frontiers and on the mountain route. It would be as well were they in commission. I shall be able to write you something much more interesting from the general rendezvous, Independence.

LAON.

— — —

Missouri River, April 23, 1846.

My dear old Friends:—Thumping and bumping upon sand bars—rushing and crushing upon snags and logs— in and out — a lick ahead and a lick back — we have found to be the unpleasant accompaniments to the navigation of the Missouri river. The stream is a grand and peculiar one enough, but it is too wide for its depth, "too big for its breeches"—"spreads" itself too much for safety and comfort. We have a fabulous account of a river Styx, but the Missouri is the real *sticks,* and I fancy there will be found no one to dispute it. The grandeur of the stream, I presume, is discoverable in the circumstance that every mile of its travel is full of danger—that while you are in a floating magazine you are over a mine, as it were, which is liable to be sprung upon you at any moment. That is grandeur for you! On the other hand its peculiarity is so strongly marked, that it is unlike all rivers of the west. Its swift current and tortuous course—the peculiar discoloration of its waters — the nature of its banks, (which, torn out or caved in, in many places, and covered with piles of drift wood, exhibit the strength of the mighty river) with their sparse fertility;—all these characteristics, and numerous others, are observable in its progress ocean-ward, even to the Gulf of Mexico. Of nearly a hundred tributaries there is not one that can, in the least, control its nature or affect its general character—it is the Missouri river at its source, and the Missouri still far out in the Gulf stream.

— — —

THE MISSOURI

Far from the mountain land, 'mid rocks and
  snows,
Thou comest rushing wildly on thy course—
  Onward—still onward, with a fearful force,
Daring thy bosom to the lurking foe,
Whose strength is terrible and fraught with
  woes.
  The noble steamer, like an untamed horse,
Plunging and snorting on its rapid way,
  Rideth thy bosom gallantly and brave—
But there's no rescue; in her proud array,
  She meets the unseen danger, and her grave;
  She lieth now beneath thy murky wave.
What carest thou for man and his high sway?
Thy sand-bars, snags and rocks are all thy own,
And from thy depths fair commerce still must
  groan.

Arrow Rock, April 23d, 1826.   LAON.

Missouri Reporter, St. Louis, April 25, 1846

FOR CALIFORNIA. — Edwin Bryant, Esq., formerly editor of the Louisville *Courier,* with a son of Dr. Ewing, and a son of John I. Jacobs, Esq., from Louisville, and a number of other young men, passed through this city yesterday, on their way to Independence, to join the Company of Col. Russell, which is about to depart for California. We wish them a safe journey, and the realization of their hopes. Mr. Bryant, we learn, intends to write a book on California, for which task he is well qualified.[22]

Missouri Republican, St. Louis, May 5, 1846

St. Joseph, April 26th, 1846.

Messrs. Editors: It has been the impression here generally this winter and spring, that the emigration to California and Oregon would not be so great as it was last spring, owing to the unsettled condition of both countries. But from present appearances it will be as large as it has been during any time past. Emigrants from various sections of the country commenced making their appearance at this place four days ago, who report others behind them. They arrive here generally in detached parties, expecting to form general companies after they have all assembled. Up to this time, seventeen wagons and sixty persons, or more, have arrived, and this morning they broke up their encampment, and twelve wagons were crossed over the Missouri into the Indian country. The balance of the company started for Iowa Point, which is about sixty miles (by water) above, where they expect to meet and join a larger company already assembled in that neighborhood.[23] Report magnifies the number of emigrants now encamped in Holt and Atchison counties to five hundred persons, and upwards of one hundred wagons. But of the number it is impossible to speak with certainty, as they occupy various encampments, far removed from each other.

They will cross the river between this date and the 4th of May, at which time one company purpose starting upon their journey. No officers, as far as I can understand, have as yet been appointed, and this necessary act will be deferred until they have assembled on the opposite side of the river. The company which passed over at this place to-day purpose to journey about forty miles and form an encampment, with the view of awaiting the arrival of other emigrants. Captain Martin, of Platte county, was commanding this party, *pro tem*. It is stated that the advance guard of the Mormons are marching, by easy stages, through the Grand River country, and that they will cross the Missouri some distance above the Council Bluffs. I do not know how many constitute the company, but suppose it to be the same company which passed the Mississippi from Nauvoo, (a notice of which was contained in a number of your paper,) and equally as large now as it was then.[24] By a reference to the map of the route usually pursued by emigrants to Oregon, it does seem that they would advance their interest more, by starting from a higher point upon the Missouri river, than they have hitherto done. They not only avoid the passage of the large streams by so doing, but they also save a distance of one hundred miles in their trip, as it is so much nearer—if the statements of travelers residing here can be relied upon. St. Joseph is, doubtless, a better point to start from than any place below, and still higher up the river may be found better places than it. My letter has become too long, so I must conclude by stating, that companies will be forming and starting to both California and Oregon, from this section of country, until the 1st of June.

— — —

Saint Joseph, April 29th, 1846.

I wrote to you on the 26th instant, but as I had no opportunity of sending the letter by a boat, as directed, I have it still with me, and will send it with this.

Since that date, thirty wagons, with upwards of one

hundred and eighty emigrants, including women and children, have arrived and crossed the river at this place. Twenty-five wagons are still on the Missouri side, having been prevented from crossing over by the very rapid rise in the river. It commenced rising on the night of the 27th, and up to this date has risen about eight feet. The current is so rapid that it is difficult for a common ferry boat to stem it—hence the delay. Those persons who have already passed the river have certainly formed a camp about twenty-five miles distant, and will not start from that point, upon their journey, until the 4th or 5th of May; and, in the mean time, they will await the arrival of others, elect their officers, &c. It seems to be the understanding, that all the emigrants who have passed on to the counties above, (Holt and Atchison,) will concentrate near the same place, though at different times, as there doubtless will be three or four companies.

I understand that the Mormons will cross at Iowa Point (sixty miles above) instead of above the Council Bluffs, as I first wrote you; but I cannot learn their number, nor whether they will join the other emigrants.

By far the greatest number of emigrants will start from Independence. As soon as they encamp I purpose to visit them, and then I can give you a more exact account.

P.S.—The number of wagons on both sides of the river amounts to fifty-five. The number of emigrants (each wagon averaging six, which is moderate,) amounts to about three hundred and thirty.

C.

Weekly Reveille, St. Louis, April 27, 1846

HO! FOR OREGON!— Quite a number of teams, with strong and stout built wagons, have been crossing at this place, (says the Quincy *Whig*) during the past week, on their way to Oregon. Most of them were from the interior of Illinois. We see that they are also cross-ing above and below this city for the same destination. Joy go with them.

— — —

CALIFORNIA. — At the last Van Buren (Ark.) dates, Mr. Leavitt, with his party, was about to start for the bay of *San Francisco*. He expects the trip to be of three months' duration, and estimates the distance (low-er route) at 1,600 miles, by far the nearest point of the Pacific. Mr L. is very sanguine, and thinks that Cali-fornia now offers greater inducements to the emigrant than either Texas or Oregon.

[GEORGE L. CURRY] TO THE ST. LOUIS *Reveille,*
INDEPENDENCE, MISSOURI, APRIL 28, 1846.[25]

My dear old Friends: — Our tent was pitched about half a mile from Independence, on the evening of the 26th inst., the day after our arrival, and we had scarcely made the necessary arrangements when a most terrific storm burst upon us. We were prepared for it, how-ever, and as we could not control the weather, we con-cluded to do as they do in Illinois—we "let it rain."

We shall gear up again for the general encampment, about twelve miles from town, on the 30th inst. As soon as we reach there, you shall understand the actual num-bers assembled, and I shall probably be able to form an idea of the character and extent of the emigration. The wagons that have passed through since I have been here—and they have been numerous—are *all* for *Cali-fornia!* It is truly astonishing to notice the enthusiasm that has seized upon people, from all parts of the coun-try, for a move to that point; indeed, the word is Cali-fornia. I have seen but one wagon for Oregon.

With Santa Fe traders and California emigrants, In-dependence seems in quite a bustle; but unless there be a better road soon made from the river, which is some four miles distant, the emigration and mountain trade will eventually find Westport the most convenient point.

Our present encampment is a very pretty one, but too near the settlements to be entirely *romantic*. Since we encamped, four *more* wagons, for the *Sacramento,* have taken up temporary quarters around us. We have a good spring of water, plenty of firewood, and good pasturage; but life on the plains and *plain living* we are yet to have. Look out for "moccasin tracks." It will be gratifying to their friends, doubtless, to state, that the invalids of our company are getting along finely, and fast recovering their health. H. A. [Hiram Ames] and E. W. P. feel, as they express themselves, fifty per cent better in health than when they left the "Mound City" My friend, Geo. McK[instry], is, I may say, in perfect health.

One thing has struck me particularly, since I have been among the emigrants—the desire *to lead out companies!* I find about a *baker's* dozen of aspirants for the office of commander-in-chief. I take it that a *round* dozen are destined to disappointment relative thereto.

An express arrived on Sunday, from Messrs. McGuffin & Co.'s Santa Fe Company. They will be in next week. I do not hear of any news.

Always, sincerely,   Laon.

— — —

Wednesday Night, 10 o'clock,
April 29th, 1846.
Messrs. [Charles] Keemle & [Joseph] Field.

Dear Sirs: The company of Messrs. Weatherhead, Jones, and a few Mexican traders, arrived here a few hours since from Chihuahua and Santa Fe. They had excellent luck in coming in, and made the trip in fifty-six days from Chihuahua, and twenty-eight from Santa Fe. They bring no news of any consequence. Trade is very fair in Santa Fe, and circumstances are as favorable there for the same as could be expected.

Great exertions are being made this spring for this trade. Col. Owens and Mr. Aull are making extensive preparations. There are, likewise, our mutual friends, Messrs. Webb and Glasgow; also, Colonel Davy and others. A very large stock of goods will be taken out. You can form some idea of the number of companies going out, when I inform you that there will be upwards of one hundred wagons—by great odds the largest effort that has ever been made in the trade. Armijo, alone, has some dozen wagons ready for a start.

Yours, truly,   LAON.

Weekly Reveille, St. LOUIS, MAY 4, 1846

OREGON AND CALIFORNIA. — We discover that a goodly number of emigrants are beginning to come in, previous to their departure for Oregon and California. From present prospects here, and from what we can learn with regard to the state of feeling on this subject elsewhere, we doubt not that the number in the companies will equal, if not exceed, those of the years previous. Many, doubtless, are deterred from going on account of the unsettled state of things there, but still others are determined to venture their all—looking forward with bright anticipations to the future.

There can be but little apprehension, from the numbers now assembling, of danger on their route onward; their force is already great enough to intimidate the fiercest foe they may meet, and if many more are added they may be even scattered along for miles in squads and parties, and still be under no fear from hostile forces.—[Independence *Expositor.*]

The Gazette, St. JOSEPH, MAY 1, 1846

OREGON EMIGRANTS. — A large number of Oregon emigrants have passed through our place within the last few weeks, and are now encamped in the neighborhood, partly on this side the river and partly on the other, awaiting the proper season for starting on the vast prairie, as also the formation and organization of companies of convenient size for the trip. We presume that in a week or ten days, some of them will bid adieu to the States and wend their way across the Mountains to the "promised land." Many of the emigrants preparing to start from this place are for California, but they travel the same route as the Oregon emigrants the greater part of the way.

Missouri Republican, St. Louis, May 2, 1846

Yesterday we saw, on Market street, four large wagons, drawn by oxen, with a large accompaniment of cows, calves, and horses, and a yet larger number of men, women and children, en route for Oregon. They were from the State of Mississippi, have been on the route about three months, and yet have from 20 to 30 days' travel before them, before they reach Independence, the point from which they expect to take their departure for the Far West. They did not appear in the least discouraged with the prospect before them, and spoke confidently of reaching Oregon this fall, in time to provide themselves with winter quarters. What most surprised us was the satisfaction and confidence expressed by the women. They appeared to be not only indifferent to the hardships and dangers of the way, but to be gratified and pleased with their prospects. In the party were a number of young men, who, it occurred to us, would make rather troublesome customers in the event of a war between the United States and England.[26]

Weekly Reveille, St. Louis, May 4, 1846

CALIFORNIA EMIGRATION. — The clerk of the *Amaranth,* which boat arrived yesterday from the Missouri river, informs us that the country around Weston swarms with emigrants, destined for Oregon and California. A perfect fever appears to pervade the whole section where they are clustering, and many Missourians, it is expected, will pull up stakes and join the tide.

Missouri Reporter, ST. LOUIS, MAY 5, 1846

The Weston *Democrat* says a much large number of emigrants are now congregating, destined for Oregon, than ever departed in any previous year. It also expresses the opinion that those hardy pioneers will reap a rich reward for all their privations.

[GEORGE L. CURRY] TO THE ST. LOUIS *Reveille,* "ON THE TRACE," MAY 6, 1846.[27]

Old Friends of the Reveille: — Here I am, at noon, on the sixth day of May, at "Russell's Encampment," twelve miles from Independence, on the Santa Fe Trace, trying to write you a few lines, which, I fancy, you ought to term "A letter from the inside of a wagon," for a regular thunder storm prevails over the prairie around us, and I am forced to the inside of a wagon, using the bottom of a washing tub for a desk, my own traps being some twelve miles beyond this, at "Harlan's camp," which I expect to reach on to-morrow.

Both emigrations, California and Oregon, are rapidly increasing. The roads into Independence are lined with wagons. I cannot pretend to form an idea of the extent of the emigration until it shall have reached the Kansas, as I think I mentioned in my last notations. As we are now fairly under way for the "El Dorado of the West"—an expression used by Mellen, the poet, the Spanish and application of which I do not care about questioning, if any one else should—it may be as well to say, that I shall always take pleasure in furnishing you the earliest information of any interest, and I trust some of the incidents of our adventure may not be altogether destitute of that which is calculated to give a relish to the popular appetite.

The first five miles of the road leading from Independence to the Trace, we found in a very bad condition for wagons. We passed several emigrant and two large Santa Fe wagons badly stalled, notwithstanding the latter had six yokes of oxen each to draw them. This may prove another reason for Westport being made the point of rendezvous hereafter, unless the evil be remedied pretty soon.

Amid the fiercest storm I have yet witnessed on the trip, I encamped last night with a party of "our folks;" and though I was literally soaked through when I arose in the morning from my grassy couch, I never slept more profoundly, nor experienced healthier feeling. Favored with pleasanter weather, we continued, after breakfast, our ride to the plains.

Here we are passing through a charming strip of woodland. The fragrant haw has put forth its numerous and beautiful blossoms, and the wild larkspur, with other forest flowers, glittering with dew, make our way most pleasant and delightful. The wood is vocal with the melody of birds—gay plumaged warblers! We have emerged upon the prairie, and threatening clouds are convolving in the distance. Never mind about delaying to gather these flowers, however so attractive, but spur up—spur up for camp. We have reached it, and our horses are scarcely staked out when the big rain drops come pattering to the earth.

The emigrants appear to be much concerned about the Mormons. There was a "camp report" that six hundred wagons of them had crossed at St. Joseph's. This report, like all "camp reports," could be traced to no reliable source. Yet such anxiety was manifested about the matter, that Col. Russell was induced to send out an express to Col. Kearney, at Fort Leavenworth, to ascertain the truth. Col. Kearney reports some two thousand having crossed the river, with artillery, &c., but peaceably disposed towards us.[28] Why should they be otherwise.

I have had the pleasure of making the acquaintance of Lieut. Woodworth, of the United States navy, bearer

of despatches to Oregon and California. I shall, probably, bear him company as far as Fort Hall. He is shrewd
and circumspect, and says nought about his mission.

Mr. E. Bryant, late of the Louisville *Courier*, is with
us. He goes out for the purpose of making a book, so I
understand. He is a pleasant and an intelligent gentleman, whose society will be an acquisition upon the
journey.

Something of "prairie life" in our next.

LAON.

NATHAN J. PUTNAM TO JOSEPH PUTNAM,
INDEPENDENCE, MAY 6, 1846[29]

Dear Father

As this is my last visit to this place I embrace the opportunity to write you, and as business should be attended
to first I will get through with that [*deleted*: first]—

I wrote to you that I had got of Dale 3 Yoke of Cattle
which come to 100 dollars, which am't I credited on his
a/c. the reason why I did not settle the whole a/c was
that he did not think he ought to pay Interest and besides he thought that the charge of Insureance was Incorrect—if upon examination you finde it is not correct
you can rectafy it. Dale sayd that he would Send you
in the balance due on the old a/c this month and also for
the bill of cards which he ordered this spring

I believe I wrote you that we had dispenced with our
large Boxes and all our Barrels as they were too heavy
to carry. I think that our wagon is as well fixed and as
well calculated to go through as any wagon of the whole
number that I have seen—

I only wish that you could have Started out this spring
with us but as that was impossible I shall say no more
about it, but if the country is such as I believe it is I will
come back to help you out. just as soon as I can. You must
try and [*deleted*: collect] save enough rects. to get you
to California if I stay there—

As to the future I hope you will not take such gloomey views as Your letters would indicate for I am determined to do all I can to see you comfortably situated and I will not rest untill I do so, as to whether we are in Lexington or California it is a small matter so that we are contended—

Tell Joseph that I will write to him after we get started in which letter I will give you all the particulars as to who is to be our Capt, how many wagons there is going &c &c.

I have not yet received an answer to my letter from Dales nor have I received an answer to any of my letters from this place—I would not advise you to write any more letters to this place as it will be extremely doubtfull whether we get them—any letters which you may have now written I will get as there will be a man left here untill the 15th of this month to bring on letters and papers—

Tell Mr John S. Wilson that I am writing from the store of his Cousin and that he wishes to be remembered to him—give him my respects and thanks for the letter of introduction which he gave me to his cousin—

I wrote to Mother by Co'l Russell in which I mentioned what disposition I wished made of the pistols in the little table drawer I also told her that I did not owe Mr Trumbull a sent—and I hope you will not pay him any thing

I shall write to you along the road as I may have oppertunity—Give to all my relations in and about Lexington my respects and to all my brothers and sisters give my love, kiss Henry & Siss for me

Tell Mother that Gov Boggs has treated us all with kindness—

John B— Charles & Buckhanan are all well—Keep up your spirits and do not be discouraged there are a thousand instances of men retriveing their circumstances who were in a worse fix than you are— I must now bring my letter to a close and in doing so I pray that god may bless you all and that I may see you in the course of a year or 2 at fartherest

N. J. Putnam

Conclusion of my letter N. J. P.

We had also to pay more for our oxen than we anticipated and in addition to that and many other smaler matters we will have to be here until the 15th of May on expenses so that I thought I had better take 3 yoke of oxen
and let the note which Charley has of W. pay you for the
am't which I have credited on Dale's account which is
$100. I have bought out Buchanan's interest in the wag-
on and oxen when we arrive in California. We will have
when we leave Independence about $150 in money which
I think will be enough for all we want. Mr. Fowler a
jentleman who lives in California says that he will ensure us $3 per day and from all I can learn I have no doubt
but we shall have plenty of land, there is in my opinion
no doubt but we will do first rate. I only wish that you
could have started with us. There are plenty of farmers
in Jackson, Clay and other countys who are sacrificing
their property and going to California, but next spring
you must be ready and if all is right I will be in to pilot
you out. The best way I discovered to go out is to have
2 horse wagons with 2 persons to a wagon, the body should
be squair, of the lightest material and little iron on them—
the material for the running gear should be well seasoned
and the *tire* instead of being nailed on should be bolted
as the nails are apt to loose out.

You must not think that by my saying that we should
use 2 horse wagons that ours is not suitable, for my own
opinion is that our mess will be the best provided and the
shurest of getting there of any that I have yet seen, for if
our wagon is heavy we have a corresponding team viz:
6 yoke of oxen and I think good ones. When we get out
on the plains we will only use 3 yoke which will be amply
sufficient and change about with the others every week
or maybe less. I stand walking first rate for I feel better
today after walking about 18 miles yesterday than I have
done for the last ten days. Give my love to mother and
all the children as though each were named. Yours af-
fectionately.

Missouri Republican, St. Louis, May 9, 1846

The [Independence] *Western Expositor* says — "We notice among those going out to California, Wm. H. Russell, Dr. Snyder, Mr. Grayson, Mr. M'Kinstry, Mr. Newton and others from below; and Messrs. Lippincott and Jefferson from New York, and from about here ex-Gov. Boggs, Judge Morin, Rev. Mr. Dunleavy, and hosts of others.[30]

The Gazette, St. Joseph, May 8, 1846

THE EMIGRANTS.

As it was last week, so it is this. Oregonites and California emigrants have been pouring in upon us by quantities. From every quarter they seem to come—prepared and unprepared to meet every emergency. We look out upon them, and are astonished to see such careless ease and joyousness manifested in the countenances of almost all— the old, the young, the strong and feeble—the sprightly boy and the romping girl, all plod along, as if the jaunt was only for a few miles instead of a thousand— as if a week's troubles were to terminate their vexations and annoyances forever. What an idea it gives us, and what an insight into human nature—HOPE, the bright, beaming star, is high ascendant in their sky, alluring them on to peace and enjoyment, and constantly betokening better prospects and more delightful days. Anticipating an interminable season of pleasure and delight, they go forward with easy tread, willing to brave all danger and run every risk, if they may but attain that favored spot, and there sit down, determined to be contented the remainder of their days.

We wish them great success in all their undertakings, and hope that disappointment of any kind may not be the lot of a single soul.

We will be able in a few days to give a full list of the number of wagons that have crossed at this point, and other important information connected with the company.

—We learn that one company will leave on Monday.

☞ A large number of our citizens are about leaving for their rendezvous across the river, on their way to Oregon. We are about parting for a long time from many old friends—may peace and prosperity go with them.

[WILLIAM H. RUSSELL] TO THE *Missouri Republican,* INDIAN COUNTRY, 20 MILES WEST OF INDEPENDENCE, MAY 10, 1846.[31]

I did not receive your favor of the 25th ult., directed to me at Independence, until after our arrival at this encampment, and as I write seated on the ground, and a knobby trunk for my desk, I cannot make my answer as acceptable as I could hope to do under more favorable circumstances.

The company bound for California is composed of as much intelligence and respectability, certainly, as ever wended their way to a new country, and the integrals are representatives from almost every State in the Union. I was just visited by a gentleman and lady each, who came from the widely separated States of Louisiana and Pennsylvania. We have, also, clergymen, lawyers, physicians, painters, and mechanics of every trade, including some jolly printers.

We will wait here for all the emigrants to come up, when we will organize, and begin in earnest our long journey, which will probably be accomplished by Monday evening so as to admit of our final departure on Tuesday morning.

The emigrants are provided with every comfort necessary for a six months trip, and the mode of travel is in light wagons, universally drawn by oxen and usually about three yoke to a wagon.

It is impossible to form any thing like an accurate idea of our number, but it is very large—far more than I had dared to hope: I can now count from my present humble seat, over one hundred wagons, and estimating each wagon to contain five souls, we have at this encampment at least 500 persons—all bound for California. The number, I think, cannot fall short of 1,000.

The Oregon fever has abated, and I think the number cannot be large that will strive for a place in the debateable land.

I have just received a letter from Colonel Kearney, at Fort Leavenworth, to whom I sent an express to know something of the Mormons, who are crossing the Missouri river in great numbers at St. Josephs. He informs me that at least 2,000 have actually passed, and that others are daily crossing. He represents them as well provided with all needful munitions of war, including a train of artillery, but thinks that they have no hostile intentions towards us, unless it be to Governor Boggs, whom he desires me to caution to be on the alert.

I design to treat them with proper courtesy, but if they will not receive our passing friendship, why they must take their own course, but they cannot bully this crowd without paying a price that even a Mormon will not relish. But I do not expect any trouble whatever with them, and it is, therefore, in bad taste to comment about it.

My mess consists of Messrs. Edwin Bryant, late editor of the *Louisville Courier,* who is preparing to write a book, and a good one may be expected; and also sons of John I. Jacob and Doctor Ewing, of Louisville, and, as the Yankees say, two helps.

R.

[GEORGE L. CURRY] TO THE ST. LOUIS *Reveille,* CAMPING GROUND, SHAWNEE COUNTRY, MAY 11, 1846.[32]

Editors of the Reveille:

I am happy to inform you that the California emigrants (encamped on a branch of Indian Creek, in the country of the Shawnee Indians,) organized to-day by the election of Col. Wm. H. Russell, and the adoption of the subjoined laws, which, thinking they may be of some interest to your numerous readers, I am induced to give in full. The committee who framed them consisted of Ex-Governor L. W. Boggs, (the only competitor Col. Russell had for the office of commander) Rev. Mr. Dunlesay [Dunleavy], Messrs. Brookey, Kuykendall and Wm. Campbell of Calloway county, Mo., B. S. Lippencott, of New York, and George L. Curry, of St. Louis:

1. The company shall be divided as nearly as may be into four equal parts; to each division of wagons there shall be a commander appointed, whose duty it shall be, under the direction of the captain commandant, to take charge of and direct the movements of their respective divisions, but messes shall not be divided. Each division shall elect its own commander.

2. It shall be the duty of the captain to cause a register to be made out of all persons subject to guard duty, and to arrange the periods and divisions of time both at day and night, so that the duty shall bear as nearly equal as possible upon all subject to it, and the commanders of the several divisions shall constitute the council of the commanding officer, whom he shall consult whenever the same may become necessary.

3. It shall be the duty of the commanding officer to cause the company to march in two parallel lines, whenever the nature of the country will admit of it, so as to form a square encampment, or *caral,* the more easily when necessary.

4. No person, unless on guard duty, or specially ordered by the commanding officer, shall keep fire-arms primed or capped.

5. Each division shall be numbered, and march alternately in advance, and the several messes shall, likewise, be numbered, and each mess shall alternately march in advance of their respective divisions—said alternation, both of divisions and messes, shall be daily.

6. A committee of five shall be appointed to inspect the wagons, teams, provisions, ammunition and fire-arms;

and so far as relates, the inspection of fire arms, the duty of this committee shall terminate only with the dissolution of the company; and, to prevent accidents, it shall be the duty of this committee to see that the provisions of the fourth article be strictly observed by each member of the company.

7. Whenever it may become necessary, in view of the scarcity of game, the captain shall have power to restrain hunting, and appoint regular hunters for the time being; and, in case of the scarcity of water and fuel, he shall, likewise, direct the mode of procuring or distributing it equally among the several messes, in proportion to their numbers.

8. The committee of inspection shall have power to arraign any person for delinquency of duty, or for the violation of any of the rules or regulations, when reported by the officers of the guard or otherwise; and the punishment for such delinq[u]ency shall be decided upon by a vote of the company.

These laws appeared to give satisfaction to the company, as they were adopted without any opposition. When put in practice, they may require some amendment, which circumstances and experience will suggest in due time.

This evening Col. Russell announced the appointment of Mr. Kuykendall to act as Adjutant of the company, B. S. Lippencott, Quartermaster, and George L. Curry, Aid-de-Camp of the commanding officer.

We have, in all, fifty-five wagons at our present encampment, that will start to-morrow morning for the Wakaousha [Wakarusa], where they will remain two days, to await the arrival of some twenty odd more, principally from Jackson county, Mo. We have in our company about one hundred and thirty-five fighting men—altogether, some two hundred and fifty souls. An encampment of twenty wagons for California, half a mile distant from us, organized to-day, and appointed Mr. George Harlan Captain, who declined the honor, and Judge Morin, as I am informed, was afterwards elected to fill the va-

cancy. The company is so small, however, that I presume
it will ultimately attach itself to the general emigration.

The Oregon emigrants have all moved on to the Kanzas river, where, I presume, they will organize.

It is midnight, and I'll to my buffalo robe. Good night.

LAON.

NATHAN J. AND CHARLES F. PUTNAM TO THEIR PARENTS,
"INDIAN COUNTRY 25 MILES FROM INDIPENDANCE"
MAY 11, 1846[33]

Dear Father

We received yesterday by the hands of Gov Boggs the
pasports and with them your letter. I am sorry to hear
that Mother's face is not getting better, but hope before
this reaches you that it will be well I am certain that if
she continued to take medicine and diet herself she will
get well—

[*Four words lined out*] I have just been out on the
Prarie to look up my Cattle and forgot what I was going to say at the beginning of this sentence

We have had an election for officers, this morning Col
Russell was elected Capt at 2 O'clock we have another
meeting to adopt by laws &c &c after the meeting I will
give you the particulars.

I have just received a letter from Mr [L.] Wheeler
and one from you I cannot to-day answer eather as we
start tomorrow but on the road between here and Fort
Leavanworth [*i. e.,* Laramie?] I shall endeavour to do
so. You need be under no apprehensions as to our safty,
there is now in Camp 141 fighting men 71 Women 109
Children and 75 Wagons. and that will be increased to
at least 200 besides there is another encampment within
about a mile of us with about 40 men—I do not believe
there is the slightest danger from any cause and I hope
you will not *bother* yourself about any thing of the kind.

As to what my intentions are as to going, I thought
you knew them before I started. I am determined to go

and I cannot think of any thing which could turne me back, except the *loss of the means to go,* and I shall take good Cair that such an occurance does not happen

I have not had for years such health as I now have I can Walk all day without feeling more fateague than I used to feel at night when I used to lock up the store—

I would like to write more but I have not now time— Charles will fill up the other side and this evening I will give you a scetch of the proceedings of our meeting

The meeting is over there was nothing of importance done that would interest you

Give my love to Mother Joseph, Isabela, Virginia, Francis, Catherine and Henry & My Respects to *Aall* enquireing friends

Tell Cousin Cincinnatus that I shall write to him shortely and Joseph also, the reason why I have not written to All is that it would be a useless expence and I suppose that all of the family read my letters

Tell Mr Loque & Hiram Shaw that when I *arrive* at Fort Laramie I will write to them—

Do not write any more as I will leave here tomorrow

Good-by

N. J. PUTNAM

Dear Mother

I have a few moments to write, but I will shortly have to go about cooking supper, we make very good bread & coffee. Tola is the best dish I ever eat, it is made of parched corn ground, & cooked in the same manner that mush is. It is sweetened with sugar. I have just finished a letter to Miss [*deleted*: C] I now wish that you & all were along, seeing the respectability of the company & the ease that we can get along & the few fears that I entertain as to the trip even supposing that war should come we will be equally as safe as though we were at home, for we would be drafted there. And if Mexico should declare war against the U. States & England was to interfere with the Californias, I am confident that the U. States

will send a force there that will quope with any that Great
Britain may send in that quarter & the Americans acting
on the defensive will be equal to five times the strength
of her enimies. But we go there not for the purpose of
creating a revolution, (though it could be easily done,
with the Americans, foreigners, & the native Spaniards
that are there & those Americans that are going this year
would be amply sufficient to defend California against
any aggression that Mexico might make

But I say as I have said above, that we go to California not for the purpose of creating a revolution, no, I
agree with Mr. Wheeler that we ought not to do any thing
that would be discreditable or dishonorable to ourselves
or our country. We are invited there by the Governor of
California & he is appointed by the Mexican Government
& he is i[n]vested with full authority so to act, & we intend to comply with his demands upon us. But should
they after inviting us there wish to impose any new laws
upon us, I am afraid that ambitious men will excite a
revolutionary spirit among the emigrants & the people
there who are already in favor of annexation to the U. S.
or an Independent Government. But I hope that all may
be done "peacibly & in good order." There is no fears to
be apprehended from Mexico at any rates, no more than
if we were at home & I think England has too much caution to go to war with this Nation for America (I believe)
will strike for every inch of ground she owns on this continent & be very apt to gain it. But war would be a curse
to both nations & the world, Even if we should gain ever
thing. I have stated these facts to show you that we are
in no more danger here than we would be there. We elected Col. Russell as our Captain by a vote of three to one
over Gov. Boggs, the two candidates walked aside with
their friends. The Governor laughed at his being so badly
beaten & afterwards drank to the health of the Col. R.
The Gov. B., is rather trickish I think, for he told me that
he did not wish the office. He told me also that he was
in favor of the Captain's choosing his own aids, but he

voted against this resolution after he found he was not elected. I have seen some wagons that were bound for [*deleted*: California] Oregon that had cooking stove in it. We have good neighbors they send milk they have butter & every thing that is necessary for comfort. There are plenty of pretty Girls along also. Sunday we had preaching by the Rev. Mr. Donleavy our tent was crowded with young ladies. We set our table and & spread a table Cloth & they eat and drank as much milk as any ladies I ever saw set down to a table. We are now on a Prarie it is the most beautiful sight I ever saw they are filled with beautiful flowers & they cover over a space as far as the eye can reach. I hope to see & be with you & all our family & many of my friends & acquaintances in these plains on our march to California

Don't give yourself any uneasiness about us, we are provided with every thing that heart could wish for. I shall write to you again soon You may let Mr Wheeler see this if you wish. Mr. Bryant was elected Chairman today & a Mr Curry an editor of a St Louis paper secretary & I have to do his (Curry's) business to-night as he is on guard. Give my love to all

from your son
C. F. P

I have written over this letter, so that I will have to put an envelop over it "The more haste the less speed" I have not time to write more There is a prospect of a wedding in the Camp not me or any of us

MRS. GEORGE DONNER TO ELIZA POOR, INDEPENDENCE, MISSOURI, MAY 11, 1846[34]

My dear sister

I commenced writing to you some months ago but the letter was laid aside to be finished the next day & was never touched. A nice sheet of pink letter paper was taken out & has got so much soiled that it cannot be written upon & now in the midst of preparation for starting across the mountains I am seated on the grass in the midst of the tent to say a few words to my dearest only sister. One would suppose that I loved her but little or I should have not neglected her so long, but I have heard from you by Mr Greenleaf & every month have intended to write. My three daughters are round me one at my side trying to sew Georgeanna fixing herself up in an old indiarubber cap & Eliza Poor knocking on my paper asking me ever so many questions. They often talk to me of Aunty Poor. I can give you no idea of the hurry of this place at this time. It is supposed there be 7000 waggons start from this place, this season [?] We go to California, to the bay of Francisco. It is a four months trip. We have three waggons furnished with food & clothing &c. drawn by three yoke of oxen each. We take cows along & milk them & have some butter though not as much as we would like. I am willing to go & have no doubt it will be an advantage to our children & to us. I came here last evening & start tomorrow morning on the long journey. Wm's family was well when I left Springfield a month ago. He will write to you soon as he finds another home. He says he has received no answer to his two last letters, is about to start to Wisconsin as he considers Illinois unhealthy

> Farewell, my sister, you shall hear from me as soon as I have an oppertunity, Love to Mr. Poor, the children & all friends. Farewell
>
> T[AMSEN]. E DONNER

Weekly Reveille, St. Louis, May 11, 1846

FOR CALIFORNIA. — We received several visits, yesterday, from parties anxious to overtake the California emigrants, now about starting from Independence. The late news will attach new interest to the fortunes of the present adventurers.

[*The same page of the* Weekly *has a report from the* Picayune *of "Capt. Thornton's Disaster" on the Rio Grande.*]

Weekly Reveille, St. Louis, May 11, 1846

St. Louis to California. — Our correspondent, now on his way to California, writes us, 5th inst., from Independence. He was in the very act of leaving for the plains, whence his next letter will come. He says: "Ex-Governor L. W. Boggs and Col. W. H. Russell will probably command the two expeditions for California. Emigrants are constantly arriving, and there seems to be no end to them. It will be hard to tell the extent of the emigration until after we cross the Kansas," &c.

The last Independence *Expositor* speaks of the "crowds coming up," and mentions many of the emigrants by name:

"Among the number is Mr. George L. Curry, who has been connected with the St. Louis *Reveille* since its commencement. We do not know what Mr. C.'s object is, but we learn that he will be a regular correspondent of that paper, and we may look for something intelligent, spicy and adventurous. We suppose his letters will come under the head of '*Curry*-ings by the Way.' "

— — —

[The same issue of the *Weekly Reveille* reprints, probably from the *Daily* of May 5:]

The Californians. — The Independence *Expositor* says that emigrants are absolutely pouring into the town. "The company to California seems to be increasing in numbers much over that to Oregon; this point (California) has had decidedly the preference in the minds of a majority, and we would not be much surprised if, when the separating time comes, *en route,* that all will be merged in one, and the fairer southern spot, even at the risk of expatriation, will be the one chosen.

"Two or three more such companies as those that have gone out for a year or so past, and will go this, will do more to settle the vexed question of territorial right, than millions of blood and treasure, when expended in the most judicious and economical form by our national worthies."

— — —

[On the same page of the *Weekly,* evidently from the *Daily* of May 6:]

FOR OREGON. — A party of emigrants, with plentifully stored wagons, passed up Market street yesterday, who were *en route* to the far-off Pacific. Some of the by-standers were disposed to pity them, but the party appeared to look upon the three thousand mile journey as a small affair, and the show of sympathy for their prospective dangers a waste of feeling.

Missouri Republican, ST. LOUIS, MAY 15, 1846

Independence, (Mo.) May 11, 1846.

Our town for the last few weeks, has presented a scene of business equal to a crowded city. Emigrants to Oregon and California have been pouring in from all quarters to this point, which is made their general rendezvous. It is here that most of them lay in their outfits, comprising all sorts of merchandize, groceries and provisions— wagons, oxen, mules and harness. There are, this spring, two distinct companies, one to Oregon, and the other to California; heretofore they have made but one company until they have crossed the mountains; but at present the number to each expedition is sufficient to organize and protect themselves from the Indians.

The number of emigrants is not yet known, nor can it be until they reach their general encampment on Kansas river, about 100 miles west of this place, and where a census will be taken. A finer looking body of emigrants than the present, I have never seen-–manly and bold in their appearance, and generally well equipped for so long and tedious a journey as they have before them. Among them are persons of all ages, even to the old man following his grandchildren. I saw a venerable man, 72 years of age, who has been a sea captain, and was born upon a cape of our Atlantic coast, now going to bury his bones upon the shores of the Pacific. He is a patriarch indeed— has his children and grand children with him, and ten wagons to convey them—a small fleet for the plains.

Some of the emigrants have waggons fitted up in the best possible style, carpeted, with chairs, bed and looking-glass, for the convenience of families. There are numerous young girls, just blooming into womanhood, and man[y] of them beautiful, neatly dressed, and bound for Oregon and California. Young men going to those distant countries need have no fear of not being able to get a wife; for I assure them that the assortment of girls in the present companies is by no means indifferent. Some of the wagon covers have on them "Oregon—54 40—all or none!"—and say they are willing to fight for it if necessary. Part of the Oregon emigrants have started, and others will start tomorrow. Their present camp is 18 miles southwest of Independence.

The California emigrants will not leave for a few days. In my next, I will give you some statistical information of the present companies—their number, commanders, number of wagons, amount of provisions, &c. &c.

A number of Santa Fe companies have come in this spring, and some have gone out. Magoffin's company will be in to-morrow, or next day, from Chihuahua. Nearly double the amount of goods will be taken out this year to any previous year. It is thought that upwards of four hundred wagons will leave Independence for Mexico this year, and they may be safely set down at four thousand dollars per wagon. Col. S. C. Owens has not yet left. He has a very large amount of goods directly imported from England, thereby having the duty taken off at this point, if they pass through in the original package. Most of the traders are beginning to take the benefit of the drawback, by purchasing foreign goods in the original package. Speyers & Co., are to leave to-day, with a very large lot of English goods. I will give you, shortly, some statistical information of this important trade—a trade that, I believe, could be made of the utmost importance to Missouri. The amount of specie brought in annually to this point is very great, and might be greatly increased.

I have hastily given you a sketch of these things, but will, in my next, enter into the details and give you facts as they stand.—

CHARLES T. STANTON TO SIDNEY STANTON, INDEPENDENCE, MISSOURI, MAY 12, 1846[35]

My Dear Brother

In my last I wrote you from St. Louis stating that I should leave the next day for this place—Well what may surprise you perhaps is that I am going to start for California tomorrow I met with a good opportunity and, thinking it doubtful whether I should find anything to do in this country I concluded to go

I have thought the matter all over and think it be best steps I can take I am in hopes that the trip with the excitement may have a tendency to restore some of my dormant energies which have been so long asleep. When I left C[hicago]—I had not this design in view, but traveling had such an agreeable effect on me and having once got afloat that I have found it as hard to stop myself from going as I did in the first place to set myself in motion—On my route should I have an opportunity I will send you a sketch of my progress on my arrival in that land of promise I may send you a large package Should I meet with an oppertunity by any of the vessels that may be sailing round Cape Horn—So good-bye for the present Give my love to Fanny and the Children and believe me your

Affectionate Brother
C T STANTON

My Dear Sister [Almena][36]

You will see by what I have written to Sidney my future course for the next four or five months is marked out. You may recollect that before your leaving Chicago of my reading "Farnhams travels to Oregon" and of my expressing a desire to travel through that wild region, and that you also wished that I would go and take you along

This desire has never left me and it has seemed to me that if I ever intend to go I could not go at a better time than the present. Home seems as dear a home to me at one place as another except I have an irresistible desire to see you Van Renselar [Philip R. Van Renselar Stanton] and Sidney & family And now that I have decided on going I feel rather mournful at going away so far from *you* my dear and only friends, but I trust I may get through safe and get back so as to see you next year. It is true this is but a mere wish. But wishes are some times realized In my long letter I have written some of the incidents of my travels up to this place, which I trust you will over look the many errors that you may find as it has been written all in one night being anxious to complete or bring up my narative to this point before starting. Should David Hatch bring my trunk from C[hicago] —as I have requested him to do you will find a long letter in it for your self written after my return from Michigan which I never sent. You will find among my composition Lines "To My Mother" which Dodson to whom I showed them thought were very good You will also find lines "To my Sister" which will describe you my feelings when you requested my aid and I could not give it I cannot ask you to answer this letter not knowing that I should ever get it except you write to Van Ranselar and get him to send it around to Monteray by some vessel that may be going round So now my Dear Sister a long farewell I shall take occasion to write home by every opportunity.

Daylight is just breaking. may we trust it is a light of peace and Joy that will eventually cheer us both So once more my dear sister adieu and may God watch over and protect you

Your affectionate Brother
C T STANTON

* * *

My Dear Brother

You will [see] by the foregoing what are my future intentions. I dont know whether you will blame me or not for this course. Should prefered consulting you on so important a step before taking it but that could not be and I have been compelled to act on my own judgement The most I regret in this long Journey is that I shall not have the privelege of corisponding with my dear Brothers and Sister but now I am to loose all that but I think I shall enjoy myself much better in this active busy life upon which I am about to enter than I have done in the dull monotonous one I have so long led. If you have never read Hastings Oregon & California get it and read it.— You will then see some of the inducements which led me to this step I am in hopes to get through safe which I think there is little danger as we go in such large crowds that we shall be law unto ourselves and a protection unto each other I have hinted Almena how she might send a letter to me as a matter of course You and Sidney can take the same channel A letter to Montery the Capital of California or the Bay of San Francisco would reach there (Via Cape Horn about the time I should) Imagine how pleasant it will be to me to get letters from you all, on my arrival in that distant country.

So now my dear Brother a long long, adieu till I hear from you

Your affectionate Brother
C T STANTON

P R Van Renselar

Missouri Republican, ST. LOUIS, MAY 21, 1846

Independence, Mo., May 16, 1846.

Since my last, the scene has entirely changed in our town. Instead of a great bustle of emigrants for Oregon and California, with their wagons crowding our streets, laying in their outfits for their journey across the plains, we have a great crowd of Mexicans and traders to Santa

Fe and Chihuahua. It is supposed that we have at least two hundred Mexicans in the town and vicinity, at this time. Messrs. AGUIRA and SKILLMAN arrived here a few days since in advance of the main company, making the trip from Chihuahua in forty-six days. The present week several companies have arrived—among them, PEO SEMLRANE, JOSE GONZALES and LOUIS YAULWAGER, Mexicans, who are on their way to the east to purchase goods. They came in the early part of the week; also, JAMES MAGOFFIN, with others from Chihuahua, have also reached here. These various companies have brought in an immense quantity of specie, amounting to about three hundred and fifty thousand dollars. These Mexicans had to make forced marches between Chihuahua and Santa Fe, owing to the hostilities of the Indians, who pursued them for the purpose of robbing them, and were much pressed.

About forty wagons have left for Santa Fe and Chihuahua this week, and others are preparing to leave shortly. The late war news from Mexico does not seem to intimidate the traders . . . .

The Oregon emigrants have gone in advance of the Californians, to their great encampment on the Kanzas river, about one hundred miles west of this.[37] We have not yet received a census of their company, but will in a few days. The California emigrants held a meeting twenty-five miles west of this place, on Indian Creek, and elected their officers—Col. WM. H. RUSSELL, of Callaway, was elected their Captain. They have 141 fighting men, 71 women and 109 children, and 128 wagons. Ex-Gov. BOGGS and Rev. JAS. DUNLEAVY, of this county, are among them, with their families. There are many Kentuckians with them, who evince the same daring spirit that characterized their fathers in the settlement of that highly favored region, the land of their birth . . . .

Yours, &c.
B.

Missouri Republican, St. Louis, May 27, 1846

Weston, May 17, 1846.

Messrs. Editors—

I have at a good deal of trouble, visited the camp of the Oregon and California emigrants above this, and found them pushing forward with all possible expedition. They have been crossing the Missouri river, at as many different points as there are ferries between here and the Bluffs, but the largest body crossed at Iowa Point, Elizabethtown and St. Joseph. I found it impossible to ascertain the number of individuals, as no account was kept at any ferry, except of the number of wagons. They have all passed the Agency of the Iowa and Sioux villages, except forty-two wagons, which have crossed at the mouth of the Nishnebotna,[38] the roads from all the ferries leading by and to this point, except the above. Many, if not all the wagons which were to cross at the Bluffs, came down to the Nishnebotna, partly to avoid the numerous small streams which empty into the Nebraska on the north bank, and partly to avoid the Sioux, Pawnee and other Indians who are about to make war on each other. There has been nothing like that organization which heretofore has been deemed necessary; as they have crossed they continue upon their long journey without stopping. There was no election of officers, no systematic combination, no meeting even to adopt anything in common, and the road from the Iowa village to the Pawnee is strung with them like some great thoroughfare in the States; their numbers and supplies of all kinds having inspired them with a confidence of security. The road which they go, is said to be very good, being as well supplied with timber and water as any route on the prairie, without any stream to impede them until they reach the Nebraska. The weather has been as favorable as could be expected at this season of the year, and the grass on the prairie has been good for two weeks past. They commenced leaving about the first of the month, and continued passing the

Iowa Agency daily until about the 10th, when the last of the main body left that place. All have left and are at least seven or eight days journey from the frontier, except forty wagons which were to have been at St. Joseph last night; I saw three of them, who told me they were one day in advance of thirty others, with whom they started from Iowa and the country east of it, and had been delayed by bad roads. There were seven others in the neighborhood waiting for enough to form a company. This I think will form the rear, as I could hear of no others.[39]

One hundred and seventy-four wagons have passed the Agency, forty-two crossed above at the Nishnebotna, and there are forty still to cross at St. Joseph. This will give two hundred and fifty-six wagons, exclusive of any which may have crossed at the Bluffs; all that have passed the Agency were ox teams, with generally four yoke of oxen to each team, and the emigration from the upper country consists principally of families, and many of them large; allowing five to a wagon—and all with whom I conversed thought this a fair estimate—about 1300 souls have left these points, exclusive of the number from Independence and the Bluffs, from which latter place I have no doubt from all I can learn, at least from ten to twenty wagons have gone. They are all as well provided as the nature of the journey will admit of; the quantity of loose stock is very great, probably double the number in the teams; including work oxen, at least 5000 head have gone out.

I learn from good authority that nine hundred lodges of the Sioux Indians are on their way to make war on the Pawnees, who are preparing for them; if so, they will meet the emigrants, and I fear the next news we hear from them will be that the Indians have murdered and robbed some of them strung out as they are on the road for two hundred miles.

Of the one hundred and seventy-four wagons which passed the Agency, twelve were supposed to be Mormons, with a large lot of loose stock, which it was believed they intended to herd on the prairie and fatten, until the main body came up; this, however, is only conjecture. A good deal of excitement has prevailed on this frontier and amongst the emigrants, by reports that large bodies of Mormons, well armed, were on their way, but I can hear of none except the above, and it is now believed they will cross at the Bluffs, if they go at all . . . .[40]

Weekly Reveille, St. Louis, June 15, 1846

THE CALIFORNIANS.

The following letter is from a friend—one of the California boys. It was written after leaving the settlements, and gives a very good idea of the grand prairie picture, humanized by the string of emigrants and their rude appointments.

"I am now seated on a saddle, on the shady side of the wagon, leaning against the spokes; the wind sweeping over the prairie and fluttering my paper.

"We have passed through the Shawnee, Pottowatamie, and are now in the Kaw nation—said to be great thieves— and we are obliged to keep a strong guard out to protect our animals. I will place you at Independence, the last of civilization; the town full of mules and oxen, for sale. Here comes a long, low, raking, black wagon, that might be taken for Whitney's locomotive, a stove pipe projecting some two feet above the top, under way, and the smoke rolling out; on the side of the cover is painted, 'OREGON —54 40;' and in the course of the day dozens of others pass on for the plains, to wait for organization. Now we will leave for Indian Creek, say thirty miles; the election comes off—great excitement; 'the time for action has arrived;' speeches are made; a fuss kicked up; part leave the ground with the yells of the Indians; Gov. Boggs and Col. Russell candidates for the high honor; Russell elected by a large majority; committee go out to draw up laws; Col. R. "treats" at his marquee; a few slightly inebriated. Two o'clock—horn blows; committee's report accepted; adjourn; orders given to march at sun-rise; now the old barrels and boxes suffer. Morning—and we are under way, the line stretching some four or five miles over a most beautiful rolling sea of land; nothing but prairie as far as the eye can extend. Imagine yourself, now, alongside of Grayson, Curry, McK., and some dozen or two young Kentucky bloods on fine horses.

"Next we ascend a ridge and before us we have some eighty large wagons, drawn by four, six and eight yoke of oxen; alongside, a reckless young operatic blood sings out at the top of his voice, 'I see them on their winding way;' another one, a little sorry he put his foot in the expedition, follows with, 'Oh, I am goin' back to Old Kentuck'' another rattles in with 'Old Joe with the yaller gal raring up behind,' and you are in our crowd. Apply the spur now, and we are up with the line. Here is a young dare-devil, not long from the counting room, with long gad in hand, stirring up some four or five yoke of oxen. Look inside, and there is a lady and some two or three children, reclining on a tumbled lot of coats, blankets and buffalo robes. Who is that ahead, with slouched white hat, sitting with the 'ribbons' in hand, 'behind *four mules?* he has been on the Third Avenue and Bloomingdale road before to-day. Alongside, 'go it Lip!' cries one of our boys; that is Mr. Lippingcott, from Pearl street, on his way to California. Now we are at the head of the line— here is a little old man in buckskin, a long rifle over his shoulder, and a large determined man by his side—they are the guides. We travel some twelve or fifteen miles, and form "caral" for the night—wagons in a circle; wheels chained together; tents on the outside; cattle in— now the cooking is 'done up brown;' horn blows; guard mounted; pipes smoked, and we retire to our dreams."

"The Buffalo Hunt"

The Plains

[GEORGE L. CURRY] TO THE ST. LOUIS *Reveille,*
MAY 15, 1846.[41]

Friends of the Reveille: Here we are, May 17th
[15th?] in a beautiful encampment on the Wakanisha
[Wakarusa] river, all in the enjoyment of excellent
health and a fine flow of spirits. The recent rains have
made the roads very bad; indeed, for three miles before
reaching the elevated ground upon which we are encamped, it was a complete swamp. By assisting each
other, however, we all got through without experiencing
any accident that we could not ourselves repair; the rear-
most division, comprising seventeen wagons, all getting
into camp by nine o'clock last night. We shall remain here
one day, to repair damages and roads, and then hasten
on to the Kansas. I understand that there are some thirty
wagons for California about a day's travel behind; they

will probably join us to-morrow.

The company assembled under Mr. Harlan, on Indian Creek, numbering twenty-seven wagons, we passed on the Santa Fe trace last Wednesday [May 13]. They have elected Judge Morin, of Missouri, their commander, and contemplate pushing through to the Sacramento by themselves. Our company number sixty-four wagons, and receives augmentation almost daily. Our strength averages about two men and a half, capable of bearing arms, to each wagon. The company is a most agreeable one, each laboring for the good of all.

Life on the plains far surpasses my expectation; there is a freedom and a nobleness about it that tend to bring forth the full manhood. A man upon the horizon-bound prairie feels his own strength and estimates his own weakness. He is alive to every thing around him. For him there is a joy in the "lone elm" grandeur on the mounds, beauty in the grassy and flower-besprinkled couch on which he rests, and a glory forever round him, stretching his spirit to its fullest tension. Bacon and hard biscuit may occasionally interfere with his *fairydom,* but that only occurs twice a day, and the influence is but momentary. To-day we have ripe strawberries upon the prairies—we eat them with cream too, at that; think of it, and "begrudge" us. There are other features in our "plain living," which I intend to speak of hereafter. I have been writing these few lines whilst the bearer, who takes them to the settlements, was saddling his horse; he is ready and waiting, and I have scarcely commenced, but more anon.

LAON.

Niles' National Register, JUNE 27, 1846

EMIGRATION TO OREGON. — By a member of Congress, the *Argus* has received the following interesting letter.—

Weston, May 18, 1846.

I have just returned from the Oregon Camps above this, which I visited to inform myself concerning the emigration to the Pacific. The party in front, must at this date, be nearly 300 miles from this frontier.—In fact, they are strung along the road from the Iowa village to the Paronees [Pawnees], on the Nebraska. I have been a week over with the Iowas and Saucs, from whose villages they start on the great Prairies. They have left this season well provided with everything, except Pilots. But without any organization. The consequence of which, I fear, will be that the Pawnees, Sioux and other wild Indians of the Prairies, will not only rob, but kill many of them off, as they find them in small parties. The next news we have from them, I fear, will be that some disaster of this kind has happened. They are all on the plains except 40 wagons, which I left at St. Joseph to cross to-day and to-morrow. They will go together, and I think will be strong enough. Two hundred and sixteen wagons, exclusive of these, have left the Iowa agency and mouth of the Nishnebotina, making altogether 356 [256] wagons—each wagon has in general 4 yoke of oxen, which added to the loose stock, would make 2000 head of cattle taken. The number of souls could not be ascertained, but it will average about 5 to a wagon, which would give about 1300, which added to those who leave Independence, would make about 2000 souls going out from this frontier to the Pacific, well provided with arms and necessaries. They could muster, I should think, when together, 800 able bodied men of resolute spirits.

On yesterday I for the first time, heard the news from Mexico, it did not surprise me though in the least but I wish an express could be sent to overtake the emigrants after Congress has acted, and authorise them to make the conquest of California. They could and would do it, and take it for granted our Government will declare war—all they want is a chance.

WILLIAM H. RUSSELL TO THE INDEPENDENCE *Western Expositor,* "FOUR MILES WEST OF KANSAS RIVER" [MAY 18-19, 1846][42]

Messrs. Webb and French:—

In compliance with my promise, I proceed to give you a hasty and brief account of the journeyings of the California emigrants to this point.

Our numbers cannot even yet, be accurately ascertained, in consequence of the irregular manner in which they come in, but they are numerous, and cannot fall short of one hundred wagons.

We have had a pleasant march thus far without any kind of accident, and much less disturbance than could have been expected, from so large and promiscuous an assemblage.

Our movements being so unwieldy, in consequence of our great numbers, we deemed it expedient this morning [May 18], to separate; we done so in the most amiable manner, and I entertain the fullest confidence that we shall proceed with great despatch, and I am satisfied with the utmost harmony.

Our journeyings are so monotonous that I have nothing to communicate by way of episode, save the birth this morning [May 19] in our camp of twin infant boys, one of whom was called after the accoucheur, Doct. Reuben P. Rubey, of Independence, and the other he [Reason Hall] done me the honor to call after me, so that the youngest emigrant that will arrive in California will be one of my namesakes.

We have had intelligence of the difficulties of our Government with Mexico, but it has created no alarm in our camp. Our women and children seem to anticipate pleasure rather than otherwise in the conflict with the Mexicans, when we arrive in California.

I have so few facilities for writing, that I write but little, and always with great labor and must now close this hasty and uninteresting letter.

Your ob't servt.
WM. H. RUSSELL

WILLIAM H. RUSSELL TO THE *Missouri Republican,*
"FOUR MILES WEST OF KANSAS RIVER. 120 MILES
WEST OF INDEPENDENCE," MAY 19, 1846.[43]

Col. A. B. Chambers—

We crossed the Kansas yesterday, and the two or three
last preceding days being excessively warm, and our animals a good deal jaded, I considered it proper to halt
to-day, which affords me another opportunity, and perhaps the last one for some time, of giving you an imper-
fect account of our travels.

You have been informed, I suppose, that the company,
by a large majority, were indiscreet enough to select me
as their commander, to justify which flattering distinc-
tion as far as I could, I have imposed on myself incessant
labors by day and by night, and if blessed with health, I
shall not intermit my watchfulness until we reach the point
of our destination.

Nothing at all of interest has transpired since my last
letter. Our journeyings are regular but very slow, not
averaging more than fifteen miles a day. I considered it
proper on yesterday, to divide the company, in consequence of the great numbers of wagons and the amount
of stock. I retain with me ninety-eight efficient men, forty
women, fifty-seven children, three hundred and twenty
oxen, fifty horses, and forty-six wagons, a company quite
large enough of itself, but I have my other divisions always within convenient reach, so as to enable me to concentrate, in a few hours, at any time, though I have no
fears that such an emergency will ever happen.

Our peregrinations, though provokingly monotonous,
so far as driving oxen and forming carals are concerned,
is yet occasionally mingled with a good deal of excitement, and racy wit. We are attracted almost every hour
by numbers of the prairie denizens, most gaudily dressed,

mounted on the wild, outlandish ponies, passing and re-passing our column, bantering our boys for swaps.

It is a great mistake in supposing that the Indian is devoid of curiosity. I think we are chiefly indebted to that quality of mother Eve for their frequent visits. As yet, I do not think they have stolen anything from us; but perhaps we have been saved by the vigilance of the guard.

Our party, without a single exception, ladies and gentlemen, continue to enjoy most robust health, as is proved by appetites that would do justice to a subject of a menagerie. If we come across buffaloes, the poor slaughtered animals will have just cause to regret our invasion of their far distant pasture ground.

We have learned the probability of our difficulties with Mexico, but it has created no alarm among our ladies; and as I shall go on, and if attacked, the Anglo-Saxon blood may be spilled, but they will not be captured, that you may rely on positively.

I am so badly situated for writing that I must of necessity come to a close, but I must first tell you how we increase our numbers, which process, we hope, will continue in our projected new home. A worthy lady was brought to bed yesterday on our march, by a cause not complained of by those "who love their lords," and in a short time my Adjutant reported twin boys added to our numbers, one of whom was named after the attending physicians, and the other after your humble servant. If we continue this way, how long will it take to people California. I am, in haste, with high respect, your obedient servant,

WM. H. RUSSELL.

[GEORGE L. CURRY] TO THE ST. LOUIS *Reveille,*
"AMONG THE INDIANS," MAY 19, 1846.[44]

Friends of the *Reveille*:

We crossed the Kanzas river on yesterday, by placing the wagons on flat boats and swimming our horses and oxen. We accomplished it with considerable despatch, too, crossing forty wagons in about four hours, which number of wagons now comprise the advance company of the California emigration. The company that elected Col. Russell commander became so large as it progressed towards its destination—swelling into upwards of one hundred wagons—that it was found actually necessary to form into two companies in order to travel with any thing like the usual speed. Col. Russell is with us, and makes a most popular commander. We are waiting to-day for some eight or ten wagons that are behind— the emigrants attached to which, finding themselves alone on the road, sent forward a request that we should wait for them to come up, which we are now doing, four miles west of the Kanzas. As soon as they have joined we shall number fifty odd wagons, and shall push forward with unusual despatch. We have one hundred men capable of bearing arms, in the company.

We found the Caw or Kanzas river in a very low state, and if we had chosen to go six miles out of our course we could have forded it without difficulty. It was a grand sight to see the emigration defiling from the wooded banks of the river, and the wagons plunging through the sand, which at high water is a portion of the river's bed, as though they were drawn by any other power than that of the ox. The ox is a sure and faithful animal, and although a slow moving one, is decidedly the best beast of burden for the emigrant, when all things are taken into consideration.

We heard the "war news" some twenty miles back of this, but the particulars we did not receive until last evening, when, through the politeness of Mr. Buchanan, Postmaster of Independence, and Mr. Webb, of the *Expositor,* who came out to us, we received the mail. The only thing it contained for myself was a *Weekly Reveille* of the 11th inst.; and though I felt a little disappointment in not hearing from one of my numerous friends and acquaintances, I could not think that I was entirely alone or neglected, however, when I had the privilege — the luxury—of reading a *Reveille*. I stole to a remote part of the *caral,* threw my self upon the grass, and in the glory of the setting sun—the setting sun of the prairie, oh, how magnificent!—held sweet converse with my much-loved friend. Our mutual oracle was responsive to my every thought. I needed not to ask—the answer was before the question. I was with you again — the "our Senior," "Straws," "Solitaire," and all. No reader of the *Weekly Reveille* of the 11th of May read it as I did—page, column, line and word, were pressed upon the brain. I was recalled to myself and duties by the sounding of the bugle for the night-guard.

So far as our company is concerned I can assure you that the war intelligence does not *shake* us in the least. We will move steadily forward, prepared for any emergency; and there is no power that can cope with the spring emigration when it shall have reached the western slope of the "Stony Mountains." Texas is ours—is it impossible that California can be? The very echo of the "can?" is most decisive. There *shall* be another star added to our constellation. As our friend "Solitaire" would say, "it's jest as sure as shootin'." We carry with us peace and war—let the Californians choose which they please.

I neglected to state that on the day of the organization of the California emigration, Mr. Grayson withdrew his name as a candidate for the office of commander, and gave his vote and influence for Col. Russell.

The number of wagons that will go out to Santa Fe and Chihuahua this spring and summer, will number over *three hundred.* I state this fact here, in order to correct an error that was made in one of my letters, wherein you made me say that something like *one* hundred was the number. It is expected that the trade will be "used up" for the next season, at least. Again, when opportunity offers.

Yours, always sincerely,
LAON.

Missouri Reporter, St. Louis, May 19, 1846

About 1000 emigrants have left Independence, the place of rendezvous, for California. The number of emigrants to Oregon is not so large, as was anticipated; California having become the principal point of attraction.

— — —

Messrs. Shaw and Pope, from Fort George, on the Little Missouri [Bad River], report the streams very low, with but little snow on the mountains. They met a number of emigrants on their way to Oregon and California.

Missouri Reporter, St. Louis, May 20, 1846

FROM THE MOUNTAINS—We learn from Mr. Robert Pope, a gentleman recently from Fort Laramie—which place he left on the 31st of March—that large quantities of snow fell in the mountains during the winter. Mr. P. met Ex-Governor Boggs and company — including Messrs. Jacobs and Ewing, of Louisville— on the Santa Fe trace, destined for California. He also met about 500 wagons on the Santa Fe road, though the emigration to Oregon seems not to be so great as at former periods. One Santa Fe trader, Samuel C. Owens, of Independence, takes out the present season, $50,000 worth of merchandize to Santa Fe and Chihuahua. Mr. McGuffin, with 30 wagons, arrived at Independence from Chihuahua about the 14th inst. It was expected at Independence that 500 wagons more would depart for Santa Fe during the present season.

Our informant also states that a strong disinclination [*i. e.,* inclination?] is manifested among the people of California, to throw off the Mexican authority, and to come under the government of the United States. American emigrants that have settled there, are well pleased with their situation and prospects.

The Gazette, St. Joseph, May 22, 1846

EMIGRANTS.

Some thirty wagons of emigrants bound for Oregon and California, passed through this place yesterday and to-day. They purpose joining a fraction of a company encamped on the opposite side of the river, and will take up their line of march in a few days. The company will number some fifty wagons. This will be the last company that will leave this season. We expect to be able in a few days to furnish a list of all the emigrants that have crossed here, and at the upper ferries.[45]

Missouri Republican, St. Louis, June 1, 1846

Independence, Mo. May 25.

A gentleman who has just arrived from the California camp on Kansas river, informs me that the company had organized before reaching that point, but had divided, owing to a slight altercation which took place between Capt. Russell and Rev. Mr. Dunleavy.—Russell called off all that were willing to go with him as their commander, leaving a large party who chose Dunleavy as their captain. It was generally believed that Governor Boggs would return. They had received news that several thousand Mormons had crossed the river at Iowa Point, on their way to California. As Boggs apprehended some danger of being assassinated by them, he began to talk strongly of returning. It was impossible to obtain a correct estimate of the number of wagons and souls in the emigrating parties up to the time our informant left, two hundred and thirty wagons had crossed the Kansas River. It was supposed that there were about sixty yet to cross. The number of souls in both the Oregon and California companies, in the aggregate, is estimated at about 2,000.

Several companies of Mexican traders have gone out since the war news reached here, and are making rapid pace across the plains to get into Mexico as soon as possible. They fear the U. S. troops at Fort Leavenworth will be ordered to intercept them. Several companies yet to go out are hesitating whether they will go or not; but the boldest will venture at any rate . . . .

Business is quite brisk here; crops very promising— wheat never looked better in the country at this season than now.

Yours,

B.

Missouri Republican, St. Louis, June 11, 1846

Weston, May 25, 1846

Since I last wrote you, we have had no news from the emigrants to the Pacific from points above this, though a rumor has been current for the last two days that a company of thirty were returning, who had been robbed of everything by the Indians. I have been anticipating something as bad or worse, but as yet the rumor wants confirmation. The wagons which I informed you were at St. Josephs are still there, and may ultimately abandon the trip, as it is now getting late. I can hear of no Mormons on this frontier, though various rumors have been afloat at different times of great numbers coming. If they have reached the river, or even its neighborhood, it must be beyond the limits of this State, and unless they have recently arrived, they are not even at Council Bluffs . . . .[46]

G.

Weekly American, St. Louis, June 5, 1846

MORMON AND CALIFORNIA EMIGRANTS.—We learn from the officers of the steamboat *Radnor,* in from Missouri river, that a messenger arrived at Kansas from the plains, who reported that a collision had taken place between Gov. Boggs' party of California emigrants, and the Mormons, who are on their way to the same destination.— Boggs and several of his party were killed in the encounter. The settlers on the Kansas were arming to go to the assistance of the emigrants. We know not how true the story may be—a few days no doubt will bring us the facts.

Weekly Reveille, St. Louis, June 8, 1846

IMPORTANT RUMOR.—*Collision between Mormon and California Emigrants.*—The officers of the *Radnor,* which steamer arrived from the Missouri river, reports that a messenger arrived at Kansas, from the plains, while they lay there, who reported that a collision had taken place between the party of Mormons now emigrating to California, and Gov. Bogg's party journeying to the same destination. In the encounter, Boggs and several of his company were killed. The last intelligence we had from the plains spoke of a threat which had been made against the California emigrants by the Mormons, and this may have given rise to the report of a collision. We give the intelligence as we received it. A few days will bring us more particulars, if the messenger's story be true. The settlers at Kansas were arming to go out to the assistance of the emigrants.

RISE IN THE MISSOURI.—The *Radnor* reports the Missouri rising all the way down, at the rate of three inches per hour—it threatens to again overflow the bottoms.

A party of mountain traders, from Fort Laramie, came down upon the *Radnor,* bringing with them a quantity of furs.

Missouri Republican, St. Louis, June 6, 1846

The report that the Mormons had attacked a body of California emigrants on the plains, and killed Gov. Boggs and others, turns out, as we expected it would, to be a hoax.

Weekly American, St. Louis, July 17, 1846

OREGON AND CALIFORNIA EMIGRANTS.—The Independence *Expositor,* of July 4th, says:

"A gentleman of our town received a letter this week, from Ex-Governor Boggs, now on his way to California, under date of June 2d. The letter was sent in by a Shawnee Indian and is without doubt the latest news from the Oregon and California emigrants. It is written from a branch of Blue river, about 250 miles from this place. The letter states that no accident of any kind had happened to interrupt them seriously on their trip, and that they were getting along well. Two deaths had taken place amongst the California emigrants—one a small child, the child of Judge Morin, and the other a Mrs. Keys, from Springfield, Ill., quite an aged lady and, had been laboring under consumption. We will endeavor in our next to give the particulars of this letter which from the late time at which it was received we were prevented from doing. We will add, however, that Gov. Boggs says nothing in his letters about the Mormons, which will settle many rumors going through the land about this people."

Missouri Republican, St. Louis, June 11, 1846

St. Joseph, (Mo.) June 7, 1846.

I have not written to you for some time past, owing to the difficulty I have encountered in ascertaining the exact number of emigrants who have crossed the river at this place and above, for Oregon and California. Two hundred and twenty-four wagons have passed, up to this date, the great Nemahaw Sub-Agency, including those which have passed here and at the intermediate points. The emigrants have commenced their journey in detached parties, and, except in a few instances, have not elected any officers. Captain MARTIN, of Platte City, who passed over early in the season, was elected Captain of the first company that started, and another (name unknown,) was elected captain of a subsequent company.[47] It is supposed that about seventy-five wagons crossed over at points above the Nemahaw Agency, making in all about three hundred wagons. About two-thirds of this number are bound to California, the balance to Oregon. They average five or six souls to the wagon.

NATHAN J. PUTNAM TO JOSEPH PUTNAM, "PLATT RIVER 370 MILES FROM INDEPENDENCE," JUNE 10, 1846.[48]

Dear Father

I have an oppertunity of writeing you a few lines by a party of Fur Traders desending the Platte—[49]

I have had unusual good health so far and can now walk 10 or 15 miles without any difficulty the whole company have enjoyed the same Blessing—

Buch hanan & John B. are well Charles is himself writeing we shall cross the south fork of the Platte by the eighteenth of this month and by the 4th of July we shall have passed Indipendence Rock beyond Fort Laramie so that when you heare the cannons fire in the morning on the 4th you may know where (or nearly so) we are

Give my love to Mother and to all the family and my respects to all enquireing friends

I am writeing on the ground as we have stoped to noon on the Banks of the Platte—Saw today 9 antelope and Buchhanan saw one Bufaloe I can write no more as the man who is to take my letter to the boat is about leaveing

Good by

N. J. PUTNAM

[GEORGE L. CURRY] TO THE ST. LOUIS *Reveille,* PLATTE RIVER, JUNE 12, 1846.[50]

Messrs. Keemle & Field:—We have just met a party of mounted men, in the employ of Pierre Chouteau, Jr., & Co., who are on their way down the Platte from Fort Laramie, ladened with peltries, &c. I take advantage of the opportunity to send you a few hurried lines, that you may know our whereabouts, and how we fare. We are now about seventy-five miles from the Crossings of Platte, and averaging some twenty miles a day in travel, and in good health and spirits.

Since I wrote you at Black Warrior, or Soldier Creek, we were compelled to lie by at the Crossings of Blue four days, in consequence of the river being too high to ford. We were finally obliged to make canoes, and cross our wagons by means of them. We crossed fifty-four wagons in one day, in the midst of a cold, heavy rain, too. That is what might be called driving things. We have had, since then, fair luck and pretty good roads. The weather, however, has been excessively warm lately, and the musquitoes dreadfully annoying. We are without incidents of any importance, as yet, and have not seen an Indian since we left the Kaw Village—which Indians, by way of parenthesis, I would say, are as miserable and "loafing" a race of beings as one would care to behold.

We struck the Platte on Monday evening [June 8], and were rejoiced to escape the confinement of the sand hills that form the southern boundary of the floor-like bottom land upon which we are now travelling.

We have seen no buffalo yet, and our friends from the Fort tell us it will be three or four days before we are gratified in this respect. Antelopes we have seen, in any numbers, and have been fortunate enough to get some into camp. I prefer the meat to venison; it is juicy and tender. We supped last night on curlew, snipe, plover and duck—that's a prairie bill of fare for you! Don't your mouths water?—but they need not, if you let your minds take in the idea of the number of mornings and nights that plain middling meat, crackers and heavy biscuit comprise our fare. A world for a meal at "The Empire," and another for a "sherry cobler," after Austin's best style, with Fuller standing by, entertaining you with his pleasant chit-chat. But these may not be dreamed of, even, now.

It may be as well to say here, that a trip of this kind is the best thing in the world, perhaps, to knock the romance out of a fellow—I mean travelling with emigrating companies. There are so many little things—trifles, in the main—constantly occurring, of an unpleasant character, that one must call in a good deal of philosophy to his aid not to be entirely disgusted, and driven to take the back track. But then we have a glorious time of it in the still night, upon the broad prairie; the solitude gives a profundity to thought, and fancy has no limits. The glorious night upon the prairies it would be useless for me even to *attempt* to describe.

I took a skir[mish] among the hills yesterday, in hopes of finding buffalo, and discovered, among other things, a species of the cactus plant, with a most admirable flower; likewise *green peas.* Just think of it, green peas in a hollow among the sand hills, miles away from the emigrant route. They resemble the cultivated pea in every respect, excepting that the leaf of the vine, or bush, is entirely different.

I shall send some "dottings" back from Fort Laramie, among which shall be a few serious words to emigrants.

The party from the Fort, numbering thirteen mackinaw boats, are under the charge of Mr. [P. D.] Papin, who has long been the popular and efficient superintendent of affairs at the Fort. We saw eleven of the boats yesterday morning, on the western side of the river, with whom, as we are informed, is Mr. P. The Platte is now so low and difficult of navigation that the party despair of reaching the mouth; they have been since the 7th of May making this distance. Wagons will probably be sent to them from Council Bluffs, to which place, as I understand, an express has already been sent.

The company are through with their "nooning," and I am forced to close, as the line of march is again resumed.

                                                    LAON.

CHARLES T. STANTON TO SIDNEY STANTON,
"EMIGRANTS' TRAIL," JUNE 12, 1846 [51]

For the past few days we have got along finely, having travelled at the rate of from 20 to 25 miles a day. We are now encamped upon the Great Platte, 500 miles from Independence, and 300 from Fort Laramie.

My last was dated June 2, soon after crossing the Blue Earth River, where we were detained by high water several days.

After travelling one or two days, we encamped upon the Little Blue which abounds in fish, and my skill as a fisherman was here put to the test; but I succeeded in catching one of the finest cat you ever saw, which we had the next morning for breakfast. I have eaten of the salmon, the Mackinaw trout and the celebrated white fish, but I think I never ate anything better than the fine fish caught from the waters of the Blue.

We journeyed for several days up this delightful stream, and every night found romantic camping ground. The scenery was most beautiful—the eye wandered over fair prospects of hill and dale. A strong north wind prevailed for two or three days; all of the men wore their over coats to keep warm, and the women wrapped themselves up in shawls, or walked on foot, to do the same.

In our encampment we had several Oregon families, constituting twenty wagons. Some little disturbance arising, they concluded to withdraw from our party and go on their own hook, forming a company of their own, mustering a force of some twenty fighting men.[52]

They went on ahead, and for several days encamped within one or two miles of us. In their party there were many young ladies—in ours, mostly young men. Friendships and attachments had been formed which were hard to break; for, ever since, our company is nearly deserted, by the young men every day riding out on horseback, pretending to hunt, but instead of pursuing the bounding deer or fleet antelope, they are generally found among the fair Oregon girls! Thus they go, every day, making love by the road-side, in the midst of the wildest and most beautiful scenery, now admiring the meanderings of some delightful stream, or course of some noble river!

This little party, one day before they reached the

Platte, were surprised by a band of 20 or 30 Pawnees, drawn up in battle array, coming down full sweep to attack them; but they were no sooner seen than the men formed in order of battle to meet them. The cunning Pawnees, seeing this little band drawn out, and fearing the deadly rifle, immediately turned their war party into a visit—shaking hands, hugging men, and attempting to embrace the women. After receiving some presents, they went away apparently as well pleased as if they had taken all of their scalps.

Every one was anxious to reach the Platte. It was in every body's mouth "when shall we get to the Platte?" We had now travelled four days up the Blue, and one day's march would take us to that great river. This day's march, therefore, was resumed with alacrity. We had to cross a high elevated plain, the dividing ridge between the waters of the Kansas and the Platte. About eleven A. M. we could perceive, as we crossed the highest elevation, that the land gradually descended both ways, and far in the distance could see the little mounds or hillocks, which formed the ridge or bluffs of the noble river. Here we stopped "to noon," after which we journeyed on, a part on horseback, going ahead (myself among the number) to catch the first view of the river. It was about two P. M., when, in ascending a high point of land, we saw, spread out before us, the valley of the noble Platte. We all hallooed with pleasure and surprise. The valley of the Platte! there is none other like it. The bluffs are from ten to fifteen miles apart, the river, of over a mile in width, flowing through the centre. The bluffs suddenly fall down from 50 to 100 feet, when there is a gradual slope to the water's edge. There is not a single stick of timber to be seen on either side of the river—it is one interminable prairie as far as the eye can extend; yet there is a relief found in the numerous islands of the river being generally covered with wood. We encamped for the first time, on the 9th instant, on the Platte, and for three days have been travelling up its beautiful valley.

About noon to-day we met some few [fur] traders going down with boats, loaded with buffalo and other skins. By them I shall send this letter to you. They are staying in our encampment tonight. To-morrow morning they will leave for the East, and we, on our long journey, for the West. Adieu, for the present. I shall write you again from Fort Laramie.

S. T. C.

WILLIAM H. RUSSELL TO THE *Missouri Statesman,* "NEBRASKA OR BIG PLATTE RIVER, ABOUT 400 MILES WEST OF INDEPENDENCE," JUNE 13, 1846 [53]

Col. Wm. F. Switzler:

Dear Sir:—I remember that I promise to write to you somewhere on the road, and give you an account of our progress, and such of the incidents of our wilderness life, as I supposed might interest you and your readers, and having stopped to-day to repair wagons, recruit animals, &c., I have concluded to begin a letter, which, in all probability, I shall not close or meet with an opportunity of sending back before we get to Fort Larima, at least 300 miles further on our journey.

Well it is a queer life we are living, all our teams are oxen, and our travel of consequence is vexatiously slow not averaging more than 16 or 17 miles a day. We get up at daylight, get breakfast as soon thereafter as practicable, always mean to start or break up the caral at 7 o'clock. At 12 we stop and noon it, rest about an hour, and then travel until between 4 and 5 o'clock, P.M., when we stop for the night.

I keep up a regular guard, and if I could only keep the militia from falling asleep on their post I should be secure against surprise.

My duties as commandant are troublesome beyond anything I could conceive of. I am annoyed with all manner of complaints, one will not do this, and another has done something that must be atoned for, and occasionally, through variety, we have a fight among ourselves *only* to *show* what they can *do,* should the Indians attack us.

I sometimes get out of patience myself, and once I threw up my commission, but to my surprise after I had left the caral I was again unanimously re-elected, and a committee with Gov. Boggs as chairman raised to request a renewal of my duties. My vanity of course was flattered, and I again after a general lecture resumed the yoke, but how much longer I can consent to serve is very problematical.

The country through which we have traveled from Independence has been almost an unbroken plain and prairie, with the exception of the margin of the streams we have crossed, consequently we are put mightily to our shifts for fuel to cook with, and are now relying chiefly on buffeloe *chips,* a resource that we hope will not fail us.

The Platte, a stream sometimes over a mile in width, which we travel up at least 170 miles is entirely destitute of timber.

Our hunters are beginning to kill buffalo, elk and antelopes, the latter are very abundant, and I expect to dine to-day on the hump of a fine buffaloe.

I cannot state the precise number of emigrants for California and Oregon, but all told it cannot fall short of 5,000 souls. I have not had less than 150 wagons under my command since our organization at Indian Creek, but the number being so bulky and unwieldy I have been compelled to seperate, and I have not at this time more than about 40 wagons, and yet it is too large for harmony and despatch.

I have with me Mr. E. Bryant, a noble brother chip of yours, who will, in a book, record our proceedings in a style worth reading; also young Jacobs of Louisville, Ky., a fine little fellow; Gov. Boggs and family; Alphonzo Boone and family; Mr. Greyson; also Mr. West and his fine family from Callaway; also Mr. Branham and his, and a host of other most excellent and respectable people.[54]

We have heard nothing of the Mormons and see no trace of them being before us.

I write so inconveniently that I must stop from sheer exhaustion, and may add a few lines hereafter when further on the road.

Truly your friend,

W. H. RUSSELL.

South Fork Platte, 16th June.

I have just met with a company of Oregon visitors on their return to Missouri, and will carry this.[55] We are advanced 60 or 70 miles since the date as aforesaid. We find thousands of buffalo, and kill more than we can destroy [eat], it is really fine sport.

W. H. R.

EDWIN BRYANT TO A FRIEND, "SOUTH FORK OF PLATTE RIVER, 500 MILES FROM INDEPENDENCE, MO.," JUNE 16, 1846 [56]

My Dear Sir: Presuming that you would like to see a line written 500 miles from civilization, I avail myself of a few moments of spare time to write, and send you a note by a small company of Oregon emigrants, whom we met this afternoon, returning to the States. They are eight in number, and left Oregon on the 1st of March, and appear, I suppose, much as I shall appear before I reach California—that is, like savages. They seem, however, to be clever and intelligent men.

We left our place of rendezvous, in the neighborhood of Independence, on the 12th of May, and have been detained in several places by high water, or we should have been about 200 miles farther advanced upon our journey. The weather at first was very rainy, and the roads wet and miry, but no rain has fallen on us for the last three weeks, and now the roads are excellent, and we march from 20 to 25 miles per day. The country through which we have passed thus far is totally unlike any that I have ever before beheld. I have no time; suffice it to say, that much of the scenery combines more of the sublime and beautiful than any that I have ever beheld.

For a distance of 300 miles after we left Independence, the prairies presented to the eye a rich and varied landscape, surpassingly beautiful and grand. It would almost seem as if the Deity had lain himself out in arranging a garden of illimitable extent to shame the puny efforts of man. For 200 miles up the Platte river the scenery has been less picturesque and the land flat and the soil poor; but the singularity, the strangeness of everything you still gaze upon, still render our journey interesting; and the days appear shorter than I ever knew them.

We are now in the midst of buffaloes, and buffalo meat is as "plenty as blackberries." I have seen not less than 1000 of these animals to-day, without going off from the wagon trail. I assisted in shooting one about two hours ago. He fell about 200 yards from our encampment to-night. Antelopes are very abundant, but hard to kill. They are almost as fleet as the wind, speaking literally, and it is only by stealth that they can be approached. We have not seen an Indian since we left the Big Blue river— 17 days.

In that region, large numbers of the Kansas Tribe followed our caravan several days for the purpose of begging and stealing, but thus far we have lost nothing, and had no encounters with the savages. The district we are now in belongs to the Pawnees.

If you were to see me now you would scarcely know me. Indeed, when I look in the glass I do not exactly recognize myself. I am as dark, apparently, as the darkest Indian I have yet seen, and bear in many respects a strong resemblance to them. My health has generally been good, although there has been much sickness among the emigrants. The numbers of emigrant wagons upon the road is 470, each wagon averages about 5 or 6 persons, men, women and children, and the number of cattle besides oxen in the teams, is about 10 to each wagon.

These wagons are scattered in companies of from 20 to 50, over a space of 300 miles. Our company consists of 40 wagons, and now is in the rear. We have preferred to spare our teams at the outset. So you see we are a "mighty host." I have slept on the ground now more than a month, and have become so inured to it that I doubt if I could sleep in a bed. We expect to cross the south fork of the Platte to-morrow.

After doing this, I shall, in company with four men, proceed on horseback to Fort Selomie [Laramie]; a distance of 200 miles. Here we intend, if we can, to swap our oxen and wagons for mules, and pack our provisions the remainder of the way on mules. By this arrangement, we shall gain at least 10 miles per day.

Yours, very truly.

E. BRYANT.

MRS. GEORGE DONNER TO A FRIEND IN SPRINGFIELD, ILLINOIS, "NEAR THE JUNCTION OF THE NORTH AND SOUTH PLATTE," JUNE 16, 1846 [57]

My Old Friend:—

We are now on the Platte, 200 miles from Fort Larimee. Our journey, so far, has been pleasant. The roads have been good, and food plentiful. The water for a part of the way has been indifferent—but at no time have our cattle suffered for it. Wood is now very scarce, but *"Buffalo chips"* are excellent—they kindle quick and retain heat surprisingly. We had this evening Buffalo steaks broiled upon them that had the same flavor they would have had upon hickory coals.

We feel no fear of Indians. Our cattle graze quietly around our encampment unmolested. Two or three men will go hunting twenty miles from camp;—and last night two of our men lay out in the wilderness rather than ride their horses after a hard chase. Indeed if I do not experience something far worse than I have yet done, I shall say the trouble is all in getting started.

Our waggons have not needed much repair, but I cannot yet tell in what respects they may be improved. Certain it is they cannot be too strong. Our preparations for the journey, in some respects, might have been bettered. Bread has been the principal article of food in our camp. We laid in 150 lbs. of flour and 75 lbs. of meat for each individual, and I fear bread will be scarce. Meat is abundant. Rice and beans are good articles on the road—cornmeal, too, is very acceptable. Linsey dresses are the most suitable for children. Indeed if I had one it would be comfortable. There is so cool a breeze at all times in the prairie that the sun does not feel so hot as one would suppose.

We are now 450 miles from Independence. Our route at first was rough and through a timbered country which appeared to be fertile. After striking the prairie we found a first rate road, and the only difficulty we had has been crossing creeks. In that, however, there has been no danger. I never could have believed we could have travelled so far with so little difficulty. The prairie between the Blue and Platte rivers is beautiful beyond description. Never have I seen so varied a country—so suitable for cultivation. Every thing was new and pleasing. The Indians frequently come to see us, and the chiefs of a tribe breakfasted at our tent this morning. All are so friendly that I cannot help feeling sympathy and friendship for them. But on one sheet, what can I say?

Since we have been on the Platte we have had the river on one side, and the ever varying mounds on the other— and have traveled through the Bottom lands from one to ten miles wide with little or no timber. The soil is sandy, and last year, on account of the dry season, the emigrants found grass here scarce. Our cattle are in good order, and where proper care has been taken none has been lost. Our milch cows have been of great service— indeed, they have been of more advantage than our meat. We have plenty of butter and milk.

We are commanded by Capt. Russel — an amiable man. George Donner is himself yet. He crows in the morning, and shouts out "Chain up, boys!—chain up!" with as much authority as though he was "something in particular." John Denton is still with us—we find him a useful man in camp. Hiram Miller and Noah James are in good health and doing well. We have of the best of people in our company, and some, too, that are not so good.

Buffalo show themselves frequently. We have found the wild tulip, the primrose, the lupine, the ear-drop, the larkspur, and creeping hollyhock, and a beautiful flower resembling the bloom of the beech tree, but in bunches large [?] as a small sugar-loaf, and of every variety of shade, to red and green. I botanize and read some, but cook a "heap" more.

There are 420 [470] waggons, as far as we have heard, on the road between here and Oregon and California.

Give our love to all enquiring friends—God bless them.

Yours truly

MRS. GEORGE DONNER

GEORGE L. CURRY TO THE ST. LOUIS *Reveille,* "SOUTH FORK OF PLATTE RIVER," JUNE 16, 1846 [58]

Friends of the Reveille:—

As I have no time to write you in full, I beg to refer you to my friend, Mr. Wall, whom we have just met on the road, on his return from the Sandwich Islands, *via* Oregon. He will take pleasure in giving all the information he can in relation to matters and things on the Pacific. (See a letter from Mr. W. in another part of the paper—*Eds.*) [59]

We have met no Mormons, as yet, nor have we heard of any being on the road since we came out of the settlements. We are all well, and within fifteen miles of the crossing of the South Fork, and two hundred of Fort Laramie. I wrote you a long letter by some voyageurs from Fort Laramie, which you may not receive until some time after this, as they were bound down the Platte in Mackinaw boats.

I am in good health, and enjoy the trip as much as its privations will permit. My pony and myself are greatly attached to each other; he has proved himself a most valuable animal. I tried him in a buffalo hunt yesterday, and he beat all the horses. He laid back his ears—flew over the ground with a rapidity that soon brought me into the midst of the band, and all I had to do was to make my choice, and kill. I will write you more fully from Fort Laramie.

Truly yours, G. L. C.

NATHAN J. AND CHARLES F. PUTNAM TO THEIR PARENTS, JUNE 17, 1846 [60]

Dear Father

After writing a short letter to Cousin Cincinnatus I have commenced a similar one to you—I am at the time I write you some 400 miles or upwards from Independence and about 18 miles above the Junction of the South & North forks of Platte River tomorow if the River is favorable we will cross it some 20 miles above where we are now encamped—

I wrote you a short and I fear rather unintelegable letter which I sent to the States by some Hunters retureing with their Buffalo Robes & Fur skins. I suppose you will receive it, this I send by some jentleman returneing from Origon with the intention of takeing their familys out the ensueing spring they speake in glowing Colours of *Portions* of Origon

For the last 4 or 5 days we have all been feasting on Buffalo & Antalope and although when we stop at night we are very tired yet when we start out in the morning we feel well and able to go through with an other day

We are the last company on the road out of 470 Wagons but the detentions which we have met with will ennable us to pass all but one Company which started out in April for our Cattle are all in good order and those

of the formost Companies are in a terible Condition to-
day we passed 2 of their Cattle which they had left to
die on the road—

The whole company are in good spirits and determined
to go through with our long journey and I have no doubt
but we will do so

For two days past we have been cooking with Buffalo
Chips I think with Col Russell that it is rather a hard
matter that the Buffalo should furnish the meat and then
the Fuel to Cook it with but nature seems to have so ordered

Before I forget I hope you will explain to any of my
Friends or relatives who complain of my not writeing
how I am situated now tonight after Traveling 20 miles
I had to cook supper wash dishes stand guard &c &c this
to any one who has common sence will be sufficient and
to those who have not do not, if you please give any excuses—

I do not think now that it will be possible for me to
returne this year for we cannot get to California before
October and then by the time I could get half way back
to the *states* the Grass on the Plains would be covered
with snow—if therefore I or Charles should not return
before this summer a year do not be alarmed or dis-
apointed if we like the country one of us will shurely
returne and if we do not both of us will of course, & as
soon as possible—

If you should come out or make arraingements to come
have *light* 2 horse wagons made that is light with the exception of the running Gear have the axel tree at least
4 inches at the largest point and $2\frac{1}{2}$ at the smallest—
the tire should be not very heavy but about $2\frac{1}{2}$ inches
wide and fastened on with bolts instead of nails — the
bodie should be as light as possible with little iron on it
the Flour, Crackers, Meal and such things as could be
stowed in bags should be so stowed the cover of the wagon should not be painted but should be of Cotton drilling of the heavyest kind and so arrainged that you could

raise the sides like those of a Carriage—the houns[?] of the wagon should be made strong made to fall, I suppose you have seen the falling houns [?] made some what like the splendid drawing below

The timber in the running gear should be of the best kind and *well Seasoned* You should have a *Privy* arrainged in one of the wagons made in the hind part the wagon—100 lbs of Bacon is none to much for one person and 200 lbs of Bread Stuff's Parched Corn Ground into meal and sifted is first rate, you should bring some it will keep for 10 years do not if you start bring any kind of meat except *Clear* sides Pickle meat porke would go fine you ought to have Molasses—but as I shall be in this summer a year to come out with you I need not be so particular you must not come till I see you or you hear from me—

I will be at fort Laramie in about 12 days when I will probably write again but when we lay-by I have to do my washing, survey [?] provisions & so many other things that I hardly have time—15 hundred weight is as much as should be put in a wagon—

I am keeping a kind of a journal which when I see you will shew you but I cannot give it to you now for time nor my fateague will permit it give love to Mother Virginia, Frank, Joseph, Isabela, *Siss* and Henry. Respects to Mr Wheeler & all Friends—

Yours

N. J. Putnam

Mr. Joseph Putnam

Dear Mother

It is now too late or I would write you a long letter. I shall decist therefore from doing so untill a more convenient opportunity. Nathan has given you all the important information. Mr Russell intends returning next spring in time to bring his family to California. if he likes the country. I have written to Cousin R. Marsh.

I must close by wishing this may find you & all in as good health & spirits as we are

Your son

C. F. PUTNAM

Oregon Spectator, OREGON CITY, JUNE 25, 1846

PUBLIC MEETING.

A meeting of the citizens of Oregon was held at the City Hotel, in Oregon City, on Monday the 15th June, 1846, for the purpose of sending an express to meet the emigration from the United States to this country, in order to prevent their being deceived and led astray by the misrepresentations of L. W. Hastings, who is now on his way from California for that object; when the following proceedings were had: Gen. McCarver being called to the chair, and J. S. Rinearson appointed secretary, on motion of Col. Taylor, the sense of the meeting was taken with regard to the propriety of sending such express, and decided in the affirmative.[61]

On motion, a committee was appointed to select persons to proceed to the Soda Springs to meet the emigration, and also to ascertain what amount of funds can be raised to defray expenses. Col. Finley, Col. Taylor, P. Foster, Samuel Parker, and A. Hood were appointed said committee.

On motion, resolved, that the express start as soon as the 25th inst.

The committee reported they had selected Colonel Finley, J. S. Rynearson, and W. G. T'Vault, as suitable persons to go on said express, which was accepted by the meeting.

On motion, a committee of three was appointed to take depositions, and procure such information as will further the object of the meeting, and to have the same published. A. L. Lovejoy, D. C. Ingles, and F. Prigg, to be said committee.

After many animated addresses relative to the subject, on motion, it was ordered that the proceedings of the meeting be signed by the chairman and secretary, and handed to the editor of the *Spectator* for publication.

On motion, the meeting adjourned to meet on Saturday evening next.

M. M. McCARVER, CHR'MN.

J. S. RINEARSON, SEC'Y.

— — —

In conformity with the above, the committee waited upon several individuals, who have recently returned from California, and received the following statements.

We, the undersigned, left the United States in 1845 to proceed [to] Oregon, and upon our arrival at Fort Hall, having been told by Capt. Grant that the road to Oregon was so bad and destitute of grass and wood, by his advice and others, we were induced to leave the Oregon trail, and go to California. When we arrived at the plains of the Sacramento valley, we found the whole country burnt up by the sun, and no food for either man or beast; having been deceived ourselves, our object is to prevent others being deceived in like manner. Owing to the drought, no vegetables for sauce of any amount can be raised. Flour is from 10 to 12 dollars per hundred, and unbolted at that; from 5 to 8 bushels of wheat to the acre, is about the average raise in California; the rain commences in January, and ends about the 1st of March, and then no more of any consequence till the year rolls round; four months grass and eight months drought. There is no timber but scrub oak, except on the mountains, from 10 to 50 miles from the settlements; lumber is from 40 to 80 dollars per thousand, and most of the buildings are dobe, covered with tooly. The country is so flat and marshy that, in the winter, one-fourth is inundated, and leaves the swamps full of water, which dries away in the summer, and causes intermittent complaints to be prevalent. There is no good society at all, and it is very difficult for a man to keep his own. The Roman Catholic Institute is destroyed; no land can be obtained by foreigners without purchase, and then a poor title; and it is almost impossible to get any clothing—the duties are so high, that no shipping comes in. When we left California for Oregon, Lansford W. Hastings started to meet the emigration from the states, to try to persuade them to go to California. He told us publicly that he and Capt. Suter intended to revolutionize the country, as soon as they could get sufficient emigrants into California to fight the Spaniards; this plan was laid between Capt. Suter and L. W. Hastings, before said Hastings published his book of lies in 1844.

We have now traveled this side of the Umqua mountains 80 or 90 miles before we reached the settlements in the Willamette valley, and we can say we have found the most splendid and beautiful country, with rich prairie land and timber adjoining, together with good water and springs; there is probably one thousand farms can be had convenient to the Willamette river, such as will suit the fancy of any farmer, and far exceeding anything we have seen in California.

TRUMAN BONNEY,
JAMES BONNEY,
(corroborated by) ABNER FRAZER.

Signed at Oregon City, June 17, 1846, in presence of A. L. LOVEJOY AND F. PRIGG.

— — —

The undersigned was a resident in California eight years, during which time he only witnessed one fair crop, and two half crops raised, the balance of the time the seed was barely returned, except in a very few instances. Wheat, in a great portion of the country, may be seen in ear 6 inches high; potatoes can only be raised near the coast, and then by irrigation—have known Capt. Suter endeavor to raise potatoes without irrigation, and it was a complete failure. The principal article of food, and in

most instances the only one, is dried or jerked beef —
generally well mingled with sand.

The fever and ague is very prevalent during summer
and fall, scarcely any foreigner escaping, and the symp-
toms are usually severe. The state of society is very lamentable, and you are only sure of your horse, but when
you have hold of the rope. There is no money in the country, and clothing is difficult to obtain. There is no timber
but in the mountains, and from what I have seen of Oregon, consider there is no comparison between the two
countries for farming purposes.

JOHN CHAMBERLAIN.

Signed at Oregon City, 17th June, 1846, in presence
of A. L. LOVEJOY AND FREDC. PRIGG.

— — —

To the Oregon Emigration:

I arrived in this place to-day, and at the request
of some friends, I make this statement to you concerning California, and the operations of men there: Captain Hastings left the 4th of May to meet the company
from the United States, for the purpose of persuading
them from their path, and enticing them to California.
Now, this I can say to you that may hear Hastings tell
of the wonders of California, there is a scarcity of timber and water, and though the hills are set with oats and
the valleys with clover, it is all short feed, as the sun burns
the clover down by the 15th of July, and the stock have
to live on the seeds in the winter. I have seen enough of
Oregon to perceive that it is the best grazing country of
the two, and for agriculture they wont compare.

ROBERT C. KEYES.[62]

Oregon City, June 17, 1846.

— — —

To the Oregon Emigration:

I wish to state to you, that I have just returned from
California, where I remained one year, and as to the spontaneous growth of fruit, it is all false. Flour, if flour I
could call it, without bolting, is $10 per hundred pounds;

beef 6 cents per lb.; coffee and sugar is 50 cts. per lb. when there is any in the country; goods of all description are very scarce and very high prices. My objection to that country, is the scarcity of timber and water, in the summer it is parched up, and in the winter it is every where flooded; there is no chance to raise any vegetables without watering. Iron is very scarce in that country and 50 cents per lb. Horses $25 a head, and milch cows $15, and poor at that—that is in trade, for money there is none in the country. I speak now of the Sacramento country, and that is all the place you can settle.

ALLEN SANDERS.

Oregon City, June 17, 1846.

Oregon Spectator, OREGON CITY, JUNE 25, 1846

OVER THE MOUNTAINS.

Whilst on the one hand we learn with regret, that the company of road hunters which arrived from Polk county, has returned unsuccessful and discouraged; on the other, we are cheered with the intelligence, that another party from Champoeg county is forming, and will soon be prepared to start, under the command of an able and experienced pilot.

When all are impressed with the conviction, strengthened in many instances by painful experience, of the vast importance of obtaining an easy and safe road to the Willamette Valley, by a southern route, and thus avoiding the numerous and heartbreaking difficulties of the Columbia, it will afford us no small gratification, to be enabled to give the names of the patriotic little band, who inspired and directed by the public safety and welfare of their country, engage in this arduous and praiseworthy undertaking; that the hopes and wishes of the community will be with them there is no doubt; that there is great probability of success, is the opinion of the oldest and most experienced of our mountaineers and trappers; that they will richly deserve our praise and gratitude, no one will for a moment question, and we have no hesitation in venturing our belief, that all interested (and who is not?) will manifest the same, not merely in empty plaudits, but in a manner demonstrative of the value at which their exertions are estimated, as well as to testify, that those who render valuable service to the state, when she needs it, shall not labor without reward.[63]

Oregon Spectator, OREGON CITY, JULY 9, 1846

THE MOUNT HOOD ROAD.

We are happy to learn from Capt. Barlow, who has just returned from the Cascade mountains, where he has been constructing a road to admit the passage of wagons direct from the Dalls to this place, that the road is now complete, and that the wagons which were left in the mountains last fall, are on the way, and will reach this place in the course of two days. We have not room in this number to say more of this laudable enterprise.[64]

[GEORGE L. CURRY] TO THE ST. LOUIS *Reveille*, FORT BERNARD, JUNE 25, 1846 [65]

Editors of the Reveille:—

I arrived here on the 23d inst., having come through on the "outside" of my pony from "Ash Hollow"—a distance of one hundred and forty miles—where I left the caravan drawing its "slow length along." We found the road lined with emigrants, moving steadily onward to Oregon and California. My friend Mr. I [J]. B. Wall, whom I had the pleasure of meeting a few days since, on his return from Oregon, had a good opportunity of forming a correct estimate of the extent of this spring's emigration, and he sets it down at four hundred and ninety wagons, which would give, at a fair average, an effective force of upwards of *one thousand men*. The companies, generally speaking, have got along remarkably well this year; they have lost but a few head of cattle in comparison with previous emigrations. Some hundred head strayed away from the advance company—through sheer carelessness on the part of the company, however. We stopped but a few minutes on our arrival at this post, and, promising to return and partake of the hospitalities politely tendered us by its commander, J. F. X. Richards, Esq., we hastened on, in the midst of a heavy rain, to Fort Laramie, eight miles above, which we reached in safety, though thoroughly soaked. Fort Laramie has quite a commanding appearance, being situated in the bosom of a range of heights which form the commencement of the Black Snake Hills, and near the junction of the Laramie and north fork of the Platte rivers. The plains surrounding the fort were covered with the lodges of the Sioux, who are preparing to send out a large war-party against the Crows. There were about two thousand in number when we passed through their encampments, but on our return, the next day, from an emigrant camp some six miles up the river, we found them crossing to the northern bank of the North Fork; and, upon inquiry, ascertained that they had taken up their line of march for the mountains, and the achievement of their purpose—the thrashing of the poor Crows, or the plunder of the emigrant—more probably the latter. Their cavalcade, if it may be termed so, was imposing as well as grotesque; here came a party of forest warriors, looking nobly — well mounted, and riding as fast as horse flesh could possibly carry them. Following them, came a long string of pack animals—ponies, and a considerable many *dogs,* attended by women, whose duty it appeared to be to do all the drudgery of the removal. The queerest kind of go-carts, too, had been impressed into the service; long poles were lashed to the sides of the dogs, across which were bound their burdens, while many of the ponies seemed to be lugging an unnecessary pile of lumber after them, solely for the purpose of accommodating a few little light articles which were bouncing about on top. Dogs, by all odds, were their principal beasts of burden, for they literally were "loaded down to the guards." All the while any number of Indians were furiously riding back and forth, without any object unless it were to display their horsemanship, which most certainly was admirable. I am informed that they contemplate travelling some considerable distance before leaving their women and children, and setting out upon the war-path. There are a good many of the same tribe who have not yet come in, being encamped in the country along the head of "Horse Creek." I learn that fifteen hundred of the Sioux came in about a fortnight since, with thirty-five Pawnee scalps, having lost only one man in the fight. The battle, however, was altogether an unfair one. The Pawnees were out in small force, and engaged in buffalo hunting, when a portion of them were set upon and cut off by the powerful numbers of their inveterate foe. The more I see of the Indians the more I lose any sympathy I may have possessed in their favor. With the buffalo, [t]heir only means of sustaining life, they are fast disappearing, and will hereafter be known but in the stories of their horrible barbarities.

The advance company of emigrants, which were for Oregon, under charge, I believe, of a Mr. [Elam] Brown, comprising forty wagons, were *stopped in the road,* on arrival at Laramie, by the Sioux, *and not permitted to pass until tribute had been paid.*[66] The Sioux say they must have tobacco, &c., for the privilege of travelling through their country. Their country, forsooth! Did they not steal it from the Cheyennes, and do they not hold possession of it because they are the more powerful? (*Naughty* savages, to be so *unchristian!*—EDS.) This may cause trouble, and Government should attend to it at once, lest the reply of the emigrant to this demand for the payment of a tax may be made through the medium of powder and lead, and so bring on fearful consequences.

I returned to Fort Bernard yesterday, and have received much attention from the gentlemen of the establishment. This post was almost reconstructed last year by J. F. X. Richards and brothers, of St. Charles, Missouri, is yet in an unfinished state, but when completed it will be an admirable place for the transaction of mountain commerce. Already it has become, though situated so near its more powerful rival, a position of no small importance. Its proprietors and inmates are agreeable and courteous in the extreme, and among them a stranger feels himself at home.[67]

It is my intention, if it can possibly be carried into effect, to leave the wagons at this point, and with fifteen others, all young men, perform the remainder of the journey with pack animals. To procure animals was the reason for my pushing ahead to this place. I am tired of the snail-like travel of the wagons, and the dissension and disunion which exists throughout the entire emigration—in relation to which I shall inform you more fully hereafter. I shall be off to-morrow or next day, at furthest.

Yours, always sincerely,
LAON

— — —

June, 26, 4 o'clock, P.M.

Post Scriptum.—Mr. Kinney and three other persons have just arrived here from California.[68] They bring bad news. Mr. W. B. Gildea, nephew of Dr. B. B. Brown, of your city, died of fever and ague at Captain Sutter's, on the 8th of February last, after being sick some time.[69] He was an acquaintance of mine, and a most estimable young man. Mr. Hastings, I understand, administered upon his effects, which were bought by Captain Sutter. Mr. Kinney has intimated that the proceeds of the same, if there were any, will never reach his relations. He charges unfairness in the settlement of the matter. I herewith send a package of letters for Dr. G., which I received while on the route, back to Dr. Brown.

Mr. Kinney represents the country to be by no means that which Hastings and others have cracked it up to be—that there is more or less sickness there—that numbers of emigrants have arrived there who would be glad to get back to the States if they could, but that they cannot command the means to do so—that the character of the American settlers there is not so unexceptionable as could be wished—that there is not theatre for enterprise there that has been represented—that the country is but nominally independent — that foreigners are arrayed against foreigners, and that there is little community of interest existing there. Enough, however, of such dark news. I shall test the truth of it.

Two trappers, named Leamai and Buck, or Burk, were murdered on Bear river recently, by an Arrapahoe Indian.[70]

The practicability of wagons getting into California from Fort Hall, *has been* tested—*successfully tested*. Fifty arrived there last year, and some twenty the year previous.[71] I leave to-morrow, which pack animals, for Oregon, thence to California and the Sandwich Islands.

Yours, always sincerely,

L.

GEORGE DONNER TO A FRIEND, FORT BERNARD, JUNE 27, 1846 [72]

My Friend—

We arrived here on yesterday without meeting any serious accident. Our company are in good health. Our road has been through a sandy country, but we have as yet had plenty of grass for our cattle and water. Our fires have been kept up, but they have burned feebly sometimes, though we have had enough to cook every meal. Our journey has not been as solitary as we feared, and we have seen several on their return to the States. Several companies are just ahead. Two hundred and six lodges of Sioux are expected at the Fort to-day on the way to join the warriors on the war against the Crows. The Indians all speak friendly to us. Two braves breakfasted with us. Their ornaments were tastefully arranged, consisting of beads, feathers, and a fine shell, that is got from California, bark variously colored and arranged, and the hair from the scalps they have taken in battle.

I can say nothing except bear testimony to the correctness of those who have gone before us. Please show this letter to our Springfield neighbors and friends and to our children. Our provisions are in good order, and we feel satisfied with our preparations for the trip. Our wagon sheets have shed the rain as yet.

Yours,

GEORGE DONNER.

[CHARLES T. STANTON TO SIDNEY STANTON]
FORT LARAMIE, JUNE 28, 1846 [73]

My last letter was dated at the Twin Springs, where we had encamped in a most beautiful place, and near which a large buffalo had been killed.[74]

The next day we reached the junction of the north and south forks, which form the great Platte. We travelled up the south fork four or five miles, when we crossed that stream, which was done not without some little difficulty, it being at this place nearly a mile wide, and deeper than usual, owing to the late rains. We arrived at the ford about the middle of the afternoon, and by sun-down the wagons were all over, the water in many places coming above the wagon beds. The next day we travelled up the south fork ten miles, and encamped. This is a most beautiful stream. There are no islands in it as in the Platte— the bluffs are smooth—the bottom lands from three to five miles wide, gently sloping down to the water's edge. Timberless, the prairies make a broad sweep over the bluffs, up and down the valley, and across the broad river, which winds its silver course through as lovely a scene as the eye ever dwelt upon.

From this point the road leaves the river and runs to the north fork. A distance of fifteen miles brought us to "Ash Hollow," one of the most remarkable places we had seen on our route. The level prairie over which we had travelled nearly all day, suddenly sank down into a deep gorge. It was a wild dell, and I was told had been the battle ground of the Sioux and Pawnees. For five miles our wagons wound around among hills and steep declivities to a little spring, half a mile from the north fork. Here we stopped to enjoy a refreshing draught of water after the fatigues of the day, in riding through this valley of sand and water. At this river we found a company of twenty wagons encamped. They had had considerable sickness, and this day had buried one of their number.[75] We continued up the north branch some three miles, when we encamped for the night. We heard today that Dunbar's company of 20 wagons, which had left ours a week or ten days previously, had gone up the south fork farther than we had, for the purpose of finding a better crossing, but that the water had risen so that it was impossible for them to cross. Their only way of getting across will be to kill buffalo, take their skins, and make what is called "bull boats," and with small freights in each, they will thus be able to get over. Most of our company felt pained at leaving this Oregon party behind, particularly our young men, as there were many fair and amiable young ladies among them.[76] The next day we travelled over a sandy road most of the way. About 10 A.M. the Chimney Rock was discovered, some forty miles distant. I saw it. It looked like a small spire, standing out in bold relief against the sky. Two days more we reached this celebrated rock, and arrived to it about noon. Its height was variously estimated by our guessing company, from two to eight hundred feet. I suppose it to be three hundred feet high. It is round, gently sloping up, and coming to a point at the base of the chimney, 250 feet; then the chimney commences rising in an oblong square, of 10 by 20 feet, 100 feet more. Yesterday we passed a greater curiosity in my view than this; some called it the Court House, others the Fortress, and others the Castle Tower. But before describing this, it may be necessary to give you some idea of this valley of the Platte, which possesses many and singular peculiarities.

In one of my former letters, I have noticed the rough and hilly nature of its bluffs. In travelling up the river to Fort Laramie, I have remarked that their knobs, or hills, or bluffs, or whatever else they may be called, are only to be found upon one side of the river at a time, sometimes on one side and then on the other. Consequently, while one side presents a rough, ragged appearance, the other is smooth and even as a gently undulating lawn. The wagons will often wind along under these bluffs, and, in their broken appearance, you can trace houses, castles, towns, and every thing which the imagination can conceive. These suddenly disappear, and the bluffs become smooth and even; but the ragged bluffs, with their castles and towers, are again seen upon the opposite side of the river, where they appear in greater splendor, as 'tis "distance lends enchantment to the view." This was the case before reaching the "court house," but here they suddenly jumped across the stream, and the first building we saw, was the immense mass on the tops of the Bluffs, 200 feet above the river. There it stood, solitary and alone, in solemn grandeur. It looked to me very much like the forts on Governor's or Staten Island, and seems to have been placed there for the express purpose of guarding the genii and spirits which dwell in the caverns and deep recesses of the ragged peaks, which immediately follow in its train, and line the bluffs up as far as Fort Laramie.

I have to leave this part of my subject, as well as my letter, unfinished, for want of time. I may finish it in a day or two. I send this by a party of Californians on their return to the "States." [77]

S. T. C.

B. F. E. KELLOGG TO PRESTON G. GESFORD, "PLATTE CROSSING, 15 MILE FROM FORT JOHN," JULY 5, 1846 [78]

Dear friends,

Finding another opportunity of letting you hear from me I sit down to write our adventures. Since I last wrote we have got along well. Our teams stand well and are in good order. Some of them got footsore and I had to shoe them. We found the grass much better than is common on the plains. Being but few nights without plenty of the best. We found buffaloes scarce as well as other game, and we had but little until now. We have not been troubled by the Indians but very little. They are friendly disposed and no disposition to hostility is shown. They, however, steal all they can but as yet they have not got much from us. We have met several from Oregon and also California. Some well pleased and some not so well pleased. We are all well and trying to do the best we can except John. He curses and swears and beats the cattle for which I had to take hold of him and talk straight to him. He was all up for leaving, packed up his trunck and cleaned his gun, etc. but finding I was going to keep his trunk and clothing until I got my pay he cooled down and has done some better since. When we got here, I found my brother Philander who had been out trapping in the mountains and caught about $700 worth of fur but unfortunately had 3 mules and 2 horses stolen by the Apaches and came up to the road to buy horses of the passing companies which he did. [79] Meanwhiles, hearing of our coming, he waited 5 days for us and we were glad to see each other. Orville has the note you gave Frederick for the borrowed money. We have been laying here for four days drying buffaloe meat which Philander killed for us to the amount of 20 buffaloes. Yesterday being the 4th of July, we made a large pot pie out of the brisket of a large buffalo and enjoyed the day. In the evening, we fired 150 guns and was answered by 5 or 6 hundred more. There have been 5 companies pass here since we stopped, but tomorrow we shall start and soon leave them behind us as we have done before. I have found several of my old acquaintances here since we stopped. Eren Browns [Elam Brown?], Abentore and others. Imus and Hecock are eight days before us.[80] Gesford, you must excuse me when I ask you to favor my brother Orville B. Kellogg, State of Illinois, Stevenson County, Onico with a copy of this. Also collect all of the information contained in former letters to Pap Elias in Scott County. It is a strange way of writing but the short notice of the company coming from Oregon[81] that I can write but one and hardly time for that and I am sure that the Major will not think it a task to do a few lines and when I get a chance I will write separate letters. Let them all know the reason of my writing this and beg them to excuse me until I get a chance to write again. Louisa, they say chickens in California are worth 50 cents a piece and cost nothing to grow them there. So you can make your fortune there. Gesford can take them to the harbor so you will both have something to busy your selves in this land of laziness and comfort. James' elk skins are worth $2.00 and so plentiful that a good hunter may kill from 1 to 10 in a day and so come out and get rich. Emily and Polly Venable will be useful in the establishment of schools and will do well to come. Tell old Sam, women are plentiful and easy to get acquainted with. Orville, they say wagons are worth from 2 to 3 hundred dollars and blacksmiths are worth $5.00 a day so you and I can do well. The American girls are in great demand and the purchasers aplenty. In short, all good folks and all good things are desirable articles for trading and you had better come. Wait first until you hear what I say of it until I see it myself. There has been 6 deaths in different companies including one in ours. One marriage among the deaths. A pair of twins. Three wagons left our company this morning and 3 come in tomorrow. One of our company killed a grissly bear yesterday. Rebecca says she wants to see you all, especially Delilah, Polly, Martha, Louisa, Cynthia Anne and particularly to Father and all our friends in Scott. Give my love to all and be assured you are not forgotten. Bill turned the big wagon over and it took me all of one afternoon to mend it up again. I have no more to write. I would be glad to see you all. I shall look for you all to come out when you hear from me. Philander would have gone with me if he had known it in time. He says I may look for him in one or two years. He sends you his love and respects, especially to Orville, Abigal and Emeline. Orville, when you come or the year before send Philander a letter. Major, you and all our folks there must not forget our old acquaintances which may I hope be renewed in California. So farewell for the present.

F. E. KELLOGG.

[CHARLES T. STANTON TO SIDNEY STANTON]
"ENCAMPMENT ON BEAVER CREEK, NINE MILES FROM
FORT LARAMIE," JULY 5, 1846 [82]

On our route to this place we met a small party from Oregon, on horses and pack mules. I much regretted that I had not a letter already written to send to you, and I resolved to write one the first time I could get to spare, so that if I should meet with another opportunity of sending, I could do so by the next company we might happen to meet.

Yesterday we laid by to spend the Fourth, to day we do the same to keep the Sabbath, the only Sabbath we have kept on the road. I determined to keep a portion of it in writing to you.

We left our encampment at the Fort on Sunday [June 29], and went up the Laramie Fork two miles and encamped, where we found better grass for our cattle and horses. Here I wrote the other half of my letter to you. But I [did] not finish it till the next morning [June 30], and even then, not until our company had left. I waited behind over an hour to finish it. I sent the letter by Mr. [Robert M.] Ewing, a young gentleman from Kentucky, who with a party of four or five other young men, remained behind this morning, intending to change their course of travel by going to Taos and Santa Fe.[83] I have since regretted that I did not give him positive orders to leave the letter at Fort Laramie, as from this point you would get it sooner than from any other. They were already on their mules, ready for a start, when I handed Mr. E. your letter—we bade each other good bye, and I was left alone in the prairie. The last of the wagons had long since disappeared behind the hills which bore off to the North West, towards the north fork— the company of young men were galloping fast to the Fort, and I alone was trudging on foot to overtake the wagons.

I soon reached the main road, when I beheld it lined with Indians on horseback, coming back from the wagons which they had accompanied a considerable distance on their journey, for the purpose of securing what presents they could obtain and swapping horses. All of the Indians that we have seen on our route are most inveterate horse jockies, swapping horses whenever they can get a chance, often times getting the worst of the bargain, by giving a good horse for a poor one, so fond are they of this species of trade. I was soon surrounded by ten or a dozen Sioux. I believe there are few men, no matter how brave, that would not have a queer sort of feeling come over them, by being thus suddenly surrounded by these children of the plains. I could not understand a word they said, nor but a few of their motions. They all rode up and shook me by the hand, and wanted something which I could not understand. One or two drew their knives across their throats. This struck me as not being a very pleasant amusement, especially if they were to amuse themselves in this manner on me. I finally presented them with a few pieces of tobacco, which they gladly accepted, and rode off seemingly well pleased.

I was now left to my solitary walk—but I was soon surrounded by another party, and then another, and still again another until I caught up with the wagons. Here I felt in perfect safety. The Indians seldom attack a large body, but only straggling parties of one, two or three. These they seldom kill unless they resist, but strip them and send them back naked to the camp.

I was informed by Mr. McKinstry, who joined us in the course of the day from the Fort, that before he left, 2,000 Sioux had arrived there *en route* to fight the Crows. He says, as they approached the Fort, they presented a fine appearance. They were drawn up in battle array, in three columns, with music and colors flying. The warriors or braves were splendidly dressed, principally in white tanned buffalo skins, richly ornamented with beads. Mr. McK. also brought the information that some Frenchmen had arrived at Fort Bernard, who stated that the Mormons, a thousand or more, had crossed the Mississippi [Missouri] at the mouth of the Platte, and were on their march westward, and that there were a party of emigrants, consisting of 40 wagons, some four or five days behind us. That while they were travelling up the Platte, near the place where we met the boats, (which I mentioned in one of my letters,) three of their party went out in the morning on horseback to drive up the cattle, when they were attacked by some Pawnees. Two of the men gave up their horses — the other refused and resisted, and was immediately shot. The other two were permitted to go back to their camp. The Pawnees secured the three horses, and made their escape. An express was sent back, in the hope that our government would take some steps to bring these murderers to justice.[84]

On coming up with the wagons, I found that the Oregon company had joined us. Since they left us, three marriages had taken place, and one or two more were on the tapis. We were all glad to see each other after our long separation, and good feeling seemed to reign throughout.[85]

We had not travelled far before we commenced the ascent of the Black Hills, and had a fine view of Laramie's Peak—the highest in the range. Pike and Long's Peak lies off to the south of this. Fort Laramie may be said to be at the base of the Rocky Mountains—the Black Hills being a spur of them. The views which Fremont gives in his large book of the Chimney Rock, Scott's Bluffs, Fort Laramie and Laramie's Peak, are all correct delineations.

We travelled 15 miles and encamped on a clear, cold stream. At this place a debate occurred whether we should lay by the next day, or go on till the 4th, and then stop and celebrate; but the Independence party prevailed, and the next day we rolled on as usual. The Oregon company remained behind, and we are again separated. This day the road became more hilly, with Laramie's Peak in view all day. We encamped by a fine spring, in a delightful valley, surrounded by high hills. The next day, Wednesday [July 2], in the morning, I walked on ahead, travelling over a high hill. When I reached the top, I beheld one of the finest views I ever saw. It was a succession of hills and vallies stretching off to the right, covered with grass and dotted all over with small pine trees — to the left, the same view extended up to the base of Laramie's Peak, which did not appear over five miles off. Towards night we passed through a pleasant valley till the road wound up to the top of the bluffs, through a deep gorge in the hills, running up almost perpendicularly on either side, leaving a place just wide enough for the wagons to pass. On the right side of the road a small stream rippled down, along the line of which a small growth of timber stands, in fine relief to the arid hills. About half way up we found the spring. It was cold, but had such an unpleasant mineral taste that few would drink it. After arriving at the top of the hill, we again descended into a pleasant little valley, and encamped for the night.

In the morning [July 3] I started on ahead again, with the intention of walking a few miles and then waiting for the teams to come up. I had walked but a few miles when I met a small party from Oregon. Although I had never seen either [any] of them before, or they me, yet we shook hands all round, and were as glad to see each other as though we had been old acquaintances all our lives. On being told that our company was bound for California, they shook their heads, said it was a poor country, but thought Oregon was the Paradise of the world.[86] After a few moments chat, I bade them good bye, and went on my lonely way. The air was bland and balmy—it was bracing. I felt lighter of foot than I had done since I started, and I walked to a small stream ten miles before I was aware that I had gone five. I waited here two hours for the wagons to come up.

Our company again "rolled on," and finally encamped in a pleasant valley, at the bottom of which a small stream was running. High bluffs encircled it all around. The hills were composed of the red pipe stone, and as the declining sun shone upon them, it gave them the appearance of gold. So much was I struck with the beauty of this place, that I gave it the name of the golden valley.[87]

Yesterday, as I said before, we celebrated the 4th of July. The breaking one or two bottles of good liquor, which had been hid to prevent a few old tapsters from stealing, (so thirsty do they become on this route for liquor of any kind, that the stealing of it is thought no crime), a speech or oration from Col. Russell, a few songs from Mr. Bryant, and several other gentlemen, with music, consisting of a fiddle, flute, a dog drum—the dog from which the skin was taken was killed, and the drum made the night previous—with the discharge of all the guns of the camp at the end of speech, song and toast, created one of the most pleasurable excitements we have had on the road.

Deer and elk have been seen in the vicinity of the camp; but none have been killed. The bread root is here found in abundance. It is about as large round as a hen's egg, and twice as long. To obtain it, you have to dig to the depth of six or ten inches in a hard soil. It is perfectly white, and has a pleasant though rather insipid sweetish taste. When dried, the Indians pound it up into a kind of flour, from which they make bread, or mix it in their soup, the general way of cooking among them. Some of our company have been back among the hills which surround us, and tell of the most delightful place imaginable. I am going out, by-and-by, to view, and if it is anything worth describing, I will speak of it in my next.

We are now among the mountains—Laramie's, Pike's, and Long's Peaks lie off to the south. In a short time we shall be at Independence Rock, and the South Pass. The days are extremely warm, and the nights exceedingly cold.

S. T. C.

Missouri Republican, St. Louis, July 7, 1846

FROM FORT JOHN.—Eight Mackinaw boats, laden with buffalo robes, &c., with a company of thirty-six men, under the charge of Mr. P. D. Papin, arrived at Fort Leavenworth on the 2d from Fort John, at the junction of the Laramie and Big Platte rivers. The crews and cargo were there transferred to the steamer *Tributary,* which arrived here yesterday morning. The cargo consists of 1100 packs buffalo robes, 10 packs of beaver, and 3 packs of bear and wolf skins, and was consigned to P. Chouteau, Jr. & Co. We learn from Mr. Papin that he had great difficulty in descending the Platte on account of the low water, and was obliged to transfer the cargoes from three of his boats and leave them behind. Two boats which left the Fort before him, he thinks will be unable to get down, not having men enough to haul them over the shoals.

During the absence of the Pawnees, on a hunting excursion, about two weeks ago, a large war party of Sioux, several hundred in number, destroyed their crops of growing corn, and turned loose their horses. A Missionary and his family living in one of the villages, was shot at several times,—one of the balls passed through his clothes, barely missing him, and he was obliged to retire to Council Bluffs.[88]

The Sioux are greatly dissatisfied at the passing of the California emigrants through their country; complain that they kill all their game, and declare that no more shall be permitted to intrude, unless they pay them for the privilege. They have made the same complaints to the mountain traders, and strongly urge their claims for payment, and desired to hold a council with Col. Kearney [Stephen W. Kearny] on the subject.

The Pawnees were practicing their thievish propensities on the emigrants, following them in small parties and stealing their horses, cattle, &c., when left unguarded. One man, who had strayed from the camp, was found by a body of twenty or thirty, and completely stripped of all that he had, was then badly flogged, and afterward allowed to return to the camp. Game is said to be very scarce, and many of the Sioux and other tribes are in a starving condition.

The emigrants were understood to be progressing slowly, divided in parties of thirty or forty wagons, for the purpose of better procuring game and water. The leaders of the Mormons were at Council Bluffs. About one thousand wagons, belonging to Mormons, had arrived there, and they were waiting for the remainder to come up, when they intended to proceed to Great Pawnee Island [Grand Island], on the Platte, and there encamp for the winter. They had already commenced crossing the Missouri at the Bluffs.[89]—Messrs. [Louis] Vasquez & [James] Bridger, from Fort Hall [Bridger], on Green river, one of the extreme western posts in the mountains arrived at Fort John before Mr. Papin and his party left, and reported all quiet in that country.[90]

Missouri Reporter, ST. LOUIS, JULY 7, 1846

We learn from a gentleman who came down from Fort John, in Mr. Papin's company, that the Sioux Indians recently attacked a Pawnee village on the Platte, while the braves were absent in the chase, and drove off the inhabitants, including two missionary families. They also destroyed the growing crops of corn.

— — —

The cargoes of eight Mackinaw boats were brought down by the *Tributary* from Fort Leavenworth. They comprize 1100 packs of Buffalo robes, 3 packs of Beaver, and sundry other peltries. Thirty-six mountaineers, also, under charge of Mr. Papin, came passengers. They are from Fort John, on the Big Platte. They report the Platte very low. A timely rain, on Sunday week [June 21], facilitated their getting out into the Missouri, otherwise they would have been detained from lowness of water.

Missouri Reporter, ST. LOUIS, JULY 11, 1846

NEWS FROM THE FAR WEST.[91]

On Tuesday [June 30], Messrs. J. Bond, W. Parkinson, W. Delany and two others, arrived in our place [Independence] almost direct from Oregon.[92] They left Oregon city on the 1st March, 1846, for the States—were much delayed in the early part of their route, especially when crossing the summits of the Rocky Mountains, by severe snow storms; afterwards progressed tolerably well. On the 10th of June, they met the company of emigrants from St. Joseph at Fort Laramie—all of them having gotten along pretty well and in good spirits. The companies which left here were found at different points between Fort Laramie and the Big Platte, considerably scattered, but still going along, probably more advantageously than if they had all kept together. They met with some considerable loss of stock (oxen and mules) after they had reached the main prairies, partly owing to neglect. After these companies had gone along, they saw forty-three wagons, said by the emigrants to be Mormons—whose teams and stock appeared to be very indifferent, and they in consequence, were getting along but slowly.[93] In the route thus far [Elam] Brown's company had lost 120 head of cattle (60 yoke of them oxen and the remainder loose cattle.) Yet, despite of all "go *ahead*" seemed to be the motto.

On the 14th of June, these four [five?] men were charged upon by some 200 Indians, (Ottoes,) who supposed them to be their enemies, (the Chiens,) but as soon as they discovered them to be Americans, they did not molest them, but came up to them, exchanged civilities and departed; also, while crossing Snake river, the Snake Indians charged on them and even fired a gun or two, but seeing signs of fight among them and no exhibition of fear, though so few in number, they soon dispersed.

A company has undertaken to cut a road through the Cascade mountains, and even bound themselves in writing, in the sum of $5,000 for the fulfilment of it. It is to be completed this spring, by the time the emigrants arrive. In the spring of 1845, 75 persons died in crossing the plains, caused by getting lost while following Pilot [Stephen] Meek from Fort Bosieu [Boise] to the Dalles on the Columbia river. Thirty wagons in the company went into the Cascade mountains, and there remained until the spring had fairly set in, and were then able to come out.

When these men left Oregon, wheat and every thing were very plenty, enough to furnish all the inhabitants and emigrants subsistence, and much to spare. Some of these men, just arrived, intend returning next spring, and some do not, some being well pleased and some not.

Weekly Reveille, St. Louis, July 20, 1846

FROM OREGON.

CALIFORNIA EMIGRANTS.

We have received a deeply interesting letter from a young friend who has just returned from the Territory of Oregon, but can only find space to-day for that portion referring to his encounter with the California emigrants. It contains matter of moment to those embarking for the plains, and will be read with avidity. He says:

"We met the first party of California emigrants at Fort John, on the north fork of the Platte, and the last company fifty or sixty miles below the south fork — a distance of about two hundred and fifty miles this side of Laramie, or Ft. John. In this company were a few Mormons, bound for—they knew not where.[94]

"On the 18th of June we met Smith's company,[95] about thirty miles below the crossing of the south fork, lying by, hunting their cattle, which had nearly all been run off, as they supposed, by the Pawnees. Soon after we had camped that evening, (some twenty miles below,) two of Smith's company passed our camp in search of the lost cattle, but in a short time they returned to us, and reported the murder of one of their party by the Pawnees, about six miles below. It appeared that a Mr. Edward Trimble, of Henry county, Iowa, and a young man, named Harrison, who had gone on in advance of them, had found a part of the cattle, and were returning to camp with them, when a party of Indians, who had been concealed in the high grass near the road, charged upon them, killed Trimble, and took Harrison prisoner, whom they were in the act of stripping when the other two of their party discovered them. As soon as they saw the Indians, they raised the yell, and charged. The Indians, supposing, no doubt, that they were backed by a strong party, left their prisoner, and fled to a neighboring bluff; while one of the California party took Harrison behind on his horse, and they fled with all possible speed to our camp, lest the Indians should discover their number and pursue them. As soon next morning as it was light, we raised camp, and moved on to where Trimble was murdered. We found where the poor fellow had weltered in his blood, but the Indians had borne off the body. We made a search for it, but no further traces could be found. Mr. Trimble was, it is said, one of the best and most estimable citizens of the county in which he lived. He has left a widow and four small children to mourn his loss. His widow and family would have returned with us to their friends in Iowa, had not her delicate situation [pregnancy] made it imprudent for her to travel without being accompanied by some of her female friends. It is her intention, however, to return to the States whenever circumstances will permit.[96] The Pawnees have also committed several daring robberies this spring. A war party fell in with Messrs. Sabille [Jean Sibille] and [Joseph] Bissonette, who were accompanied by three men in their employ, on a trading expeddition from St. Louis to Laramie, whom they robbed of a considerable amount of goods, and would, no doubt, have taken all they had, had they not been deterred by being told that a large party of Americans were close behind them, and that they would kill the whole of them.[97] We think it is high time the attention of the Government was called to the matter, and that they should use some other measures with the Indians than making them presents, and smoking with them the pipe of peace.

"The company finally procured the greater part of their cattle. There were, however, four families who lost their livestock, and were unable to procure a sufficient number to ensure them provision on the route; they, consequently, were compelled to return to the States. Our party accompanied them through the Pawnee country, and they are now, in all probability, within three days' travel of the State line."[98]

[The above was doubtless part of a long communication by I. [J.] B. Wall, dated St. Joseph's, Mo., July 7, 1846, printed in the *Weekly Reveille,* July 20, 1846, with "Laon's" letter of June 16. Occupying nearly three columns, the letter begins:]

Editors of the Reveille:—We reached this place this morning, on our overland trip from the Pacific to the United States. We left the seat of Government of Oregon, (Oregon City) in company with a small party of emigrants, on the 5th of March last. At that time spring was fairly established in the seat of old winter, who had been completely put to flight by the mild advances of his more genial supplanter. The woods were vocal with the songs of innumerable warblers; the grass had started from its sleep of months, and the tender buds had put forth to "woo the gentle kisses of the balmy breeze;" and, in short, all nature bore indications of a much earlier resuscitation from the effects of winter, than is to be seen on the Atlantic side of the continent in the same latitude.

[After describing at length conditions in Oregon, and the experiences of those who took the Meek cutoff in 1845, the letter concludes:]

The emigration to Oregon the current year, I think, will number about twelve hundred souls—being about one half as large as it was last year; and that to California will, perhaps, amount to four hundred and fifty or five hundred souls. This year's emigration will not bear a very favorable comparison with that to California, as far as I am able to judge, in point of respectability and talent.

The Gazette, St. Joseph, July 10, 1846

FROM OREGON.

On Tuesday, the 7th of July, we had an arrival from Oregon. The company, which consisted of eighteen men, left Oregon city in March, and travelled over the mountains and through the prairies, without accident or unusual trouble. They brought a large package of letters, and three numbers of the *Oregon Spectator*. The *Spectator* was commenced in February, is published semi-monthly by an association of gentlemen, and is a neat, compact little sheet. The articles are all original (they not having the advantage of exchange papers) and most on the subjects of agriculture, temperance, and religion. It seems that the people are not engaged with politics, and the discussion of that matter is forbid.

One of the gentlemen who came in informs us that he met the advance company of the 1846 emigrants at Fort Laramie, and the whole emigration consisted of about 15 companies, strung out at short distances. The emigrants had met with no extraordinary difficulties, except that the Pawnee Indians had killed one man. Their mode of procedure is to drive off from camp a number of cattle during the night, with the expectation that small companies will go out for them in the morning. If so, and they encounter the Indians, they are robbed, and if necessary shot. The emigrants must be protected from the depredations of these Indians.

We are pained to learn that about seventy of last year['s] emigrants sunk under the severe exposure to hardships and dangers. A portion of the company were induced by the representations of persons belonging to the Hudson's Bay Company to take a new road beyond Fort Bogy [Boise] which proved to be a wrong one. They got lost and remained so for several months, during which time about thirty persons died, and shortly after reaching the settlements forty more died. Starvation, unwholesome food, and excessive fatigue were considered the causes of this fatality.

We also learn that four wagons will reach the settlements in a few days, a portion of a company which were disturbed by the Indians. They will wait here until spring and again undertake the journey in company with other emigrants.

☞ The emigrants that returned from Oregon met

Martin's company at Fort Laramie. They were in advance of all the companies, and getting on well. The report in circulation some time since that his company had been cut off is unfounded.

JOEL PALMER TO THE ST. JOSEPH *Gazette,*
JULY 10, 1846 [99]

Mr. Editor—

Sir, I see in the *Gazette* of this morning, under the head of "From Oregon," a statement that a portion of last year's emigrants were induced by the representation of persons belonging to the Hudson Bay Company, to take a new road beyond Fort Boises, which proved to be a wrong one, and that the disastrous consequences which followed was owing to their getting lost, &c. Now I am not a member of that company, nor have I any very good feelings towards them, but justice requires that facts should be stated. It was a man by the name of Stephen L. Meek, from Jackson county, Mo. who induced the company to take that route. He stated that he could shorten the distance 150 miles over the old road, and that he was perfectly familiar with the route. But unfortunately it proved otherwise. Captain [Richard] Grant, the person in charge at Fort Hall, advised us not to take that route, as also did the person in charge at Fort Boisea.—In the same paper under the head of Oregon, you state that the gentlemen from Oregon gives it as their opinion, that the residents of that Territory will generally be much displeased with the Compromise.— To this I have to say, that if the compromice gives to Great Britain the whole of Vancouvers Island, the statement is correct, for it is generally supposed that the 49th parallel divides the Island east and west nearly in the centre, and as the southern half commands the entrence to the harbor of Pugot Sound (the only natural and safe harbor in Oregon) the people would be unwilling that it should be ceded to any other government. But if the 49th parallel is the boundary fixed upon, they will cheerfully acquiesce, for the sake of peace, but would have been willing to shoulder their muskets and rifles and contended for the 54 40. You also state that they inform you, that the best portion of that Territory is north of the 49th parallel, and that the division will spoil the whole country. This is also a mistake, I never travelled over any portion of the country north of 49, nor has any one of our party, but from all the information I have been able to gather, the most of the valuable portion of Oregon is south of 49. There is doubtless some good land on Frazier's [Fraser] river, as also upon some other streams north of that degree, but the amount is limited, it is tolerable only on account of timber, fish, and fur, it being a mountainous country.

Will you have the goodness to make these corrections.

Very respectfully your humble servant,

JOEL PALMER.

P. S. Your informant has doubtless unintentionally misinformed you.

J. P.

Jefferson Inquirer, JEFFERSON CITY, MISSOURI, JULY 21, 1846

From our Extra of Wednesday last.

LATE FROM OREGON.

THE EMIGRANTS IN GOOD HEALTH

MURDER BY THE PAWNEE INDIANS OF ONE

OF THE EMIGRANTS

THE FLOURISHING CONDITION OF THE TERRITORY, &C. &C.

We have conversed with Mr. Palmer, formerly of Indiana, and Mr. Smith, formerly of Ohio, who passed our city on the steamer *Balloon* yesterday evening [July 14], on their route from Oregon City, which place they left on the 5th of March last.—They travelled through without much difficulty. The Indians on their way were friendly and made no hostile demonstrations against their party, which consisted of eighteen men. They met the first party of emigrants at Fort Laramie, on the 10th June, under the command of Capt. Martin, of Platte county, and continued for two hundred miles to meet other parties, having from six to forty wagons. A band of emigrants with 212 wagons were bound for California. The number of wagons accompanying the several parties which they met, amounted to 541, and an estimate of five persons to each wagon, was not considered too large. The emigrants were generally in good health and fine spirits. The party under the command of Col. W. H. Russell, was met 160 miles this side of Fort Laramie. There was no truth in the report of the death of Gov. Boggs.

A company under the command of Capt. Smith, of Iowa, lost 150 head of cattle, supposed to have been frightened off by the Pawnee Indians, with the design of theft. A gentleman by the name of Trimble, of Iowa, accompanied by a young man from the same Territory, named Harrison, started in search of them. They returned about 40 miles and found five head of the cattle, which they drove back for about ten miles, when they were suddenly attacked by 12 or 15 Pawnees who were lying in ambush. In the struggle which ensued, Mr. Trimble was killed, pierced by three arrows. A gun was fired at him by the Indians, and he was seen [to] fall from his horse. The Indians were in the act of stripping Mr. Harrison, when two of the emigrants appeared and they immediately dispersed, taking with them the horses of Messrs. Trimble and Harrison. Early in the morning of the next day, nine of the party of Messrs. Palmer and Smith went in search of the body of Mr. Trimble. They did not find it, but discovered pools of blood, two bloody arrows, his pocket knife, hat and whip; all of which circumstances confirmed the fact of his death. About twenty of this party, with four wagons, returned to the frontier, guarded by a company of Messrs. Palmer and Smith.

Messrs. Palmer & Smith estimate the population of the Territory at about 6000, and rapidly increasing. There is an abundance of provisions and a surplus of agricultural products. A brisk commerce is carried on with the Sandwich islands. The barque *Toulon,* Crosby master, (of New York,) left the mouth of the Columbia river, bound to the Sandwich islands, about the 1st of March, and freighted with a full cargo of fish, lumber, flour, &c.

George Abernethy, formerly of New York, is Governor; John E. Long, of Kentucky, Secretary, and Peter H. Burnett, of Missouri, Circuit Judge of the Territory. The Iowa laws have been adopted as the provisional code of the Territory.

A party, among which was one of our informants, had explored the country north of the Columbia river as far as Puget's Sound. The silly tales about its sterility, are grossly false, and have with many others of a similar character been manufactured by the Hudson Bay Company. It is a fertile country, admirably well suited to the production of wheat and other small grain. Its general features are rolling and mountainous, but interspersed with the most fertile valleys, covered with heavy and valuable timber,—with occasional plains and prairies, well watered and the streams abounding in fish. A belt of country from 40 to 60 miles in width, extending around the southern portion of the sound, is of a level character. It is believed that there will be a large settlement of Americans on the north side of the Columbia the present season.

The Hudson['s] Bay Company at their fort at Puget's sound, have extensive and well cultivated farms. In December last they slaughtered about 500 head of the finest cattle, fattened entirely on "the range."

The British brig *Modeste,* 18 guns and 160 men, has been laying all the winter in the Columbia, at Fort Vancouver. It was supposed she would remain there until relieved. The armed British ship *America,* was at Puget's sound in September last. Several American whalers laid in the straits of St. Juan de Fuca last winter. So far, they had met with but little success.

Mills at present are scarce in the country.—There are 6 grist and 8 saw mills in operation.—Dr. McLoughlin's merchant mill, with three pair of burrs, situated on the Williamette, will compare both in the quantity and quality of the flour manufactured by it, with any mill of the same size in the United States.

Messrs. Palmer & Smith brought with them between 600 and 700 letters.

We have seen the two first numbers of the *Oregon Spectator,* dated the 5th and 19th of February, and published in Oregon City. It is a neat sheet, and is edited with spirit and ability by W. G. T'Vault, Esq.

Missouri Reporter, St. Louis, July 17, 1846

FROM OREGON.—We enjoyed the pleasure, yesterday, of a few minutes' conversation with two gentlemen who had just arrived from Oregon, Messrs. Palmer and Smith. The intelligence which they bring is not particularly interesting, further than that it evinces the general prosperity of the country. They started for the United States on the 5th day of March, but spent twenty days at the missionary establishment of Dr. [Marcus] Whitman, and several days with the Rev. Mr. [Henry Harmon] Spalding, some hundred and fifty miles distant. The missionaries are represented as doing much good at their respective stations, but need aid in the prosecution of their labors. The Indians generally, on the other side of the mountains, are quite friendly to emigrants.

The party met, during their journey, three hundred and twenty-nine wagons bound for Oregon, and two hundred and twelve for California. The emigrants were getting on finely, and had lost but one of their number from Indians. This person was killed by the Pawnees.

Our informants have resided in Oregon some eighteen

months or two years, and represent the climate as salubrious and the soil exceedingly productive. One of them showed us a specimen of Oregon wheat, the finest we ever saw, and this he assured us was inferior to much that is produced.

The people of Oregon are quite anxious that the laws of the United States should be extended over them. Being composed, as they are, of people from every section of the Union, they feel that the mere laws of Iowa are inadequate to their situation.

Messrs. Palmer and Smith go eastward, but will soon return on their way to the shores of the Pacific.

Missouri Republican, St. Louis, July 17, 1846

NEWS FROM OREGON.—Two gentlemen, on their return from Oregon, arrived in this city yesterday.—One of them, Mr. Palmer, belongs to Indiana; the other, Mr. Smith, is from Ohio. From the latter gentleman we have obtained some information of a very interesting character, as exhibiting the prospects of the American population in that quarter.

These gentlemen, in company with some fifteen others, left Oregon city on the 5th of March, and Dr. Whitman's Missionary establishment, on the Wallawalla river, on the 14th of April. This missionary establishment is represented as in a flourishing condition, enjoying the confidence of the Indians. Oregon city contains a population of about eight hundred. It contains two churches, one a Methodist and the other a Catholic church—two flour mills, and three saw mills. Oregon city is now the residence of Dr. McLaughlin, who has resigned his post in the Hudson['s] Bay Company, and is actively employed in measures for the improvement of the territory. The canal around the Willemette Falls, for the erection of which a bill passed the Oregon legislature last year, it is now proposed to convert into a railroad, and it is expected that this will be done in a year or two. The territory of Oregon itself is represented to contain a population of about 7,000, all prosperously employed, and those who went to that country last year are represented as well satisfied with their situation. The intercourse between the Hudson['s] Bay Company and the Americans was of a very friendly character, though great interest was manifested, on both sides, as to the result of pending negotiations for the adjustment of the question of the boundary. It is the impression of our informant, that the treaty arrangement will not be satisfactory to the Americans, but the Hudson['s] Bay company seem to have anticipated very accurately the boundary which has been established. The country north of the Columbia, which has generally been represented as of a very poor and indifferent quality, is not so regarded by our informant. It is susceptible of cultivation, and is cultivated to a very considerable extent by the Hudson['s] Bay company, who find a market for Wheat, at $2.50 per bushel, in the Russian possessions.

This party pursued in the usual route, returning home. It is a broadly marked wagon road, some of the difficulties of which, are soon to be obviated by contemplated improvements, in the region of the Cascade mountains.

Mr. Smith gives a most melancholy account of the progress and sufferings of the *St. Joseph's company* of emigrants, which left in 1845, under the pilotage of Mr. [Stephen] Meek. This company lost their way and endured incredible hardships. They were out forty days longer than usual, and before their arrival at the Dalles of the Columbia, some seventy-five of the company had died. A short supply of provisions, and that of the worst quality—very poor cattle—produced what was called the "Camp Fever." Frequently, too, they were twenty-four hours without water for the children or the sick. Of the number of those who died, we are supplied with the following names:

Wm. Henderson, of Mo.; John Noble, Mrs. Leggett, Miss Butts, Mr. Moore, (Baptist Preacher), John Sanders, of Ill.; Duke Wilkes, John Harris, Mr. Moore, of Ill., Mr. Wilson, of Clay county; old Mr. Pugh, his son, the wife of William, and two children of the old man; Mrs. Bryant of Mo.; Miss Stephens, of Iowa; old Mr. Hull, of Ohio; James Mallory, of Mo.; Miss R. Chambers, E. Noble, Mo.; Mary E. Harris, H. Belden, of Caldwell co. Mo.; Miss Parker, of Iowa; Harvey Croumell, of Mo.; Mrs. T. Willaker, John King, his wife and one child; Mrs. Straithoof, Mr. Earle, of Iowa; D. Watts, do.; Julia Ann Straithoof, Mrs. Jones and daughter, the latter grown, Mrs. Parker and child. Many children died whose names are not given.

On their return, the party met the advanced company of the Oregon emigrants at Fort Laramie. They were getting on pretty well, but were suffering from the depredations of the Indians upon their cattle. The Pawnees were principally concerned in these outrages, and on one occasion, attacked and killed one of the emigrants who was out in search of his cattle. The person killed was from Henry county, Iowa, by the name of Edward Trimble. He and a companion by the name of Harrison, were fired upon from the grass, and Trimble killed, and Harrison taken prisoner. They were, however, discovered by two others of the party, who raised the shout, and the Indians fled. Mr. Trimble's body was not found. He has left a wife and four small children. They would have returned with this party, but were prevented from doing so, by peculiar circumstances. Mrs. Trimble's friends may expect her return as speedily as possible.

During last winter, four American whalers were lying at Vancouver's Island. Of the number, one was the ship *Morrison,* of Massachusetts, and another the *Louvie,* of Connecticut. Six of the men belonging to these vessels stole a whaling boat, and run away with it. The Indians on the island would not permit them to land. They were compelled to put to sea—a storm arose, and three of them were drowned. Their names were Robt. Church, Frederick Smith, and Mr. Rice, of New London.

Last year five families passed over to the north side of the Columbia, at Puget's Sound—pioneer settlers on that side—and were highly pleased with it. They remained there to cultivate it. Forty or fifty others will follow their example this year. Judge Michael Simmons, of this State, intended to hunt out a road, this year, from Dr. Whitman's settlement to Puget's Sound, for the benefit of emigrants to that side of the Columbia. This will save a hundred miles of travel, and presents a far better route to those who wish to reach that point.

The stock of goods in Oregon, was very limited, and many articles were in demand. Our Yankee friends might drive an advantageous trade by sending a ship load of goods thither, and receiving in return, articles of trade which find a ready market at the Sandwich Islands. For some articles, prices are very reasonable. Sugar is sold for ten cents, and coffee for twenty cents —these articles are obtained from the Islands. Coarse boots bring $5 to $6, per pair.

The Pawnees recently lost twenty-five men, from an attack made upon them by the Sioux — and had their villages burned, and numbers taken prisoners.

"Along the Sweetwater River"

New and Nearer Routes

CHARLES F. PUTNAM TO JOSEPH PUTNAM, "SWEET WATER 220 MILES FROM FORT HALL," JULY 11, 1846 [100]

Dear Father

There is a gentleman in our camp [Wales B. Bonney] who has just come from Oregon *alone* & intends returning to the States *alone*. He arrived late this evening bringing a letter from Mr. Hastings, which stated that he, (Mr. Hastings) [*deleted*: was waiting] would wait at the Salt Lake 60 miles from Fort Hall & from thence take us a new route to California which would make a difference of 300 miles nearer. But if it *is* his design to aid in Revolutionizing the country & to get us to aid him in *immortalizing* himself, he will find *himself,* vastly mistaken. There are now 510 wagons for Oregon & California & nearly all of them contain families. There are two Bachelor wagons in this company; ours & another, the gals say there are two Bachelor wagons & kitchion. Quite a compliment. The kitcheon is a Provision wagon of Judge Moreland's [Morin's]. This is the general average of the Bachelor wagons in the different companies. If there is any danger we will not go to California. But to Umqua river in Oregon 250 miles from Suitor's [Sutter's] settlement in [*deleted*: Oregon] California a beautiful valley which is spoken of highly by Hastings & every one who has seen or written about it. This river will permit small ships up it & has a very good Harbor at its mouth sufficient for all useful purposes. A gentleman on whom Gov. Boggs & Judge Moreland have the most implicit confidence in assured them that if he was going to Pilot a company & they left it to him he would take them to Umqua Valley. This gentleman has been to both countries & has no interest in either he is also very wealthy. Gov. Boggs is well acquainted with him. He was his neighbor. If we should change our notion, which is yet uncertain until we arrive at Fort Hall we will not lose any thing by it for our oxen are worth more in Oregon than in California. our wagon will also be more valuable. This gentleman states that there is but this difference between the two countries, California has a larger Harbor & that Fruit is more abundant. & that Umqua Valley is a more regular climate & is not subject to drouts like California. He speaks in high terms of both countries. It will be in Umqua Valley where most of the Californians will go, if things are not as they anticipated when we left, in fact the *Aristocracy* or respectable portion of the companies will go to this valley if any danger is apprehended when we arrive at Fort Hall. We can get to Umqua river a month sooner than by going to California & we can also get our section of Land apiece with a good title from the U. S. & If hereafter we find it would be to our advantage to go [to] California it is but 250 miles over a road which has been often travelled. You can get Lt. Wilkes' work on Oregon & there are others that treat of this valley & Oregon but I do not recollect their names at present. One of us can return with ease next spring I think if we go to Umqua as there are a number of persons who intend returning for their families. Do not apprehend any danger for we will act with prudence & discretion in this matter.[101] I am writing on the ground in our tent. It is crowded with persons. Nathan will commence on the table when they leave & write more fully & plainly I hope. We are now in the Rocky Mountains & have a much better road than I anticipated, in fact we have had a perfect turnpike with the exception of a few days travell in sand & mud & even this was better than our dirt roads in Ky. We have been ahead of all the California companies although we were next to the last company that left the states & nearly two thirds of the emigrants started for California. I must close give my love to all & my respects to the Observer & all my acquaintances. I hope this may find you & all *in as good* health & spirits as we are.

　　　　　　　Your Son

　　　　　　　CHAS F. PUTNAM

P. S. The Mormons I understand intend to [*deleted*: remain] spend this winter at Fort Laramie or near there on the Platte. They cannot get to either country this year as they would be cought in the winter & there have to remain & star[ve to] death. We do not know for certain that they are on the road but heard that they were building boats to cross the Missouri. We know this that they are too far behind to cross the Mountains this winter. I have increased in strength health & weight & can walk 30 miles a day without being fatigued & help the girls to sing until 10 & 11 o'clock at night. we do not travell 30 miles a day but I frequently walk it when hunting. Nathan & John B. are frequently fatigued, but both of them are in better health & much stouter than when they left home.

NATHAN J. PUTNAM TO JOSEPH PUTNAM, "SWEAT WATER 220 MILES FROM FORT HALL." JULY 11, 1846 [102]

Dear Father & Mother

As it is now late and as my watch comes on at 12 O clock I shall be compelled to write you a short letter.

Charles, John, & myself are all in good health as to myself I have never [been] in as good health as I now am I am frequently compelled to wade rivers & creeks and I have had but one cold since I left Indipendence—

Buchhanan has left us to go on in Company with Russell Bryant and others on *Mules* I doubt whether they will get through, but that remains to be seen—[103] I suppose Charles will tell you that owing to various reports which we have heard about the probibility of our procureing land and the supposed unsettled condition of the country in California, that we think that we will go into Origon look around this fall and winter and if we like we will enter some land there, and then if not perfectly satisfyed we will go down into California and look at it, but if as I am told I can get from 3 to 4 dollars a day in Oregon I shall stay there for a while that is untill I returne to the states to see you all—there is a valley in Oregon on the Umqua river which is represented to be the finest in the world as respects land timber and healthyness of its climate there is as yet no settlements on it with the exception of a small trading establishment at the mouth of the river—if we go to Origon we shall probibly locate some land there as there is some ten or twelve wagons now in company who speake of getting some twenty more wagons and formeing a settlement on said river

You will of course remember me to my friends without my naming them all I want you also to remember me to Unckle John & family when you write to them

I would like to give you a discription of our journy but I have not time nore space, we have passed two or three of the curiositys of the road the chimney rock on the North fork of Platte the lakes of salt and the Bed of Salaratus

of which last we have procured a bucket full and use
it evry day in makeing our bread I like it much better than
the salaratus which you get in the Grocerys — the place
where we got what we have of it appears to be a lake of
lie [lye], it is so strong that it will take the skin off a mans
mouth and as to shoes it literaly eats them up—Indipendance rock is an other of the curiositys it looks like
an *Indian Mound* about the size of som three or four
squares of buildings in Lexington Since we passed the
above named rock the mountains have become almost entirely a mass of naked rock they are not very high but I
never saw such huge masses of rock before they appear
to have been torne and thrown about by some convulsion
of nature—

We had for supper a fine dish of soup to night made
of the hind quarter of an Antelope with some little bacon,
we live as well as any one need live lots of Bacon, Bread,
Coffee dryed fruit rice, Milk, & the finest Meat in
the world— I forgot to tell you that I saw at fort Laramie some 2 or 3000 Indians at the time I saw them they
were moveing from near the Fort across the river, and of
all the moveing ever you saw it beat all. The women mules,
horses & dogs were packed to death the men galoped
about on their ponies with their faces smeared with paint
and their persons decked off with all kinds of beads, tin
& Brass trinckits and done nothing

My time to go on guard has nearly come so I must stop
I send this by a man [Wales B. Bonney] returneing to
the States by himself I suppose he will reach there
in safety as there is in my opinion no danger— Give my
love to Joseph, Isabela, Virginia, Frank, Siss & Kiss
Henry for me—I hope that you are all well

I enclose Charleys letter in this. Give Respects to Mr
[L.] Wheeler, Hiram & Nat Shaw and when you see
Stedman tell him that the flour turned out first rate and
that when eating it we think of him and wish that we could
make him a returne in the hump ribb of Fat Young
Bufalo—

Aunt Betey & Ann I s[*torn*: suppose?] are in Madison if they are not give them my respects—
Yours

N. J. Putnam

William H. Russell to the *Missouri Republican,* "Sweet Water River, 80 miles west of Independence Rock," July 12, 1846 [104]

Col. A. B. Chambers:
My Dear Sir:
By the kindness of Messrs. Solomon Sublette, Walter Reddick, etc. etc., I am only able to furnish you with a line or two from this wild and far-distant country.

I am now within 10 miles of the valley of the Pacific, and shall hereafter drink of its waters instead of the muddy Mississippi. This is a country that may captivate mad poets, but I will swear I see nothing but big rocks, and a great many of them, high mountains and wild sage, without other vegetation to admire.

It is a miserable country we are passing through.

I resigned my command of about 150 wagons at North Platte, where I considered all safe, and am now travelling with 12 men on mules, which we procured at Fort Laramie. In my company are Messrs. Bryant and Jacobs, of Louisville, Ky., Curry, etc. etc. of St. Louis.

I have only a moment allowed me to write this much, and this on the ground. I, therefore, refer you to Messrs. Reddick and Sublette for all particulars touching our route, which they have kindly consented to communicate to you. In haste, I am, truly yours,

Wm. H. Russell.

[George L. Curry] to the St. Louis *Reveille,* "Sweet Water," July 12, 1846 [105]

Editors of the Reveille:—
Here we are, at the head of Sweet Water, (a stream most appropriately named, by the way, for its waters are,

indeed, sweet to the traveller,) and within fifteen miles
of the dividing ridge of the Rocky Mountains. We expect to noon to-day on waters that flow into the Pacific
Ocean. At Fort Bernard I apprised you, by letter, of
the change in the manner of our travel; indeed, we have
found the change a most agreeable one. I, therefore, would
advise your men, in taking the trip, to perform it with
pack animals. The reasons are obvious, as I will elsewhere
show. We have travelled from Fort Larime to this point,
a distance of over three hundred miles, in eleven days.
We have not seen an Indian since our departure from
the Fort. The emigrants, generally speaking, appear to
be getting along right well, the advance company being
some ten days' travel beyond any previous emigration.
We are daily overtaking companies of them, some of
which are astonishingly small in numbers. By this time
the leading company, numbering eleven wagons, is at
Fort Bridger.

We expect to overtake Lieut. Woodworth, the *express*
man of the Government, this evening, as he is but a few
miles in advance of us; and should we do so, I will probably accompany him into Oregon.

Hastings, the book-maker, arrived in Sweet Water
valley a few days since, from California, and, after leaving some letters of encouragement,—on the *"high felu-
tin"* order, though,—behind him, turned his face again
towards the setting sun, and, as I understand, proposes
to gather the various California companies at some point
beyond Fort Bridger, at which point an express is expected to arrive with information that will determine the
manner in which the country is to be entered. Expresses
to the rear companies will, likewise, be sent back from
this place.

I can get no conveniences for writing, from the manner in which we travel, so you must excuse brevity, &c.
From Bridger and Fort Hall I intend writing at length.

Our "Horse Company" number twelve men and
twenty-five horses and mules. The names of the party

are Edwin Bryant, R. T. Jacob, W. H. Russell, J. C. Buchanan, Hiram Miller, R. H. Holder, W. B. Brown, James McCleary, W. H. Nuttall, A. V. Brookie, Captain Wells, (a mountaineer,) and your humble servant.[106]

Mr. Sol. Sublette and company are the bearers of our letters, whom we had the pleasure of meeting last evening. He is from California, and talks *moderately* in favor of the country. Mr. Taplan [Charles Taplin], one of Fremont's company, is along; he left the Colonel, with his party, in good health, on the head waters of the Sacramento river.[107] It is true that he was "proclamationed" out of California. He did not retire from the vicinity of Monterey, however, until he had concluded the business that took him there. Yours, sincerely,

LAON.

CHARLES T. STANTON TO SIDNEY STANTON, "EMIGRANT'S TRAIL, ON THE BANKS OF THE SWEET WATER," JULY 12, 1846 [108]

My last letter was dated last Sunday [July 5], at Beaver Creek, one hundred miles from this place. I met with an opportunity of sending it to you on Tuesday morning from our encampment, on Deer Creek, twenty miles distant. A Mr. Kinney, with a small party of trappers, on their return to Fort Laramie, from the head waters of the Platte in the mountains, passed by just as we were rolling out, and I had only time to slip your letter out of my trunk, fold it, direct it to you in pencil mark, and hand it to him, when we separated.[109] I hope the letter will reach you. Should the direction get rubbed out, I requested him when he arrived at the Fort to ink it, and send it to you by the first opportunity. This letter, and the second I wrote you from Fort L., as there was a probability that the latter might go by the way of Taos, may be a long time in reaching you. I trust that you may ultimately get them, so that the chain in my narrative may not be broken. We are laying by to keep the Sabbath, and

I am keeping it as I did the last Sunday, in writing to you, with the hope that I may meet with an opportunity, while travelling along, of forwarding it on.

On the morning of July 6th, after our two days' rest, we got underway and travelled twenty miles to Deer Creek. Laramie's Peak was visible almost the whole day, off to the south east. About noon we came to the north fork of the Platte, after having been absent from it over a week. Where we struck the river, there is a fine bed of stone coal; but the great Platte, on which we had travelled so long and far, how it had dwindled down, or rather up, to a small stream. The water was clear, but I did not like it as well as I did when mixed with sand and loam when we first struck the river. Thus being mixed has a tendency to purify it, and I also think that the dirt and sand you take in while drinking, is conducive to health.

We travelled all the next day up the Platte, and camped near a small grove on the banks of the river. On Wednesday [July 8] we crossed the Platte about noon, and drove on six miles. The buffalo and other game are becoming plentiful Every day one or more is killed, and we are again luxuriating on fresh meat. I think there is no beef in the world equal to a fine buffalo cow—such a flavor, so rich, so juicy, it makes the mouth water to think of it. On Thursday morning [July 9] we left the Platte and the long range of black hills on our left, and struck off towards the Sweet Water. At noon, Col. [Alphonso] Boon came up full of excitement, stating that he had been out with some others, and had killed eight buffaloes, among which were several fat cows and calves, and requested all who wanted buffalo meat to get what they wanted. We waited some two hours for those who went out, when they came in loaded with the nice bits of the buffalo, leaving the remainder for the wolves. In the afternoon, we drove a few miles and encamped by a fine spring. The next day [July 10] we drove 14 miles to Willow Spring. At noon we heard a great firing, and shortly after young [William] Boggs came in and said they had killed one or two buffalo. Mr. Reid [James Frazier Reed] also shortly after came driving a fine buffalo bull, which he had slightly wounded, as he would an ox, up to the wagons. The next day, Saturday [July 11], we started early, having twenty miles to go. The road was very sandy, and we had to travel very slow. It was just night when we reached the Sweet Water [below Independence Rock]. All along our route to-day buffalo were in sight.

The whole region of country from Fort Laramie to this place is almost entirely barren. There is no grass except in the valleys, which, in some few places only, is found luxuriant. One seems at a loss how to account how the buffalo can live on the hills over which they range—only a few blades of grass can be seen, and that of a low, stunted growth. Over the whole region the wild sage or artemisia grows in abundance. Seen at a distance, it looks like the greenest, richest meadow, but, when you come to it, you are disappointed, as you see nothing but the wild sage in patches, and a barren soil between. The sage is not like the sage of the garden. It has more the smell of lavender, and an Englishman [John Denton?] of "our mess" sticks to it that it is nothing else. We are now in a country where there is little wood, the dry roots of which [sagebrush], being about the size of an ox whip, constitutes our only fuel.

For the last fortnight we have been travelling over, in many respects, an interesting count[r]y; the hills we have found a relief to the interminable level roads of the Platte, and almost every night we get good spring water, which we find much more agreeable than the warm muddy water of that long river. The first week after leaving the Fort, we experienced, though in midsummer, the cool mountain breezes, being necessary at night to bundle ourselves up in our overcoats, and oftentimes through the whole day. The past week, however, it has been different. It has been insufferably hot both day and night—thermometer ranging from 95 to 100 degrees.—This, I am told, is very unusual in the mountains. The sand burns your hand from the intense heat of the sun.—I was surprised to find this great heat, at an elevation of over one mile above the level of the sea. We are now about 100 miles from the South Pass, the highest point we shall ascend in crossing the Rocky Mountains. My next letter may contain a description of the country between this and that most interesting point in our destination.

I think I mentioned in one of my former letters, that the Oregon party which left us on the Platte, we passed at the South Fork; that they came up with us again at Fort Laramie, and travelled with us one or two days and then again went on ahead. This they did, but they left two or three families with us. The influence of these, with the information derived from the Oregon and California travellers, which went to lower the latter country, have cast a shade on all those that were thither bound, and induced many to change their minds. Today, a division of our company took place, Governor Boggs, Colonel Boon, and several other families "sliding" out, leaving us but a small company of eighteen wagons.[110]

Just as the new Oregon company were leaving, there was an important arrival — a single traveller, with his horse and pack mule, who came alone all the way from Oregon. As usual, we all huddled around him, to get his views of the comparative merits of the two countries. Although he was from Oregon, he gave the preference decidedly in favor of California. Of course this pleased all those who had not changed their minds, and made some of the others feel a little chagrined that they had so suddenly changed their course. But Gov. Boggs is actuated by different motives—he is afraid of the Mormons. He has heard that they are on the route, and thinks they will go to California. Should they do so, that will be no place for him. You may be aware that he was shot by [O. P.] Rockwell, and came very near losing his life; consequently, he has something to fear.[111]

Mr. [Wales B.] Bonney, the gentleman from Oregon, will be the bearer of this letter When I commenced writing it this morning I had not the slightest idea when I should have an opportunity of sending it; but here is one already supplied, and it will be on its way to you in the morning.

CHARLES T. STANTON TO SIDNEY STANTON, "SOUTH PASS," JULY 19, 1846 [112]

A week's hard travel from the date of my last letter on the Sweet Water, has brought us to this most interesting point in our route. Yesterday at noon we arrived at the "culminating point," or dividing ridge between the Atlantic and Pacific. This evening we are encamped on the Little Sandy, one of the forks of Green river, which is a tributary of the great Colorado, which flows into the gulf of California. Thus the great day-dream of my youth and of my riper years is accomplished. I have seen the Rocky mountains—have crossed the Rubicon, and am now on the waters that flow to the Pacific! It seems as if I had left the old world behind, and that a new one is dawning upon me. In every step thus far there has been something new, something to attract.—Should the remainder of my journey be as interesting, I shall be abundantly repaid for the toils and hardships of this arduous trip. But I must lead you back to the date of my letter on the Sweet Water, and attempt to give you a description of its most interesting valley.

A drive of five miles [on July 13] brought us to Independence Rock, in the appearance of which we were all disappointed, as we expected to find a rock so high that you could hardly see its top; but instead of that, in comparison with some of the high peaks surrounding it, seen from the distance, it looked tame and uninteresting. It is about 600 yards long, and about 140 feet high, of an oval shape—one solid mass of granite, rising perpendicularly from the green bottom lands of the Sweet Water.—Its sides, to the height of 80 feet, are covered with names of travellers who have passed by. There is an indentation about half way to its top, where there is a single pine tree growing. Hastings, in his trip to California [Oregon] in 1842, in attempting to climb the rock to this tree, was taken prisoner by the Indians.[113] In about eight miles further, we came to the "Devil's Gate," where we "nooned," and the most of our party walked down to take a look at it. The Sweet Water at this place makes a gap through a rock mountain, which on either side rises 400 feet from the water. The rock is of granite, single pieces of which, as large as an ordinary house, are found in this place. We drove on till sun down, and caught up with Bogg's company, which had left us the day before, and encamped. No scenery in our whole route has been more delightful than that seen in this day's drive. The valley of the Sweet Water is about five miles wide. On one [*i. e.,*—our?] right was a long line of rock hills or mountains, from three to five hundred feet in height, rising directly from the smooth level of rich meadow land. Nothing could present a greater contrast with the sterile granite mountains, than this. On our right the valley is bounded by the Sweet Water mountains, of from ten to fifteen hundred feet in height. The river is a stream about as large as Onondaga creek, and winds through this delightful valley—sometimes by the mountains on our left, and the mountains of rock, for they are literally so, on our right. In one or two instances we found this range broken into isolated hills, which were seen in their lonely beauty: the green meadow land, stretching in some instances as far as the eye could reach in and around them, still heightening the charm of this unequalled scenery.

The next day [July 14] we travelled on and encamped again on the Sweet Water, after a drive of about twenty miles, one mile ahead of Bogg's company, near the base of a large mountain of rock. The sun was an hour high, and I had a great desire to go to the top, to see if I could get a view of the Rocky Mountains; but I could find no one venturesome enough to accompany me in climbing

its steep, rugged sides, and I was compelled to give up
the jaunt, not wishing to attempt it alone. In the morning
[July 15] we drove on, and in a short time entered the
"Narrows," a place so called, where the river and the road
runs through steep rock mountains, which rise three or
four hundred feet on either side. This was a wild and romantic place.[114] On arriving at the end of this gap, the
road struck upon a rather elevated sandy ridge, and we
drove till sundown without reaching the river, and were
compelled to encamp on a small stream which furnished
scarcely water for the cattle. Here Bogg's company came
up and stayed with us; but they illy repaid our hospitality,
for in the morning [July 16] they stole the march on us
—"rolling out" first—leaving us to get along as best we
might. This movement chagrined many of our party, as
we by courtesy were entitled to the lead. We had from
this place the first view of "the snow clad mountains,"
lying off to the northwest. It was the Wind river chain,
and many of the peaks were covered with snow. It was
now midsummer—we had been travelling for the past
ten days under a broiling sun, and it was strange thus
suddenly to see this winter appearance on the distant hills.

We travelled on till noon, when we passed Bogg's company on the Sweet Water—a mile further up, Dunlavy's
—a mile further, West's—and about two miles beyond
that was Dunbar's. We encamped about midway between
the two latter. Thus, within five miles were encamped
five companies. At Indian Creek, 20 miles from Independence, these five companies all constituted one, but
owing to desertions and quarrelling, they became broken
into fragments; and now by accident we all again once
more meet and grasp the cordial hand—old enmities are
forgotten and good feeling prevails.[115]

Dunbar's company seemed to be at the head waters
of the river, for the hills from that place rose abruptly
from the stream, and crowded so upon it, that but a narrow channel was left for its waters to flow.—Therefore
I thought that this must be near its head waters, and that

on the morrow, probably, we should cross the dividing ridge; but I was mistaken, for two days after we encamped again on the Sweet Water, which appeared to be nearly as large as it did when we first struck it. This place, from the description given me by Dunbar, I have no doubt is the Kanyon spoken of by Fremont, and I have since regretted that I did not pay it a visit.[116]

The next morning [July 17] we got rather a late start, owing to a "difference of opinion" among our company (a not unfrequent thing among all companies that cross the mountains) as to whether we should lay by or go on? Those wishing to lay by were principally young men, who wished to have a day's hunt among the buffaloes. There were also a few families out of meat, who wished to get a supply before they left the buffalo country—and a further reason was urged, that the cattle were nearly worn out by hard travel, and they would not stand it unless we stopped and gave them a rest. On the other side it was contended, that if we stopped here the other companies would all get ahead—that the grass would all be eat out by their cattle, and that consequently, when we came along our cattle would starve, as there would be nothing for them to subsist on. The go-ahead party finally ruled, and we "rolled out."

One or two miles brought us to the high hill previously mentioned, up which we wound our way, and were two or three hours in reaching its summit. Many supposed, with myself among the number, that this rocky ridge was the "culminating point," and that we were now on the waters that flowed to the Pacific. The Wind River Mountains, with their snow capped peaks, lay on our right, and the Sweet Water mountains off to the south east, on our left. To the west, as well as to the east, the view was unobstructed, and every thing seemed to indicate this to be the South Pass, according to the description given of it by Fremont; but we were mistaken. We drove on till night, when we came to a pure stream, with a swift current, which we supposed might be the Little Sandy; but we were soon convinced of the contrary, as its general current was east, and we all had no doubt but that we were again on the banks of the Sweet Water.

In the morning, Saturday [July 18], we got an early start, and drove about ten or twelve miles and "nooned," without finding water for our cattle. This place was on a ridge [South Pass]. There was a large table mound on our left, covering an area of about a mile square; there was also a smaller mound on our right. The wind was strong from the west, and the day quite cold. For the past eight or ten days, we had had extremely hot weather, and we found the cool breeze an agreeable change. After our usual delay, we were again on the road, and after a few hours drive, came to a fine spring, with the grass looking green about it. The managers of our company finding it rather boggy, thought the cattle would get mired should they attempt to feed upon the rich herbage, and concluded to go on till they found better grass, before they stopped for the night. We, therefore, drove on till nearly sun-down, but came to no more water or grass. We presently came to a deep gully [Dry Sandy], where there was a little water, but no grass and were going by without paying it a passing notice, when Mr. R[eed]., who had been sent on a head to look out for a camping place, was seen returning at full gallop. He soon came up and told us that we must go back to the gully and stay, as bad as it was. It was after dark that night before we got our suppers. Mr. D.[onner?] who had been out with R. had not returned, and we all concluded that he must be lost. Guns were fired and beacons placed on the surrounding hills. About 12 o'clock, he made his appearance.

The next day, Sunday [July 19], we travelled on till noon, but found no wood or water; and it was not till the middle of the afternoon, that we reached a small stream [Little Sandy], where we encamped. This stream was of a swift current and sandy color, and its general course was westward. This surprised the most of us, as now they were willing to acknowledge that they had crossed the dividing ridge without knowing it. But it was true. The place where we had "nooned" the day before, with the table mound on our right and the little mound on our left, was the "culminating point" between the Atlantic and the Pacific; and the spring around which the grass grew so green, was the green spring [Pacific Spring]— the first water that flows westward.

Bear River, August 3, 1846.

The above was written on the spot where it bears date, since which time circumstances have prevented me from continuing my narrative further. I may not have another opportunity of sending you letters till I reach California; but I have brought you to the top of the mountains; hereafter, I will give you the descent to the Pacific.

We take a new route to California, never travelled before this season; consequently our route is over a new and interesting region. We are now in the Bear river valley, in the midst of the Bear river [Uinta] mountains, the summits of which are covered with snow. As I am now writing, we are cheered by a warm summer's sun, while but a few miles off, the snow covered mountains are glittering in its beams.[117]

S. T. C.

Dr. T. Pope Long to his Brother in Clay County, Missouri, Fort Bridger, July 19, 1846 [118]

Dr. Brother:—

We arrived here on Thursday [July 16], and are now waiting for a sufficient number of waggons, in order to take a nearer route crossing the country on the south end of the great salt lake. This route will cut off at least 250 miles, and is the one through which Capt. Fremont passed last season. It is proposed by Mr. Hastings (who has been with us for some time;) he came through on horseback, and reports the route perfectly practicable for wagons. The fort at which we are stationed, is surrounded by high mountains covered as deeply with snow as if it were the middle of winter. We have got this far extremely well. Our oxen are in good order, and travel almost as well as they did when we started. About forty wagons are now with us waiting to take the cut-off. I have met with several old mountain friends, who have treated us very kindly. * * * The different companies that started in the spring have had no difficulties with the Indians, except the occasional loss of a few horses. But difficulties are occurring almost every day *amongst themselves.* They are continually dividing, and sub-dividing. Experience has taught us that small companies, of about fifteen wagons, are the best, to travel with * * * We have received news that war is raging between the United States and Mexico. It has occasioned much speculation in our little camp, and some disbelieving the report. It has alarmed some, and will turn them towards Oregon. I apprehend no danger myself, and we are generally anxious to get to our destination. * * * We will arrive in California, I think, about the middle of September—a long and tedious trip to some, but others do not mind it. I have enjoyed myself finely; and, as the country through which we have to pass is healthy, I apprehend no sickness. We have used but little more than one half of our provisions, and have performed two-thirds of the journey to California.

LETTER FROM AN EMIGRANT TO A FRIEND IN ST. LOUIS, FORT BRIDGER, JULY 23, 1846 [119]

A letter from a young man of this city, one of the party that left for California last spring, was received by his friends yesterday, and kindly placed in our hands, from which we [the *Missouri Republican*] have extracted the following particulars. The letter is dated on the 23d of July, at Fort Bridger, which is near the head of Black's Fork of Green river, not far from Bear river mountains, and was brought in by Capt. [Joseph R.] Walker, who was returning from California [after service] with lieut.

Fremont. At Fort Laramie, col. Russell and many others of the emigrants, sold off their wagons, and with a pack containing a few articles, pursued their journey on horseback. The grass on the route from Fort Laramie was deficient, and the animals fared badly. — For one hundred miles west of the States, the country is represented as being miserably poor and barren; though fifty to one hundred miles further, the valleys of the Platte and other streams, afforded very good grazing. The soil, however, is sandy and full of salt. The parties were in the South Pass of the Rocky Mountains on the 13th of July, and had then seen no Indians after leaving Fort Laramie, and considered themselves beyond their dangerous vicinity, and only a few of the emigrants kept a night guard. From Fort Laramie, they had pleasant weather, with cool nights and warm days—though very dusty roads, till they reached Fort Bridger, and during the whole route they had not seen more than a dozen buffalo.

Col. Russell and his party, by hard travelling, reached Fort Bridger [on July 16] two or three days before the others, but his horses had their backs badly worn, and he remained there four days to recruit. At that place they were met by Mr. Hastings, from California, who came out to conduct them in by the new route, by the foot of Salt Lake, discovered by capt. Fremont, which is said to be two hundred miles nearer than the old one, by Fort Hall. The distance to California was said to be six hundred and fifty miles, through a fine farming country, with plenty of grass for the cattle.

Companies of from one to a dozen wagons, says the writer, are continually arriving, and several have already started on, with Hastings at their head, who would conduct them to near where the road joins the old route, and there leave them, and push on with his party. Russell had also started, guided by a man [James Hudspeth] who came through with Hastings. He is said to be very sick of the journey, and anxious to complete it. Instead of entering California as the commander of a half military caravan, he had been forsaken by his most cherished companions, and even his understrappers have treated him with indignity. Grayson had quarrelled with all his companions, and every one who could raise a horse had left him. Boggs and many others had determined to go to Oregon, and were expected to arrive at Fort Bridger in a day or two. Curry had also been persuaded to go to Oregon, and from thence he would go to California and the Sandwich Islands. He was still in bad health.

The Oregon route may be considerably shortened by avoiding Fort Bridger, and passing a stretch of forty five miles without water [the Greenwood Cutoff]—but most companies go that way. The emigrants were heartily tired of their journey, and nine tenths of them wished themselves back in the States. The whole company had been broken up into squads by dissatisfaction and bickerings, and it was pretty much every man for himself. The accounts they have received of Oregon and the Californias, by the parties they met returning to the States, had greatly disheartened them, and they had horrible anticipations of the future, in the country which they believed to be, when they set out, as beautiful as the Elysian fields.

The climate at Fort Bridger is described as delightfully pleasant; the days were clear and warm, refreshed by pleasant breezes, and the nights were cool, with light dews and occasional frost. Fort Bridger is said to be a miserable pen, occupied at times by Messrs. Bridger and Vasques, and resorted to be a number of loafing trappers to exchange furs and moccasins with the emigrants for flour, bacon and whiskey. The latter sells at two dollars a pint.

Missouri Reporter, St. Louis, July 30, 1846

LATE FROM CALIFORNIA.—A party of gentlemen, six in number, arrived here yesterday on the steamer *Nimrod,* who are direct from California, having left that country as late as the 22d of April last. They report having met the party commanded by Capt. Martin, of Platte City, at Red Bute, about two hundred miles beyond Fort Laramie, travelling on cheerily, having met with few impediments to their journey. Between that point and Fort Laramie, they continually met small companies, and at the Fort, met the company of Governor Boggs. All the emigrants seemed in good spirits, and highly delighted with their future prospects.

The party to which our informant belonged, consisted of sixteen, on leaving the frontiers of California. They were of both sexes, and of various ages. The gentlemen who have arrived, left the others and travelled on in advance. Those not yet arrived, were generally persons who had been but a short time in the country, but who had become dissatisfied with it.[120]

It would seem that a cause of dissatisfaction among the people from the United States who visit that country, is the impossibility, in the unsettled state of the government, to obtain good titles to their lands. Another is, that the country is far better suited to purposes of stock-raising, than those of agriculture. The soil, though supporting a luxuriant growth spontaneously, is found to be inferior for purposes of cultivation. When turned up, it "bakes," and is not easily convertible into mould.

Many of the older emigrants from the United States, however, were satisfied and determined to remain. Some of these experienced much difficulty in crossing the mountains, and met with heavy losses. Among others, a gentleman by the name of Joseph Chiles, from Jackson county, in this State, who had gone to California for the purpose of establishing extensive mills on the Sacraficios [Sacramento], lost much of his property, but eventually, by his enterprize and industry, succeeded, partially, in carrying out his plans.[121]

As in other countries newly settled by the Anglo-Saxon race, there exists in California a class of people led there solely by the love of adventure. It is these, principally, who complain of the country, and who are to leave it for other wilds, or to return to their old haunts. Our informants think that the main objections to California will be removed by a permanent change of government.

Weekly Reveille, St. Louis, August 3, 1846

FROM CALIFORNIA. — A party of six gentlemen came down on the *Nimrod* yesterday, having recently arrived on the western frontier of this State from California, which country they left on the 22d of April last. They report all quiet in that country, but a general dissatisfaction existing among the American settlers, owing to the impossibility of procuring valid titles to their lands. Some disappointment, also, has been experienced in relation to the fitness of the soil for agricultural purposes. It is believed that its *spontaneous* products are far more abundant, and of a better order, than those that are the result of cultivation. As a grazing country, however, all seem to agree that it cannot be surpassed.

The party consisted, at first, of sixteen persons, of both sexes and different ages. These persons, or most of them, had been in California but a short time, and had taken but little pains to explore the country. The six gentlemen above referred to left the main company soon after starting, and travelled on in advance. They met Captain Martin's company, from Platte City, about 200 miles beyond Fort Laramie, and Governor Bogg's company at the fort. For several days after leaving Laramie, they met parties of emigrants. They saw few Indians, and got in without encountering serious molestation.

New Era, St. Louis, July 30, 1846 [122]

FROM CALIFORNIA.—A Mr. Crosby and five other persons arrived here yesterday, in the steamer *Nimrod,* from Weston. We are informed by one of the party that a company of eighteen persons, including two or three women and children, left California about the first of May last, and that they traveled nearly the whole distance together;

but when within some three hundred miles of Fort Laramie, the company separated, and the persons mentioned above came on in advance.

Nothing of interest had transpired during the journey, and they bring no intelligence from that country of importance. About two hundred miles in the prairies, West of Fort Laramie, and in the California trace, they met Martin's company of emigrants, and at the Fort met Boggs' party—the first were moving on finely, but the latter were undetermined whether they would shape their course for Oregon or California.

Some were in favor of the former and a large portion of the latter. This disagreement as to their ultimate destination had caused some ill-feeling, but no serious misunderstanding. It was thought that the company would separate into two parties, and that each would take the course he preferred. From the short stay of Mr. Crosby and his party here, we are unable to glean any particulars concerning the country, &c. but presumed they could have added but little to what has already been published.

Missouri Republican, St. Louis, July 30, 1846

FROM CALIFORNIA

A gentleman who has passed the two last years in Oregon and California reached this city yesterday. His name is James Clymer [Clyman], and [he] migrated from Milwaukie, with a view of determining for himself the character of that country. He left California, in company with six other persons, the latter end of April, and has been ninety days on the route.[123] Mr. Clymer has kindly permitted us to glance at his *diary*—we could do no more— kept for the whole time of his absence, and to select such facts as may interest our readers. We have, of necessity, to take such incidents as occurred during his return *home,* passing over many descriptions of country, soil, places, mountains, people and government, in Oregon and California.

On the 16th [17th] of March last, Mr. Clymer refers, in his journal, to the extraordinary avidity with which news is manufactured in that country; and says, that Lieut. Fremont had raised the American flag in Monterrey—of course the town of that name on the Pacific—that all good citizens were called upon to appear forthwith, at Sonoma, armed and equipped for service under Gen. Byajo [Vallejo], to defend the rights of Mexican citizens. This report subsequently appeared, was founded on the fact, that Lieut. Fremont had raised the American [flag] at his camp, near the Mission of St. John's and that he declined to call on some of the legal authorities, when ordered to do so. It was said, in consequence of this state of things, General Castro had raised four hundred men at Monterrey; that he marched to Lieut. Fremont's camp on the 22nd of March, from which he had retreated; and that he there found numerous pack-saddles, baggage, and a considerable quantity of specie.[124] Lieut. Fremont was last heard of, after Mr. Clymer had left, on the Rio Sacramento; but as he kept his own counsel, no one knew his object in going there, or when he would return to the United States. He had lost one man, who was killed by the Indians, and had discharged others.

Mr. Clymer met, at different times and under different circumstances, parties of Emigrants to Oregon or California, who were roving about discontented, and going back and forth, as whim dictated. On the 22nd [24th] of March, he notices having met, in California, a party of one hundred and fifty persons, thirty or forty of whom were then going to the Columbia river, having become tired of *the other paradise*. On the 20th of April, Mr. [Owen] Sumner [Sr.] and his family arrived at camp, prepared for their journey to the States. Mr. Sumner had been in Oregon; from thence he went to California; and, being still dissatisfied, he was now returning, after having spent five years in traveling and likewise a small fortune.

He met, and left Mr. L. P. [W.] Hastings, the author of a work on California, at his camp on Bear Creek, a small creek running into Feather River. He was located near the road travelled by the emigrants to California. Mr. Hastings had been looking for some force from the States, with which it was designed to revolutionize California, but in this he had been disappointed. He was then, it seemed, awaiting the action of the American Government, in taking possession of that country—of which he appeared to have some intimation.[125] Mr. Clymer heard, on his return homeward, of the arrival of the several United States vessels of war at Monterrey, but knows nothing more about them.

We cannot follow Mr. Clymer and his party in their perilous journey over snow-capped mountains, on the sides of mighty precipices, in deep ravines, and places seemingly impassable. Something may be learned of the excitement and the danger of the travel, by a single scene, as roughly drawn in the *Diary*. On the 27th of April, while waiting for some of the party, the author walked out to the north-east of the valley, on the point of a ledge of rocks. "Here you have a view which is awfully and really sublime. The first thing which attracts your attention is a high, rough ridge of snow-capped mountains. Proceeding a little farther, this ridge descends in front into an impassable cliff of black rocks, divested of every kind of covering. Still farther on, and you behold a river dashing through an awful chasm of rocks several thousand feet below. Dizzy with the prospect, you turn your head to the right, and there you have ridges of snow and ridges of towering pine trees. To the left, you have a distant view of the eternal cliffs of black volcanic rocks which bound the river Eubor."

Again—on the 9th of April [May], the party pursued their way down the river Truckies, or Salmon Trout river, about six miles, to a point which they left to cross the "Great Interior Basin," as it is termed on the map, expecting to touch the *sink* of the St. Mary's river—a river not laid down on the map. Leaving the Salmon Trout

river to take a course to the North, the party struck off
to the East, and soon came near the point of a low range
of black volcanic mountains. Here they observed numerous specimens of rocks formed by concretions from
springs which must have existed some years since, but
which are no longer to be found. "In fact, it seems to me
that all the country passed over to-day must at some remote period, have been one immense boiling caldron, and
it is now strewn over with some thousands of upright
rocks which have been projected by immense bodies of
liquid steam. Quantities of mud, which now fills the whole
plain over which we passed, for several miles, was over
a white sheet of incrusted salt. We passed over, and in
sight of, large bodies of white chalk, which must also have
been involved in boiling water. A low range of black slag
lay on the left, and every thing presented the most sterile
appearance." Thus they traveled until they came to
Mary's lake, where still exists a caldron of boiling water.
No stream issues from it at present, but it stands in several pools, boiling, and again disappearing. Some of these
pools have beautiful clear water boiling in them, and
others eject quantities of mud. "Into one of these muddy
pools, my little water spaniel, Lucky, was tempted, poor
fellow, not knowing that it was boiling hot. He delib-
erately walked into the boiling caldron, to slake his thirst,
and cool his limbs, when, to my sad sorrow, he was scalded
almost instantly to death. I felt more regret for his loss
than that of any animal I had ever owned, as he had been
my constant companion in all my wanderings, and I had
hoped to see him return to his old master at Milwaukee."

Twelve days of travel up the valley of the St. Mary's
river over a most sterile country, brought them to the
point where Lieut. Fremont intersected the wagon trail,
on his route to California, last fall. On the 23d May, after
long consultation and many arguments for and against
the two routes—one leading Northward by Fort Hall,
and the other by the Salt Lake—they determined to take
Fremont's trail, by the Lake. Interesting as it is, we can-

not follow the traveler on his way, but must content ourselves with his conclusion as to the practicability of the
route. Mr. Clymer is of opinion that it is very little nearer
to California, and not so good a road as that by Fort Hall.

On the 23d of July [June], Mr. Clymer met the advance company of Oregon immigrants, consisting of
eleven wagons, nearly opposite the Red Butes. From the
North Platte they had the pleasant sight of beholding
the valley to a great distance dotted with people, horses,
cattle, wagons, and tents. Still farther on they met three
small companies—some destined for Oregon and some
for California. "It is remarkable," says the journal, "how
anxious these people are to hear from the Pacific country; and strange that so many of all kinds and classes
of people should sell out comfortable homes, in Missouri
and elsewhere, pack up and start across such an immense
barren waste, to settle in some new place of which they
have at most no certain information." At Fort Laramie
they met Gov. Boggs and Judge Morin, from Jackson
county. After a night spent in conversation, both of these
gentlemen determined to change their destination from
California to Oregon. Other parties were met, all getting
along cheerfully—suffering only from the depredations
of the Indians on their cattle and horses. The only death
among the emigrants is that of Trimble, killed by the
Indians.

Weekly Reveille, St. Louis, August 3, 1846

EMIGRANTS TO THE PACIFIC.—Our greatest surprise is
that so *few* of the emigrants to the Pacific coast become
discontented, and turn back in disgust. When we consider
the restless spirit which often alone prompts them to
move, and that when they have reached the Pacific there
is no farther "far west," without crossing the seas for it,
no wonder that the *final bound* becomes oppressive to
them. In the very immensity of their freedom they become thralled. It is change they seek, and not a home.

The small party just arrived from west of the mountains bring instances of this strange passion for motion. The diary of one of the gentlemen—alluded to in the *Republican*—has the following entry: "On the 20th of April Mr. Sumner and his family arrived at camp, prepared for their journey to the States. Mr. Sumner had been in Oregon; from thence he went to California; and, being still dissatisfied, he was now returning, after having spent five years in traveling, and likewise a small fortune." This speaks plainly in the case.

Sangamo Journal, SPRINGFIELD, ILLINOIS, JULY 30, 1846.

We saw a gentleman last week from Oregon.[126] He states that the Messrs. [William] Ide, Mr. [William L.] Todd, and Mr. [Robert Cadden] Keyes, did not go to Oregon, but went to California. He saw Mr. Nathan Hussey and the neighbors who went with him, who were well and were doing well.

DANIEL TOOLE TO HIS BROTHER, FORT HALL, AUGUST 2, 1846 [127]

Dear Brother: — I am happy of the opportunity of sending to you some further information with regard to our tedious trip to Oregon.

We arrived at this place (Fort Hall) on yesterday, which is situated in a beautiful plain on Snake river, and is certainly a healthy place if there is one in the world.

The curiosities that are to be seen upon the plains, are enough to compensate me for all my trouble. The soda springs are a curiosity indeed, the water of these springs tastes a good deal like soda, and boils up like soda when the acid is mixed; just below these soda springs is a boiling spring, which comes up through a hole in a rock; it makes a noise like it was boiling, and can be heard a quarter of a mile off. The water foams like suds, and is a little above milk warm.

The Independence rock is also an interesting sight, it is about 150 feet high, and covers something near six acres of ground. There are engraved upon this rock, between two and three thousand names; I left my name on it, July 2d, 1846. If I were to tell you that we crossed lakes of salaratus, you would scarcely believe me, but it is true; we travelled over them with our teams, and used it in our bread, and it is as good, if not better, than any you buy in the States. From Fort Laramie to this place, the road is quite rocky, mountainous, and sandy; our teams however, seem to stand it tolerably well—we have to rest them a good deal in consequence of the scarcity of grass near the mountains. The worst thing we have to encounter, is the dust, which is very disagreeable indeed. This is a long and tedious trip, and requires great patience, but I have not for a moment regreted the undertaking, for it has been a great benefit to my health, and I find health better than friends. The old men who undertook this trip for their health are getting along finely; old Mr. Linnville looks well. Those who undertake this trip should select well made cattle, as they stand it much the best; and don't be alarmed if you have to burn buffalo chips to cook by, for it makes a good fire.

DANIEL TOOLE.

CHARLES F. PUTNAM TO JOSEPH PUTNAM, FORT HALL, AUGUST 8, 1846 [128]

Dear Father

It is doubtful whether you have received any of the numerous letters that we have written to you, for the persons who return to the States have no convenient way of carrying them, being on horseback & I have found several letters on the road broken open which were directed to the States I have no doubt however but what you have received some of those we have written. Would that we had an opportunity of hearing from home, but it is impossible to hear for some time to come, you not knowing where to write & if you did, it would be about the same but it is to be hoped that you are all enjoying that greatest of all blessings—health.

A Mr. Weir [who] left Independence (Mo.) June 2ᵈ, brought a St. Louis paper of the 28ᵗʰ of May which gave an account of the victory of Gen. Taylor & the great zeal & interest manifested by the Western States in sending troops to Texas. Mr Weir is a citizen of Oregon, he returned to the States last Spring a year by Sea to Boston. He intends making the trip to Oregon city in 3 months from Independence & says he prefers travelling by land alone than by water.[129]

We are on our way to Oregon city, believing it will be to our interest to go to Oregon, on account of the unsettled state of affairs in California. In Oregon we are certain of 640 acres [of] land, provided the U. States sanctions what the Legislature of Oregon has alread[y] granted to every male emigrant of 21 years of age & every female of 18 gets 160 according to the laws of Oregon & I think there is no doubt but what it will pass both Houses of the Congress of the U. S. It passed the Lower House before we left.

We have not positively came to the conclusion as to what part of Oregon we will make our selection of land. But Nathan & Bosworth will work in Oregon city this winter (I expect). Nathan intends building a log-Cabin & hire hands to fence his farm & put in a crop. He can hire several hands with his trade. Carpenters get high wages in Oregon. There is a probability of my getting work at my trade.

A Kentuckian has came into camp [*deleted*: for the purpose of Acting] from Oregon to Pilot us. His name is [Jesse] Applegate, he is well acquainted with Ex-Governor Boggs & was a member of the Legislature of Mo. when Mr. B., was Governor. Mr. A. is a warm Whig. We stopped three days at the Soda Springs where we enjoyed ourselves as much as though we had been at Saratoga N. Y. I will return next year & give all the particulars. If you think of coming I would get three or four strong but light two-horse wagons [*deleted*: with a sufficient f] with three yoke of oxen to each wagon & a side door with steps for the family. I would also bring some fine cows, Mares, &c: they are no trouble & plenty of grass for them. Give my love to all.—

Mr. Bosworth wishes to be remembered to all his acquaintances. I hope this will find you all in good health Give love to Mother & Virginia, kiss Siss & Henry. In much haste

Your Son

C. F. PUTNAM

P. S. Direct your letters to Oregon City

JESSE APPLEGATE TO LISBON APPLEGATE, "FORT HALL, SNAKE RIVER," AUGUST 9, 1846 [130]

Dear Brother:

I arrived here yesterday alone and on foot from the Willamette valley at the head of a party to meet the emigration. We left our homes on Willamette the 22d June last to explore a Southern route into that valley from the U. S.—After much labor and suffering we succeeded in our object tho it occupied us so long that a part of the emigrants had passed our place of intersection with the old road before we could possibly reach it.

The new route follows the California road about 350 miles from here, it then leaves Ogdens or Marys river and enters Oregon by the way of the Clamet Lakes, Rogue river, Umpqua and the head of the Willamette valley— it shortens the road—avoids the dangers of Snake & Columbia rivers and passes S. of the Cascade Mts.— there is almost every place plenty of grass and water & every wagon ox or cow may enter Oregon.

I would give you a more lengthy description of this road if I had time or opportunity but I cannot escape the importunities of the emigrants who are pursuing me into every room of the fort and besieging me with endless questionings on all possible subjects—so much am I confused that I scarce know what I have written or wish to write—Suffice it to say that we fully succeeded in our object tho not a man of us had ever been in the country before—of your acquaintances, Lindsay [Applegate], David Goff, B. F. Burch & Wm. Sportsman were with me. I am well pleased with Mr. Burch he is a good boy and of correct principles—as he may not reach here in time to write tell his father that he is well and well pleased with the country and if the opportunity presented itself intended coming on to Missouri after him this fall—but as his horses were very tired when I left the balance of the company and I hear of no party going back I expect he will return with us to Willamette.

I met Larkin Stanley going to California & Oregon who told me you were coming to Oregon next year, if it is so I am glad to hear it—and gladder still that I have assisted in finding a new route. — I believe I have no reason to change any part of the directions I gave you last Spring—it is a pity you have not come sooner to Oregon—Gov. Boggs and almost all the respectable portion of the California emigrants are going on the new road to Oregon—and nearly all the respectable emigrants that went last year to California came this Spring to Oregon—and as long as you are actually coming I venture to say that *"you never will regret it"* I am better pleased every day I would write and wish to write much to you but at present I have no opportunity the emigrants will give me no peace Capt. Grant has done his best to give me an opportunity to write but all in vain.—Speaking of Capt. Grant reminds me of a favor I have to request of you and Betsy.

Capt. Grant the gentleman in charge of Fort Hall has two sons and a daughter at school in Canada he wishes them to come to Fort Hall next year with the emigration. He says his son a young man of 20 or thereabouts with little experience in the world, is his only dependence to bring his daughter a girl of 15 and a younger brother over the Mountains—He appears anxious to place his daughter in the care of some respectable lady who is coming to this country—

Now if Betsy will take the girl under her protection and you will see to the comfort and safety of the sons, you will confer a great favor upon me, and serve a gentleman to whom I owe many obligations, not only for kindnesses extended towards myself, but for the assistance he daily renders to the emigrants to Oregon. If you are coming next spring to Oregon and will take charge of these young people,—write to Richard Grant Jr. (Care of Phillip Burns esq. Three Rivers Lower Canada—) when and where to meet you which it would be better probably your own house before you leave—as in that case you could see that they were properly prepared for the journey.[131]

If I have the opportunity I will write more.

JESSE APPLEGATE.

JESSE APPLEGATE TO LISBON APPLEGATE AT KEYTESVILLE, MISSOURI, FORT HALL, AUGUST 10, 1846 [132]

Dear Brother.

Allow me to introduce to your favorable notice Mr. Richard Grant Jr.—

By my recommendation he has called upon you to rest himself at your house for a few days. That you and your family will make him comfortable I make no doubt.

Mr. Grant will give you another letter which will [quite?] fully explain his & his fathers wishes, respecting his coming out in [your?] company—to Fort Hall and perhaps all way [to the] Willamette.—

Tell Betsy and the boys that upon the new road I have been exploring they will see some of the greatest wonders of nature.—So truly wonderful is some parts of this road that I am unequal to the task of giving you a description. The immense masses of Mountains, covered in eternal Snows, the black smoke of volcanoes the boiling Springs, and deep and dark passes among the Mountains into which the sun never shines, and the high plains over which we pass, where frost falls and ice freezes every night, it is worth a years travel to see these wonders of nature, to say nothing of the immense numbers and variety of the wild animals to be seen upon the road.

In haste

JESSE APPLEGATE.

P.S. Tomorrow I start homeward. the emigrants have almost annoyed me out of my senses—and Capt. Grant who is proof against all kinds of annoyances, has out of Charity undertook to put those behind upon the right track.

JESSE APPLEGATE, OPEN LETTER "TO THE FUTURE EMIGRANTS TO OREGON, FORT HALL, SNAKE RIVER," AUGUST 10, 1846 [133]

Gentlemen:

The undersigned are happy to inform you that a southern route to the Willamette, has just been explored, and a portion of the emigration of the present year are now upon the road. Owing to unavoidable delays, the exploring party did not arrive at the forks of the road until some of the front companies of the emigrants were passed, perhaps eighty or one hundred wagons.

The new route follows the road to California about 320 miles from this place, and enters the Oregon Territory by the way of the Clamet Lake, passes through the splendid vallies of the Rogue and Umqua rivers, and enters the valley of the Willamette near its south eastern extremity.

The advantage gained to the emigrant by this route is of the greatest importance—the distance is considerably shortened, the grass and water plenty, the sterile regions and dangerous crossings of the Snake and Columbia rivers avoided, as well as the Cascade Mountain— he may reach his place of destination with his wagon and property in time to build a cabin and sow wheat before the rainy season. This road has been explored, and will be opened at the expense of the citizens of Oregon, and nothing whatever demanded of the emigrants.

Gov. Boggs and party, with many other families of respectability, have changed their destination, and are now on their way to Oregon. Some of the emigrants intend stopping in the Umqua valley—which, tho' not so large, is quite equal to the Willamette for fertility.

A way-bill, fully describing the road, will be prepared and sent to the United States, or to Fort Hall, for the use of the emigration of 1847, and no pilots will be required.

The exploring party left the upper settlements of the Willamette on the 25th of June last,—crops were most promising, and farmers in high spirits. They met a large emigration from California, consisting of the Hon. Felix Scott; late of St. Charles county, Missouri, and many others who left the United States. They give a decided preference to Oregon over California.

The exploring party consists of John Jones, John Scott, Robert Smith, John Owen, Samuel Goodhue, Henry Boggs, Wm. Sportsman, Jesse Applegate, Levi Scott, David Goff, Lindsay Applegate, Moses Harris, Wm. Parker, Benj. Osborne, Benj. F. Birch.

Editors in Missouri, Illinois and Iowa, friendly to the prosperity of Oregon will please insert the foregoing communication.

JESSE APPLEGATE.

WILLIAM J. J. SCOTT TO WILLIAM BUTINE OR JOSEPH
V. MORGAN, FORT HALL, AUGUST 14, 1846 [134]

Dear friends

I now take my Pen in hand to inform you that I am well at present and have been every since I left home I have had my health better this summer and feel stouter than I have for Several years I have got along very well so far I shal have plenty of Provisions to last me throw all of this company has plenty of Provisions to do them thare is seven wagons in our company Buckheart 2 wagons Suttle 2 wagons Johnston 2 wagons and mine all from Desmoins county I have got all of my oxen yet and Abigal two She workes well and gives afine chance of milk we have had no trouble acrossing streams it has been very dry weather hear and dusty travling we havent had but one Shower of rains Since we left South Plat River and no Drews at all it is very pleasent travling threw this country we have Sean Some Indians but our company has reseaved no injury from them thare is Sevral companies behind us and agreat many before us, one of the companys behind us had three horses Stolen from them and two wagons robed by the Sioux Indians about one hundred of them to geather you musent low no Indians to get in your wagons while they was takeing things out of the wagons the old Chief tried to Stop them all he could and Shot Several of thear horses and Stoped them from robing— look out about 12 miles the other side of the willow Springs the Soap factory it looks like it was solled on top and if you Step on it you will go under head and years and if not washed off it will take the hair off one of our girles was so misfortunate as to get in but I dont think it takened the feathers of I have had the Pleasure of Seeing the Salaratus factory— it is first rate and looks as white as Snow the Sody Spring is aquite acuriosity thare is agreat many of them Just boiling rite up out of the groung take alitle sugar and desolve it in alittle watter and then dip up acup full and drink it before it looses it gass it is frristrate I drank ahal of galon of it you will see several Spring Spouting up out ove the river it is quite asite to see the prairies coverd with Buffalow we had agreat time acilling one we Shot him and Broke his leg and then we after him we would run him awhile and Shoot him and then he would run us I must tell you acouple astoryes about tow men huting buffalow they wounded one and thought they would drive it in to camp

they got up to him saying golong yhear you Big fellow
you Pating him on the rump he turned round and tramp-
ed on the fellows heal as he whealed to rune ketched his
horn in the seat of his Britches and turned him acomplete
summer set. they rode in to alarge drove one day and one
of them droped his Bridle and commenced hallowing hay,
hay, hay and his horse throwed him of and run about ten
miles before he ketched him he cane in to the camp Owot
abig Bull got ahead so wide Stretching out his hands
more wider as dat yet Owat abig Bull.

I have not Seen father nor John yet I think it is more
than likely Some of us will Be back thare nex year I
dont no But I will Come Back my self but I cant tell for
certain til I see them but I think one ove us will certainley
come back thare to tend to the business and come out with
you if you dont come next year I would like to hear from
you but cant I Sen this letter by Mr Grant give my best
respects to all of my friends I want you to write to me
next spring and tell me all about e thing I still live in
hopes of seeing you all gain my best love to Eliza Jane
and Laton [?] I would like to see you very much it makes
me shed tears to think about you So fare well to you
all

WILLIAM J. J. SCOTT

Weekly Reveille, ST. LOUIS, AUGUST 17, 1846

FROM OREGON.—We yesterday had a conversation with
Mr. B. Genois, who, with ten others, has just arrived in
our city from Oregon. The party started from Oregon
City on the 18th of last April, and arrived at St. Joseph,
Mo., on the first day of August. They passed over the
whole route without molestation from the Indian tribes,
and report having met the different emigrating companies on their route. Mr. G. says five hundred and
twenty-four wagons, destined for Oregon and California,
passed them on their way in. They met Mr. Russell's party about one hundred and fifty miles beyond Fort Lara-

mie, and received a brief note from our correspondent, "Laon," who states that the company are all well, and progressing comfortably.[135]

Medard G. Foisey, formerly a printer in the Republican office, of this city, and who was elected a member of the Oregon Legislature, had organized a company of Canadians for a trip to California, and was to start about the 1st of last May.

On perusing the treaty, which Mr. G. read for the first time in our office, he refers to that clause securing to the Hudson's Bay Company the sites they have selected in our territory, as a most injurious portion of the agreement for the interests of the people of Oregon, because this company are in possession of not only the best sites north of 49, but, by their immense capital and power, overawe and break down all American traders who may attempt to compete with them. It was the strongest hope of the emigrants from the States, that wherever the boundary line would be established, it would entirely divide them from the influence of this company.

He reports the country healthy, very productive, and the emigrants, with few exceptions, pleased with their prospects.

Missouri Republican, St. Louis, August 17, 1846

LATER FROM OREGON.

A party consisting of ten persons arrived in our city on board the *Amaranth,* on Saturday evening [August 15], direct from Oregon City. They left Oregon on the 18th of April last, and reached St. Joseph, Missouri, on the first of the present month. The entire route was performed without interruption from Indians, or the occurrence of any serious accident. They bring nothing new from the Territory in addition to what we have already published.—The crops in many parts had been cast and promised a favorable result. On the route in, the party passed five hundred and twenty-four emigrant wagons, mostly intending to go to Oregon; a portion, however, intended to cross over into California by the Salt Lake route.—Col. RUSSELL's company, including Gov. BOGGS and others, were met about one hundred and fifty miles beyond Fort Laramie. This company when they started intended to go to California; a large portion have since determined to go to Oregon, and it is probable the whole company will go there. The general health of the country was, at the time of the departure of this company, very good.

MEDARD G. FOISY, who served an apprenticeship as pressman in this office, and who has been some time in Oregon, been a member of the Oregon Legislature, &c. had organized a company of Canadians, and was to set out for California about the first of May. Mr. Foisy is a Canadian by birth, and goes to California, as we understand, to found a colony, or make a settlement on some of the branches of the Rio Sacramento river.— He is a man of a good deal of enterprise, and in the event the United States attempts to take possession of the country, he will be with them.

Weekly Reveille, St. Louis, August 24, 1846

MURDER OF CALIFORNIANS.—It is feared that Captain Leavitt and his friends, eleven in number, who started from Arkansas to California last April, have been murdered. A party of hostile Camanches have been seen in possession of their guns and other arms, and the traders of Little River, in the Seminole country, believe them to have been murdered. A friend from Little River informs the *Arkansas Intelligencer* that Mr. Leavitt was persuaded to return, as his party was entirely too small to undertake so hazardous a trip; but he refused, and declared his intention of proceeding at all hazards.

The last *Cherokee Advocate* thinks that there is room for apprehension, and publishes a letter containing information derived from a party of Creeks, lately returned from a hunting excursion, We make an extract:

A few days since I met some Kickapoos at Mr. Aird's store, on Little River, and heard from them that the upper Camanches and Kioways were very hostile to other bands of Indians, carrying on a thriving business in the way of stealing and robbing all who were so unfortunate as to meet them. They informed me that two Creeks of the To-pof-ka town, twenty miles above, on Little River, had recently come in, who brought the news, and, also, that many of the Camanches were dying of the small pox. These Creeks were surrounded, and would have been killed, they say, but for the interposition of a chief. As it was, the Kioways robbed them of all they had. From their report, too, it is more than probable that the expedition which started for California this spring, under Captain Leavitt, numbering only eleven men, have fallen into their hands. These Creeks were only a short time behind Captain Leavitt and company in going out, and followed their course—heard nothing of them, but saw some Kioways, with guns similar (double-barrelled, which are very uncommon among Indians) to those which they saw in possession of Captain Leavitt before starting. From these circumstances we have reason to fear that they have met with an untimely end. We hope for the contrary, and would not pretend to state this as truth; for if it should not be as we fear, it would be causing a great deal of unnecessary grief to the friends of those who went, which is certainly far from my wishes. On the other hand it is given—as in the case of a ship long at sea, and reported, from circumstances, to be lost—as intelligence which should be known . . . .

D. G. W. LEAVITT TO THE LITTLE ROCK
Arkansas State Gazette, SANTA FE, JUNE 20, 1846[136]

Dear Borden:

I arrived here a few days since on my way to California, and expect to leave this place to-morrow morning.

I found the route up the Canadian entirely practicable,
better I am confident than from Independence. Wherever
the road is well defined, it can be travelled with pack
mules easily, in thirty days, another advantage is, plenty
of early pasturage, as well as wood and water. Game I
found sufficiently plenty, in many places; buffaloe were
very numerous, also deer and antelope. We saw a number of parties of Comanches but had no difficulty with
them. We were annoyed some little at Cuesta and San
Miguel by the Spanish authorities, they believed us to
be Texians; but on our arrival at Santa Fe, I immediately called upon Governor Armejo, in company with
Wm. T. Smith, Esq., a prominent merchant of this place,
and formerly of Kentucky. Gov. A. treated us with much
friendship, and proffered me a passport whenever I saw
proper to leave, to take us through the frontier settlements. His Excellency is, and I believe justly , very popular with the Americans, as are in fact the most of the
officers in command at this place—among whom I must
mention with pleasure, Don Antonio Sauer, the second in
command, who called upon me immediately on my arrival.
There are many Americans at this place and vicinity engaged in business, generally a very obliging, gentlemanly
set of people, mostly from Kentucky and Missouri. Santa
Fe, I think, to be improving at this time, it has a population of about 6,000, surrounded with many fine villages.
The gold washings are worked to better advantage at this
time than at any former period. The importation of goods
brought in this year will exceed $1,000,000. The tariff of
duties is 12½ cts. on the pound, which usually amounts to
about $600 per wagon load. Judge Tully, formerly of
Arkansas, resides at San Miguel; I saw him at this place
yesterday. I shall write to you on my arrival at California.

Yours, truly,
D. G. W. Leavitt

NORRIS COLBURN TO THE *Missouri Republican,*
SANTA FE, JULY 17, 1846[137]

Santa Fe is in a state of great excitement on account of the expected approach of Gen. Kearney's troops. There is a special session of the Council tomorrow, but I think there will be no resistance to his taking possession; all business is suspended, although the town appears lively and many people are here from the country to learn the result of the proceedings of the Assembly. They have only four hundred and fifty soldiers in this place—one thousand are on the way from the lower country, and they say they can raise 15,000 in ten days—but probably not more than one fourth would be armed.

The Indians are very annoying — the Apaches stole thirty-four mules and one horse from me, and six mules and one horse from Mr. Cooper, while we were on the way from the Pueblo fort on the Arkansas. In retaking the animals, one of our men was shot in the head by the Indians, but he will recover from the wound. Mr. [James] Waters, who has just arrived from California, reports the Indians as being very bad on the road. The Pahutes would kill as high as six or eight horses of a night, notwithstanding there was a strong guard; but the Indians were in a starving condition, and his company suffered from want of water. They lived on horse meat alone for two months.

Mr. Waters says that they have had no rain in California for near three years, and their stock was dying of starvation. The American people were anxious to leave the country. He speaks very discouragingly of California, and says the company which has just left this place, from Napoleon, Arkansas, must suffer very much before they reach their destination.[138]

The Custom-House officers are the same here as they were last year. Only one lot of Goods has been seized this year — about $3,000 worth of Tobacco, which was brought in last year.

NORRIS COLBURN

Weekly Tribune, NEW YORK, SEPTEMBER 26, 1846

FROM CALIFORNIA.

— — —

LATER FROM FORT BENT—PROGRESS OF EMIGRANTS.

— — —

The St. Louis *Republican* of the 12th instant, mentions the arrival on the preceding day, of the *Little Missouri* from the Missouri River, bringing passengers Solomon Sublette, Walter Reddick, and several fellow travelers from California. Mr. Sublette had been absent three years in Oregon and California.

In company with ten others, he left Pueblo de Los Angelos about the last of May, driving some eighty mules and horses. They traveled the road usually taken to Santa Fe. His account from Lieut. Fremont is not so late as that received at Washington, but he left him on the Sacramento, and when last heard from it was understood that he expected to reach home by the first of this month.[139]

Mr. Sublette met the first company of emigrants to California, under the command of Mr. Davis, eighteen miles on the other side of Green River, on the 8th of July last; they had eighteen wagons.[140] He understood from them that they had had no difficulties with the Indians on the route. On the 10th of July, he met a Lieutenant of the United States Navy [Selim E. Woodworth], the same who passed through this place some time ago, going as an express from the United States Government to our fleet in the Pacific; he was between Little Sandy and Sweet Water, and left this city in advance of the emigrants. Gov. Boggs was met two or three days in the rear of Col. Russell, and some 300 miles from the point where they were to separate; the one party going to Oregon and the other to California.

At the dividing place there would be two guides to lead them on their way to California. Mr. [Caleb] Greenwood, who proposed to take a route north of the Great Salt Lake, and Mr. L. P. [W.] Hastings, who preferred go-

ing south of it. Mr. Sublette prefers the former route, and
advised the emigrants to take it. By the latter route they
must travel sixty miles without any water whatever, and
the distance is nearly as great as the former.

On the 16th of July, he left the last party of emigrants
at the Willow Spring. After passing them, Mr. Sublette
met a party of Sioux warriors, about ten miles in the rear
of the emigrants, and he learned that a party of six hundred warriors were not far distant. He understood that
these Indians were on an expedition against the Crow or
Snake tribes, and if a small party of the latter were met,
it is probable that they would be killed—but their real
design, it is probable, was to rob, and, if necessary, kill
the emigrants. The Pawnees had, however, been successful in despoiling the emigrants of many of their horses
and sixty head of cattle.

Subsequently, Mr. Sublette's party was attacked by
twenty-five or thirty of the Sioux, from which they escaped with difficulty. He met a man by the name of
[Wales B.] Bonney, from Ohio, who had been robbed of
his horses and provisions, but escaped with his life and
accompanied the party to Fort Laramie. Near Fort Bent
he found fifteen families of Mormons. They had selected
their grounds, had sown patches of turnips, and were cutting logs for their habitations. They seemed cheerful, and
during the time Mr. S.'s party was with them—a week—
they had preaching, two or three baptisms, and several
dances.[141]

Between Fort Laramie and Fort Bent he met fifty
lodges of Sioux Indians, who told him that they had
determined to stop all routes for the travel of Americans
except one—that they would not permit them to be
traversing the country in every direction.

Mr. Sublette's party reached Fort Bent on the 17th
of August, when all Gen. Kearney's party had left for
Santa Fe.

Lieut. [James H.] Simpson was in command of the
military at the Fort. Many provision wagons had reached

there, and two companies were met not far distant from the Fort. In his progress homeward, he met trains of wagons all along the road.

At Pawnee Fork, Mr. S. met two companies of Col. [Sterling] Price's regiment. Col. Price himself was at Cotton Wood Fork. The battalion of Mormons was met fifteen miles the other side of Council Grove. Mr. Sublette was twenty-three days in traveling from Bent's Fort to St. Louis.

Mr. Sublette represents the Governor of California as disposed to encourage the emigration of Americans, but Gen. Castro was very hostile to it. He says that the usual quantity of rain has fallen in California during the past year, contradicting in this respect, the reports of other travelers.

Weekly Reveille, St. Louis, September 14, 1846

FROM BENT'S FORT.

We yesterday [September 11] had the pleasure of a conversation with S. P. Sublette, Esq., who came down on the *Little Missouri.* Mr. S. left Bent's Fort on the 18th of last month, and, with three others, travelled to the settlements. Mr. Bent arrived at his fort the day before the former left. On his way in, Mr. S.'s party were attacked by a band of *Sioux,* who attempted to rob them of their horses. A large party, composed of the warriors of six hundred lodges of the Missouri and North Fork tribes, have started on an expedition to meet the Snake Indians, who have sent them presents of tobacco, and a desire for peace.

A detached band of twenty-five encountered Mr. S. and his men, and commenced cutting off the packs from the horses. The owners interfered, and the Indians commenced firing upon them; they, however, after a chase of five miles, succeeded in escaping without injury, and saved all their pack horses but two. The savages stole a great part of their provisions.

Mr. S. met the two parties led by Gov. Boggs and Col. Russell; the former is destined for Oregon, and the latter company, which he met three hundred miles in advance of Boggs, is pursuing its way to California.

The Governor of California, it appears, has expressed himself in favor of the American emigration, but Gen. Castro is hostile to it. Mr. S. says, rains have been frequent in the territory the past year—this report differs from former representations.

He encountered the last party of American emigrants at the Willow Springs, and says that the Sioux were but fifteen miles in their rear, directly upon their trail, and he had no doubt that they would come up with them on the day they encountered his party, and, in all probability, rob them.

The Sioux had expressed their intention to proceed to the rendezvous appointed by the Snake tribe, and, if they found them but a small party, to attack them, instead of concluding a peace. From the disposition manifested by the Indian tribes upon the plains, there is cause to fear that emigrating parties and traders will encounter much hostility and danger, the present season, in their passage to the mountains.

Before Mr. S. left Bent's Fort he learned that letters had been sent to Armijo, the Governor of New Mexico, by *Chaves* and others of the principal citizens of Santa Fe, calling upon him to defend the city and their property against the advancing forces of the Americans. He sent them back word that, if they would come in person and aid him in such an undertaking, he would fight as long as he could stand, or they desired, but unless they did so, he should not strike a blow. The miserable show of a force which was mustered in Santa Fe, he declared unable to defend the place, even against the predatory bands of savages which surrounded them.

Weekly Reveille, St. Louis, September 14, 1846

THE SANTA FE EXPEDITION—*Californians.*—A correspondent of the *Gazette,* writing from Council Grove, under date of August 22d, says, that George R. Clark, Esq., of our city, and Col. Waugh arrived at their camp on the date above mention, the first from Bent's Fort, and the latter from Santa Fe. Col. W. reports that Gen. Kearney had left on the 3d for Santa Fe, having remained at the Fort five days. The troops had lost about a hundred horses altogether, but were still in good spirits and willing to go ahead. The company of infantry reached the Fort two days before the other companies; they had not lost a single man on the way, and were in the best possible health.

The whole regiment were on half rations, and they had but a few days' provisions with them, and the wagons that were taking out supplies to them he met some eight days behind them, and reports that when he left all was quiet there. The fears of the Mexicans, which were very much excited when the news first came that our army were advancing, were beginning to subside. They had been so long in expectation of their arrival that they had almost given them out! Upon the first alarm, they collected about two hundred men. Col. Waugh describes them as perfect ragamuffins, without arms, and presenting a most ridiculous appearance.

These gentlemen were much troubled coming in, by the Indians; they had to be constantly on the alert. They had one man shot down and killed in the encampment, and they shot three Indians, who were attempting to surprise them. They report that there are more Indians on the plains than there has been for four years, and they showed every sign of hostility. They are accompanied by Mr. Ewing, from Kentucky, who went out with a party of emigrants to California this spring, in company with Col. Russell. He went as far as Fort Laramie, and then proceeded from there to Bent's Fort. He reports that the party had divided, and that Col. Russell had started across the mountains with only six men; that they all regard it as a very rash enterprise, as several tribes of Indians, through whom he had to pass, were at war with each other, and it was scarcely thought that he would reach his destination.

Our correspondent, Mr. Curry, is with Col. Russell's party, and if they have divided, he no doubt is one of the six who has followed the Colonel in his daring enterprise. George C. will see the valley of the Sacramento, if he has to go it alone.

The Gazette, St. Joseph, September 18, 1846,

REPRINTED FROM THE St. Louis *Union*

FROM THE PLAINS.—We were highly gratified last evening, with a half hour's conversation with Messrs. Robert M. Ewing, of Louisville, and Mr. E. Hewitt, both recently from the plains. The former of these two gentlemen passed through this city [St. Louis] some months since, in company with Messrs. Jacobs and Bryant, the party being in search of adventure in the far off plains of the West.

At Independence, it was their intention to attach themselves to a company of emigrants, to be commanded by Gov. Boggs. This company, however, fell under the command of Col. Wm. H. Russell, owing to a false report, that the Mormons would sacrifice it, if commanded by Gov. Boggs—and to this company the gentleman referred to above, as well as Gov. Boggs himself eventually became attached.

We shall not be able to follow our adventurers through the trials and disappointments which, for many hundred miles, encumbered their path. Suffice it, that enough of heart-burnings, as well as less avoidable evils, harrassed them, until they arrived at Ash Hollow, on the Blue. about five hundred miles from Independence.—Here, Col. Russell, for the second time, resigned his command,

and the party struck off in subdivisions. We should have stated that on leaving Indian Creek, near Independence, the number of wagons was 75, drawn by oxen.

With twelve or fifteen persons in company, Messrs. Ewing and Hewitt started on mules, from Ash Hollow; Messrs. Jacobs and Bryant, remaining with Col. Russell, who, in a day or two, also started on mules—the destination of both parties being Fort Laramie, on the south fork of the Platte. The party of Russell, Jacobs and Bryant, consisted of eight men.

At Fort Bernard, near Fort Laramie, our informants fell in with an American, who had been a trader a long time with the Navajos, in New Mexico. The name of this gentleman was Conn. He persuaded our adventurers to join him, as he was about to start for his old trading haunts.[142] They assented. On the 4th of July, they had reached Big Timber creek, near Laramie's Peak, and here they celebrated the day with "all the honors," some good old whisky, which Mr. Conn had had corked for three years, lending its aid to enliven the occasion.—From Big timber the party proceeded to Fort Peubla, and thence to a place called Hardscrabble, in New Mexico. This is a settlement, half Indian, half white, and here a fandango was among the means of relief and recreation, after a long and dangerous travel. At Hardscrabble the party learned the danger of penetrating Mexico farther, and resolved to return. They set out, and reached Bent's Fort, one hundred and ten miles distant, just as Capt. Moore had arrived from the United States.[143]

After remaining at the Fort seven days, they started, in company with some other gentlemen about to return to the United States, some wagoners, and eleven sick volunteers, in all about thirty men, with ten empty provision wagons. On reaching Salt Marsh, some distance on this side of Bent's Fort, three of the party, Messrs. Ewing, Hewitt and Fay—the latter an Italian— dashed off to cross the marsh, sixteen miles in extent, at full speed, as the prairie fires were excessively annoying to their horses. By this means, they became separated from their party, and fell in with a number of lodges of Cheyennes. These Indians are, at this time, hostile to the whites, but occasionally show prudence enough to conceal their hostility. Previous to getting through the marsh, Mr. Fay had stopped to shoot a wolf, and suddenly found himself beset by two Cheyennes. They menaced, but did not injure him, as he was well armed. On the arrival of the main company at the Cheyenne village, the utmost good feeling was assumed with regard to the visitors, and a trade was immediately struck up for moccasins and trinkets. The parties on either side manifested friendship, and thus parted.

When near Chouteau's Island, which lies in the Arkansas, Mr. Wm. L. Swan, a gentleman of the party, discovered that a horse belonging to him was missing. Taking a fine animal belonging to Mr. Geo. Clark, of this city, he mounted and went in pursuit. After returning on their trail some miles, he came up with the horse and returned with him to near where the main body was encamped. The shades of evening had closed in, and he had arrived within seventy yards of the camp, when the reports of two guns were heard. The persons in camp had no means of ascertaining the real state of affairs before morning, when Mr. Swan was found lying dead on his back, having been shot through the heart. The alarmed horse had apparently fled in the direction he had come, and there were the foot prints of four persons in pursuit. The horse eventually was taken by a wagon master, ninety miles distant, and returned to the party. Mr. Swan was buried in the plains. The persons who murdered him were believed to be Cheyennes, though they had attempted by signs to convey the impression that they were Camanches.

At Cow creek, the party were again attacked by a large party. The intention of the assailants seemed to be the driving off of stock. In this attempt, one lost his life from the rifle of Mr. Ewing, and it was thought two others were killed. In this affair, three very fine mules belonging to a gentleman of the company, were stolen.

For the rest of the route the party met with little molestation, and arrived at Independence in safety.

Daily Union, St. Louis, September 21, 1846

NEWS FROM CAPT. FREMONT AND BENT'S FORT. — We have received a communication, by which we learn Mr. Toplin [Charles Taplin] arrived at Independence, Sept. 11th, direct from the Sacremento river, where he left Capt. Fremont on the 3d of April last.[144] Capt. Fremont had received no news of the war, but was intending to remain where he was until he received further orders from the United States, which were daily expected. Our readers will remember he was ordered out of the country, but did not intend to comply until he was ready.

Mr. Toplin was at Bent's Fort, on the 18th August. Gen. Kearney and all of his troops had been gone some days. He met a portion of Col. Price's regiment at Pawnee Fork, and Col. Price himself at Pearl Spring, with the remainder of his command. They were all in good health and getting on well. The Mormon battalion was at Council Grove on the 20th August.

Missouri Republican, St. Louis, September 21, 1846

FROM FORT JOHN.—Mr. Coburn, who left in company with Capt. Burnham, for Oregon, during the Summer, returned to this city yesterday, on the steamer *Clermont No. 2,* having left the company at Fort Pierre [John]. Thence he proceeded to Fort John [Pierre], from which place he reached the Missouri a few days ago. He represents the Pawnee Indians as being spread over the plains in small parties, for the purpose of plundering the emigrants and traders. At Fort John, some of the oldest traders had been plundered by them. One of them, in returning from an excursion, was attacked and plundered of about ten packs of furs and all his mules, and the man who had charge of the latter was shot. There was no other news.

Mr. Coburn saw two parties from Oregon, near the Kansas, on their return.

Weekly American, St. Louis, October 9, 1846

ANOTHER ARRIVAL FROM OREGON.—The Independence *Expositor,* of Oct. 3rd. says:

Mr. W. B. Bonney, of Oxford, Ohio, arrived in our town on Wednesday last, from Oregon. He left Oregon on the 13th of May, and represents the people there as being prosperous and generally well satisfied with their new homes. The election was to take place last June, for members of the Legislature of Oregon and considerable interest was felt as to the result. The great question at issue, being, as to whether the sale of ardent spirits should be permitted in the territory or not. Quite *a new question for a new country.*

Mr. Bonney brought in one hundred and twenty five letters for persons in various parts of the union, principally, from the Oregon and California emigrants, who started the present year. He says the emigrants he met were generally healthy and in good spirits, and their teams looking well. He met five hundred wagons on his route in. Some going to Oregon and some to California: The emigrants to the points above named separated at Independence Rock on the 15th of July last. Governor Boggs went to Oregon in consequence of the Mormon emigration to California. Mr. Bonney was robbed on his way in by the Indians, of his horses, provisions and clothing, and travelled seventy-five miles on foot and alone, when he was overtaken by Mr. Sublette & Co., and taken to Fort Laramie. Mr. Bonney is now on his way to Ohio, where he resides.[145]

"Sutter's Fort, 1846"

The New Land: Oregon and California

Oregon Spectator, Oregon City, September 3, 1846

ARRIVAL OF OREGON EMIGRANTS
NEWS FROM THE U. STATES.
PASSAGE OF THE NOTICE BILL.

Some of the Oregon emigrants of 1846, arrived at Oregon City on the 25th of August—also a naval officer, (Lieut. Woodworth, who is connected with the U. S. Navy,) crossed over the Rocky Mountains in company with three other gentlemen destined to Oregon, having letters for the squadron, which were left on the U. S. Sch'r *Shark,* lying in the Columbia river. Lieut. Woodworth brought us files of papers from various parts of the United States of dates up to the 23d of April, and says he brought papers of dates up to the 1st of May, as far as Fort Hall, but by accident they were unfortunately left at Fort Hall. He declares that one newspaper left by accident at Fort Hall, contained the news of the final passage of the bill through the Senate, *giving Great Britain the required year's notice of the termination of the joint occupancy of Oregon.* We notice in the files of papers received through the kindness of Lieut. Woodworth, that the bill requesting notice to be given to Great Britain, passed through the House of Representatives by a vote of *three* to *one.* When the news of the passage of the notice bill through the House reached England, great consternation and excitement prevailed throughout the whole kingdom. The prices of foreign exchanges immediately fell in the market from 1 to 1½ per cent., and the war feeling arose and spread quickly in the various departments of commercial enterprise. The opinion universally expressed by the British press appears to have been, that if the Senate of the United States should also pass the notice bill, no alternative would be left to England, but a successful negotiation in relation to a satisfactory settlement of the boundary line, or, if no successful negotiation could be entered into satisfactory to both parties, war must be the unavoidable consequence. Intelligence with regard to the settlement of the northern boundary line, either by successful negotiation, or by a direct expression of Congress in defining on what parallel our northern line shall run, has not yet reached us; but our doubts are now sufficiently expelled to convince us that the 49th degree of parallel will be the definite line ultimately agreed upon both by Great Britain and the United States . . . .

Oregon Spectator, OREGON CITY, SEPTEMBER 3, 1846

ARRIVAL OF EMIGRANTS.

Some fifteen or sixteen emigrants have arrived, having performed the last part of their journey with pack-horses. They state that between 300 and 400 waggons must be near the Dalls at this time, and nothing extraordinary preventing, they will probably arrive at Oregon City about the 25th instant. Mr. Barlow has gone to meet them in order to conduct them safely over his road. They state that between 500 and 600 waggons that were bound to Oregon and California, were counted after leaving the states. They think that between 50 and 100 waggons followed Mr. Hastings to California. Gov. Boggs, (formerly Governor of Missouri) and family, are in the company coming to Oregon. It is reported that one family in this company is bringing a hive and swarm of bees to Oregon.

These emigrants state that between 500 and 600 waggons accompanied with *Mormons* crossed over the river at St. Joseph, bound for Oregon. But it is presumed that they will not arrive here this season.

Oregon Spectator, OREGON CITY, SEPTEMBER 17, 1846

EMIGRANTS. — Several families with their wagons have arrived in our City, and appear healthy and cheerful. They traveled over Mr. Barlow's road, over which probably most of the emigration will come. There appears to be a general willingness on the part of the emigration to pay the required toll, only one individual, among a large company which has traveled over it, having refused to pay. Mr. Barlow is entitled to much credit and gratitude, both from the present emigration and succeeding ones, for the perseverance he has manifested in surveying out and making this road. Although we are informed that it can and ought to be greatly improved.

These emigrants report that the wagons will probably all arrive in town in the course of three weeks.

Oregon Spectator, OREGON CITY, OCTOBER 1, 1846

☞ The public mind has been happily put at rest, in relation to the welfare of Captain Jesse Applegate and party, by the arrival of intelligence, at Fort Vancouver, recently, to the effect, that he had succeeded in discovering a most admirable road for the emigration—one much more direct, and in every respect more preferable than the old one. We trust to be able to speak more at large in relation to this important circumstance hereafter. Captain Applegate struck the old trail in the vicinity of Fort Hall in time to turn the bulk of the emigration which are now coming on under his guidance; indeed it is altogether probable that the advance wagons have already entered the head of the Valley.

This achievement is a great piece of public enterprise on the part of Captain Applegate, and we hope that he will be rewarded accordingly.

Since writing the above, Mr. J. M. Ware, from the States, has arrived and informed us that he came in company with Captain Applegate—that the wagons, numbering some two hundred and fifty, will probably arrive in about two weeks.[146] We regret to state that Mr. Wm. [Edward] Tremble, from Iowa, was killed by the Pawnee Indians, in passing through their country.

Oregon Spectator, OREGON CITY, OCTOBER 15, 1846

☞ The emigrants still continue to arrive, almost daily, generally in good health and spirits, with their wagons and teams in very fair condition. By our next issue we shall be able to form something like a correct estimate of the size of the emigration, of which we have now no reliable information.

Californian, MONTEREY, OCTOBER 10, 1846

EMIGRATION.—We have received a letter from the Sacramento which states that emigrants from the U. States are constantly arriving. Their numbers may be guessed from the fact that they have with them one hundred and seventy five wagons. They preferred coming to California, than going to Oregon, notwithstanding the utmost efforts were made to turn them off in that direction. California is now the cry, and ten will come next year, where one came this; a high destiny awaits this country.

Californian, MONTEREY, OCTOBER 17, 1846

We have received a very interesting letter from a friend of ours, who has just arrived from beyond the mountains. It is too long for publication entire, but we give some extract which embodies most of the news. He is a gentleman we [Robert Semple] have long known personally, and we hail his arrival in California with joy, his talents and great energy of character will do much for our adopted country:

"It may not be uninteresting to you to know that the emigration by land, the present season, far exceeds the expectation of the most sanguine. Not less than two thousand human souls are now in the interior, and within two hundred miles of the settlement, winding their way over the rugged mountain's top to '*El Dorado*' of the *western world*. Many have already arrived at Mr. Johnson's farm, and are now preparing to examine the country for themselves, with a view of selecting permanent locations. This emigration introduces into the country a large proportion of talents, wealth and industry, all of which, as you are well aware, are indispensable requisites in this our infantile state. Governor Boggs was undecided as to his destination for a time, but has finally given California the preference, and is now near the settlement. The Governor comes with a determination to make California his future home; he is accompanied by his family, and a large and very respectable connexion. T. J. Farnham, Esq., is also on his way to this country, he is of the company which is said to have left Arkansas, in the month of April last, and which is said to have consisted of one thousand armed men.[147] The presumption is, however, that the number of armed men of this company is somewhat exag[g]erated, yet it is certain that a large company did set out from Arkansas, at the time above stated.

Various reports are in circulation in reference to the Mormon emigrants now on their way to this country; the number of wagons is variously estimated at 500, 600, 700, and 1,000 now en route for Oregon and California. As many of them are now located temporarily; on the Missouri river, and many are on their way to Oregon, while others are coming to this country, their final destination is still among the hidden mysteries of the future; but that many, if not a majority of them, will locate permanently in "California, there is very little doubt. A Mormon company of 40 wagons is said to be immediately in the rear of the emigration which is now arriving, and many others are said to be at the Salt Lake, where, it is thought, they will remain during the winter; but those things are unknown to all except the Mormons themselves." [148]

Californian, MONTEREY, NOVEMBER 7, 1846

EMIGRATION.—Emigrants from the United States are daily flocking into California, their land mark, after crossing the rocky mountains, is the Sacramento valley, amongst them are mechanics and labourers of all descriptions, and altho' they invariably strike for the Sacramento valley, still not one half of them will settle there, they will, as soon as they get acquainted with the country, and the winter season is over, spread all over California, and as many of these are people, who understand agriculture in all its branches, they will undoubtedly spy out thousands of acres of land, which are now considered as useless, except for grazing, and will in a short time prove to the old inhabitants that there is more land fit for cultivation in California, than ever has been imagined, by the natives; and many vegetable substances will be planted, and brought to maturity, which heretofore have never had a fair trial.

We have already had sufficient proof in various instances that the grape vine flourishes, in California, to the northward of San Luis Obispo, if not in an equal degree to that of the Angeles, at most, very little inferior, and there can be little doubt, that the industry, and intelligence of the agriculturists, which are daily emigrating to this country, will improve the nature of the soil to such a degree, as to greatly augment both the produce, and improve the flavour of this most delicious fruit, and the same may be said of all the other production of this country.

Oregon Spectator, OREGON CITY, OCTOBER 29, 1846

THE EMIGRATION.—Those of the emigrants who came by the way of the Mount Hood road, have all safely reached the valley of the Willamette, and a large portion of them are already on their claims, busily engaged in promoting their comfort and welfare. Mr. J. W. Ladd's wagon was at the head of the line, and arrived in this city on the 13th of last month, at least two months in advance of any previous emigration.[149] We have been favored by Mr. Barlow, with the subjoined statement of the number of wagons, &c., that have crossed the Cascade Mountains, by the Mount Hood road, during the present season. Five wagons only were abandoned between the Dalles and this point. The weather has been extremely favorable for the emigration, and still continues remarkably mild and pleasant for this late period of the year.[150]

In regard to the remainder of the emigration, who are coming on by Messrs. Applegate and Goff's recently explored route, we can obtain no satisfactory information, further than they are as yet a considerable distance from the head of the valley. We have understood that several families have abandoned their wagons, and come in with pack animals; likewise, that two or three parties have started out, with provisions, &c., to meet the emigration. We have a rumor that one hundred and forty wagons, of the two hundred and fifty reported to have been on this route, have turned off and gone to California; this requires confirmation, however.

Mr. Editor.—Sir, by your request, I herewith send you the number of wagons and stock that passed the toll-gate on the Mount Hood road. There were one hundred and forty-five wagons, fifteen hundred and fifty-nine head of horses, mules, and horned cattle all together, and one lot of sheep, the number not recollected, but I think thirteen. Yours, &c.

Oct. 22d, 1846. SAML. K. BARLOW.

Since the above was put into type, we learn, by the arrival of a party of the Hudson's Bay Company's servants, from Fort Hall, that there are seven more wagons *en route* for this place, in the Cascade Mountains, being the rearward company of the emigration by the Mount Hood road.[151]

Oregon Spectator, OREGON CITY, NOVEMBER 26, 1846

THE EMIGRANTS. — Our latest intelligence concerning the emigrants who are on the southern route, comes to us from some gentlemen who have recently arrived in this place, after having "packed" into the settlements. At the time of their departure from the wagons (about twenty days since,) which number altogether, as we are informed, only eighty, some few of the first were this side of the Callapoiah mountains; the most of them, however, were still engaged in crossing the Umpqua mountains. They had experienced considerable suffering, from exposure and hard labor, and bravely surmounted numerous difficulties. We regret to state that Mr. William [*i.e.,* James] Smith died instantaneously — probably occasioned by overexertion—in the kanyon of the Umpqua mountains. It is also our painful duty to record the death of David Tanner, of Iowa, and ———— Sallie, of Callaway county, Missouri, who died from wounds received in a skirmish with the Klamet Indians. In the same affair, Mr. [Benjamin S.] Lippencott of New York city, a California emigrant, was seriously wounded in the knee. We [George L. Curry] were acquainted with the parties; Mr. Sallie, had left home in a rapidly declining state of health, which was rapidly improved by the trip. He looked forward sanguinely to the enjoyment of a new life, as it were, in California, which an inscrutable Providence has prevented. Himself and two of his fellow emigrants have experienced the common lot,—"In the midst of life, we are in death." [152]

MOSES HARRIS TO THE *Oregon Spectator* OF NOVEMBER 26, 1846[153]

Mr. Editor:—As the people of the United States as well as those of Oregon, are deeply interested in the success of the company who have lately returned from exploring a southern route from the United States to this valley, it is the intention of that party in due season to give to their fellow citizens, whose philanthropy has prompted them to contribute to the success of this arduous undertaking, a full report of their travels and discoveries; and until such report is ready to be made public, it is certainly doing an injustice to those who have been engaged in this important service, to attempt to forestall public opinion, by the publication of such statements as are made in an editorial article headed "The Emigration," which appeared in the 20th number of the *Spectator* [issue of October 29].

Notwithstanding the "early and safe arrival of *all* the emigration by the Mount Hood road," it appears that some are as yet in the mountains, and many more beyond, who cannot either *safely* or *unsafely,* arrive by the Mount Hood this season, and those who have succeeded in passing the mountains have suffered losses in proportion to their numbers, full as great, as any previous emigration; some of those last getting through, having lost half, and others the whole, of their animals.

Facts, so far from proving favorable to the old road, go to show the decided advantage of the new. The emigrants on the new route, though greatly delayed by sickness, and the opening and breaking the way over timbered mountains and trackless plains, have arrived in the valley

west of the Cascade mountains more than *five weeks ago,*
and "the families who have abandoned their wagons"
amount to *one only.* This they have done by traveling a
distance not exceeding that from Fort Hall to Wallawalla, and without meeting the tenth part of the natural
obstacles encountered on the old route. From the Rogue
river valley to Oregon City, in less than ten years, there
will be continuous settlements, there being but two narrow ridges of coast mountain between; the one sixteen,
the other eight miles over.

Were you, Mr. Editor, to take the trouble to examine
the files of your paper, you would find that others, as
well as Goff and Applegate, have spent their time and
money on the public service, and are equally deserving
the praise or censure of the public. And as the hope of
pecuniary reward had no share in inducing them to undertake an expedition which was justly considered one of
great danger, labor and privation, they have with equal
magnanimity brought it to a successful issue. From the
emigrants who are traveling the new road, they have neither asked nor received any thing except by purchase;
and to those who have assisted them in opening the road,
they have bound themselves as individuals to the payment
of one dollar and fifty cents per day.

Let me tell you, Mr. Editor, the company to which I
am proud to belong, did not leave their homes to ride a
few days up the Willamette river and return with a false
report to the people: they were seriously determined to
find a road, if one was to be found; they went actuated
by the purest motives, and in the spirit of patriotism and
philanthropy, and were more than successful.

They have explored and opened a wagon road to the
western valley of Oregon which may be traveled at any
and at all seasons, by a shorter and in all respects better
route than any heretofore known.

They have made it easy for wagons to pass between
Oregon and California, which has hitherto been impracticable.

They have found a way by which the southern rivers of Oregon may be connected by rail road to the bay of San Francisco without crossing a single hill.[154]

On the road they have found a mail may be carried at all seasons, and a rail road may reach the Bay of San Francisco from the U. S. without crossing the Siera Neveda, or, to the Willamette, without crossing the Cascade Mountains.

And lastly, by their own unassisted means, they have succeeded in establishing a connecting link between the waters of Oregon, and those of the great interior basin of California, before unknown, and which one of the ablest explorers in the service of the United States [Fremont] attempted, without success.

Such, Mr. Editor, are the achievements of the exploring party, which envy and cupidity would render nugatory!!!

As I have stated nothing that I am unable to establish, I have nothing to conceal from the public.

MOSES HARRIS.

— — —

"GREAT CRY AND LITTLE WOOL." — In another column will be found an article over the signature of "Moses Harris," in which we are charged with an "attempt to forestall public opinion," inasmuch, as in the discharge of our editorial duties, we had occasion to prepare and publish an article in which we simply gave, in a statement of facts, all the intelligence that we could obtain concerning the emigration, without any reference, in word, or even in thought, as to the comparative merits of the routes by which emigrants have arrived here this season. We do not know, however, that we would have hesitated in giving the information in question, had it actually been necessary to have gone into an argument as to the merits of these routes. We are not easily deterred in the performance of any thing that we esteem to be a duty. As to the charge of forestalling public opinion, we refer our readers with a great deal of pleasure, to the article complained of, and feel well assured that every unprejudiced mind cannot fail to perceive how unfounded is the charge.

We have a "bone to pick" with Mr. Harris: for, by the article over his signature, he makes it our unpleasant duty, not only to deny some of his asseverated *facts,* but to prove that which is quite the reverse. It is hardly worth while to state, in passing, that in no single instance has Mr. Harris quoted our language correctly; almost any sentence can be so perverted as to mean what was not intended. There is no occasion to quibble or use sophistry in this matter. If the emigrants by the southern route "arrived in *the* valley west of the Cascade mountains more than five weeks ago," what then? They might suffer and starve on this side just as easily as on the other; — the settlements, Mr. Harris, the settlements, what time *did* they arrive at the settlements, their destination? or, have they yet arrived? What's the use of saying "the families who have abandoned their wagons amount to one only"? Did not Mr. James Campbell abandon two, [Andrew?] Davidson, one, [Meadows] Vanderpool, one, [John?] Long, one, [Lazarus] Van Bebber, one, and Watkins, one? [155]

They did, and we have evidence to establish the same. It is not wise to live in glass houses and throw stones.

We are not aware that there are any emigrants by the Mount Hood road, who are yet in the mountains and unable to get through this season, as intimated by Mr. Harris; on the contrary, we know that there are none. The rearward company, consisting of seven wagons, arrived here during the first week in the present month. [156]

We have not the space, if we had the inclination, at this time to argue as to the advantages or disadvantages of either route; the pleasure, therefore, of surprising Mr. Harris and his friends with an exposition of our views thereupon, is unavoidably deferred to some future occasion. Far be it from us to speak disparagingly of any scientific undertaking—much less of one that promised such important beneficial consequences to Oregon. Nor would we withhold from any member of that exploring party, a single iota of his deserts. We mentioned Messrs. Goff and Applegate, because theirs were the only names that we knew of the party; nor do we now know the number or names of the gentlemen who composed the expedition.

A word more and we have done. We do not love to be found fault with without the shadow of a cause, nor will we permit ourself to be charged falsely and unjustly, especially by those whose fears would seem to be the only source of their imputations.

As the editor of this paper, we write and publish that which we believe to be the truth, with the promotion of the general interest always in view; and it is hoped that we shall continue to have nerve enough to pursue this course regardless of consequences.

[GEORGE L. CURRY] [157]

GOVERNOR GEORGE ABERNETHY, MESSAGE TO THE
LEGISLATIVE ASSEMBLY OF OREGON, OREGON CITY,
DECEMBER, 1846. [158]

. . . Another emigration has crossed the Rocky Mountains, and most of the party has arrived in the settlements. About one hundred and fifty-two waggons reached this place very early in the season, via. Mr. Barlow's road, for which a charter was granted him at your last session. About one hundred waggons are on their way, if they have not already arrived in the upper settlements, by a southern route, they have no doubt been detained by travelling a new route, the difficulties attending the opening a waggon road are very great, and probably will account in some measure, for their detention. The emigration falls far short of last years, probably not numbering over one thousand souls. This is accounted for by a great part of the emigration turning off to California, we trust that those who have come in among us, may have no cause to regret the decision that brought them to Oregon . . .

Oregon Spectator, OREGON CITY, DECEMBER 10, 1846

THE EMIGRANTS—SOUTHERN ROUTE.—We have no further information to give concerning the emigrants on the
Southern route, excepting that which is contained in the
following letter, received a few days since:

> Settlement of the Rickreall,
> November 30, 1846.

Editor of the *Spectator*: — I have just arrived in the
settlements of this valley from the Kenyon in the Umpqua mountains. I left the people suffering beyond any
thing you have ever known. They must perish with hunger unless the people of the settlements go to their relief
with pack horses and provisions, and bring them in. They
will have property with which to pay for such services.
If they are not brought away they must perish. Before
I left, they had already commenced eating the cattle that
had died in the Kanyon. At least one hundred head of
pack horses should be taken out immediately. I implore
the people of this valley, in the name of humanity, and
in behalf of my starving and perishing fellow travellers
to hasten to their relief.

In haste, I am sir, yours &c.

J. QUINN THORNTON.[159]

We have understood that a considerable band of horses
have been sent out from Champoeg county, sufficient,
probably to bring in all or most of the emigrants.

Oregon Spectator, OREGON CITY, FEBRUARY 4, 1847

THE IMMIGRANTS. — We are glad to state that all the
immigrants have at length arrived safely in the settlements, excepting four families, who have concluded to
remain with their property until Spring, in the Umpqua
valley, on the northern side of the Umpqua river. We
are informed by some of the immigrants who have reached
here, that accounts of their condition have been exag-

gerated; and they ascribe much of their detention to their own mismanagement and delay. Of ninety wagons, which were all that were upon the southern route, fifty are this side of the Umpqua mountains, including twelve that had reached the first settlement at the head of the valley.

J. Quinn Thornton to the *Oregon Spectator,* February 13, 1847 [160]

Mr. Editor—

I have read an editorial article in the *Spectator* of the 4th instant, in which I could not fail to observe that you had been so far led astray by the rash, not to say willful misrepresentations of thoughtless or designing and interested persons, as to make no less than seven incorrect statements in the first eleven lines of an article of thirteen. I am thus particular for the purpose of showing how many inaccuracies may be crowded into so small a compass. The article in question, when analyzed, will be found to contain nine averments, viz:

1st. That *"all the immigrants" "excepting four families,"* have arrived in the settlements. This is incorrect. Mr. Duskins was, it is believed, among the last persons who returned with direct intelligence from the families "in the Umpqua valley." When he left, there were five or six families—one consisting of Messrs. Geddes and [Chauncey] Nye, the Rev. J. A. Cornwall's, Mr. Kennedy's, Mr. [Henry] Croizen's, and Mr. [Reason] Hall's. There was also the family of one whose name is not now remembered—believed, however, to be [Samuel?] Davis or Wood; making in all about thirty souls.[161]

2d. That the *"four families"* excepted, had *"concluded to remain with their property until Spring, in the Umpqua valley."* This also is incorrect. They had not *"concluded"* to remain. They remained because the hard hand of necessity was upon them. As well might it be said of the unhappy man who is being led to execution, that he has *"concluded"* to be hung.

3d. *That those who have arrived in the settlements, have* "ARRIVED SAFELY." This also is incorrect, if any thing is meant by the expression, *"arrived safely"* beyond the simple announcement of the fact, that many of the immigrants, after traversing a country dangerous in consequence of the hostility of the savages, have at length arrived in a very enfeebled condition to which they had been reduced by hunger, cold and nakedness. In addition to this, it may be affirmed, that almost every man, (perhaps indeed, every one) who came into Oregon by the southern route, is, in a pecuniary point of view, ruined by doing so. Do men arrive *"safely"* who lose their wagons, teams, tents and clothing; and who freeze their feet, and come in looking like famished wolves?

4th. That *accounts of the condition of the immigrants "have been exaggerated."* To exaggerate this account, it is feared, would be a difficult task. It is probably one which could be accomplished by those only who are the sources of your information. It is a fact well known among the immigrants, that as early as the 11th of November last, an ox that had become too lean and too much exhausted to be able to go any further, and which had finally died in the kanyon of the Umpqua mountains, (supposed, I believe, for sometime, to have belonged to Rice Dunbar) was found with its hind quarters skinned and carried away. By whom, and for what purpose was this done, if it was not done by some unhappy father who saw his children famishing for want of food? It was to this circumstance I referred in my communication of Nov. 30th, in which I observed that the immigrants previous to my leaving the disastrous kanyon, had commenced eating the cattle that had died in it. I did not, indeed, see the ox skinned or eaten, as before mentioned, but the fact was not questioned while I remained at the kanyon, nor was it ever denied until improper and unworthy motives suggested the idea of keeping the people of the valley in ignorance of the extent of the sufferings of the immigrants. I did not, in stating the fact in my

appeal to the people, in behalf of the sufferers whom I
had left behind me, intend to censure any one of the gentlemen who had been instrumental in placing a multitude
of men, women and children in such a situation, I would
have eaten my bread in bitterness until I had rescued
them, instead of attempting to amuse the public mind
either by speculations with regard to the practicability
of some other route, or by wickedly attempting to produce the impression that *accounts of the condition of the
immigrants* "HAVE BEEN EXAGGERATED." I
say *wickedly,* because I believe that, had not some persons, influenced by improper motives, succeeded to some
extent, in producing this impression, all the immigrants
would by this time have been in the valley. As circumstances now are, there is much reason to fear that the
coming Spring will reveal a tale of the sufferings of those
in the Umpqua valley, that will make sick the heart of
every man who has one.

The sufferings then, of the immigrants have *not "been
exaggerated."* Indeed, I doubt whether the half has been
told. By the very last intelligence we have of those *"who
have concluded to remain,"* we learn that an estimable
old man and his wife and grandchild, had subsisted three
days upon three mice.

5th.   That *much of the detention of the immigrants
is to be ascribed to "their own mismanagement."* How
did it come to pass, that all the good managers traveled
the old road, many of them arriving in Oregon City as
early as Sept. 13th, with their property; while all the mis-
managers took the route indicated by Messrs. Applegate
and Goff, losing all their property and arriving in the
settlements in December, looking more like the shadows
of ghosts than the substantial forms of living men? Mr.
Applegate met the company in which I traveled, August
8th, a few miles on this side of Fort Hall. Although
among the first of my company to get in, I did not arrive until Nov. 29th; while others who had entered upon
the old road only about forty eight hours before Mr. Ap-

plegate arrived at the point where the old road to Oregon turns off to the right from the California road, arrived Sept. 13th—two and a half months earlier.[162]

6th. That *much of the detention of the immigrants is to be ascribed to their* WILLFUL *delay*—for in no other sense can the word *"delay"* be understood when read in the connection in which it appears. If those to whom you refer as being the source from which you derive your information, and whom you describe as being "some of the immigrants who have reached here," mean to speak of themselves only, nothing can be objected to their making themselves as clear as they desire. But if they intend to be understood as speaking of other emigrants than themselves, then a regard to truth and justice constrains me to pronounce their statement to be untrue in all its length, and depth, and breadth.

7th. That the averments made under the last three heads, rest upon the authority of *"some of the immigrants who have reached here."* I am not careful to know what motive prompted *"some of the immigrants who have reached here,"* thus to slander their fellow travelers. I hope, however, that it does not spring from that base and mean spirit which characterizes a class of individuals known by the expressive, though not very elegant epithet of *"bootlicks."*

8th. That ninety wagons were *"all that were upon the southern route."* While I can affirm that ninety wagons were *not "all that were upon the southern route,"* I will not take upon myself to say certainly what was the precise number. Relying upon memory, an attempt will, however, be made to approximate to it. Seventy-five wagons had been turned into the new road previous to the company, in which I traveled, coming up. In this company, if I am not mistaken, there was eighteen wagons. Mr. [William] Lard and his son-in-law had two wagons. James Savage had one. I have been informed that the company of Messrs. [Elam] Brown and [David] Allen contained eighteen wagons.[163] This would make one hun-

dred and fourteen. I may have made some mistake as to
precise numbers, but I do not doubt that many wagons
have entirely escaped my memory.

9th. That of the ninety wagons affirmed to be all that
were upon the southern route, *"fifty are on this side of
the Umpqua mountains, including twelve that had reached
the first settlement at the head of the"* Willamette valley.
But where are the forty wagons making the difference
between fifty and ninety? It is answered that they lie in
scattered fragments upon the sides of the hills, upon the
tops of the mountains, and along the rocky glens and the
almost impassable kanyons which mark that disastrous
"cut-off," leading us, as I am of opinion it did, as far
south as lat. 40 north latitude. And where, too, are the
twenty-four wagons which make the difference between
one hundred and fourteen? It is answered that Gov.
Boggs, having two wagons, William Boggs, one wagon,
Mr. Lard and his son-in-law, two wagons, and James
Savage, one wagon, disappointed as to the distance down
Mary's river, the quality of the water, and the quantity
of grass along that stream, become alarmed, and believing that it would be periling the lives of their families to
leave the California road and take that indicated by
Messrs. Applegate and Goff, determined to go directly
into the Mexican settlement.[164] This determination was
precipitated by its being believed that the point at which
the road turns off to lead to Oregon by the way of the
Black Rock, was only about sixty miles from the sinks
of Mary's river.

Of the eighteen wagons, of which it is believed the company of Messrs. Brown and Allen, consisted, nothing
definite has been heard. But it is feared that all have been
cut off by the savages.

I do not desire, nor do I deem it necessary at this time,
(if indeed at all) to examine into the merits of the southern route as compared with the one in the north. This is
entirely beside the purpose in view—that of repelling a
gratuitous slander resting upon the authority of "some of

the immigrants who have reached here."

I am sir, respectfully yours, &c.

J. QUINN THORNTON.

Oregon Spectator, OREGON CITY, MARCH 4, 1847

☞ The following letter has been received in this city and handed us for publication. The information which it contains may be considered reliable and we therefore hasten to publish it.

Umpqua Valley, Dec. 27th, 1846.

Dear Sir—

At the suggestion of a Mr. [Thomas] Holt, who says he is personally acquainted with you, I am induced to write to you, and through you to arouse the sympathies of the good people of Oregon, in behalf of a small company of emigrants who are unable to cross the Callapoia mountains before sometime next season — myself and a large family among them. We are not, it is true, in a state of actual starvation, as yet, but of great want, and we do not know what the consequence will be, unless we receive some aid from the settlement, as soon as practicable.

We are in number about 25 or 30 souls, who are the last of the unfortunate ones who took the route to Oregon recommended by Mr. Applegate, and have lost nearly all our property, and almost every means of subsistance. And indeed, about the one half of the company was just at the point of starvation, when Mr. Holt, (whose liberality we shall not easily forget) helped us to three tolerably good beeves. We have scarcely any flour or salt in the camp; and nothing in prospect but a little poor beef, and occasionally a poor venison—which is quite uncertain, for deer are very scarce, as well as very wild.

We have made an effort to go to the Fort near the mouth of the Umpqua, to try to procure some provisions, if possible; but it proved ineffectual, as the waters were very high, and none of us know the way. We shall try

again, but from information, it is very uncertain whether
we shall be able to procure any assistance from that quarter or not.

Some say it will be May or June next, before the road
will be dry enough for us to reach the settlements, and
that we shall be detained here at least some three or four
months. And in conclusion, we are sorry to say, that we
have been credibly informed, that some of our fellow emigrants, who were more fortunate than ourselves, and had
crossed the mountain, actually misrepresented our condition, to prevent bringing us supplies and pack-horses, by
stating that we had plenty, and might have reached the
settlements long ago, had it not been for our indolence,
in order to receive fresh aid themselves, though so near
the settlement.

Now, in conclusion, we wish you to use your influence
in our behalf, and try to induce some hardy young men
to bring us some provisions, such as beef, flour and salt,
as soon as the weather will permit. In doing which, you
will confer a lasting favor, which we will, as soon as possible, endeavor to remunerate.

Yours, respectfully,

J. A. CORNWALL [165]

☞ In another column will be found a letter from
the Rev. Mr. Cornwall in reference to the immigrants
upon the southern route. Since it was put in type, we are
happy to state, that the person in charge at Fort Umpqua, by his recent arrival, brings us the information that
the several families had succeeded in reaching that post.

Oregon Spectator, OREGON CITY, MARCH 18, 1847

☞ A subscription has been opened at this office for
the relief of Thomas Holt and others, who went to the
succor of the emigrants by the southern route, and thereby incurred indebtedness which they cannot sustain. Call
and subscribe.

☞ We are happy to state, that Messrs. Brown's and Allen's companies of immigrants, for whose safety fears were entertained, have arrived safely in California.

☞ We see by the news from California, that our old and esteemed friend, Col. William Henry Russell has received the appointment of Secretary of State, for California. He has our hearty wishes for his welfare and success.

— — —

LATEST FROM CALIFORNIA.—By the arrival of the H. B. Company's Schr. *Cadborough,* from California, a letter has been received by a friend in this city, dated Yerba Buena, Feb. 6th, 1847. The writer is one of the recent immigration to that country. We have been kindly permitted to make the subjoined extracts. After speaking favorably of the country, and remarking upon the numerous improvements then in progress, the writer adds—

"Nearly the whole of the immigration have been off with Col. Fremont, who has command of all the land forces. But I am happy to state, that to-day we have some news of a very important nature.

The *Independence,* 74 guns, has arrived at Monterey, with a transport ship with troops: several vessels with stores and troops from the States are expected every day. By the news just received, every thing is quiet below, and I hope the news will prove to be true.

I am sorry to hear of the situation of some of the immigrants who came your new route. I see in the paper, that your wagon was among those which were left.[166] Mr. Reed's company is yet in the mountains, covered in snow. We held a meeting to-night, and gathered some six hundred dollars. Some persons here will start after them straightway. Messrs. Doland and Brinn [Patrick Dolan and Patrick Breen] are among them.

Gov. Boggs is residing on the opposite side of the Bay from us [at Sonoma]. His son William has gone below to the war. Every thing is very high here—produce is extremely so. If you come, you would do well to bring provisions of any kind. Flour is worth $15 00 per barrel, and will continue so. Write me as soon as possible. There will be vessels coming now regularly."

DAVID GOFF TO THE *Oregon Spectator,* RICKREAL VALLEY, POLK COUNTY, OREGON, APRIL 3, 1847 [167]

Mr. Editor—

In the 3d No. of 2d vol. of the *Spectator,* I have seen an article over the signature of *"J. Quinn Thornton,"* which, under the guise of contradicting an editorial article of a former number of the *Spectator,* is in reality a most bitter and false attack upon myself and my associates who were employed last season in exploring the southern route to Oregon.

Supposing you held yourself responsible for such matter as appeared under the editorial head of your paper, I expected you would have given to Mr. Thornton at least a passing notice. Though a full knowledge of the character and standing of Mr. T. would justify you, with the most fastidious on the subject of honor, in treating him and his tirade with the contempt they merit, yet I think as the article appears in a paper under your conduct, and the author is in the same sheet announced Supreme Judge of Oregon, at a distance where the author is not known, your silence may be construed.

Supposing you suffered Mr. T's charges to pass in silence, because, as the Editor of the only newspaper in Oregon, you did not wish to be drawn into a personal dispute, I have ventured to point out some of the inaccuracies of this great advocate of "truth, and justice," and to give the public a small peep under the ermine.

However incorrect the article this literary chimist submits to the torturing process of decomposition, I think he is the last man who should undertake to expose the errors of others. For his name first appears in your paper subscribed to a falsehood, and the first act of his *honor* was to confess it: and while on the subject of the *dead*

cattle being eaten at the Umpqua mountains, I will merely remark, that although he acknowledges he published
what he did not know to be true, his explanation is as
false as the original, and can only be regarded as a slander on his fellow immigrants, and his attempt to fix the
stigma on a particular individual (Mr. Dunbar) could
only be dictated by that fiendish spirit of envy and malevolence with which this man appears to overflow. Mr.
D., to an unblemished character, added the respect of
his fellow travellers, whilst Mr. Thornton was the comparative of every thing that was dishonest and mean.

That the "immigrants were in a starving condition,
and already eating the dead cattle in the kanyon," is a
slander upon the immigrants themselves, is easily seen:
for it is well known that there were belonging to the immigrants loose cattle, which were in good condition enough
to have fed them for months, and he thus covertly insin-
uates that those who had cattle would see their fellow
travelers starve rather than relieve them. An ox crippled
by accident was shot by his owner, and one of the quarters taken off—and this is the whole foundation upon
which he builds the revolting story, and this Mr. T. knew
or might have known had he been as anxious to state
facts as to misrepresent them.

To notice his *analysis* in order. He carries his point in
his first *averment,* by making a family of two bachelors
[Geddes and Nye]. Query—who is the head of that family? or has it two heads and no body?

Averment 2d *analysed,* means—That the people remained in the Umpqua valley because they could not get
away without assistance. A majority of people left in this
deplorable condition are here to prove this assertion a
falsehood. They came without any assistance, bringing
with them their wagons, teams, and loose cattle, which
are in much better condition than any wintered in this
valley. They crossed the Calapooia mountain in February, and found no snow to impede or obstruct their passage, though the valleys of the northern portion of the

Territory were still wrapped in their wintry covering.
They report Mr. Hall, who Mr. T. was going to shoot
for splitting wood near his camp, to have gone to the
Fort, and that the Rev. Mr. Cornwall, and perhaps the
bachelor family remain in charge of the property left in
their care, *as they agreed to do.* So this subject for Mr.
T's communication is lost.

Under his 3d head, he says—"Almost every man (perhaps indeed every one,) who came into Oregon by the
southern route, is in a pecuniary point of view ruined by
so doing." To prove this false in the general, may most
easily be done, by proving it false in a special case; for
example—Mr. Thornton himself, who had nothing *of his
own* to lose. I cannot see how "in a pecuniary point of
view," a man can be ruined, who leaves the U. S[t]ates
hid in the bottom of a wagon owned, or at least claimed
by another person, unless "indeed" he is disappointed in
defrauding those who have assisted him in defrauding his
just creditors.[168]

The "mice story" I suppose is about *half true,* which
does very well for Mr. T. The mice were actually eaten;
but as I can state on the authority of one of the immigrants, (Mr. Whitley) that the "estimable old man and
his wife and grand-child" had plenty of beef at the time;
the "small game," I presume, were eaten by way of a
desert.

For a man *appointed* to the highest judicial office in
the Territory, and a *professed* worshipper of the God of
truth, so far to forget what was due to the dignity of his
new appointment, and to the sanctity of his new profession, as to make statements so grossly and notoriously
false as are contained in the 5th division of his tirade, is
to be unaccountable.

After asserting in his first sentence that immigrants
on the southern route lost *all* their property, he goes on
to say—

"Mr. Applegate met the company in which I traveled,
August 8th, a few miles on this side of Fort Hall. Al-

though among the first of my company to get in, I did
not arrive until Nov. 29th; while others who had entered
upon the old road only about forty-eight hours before
Mr. Applegate arrived at the point where the old road
turns off to the right from the California road, arrived
Sept. 13th—two and a half months earlier." I do not
quote this long sentence to deny its truth, for that I think
is useless; but to give to the public some information on
that subject, which it appears to be the disposition of
some persons more deserving of notice than Mr. T. to
suppress.

Maj. Harris and myself met Mr. [Meadows] Vanderpool's company at Goose creek, where they had encamped
on the 5th day of August.[169] As Goose creek is two days'
travel for wagons on this side of the forks of the road,
and the rear of the immigrants on the old road (except
the Iowa company,) were a day ahead of them, it follows
that they must have arrived at the forks of the road on
the 2d day of August. Mr. Applegate arrived at the forks
of the road on the morning of the 6th, and Mr. [Harri-
son] Linville's company, who were the first who turned
into the new road, arrived there the evening of the 7th
of that month, being 5 days travel, or nearly 100 miles
behind the rear of the immigrants on the old road. Mr.
Linville's company united to that of Mr. Vanderpool's
alone broke and made the road to the Sacramento river;
and besides losing much time in awaiting the coming up
of the rear companies, they were further delayed in re-
opening the road over the Cascade mountain which a fire
had filled with timber. Yet they arrived in the Rogue
river valley west of the Cascade mountains, and within
175 miles of this valley, *on the 9th day of October,* while
the rear of the immigrants who were 5 days ahead of
them at the forks of the road, did not arrive at Oregon
City, until about the 20th of that month; and of the Iowa
company, who arrived at Fort Hall, but two days after
Mr. A. left that post, 6 or 7 wagons, by using the greatest diligence, reached Oregon City the first week in No-

vember, and the remainder were unable to cross the mountains at all. Does this look like the southern route is a further and worse road than the old one? Again, Gov. Boggs's company in which Mr. Thornton was traveling, left their camp a few miles from the forks of the road on the morning of the 13th of August, being 11 days or nearly 200 miles in the rear of the hindmost immigrants on the road. A part of this company, according to the journal of Mr. Isaac Kuyhendall, arrived at the Umpqua mountain within 85 miles of this valley, on the 6th of October, which shows that in despite the burning of the grass, and other annoyances and delays to which they were subjected by the Indians, they not only kept even pace with those on the old road, but actually gained nearly 100 miles upon them.

That the road through the Umpqua mountain is at present a bad one, no one has denied or wishes to deny; and that the necessary labor will make it a good one is as generally conceded. That much property was left there, that may be lost or destroyed, and that some individuals were severe sufferers, is true, and to be regretted: but that the road hunters are to blame for it, none but fools believe or liars assert.

The immigrants were told it would require much labor to open the road — that the Umpqua mountains alone would require the labor of 20 men 10 days to make it passable, and the necessity of sending forward a sufficient company to open the road before the wagons, was urged upon every company and almost upon every man. They could not spare the men, and the road hunters did all they could to supply the deficiency with their own labor; but unhappily for Mr. Thornton, the terrible *kanyon* cannot be made available in his case; long before he reached that place of disaster, he had willfully and maliciously threw away and destroyed some property left in his charge, and to make the loss certain to the owner, he forbade any person to bring it along.

Mr. T. cannot even tell the truth in a matter of so little

importance as *his own* arrival in the settlements. He was in the Rickreall settlement on the *28th November,* which is 70 or 80 miles below the first house the road passes in this valley.

If the cool contempt with which his ready praises of the road were received, and his proffered services rejected by one of the road company, may excuse his resentment towards that individual, his conduct to me has been marked by the basest ingratitude. At a time when this man's conduct had made him so odious to the company with which he traveled, that scarce a hand would have been raised to defend his life or a hole dug to hide him when dead; and when he had actually been abandoned, and his wagon remained out all night at the mercy of the Indians, I spent a whole day in bringing him up to the company:[170] for this service he has repaid me by inventing and circulating a slander on my character! But he has yet to receive his quittance, which he may rest assured shall be written in plain characters.

In conclusion, I would say to Mr. Thornton, than [that] I consider him merely a "volunteer" in the cause of his "injured fellow travelers;" for if they had felt themselves aggrieved by the road party, or your editorial, and wished an advocate, they would have chosen one, who had at least a character for honesty and truth.

If his object has been to gain popularity, and to recommend himself "where thrift may follow fawning" he has certainly missed the mark by doing too much. He should have remembered that, the traitor, the assassin, and the *liar* are despised even by those for whom they do their dirty work. That the quibble, subterfuge, and falsehood which might pass unnoticed in the pettifogger, become conspicuous in the judge, and his present elevation, like the monkey on the pole, only shows the plainer, that the robe of ermine but half conceals the dog.

Instead of the triumphant advocate of an injured immigration, and by exagerating the length and difficulties of the southern route, and enlarging upon the losses and sufferings of the immigrants, create a sympathy in his favor and bias the judgment of a jury that is soon to sit upon his conduct: he must stand before them the *exposed liar,* and the verdict of that jury will finish his character by adding *cheat and swindler* to his other "blushing honors."

The men in whose cause he volunteers his services, are beginning to see for themselves, and to understand the motives of many who have, like Mr. Thornton, become "tender hearted on a sudden," in their behalf. They see that "vested rights" and "location claims [?]" have produced much of this incredible [?] [*one word obscured*] They find the road they have to travel, by passing 150 miles through the rich valleys of the south, enters that of the Willamette at by far the most valuable portion for settlement, and whatever their losses may have been, they have *now alive* more cattle than those who came by the way of Mt. Hood.

They see parties again preparing to brave the "hostile savage" on their return to meet their friends and relations to conduct them over the mountains and "along the rocky glens and almost impassable kanyon which mark this disastrous cut off."

They see the immigrants for California for the first time preparing wagons for their conveyance to that country, over the most dreadful part of this most dreadful road, and by referring to the map they see that by the discovery of the new road, that the route to Oregon from the Platte to the Pacific, lies for the whole distance between the parallels of 41 and 43 degrees of north latitude, and the conviction is forced upon their minds that they have not only traveled the best, but also the nearest route to Oregon.

Excuse the length of my epistle, and if there be in it any expressions which may sound harsh to delicate ears, I hope you and your readers will excuse an old man who has been always accustomed to call things by their right names.   DAVID GOFF.

Hezekiah Packingham to his Brother, Willamette Valley, March 1, 1847[171]

I arrived in the Wallamette Valley on the 30th of September, and my calculations are all defeated about Oregon. I found it a mean, dried up, and drowned country. The Yam Hill is a small valley, destitute of timber. I soon got sick of this place, and then went to the mouth of the Columbia river. I can give Oregon credit for only one or two things, and these are, good health and plenty of salmon, and Indians; as for the farming country there is none here—wheat grows about the same as in Illinois; corn, potatoes, and garden vegetables cannot grow here without watering. The nights are too cold here in summer. The soil is not as good as in Illinois—the face of the country is hilly, and high mountains covered with snow all summer, and small valleys—the mountains and hills are covered with the heaviest timber that I ever saw. We have had a very hard winter here, snow fell two feet deep, and lay three weeks, by reason of which hundreds of cattle have died of starvation. The thermometer fell to three degrees above zero.—Prairie grass here is the same as in Illinois. There is no timothy nor clover. Mechanics are very numerous here. Of the ships that sailed from New York last April, but one arrived, and she was ice bound for 50 days, in latitude 50 1-2. It is supposed the other has gone to her long home. A United States man-of-war [*Shark*] was recently wrecked at the mouth of the Columbia. Money is very scarce here—and they have a kind of currency here (orders on stores and scrip)—they value property very high, but if they would put things at cash prices, they would be about the same as they are in the States. Oregon is rapidly filling up with young men, (but no girls,) of whom two-thirds are dissatisfied and many would return to the States if they were able, but the road is long and tedious, and it is hard for families to get back; my trip was pleasant until I got to the South Pass—after that the country was rugged, and bad roads.

Tell young men if they intend coming to Oregon, to drive no teams unless it is their own. We were uninjured by the Indians, though they were very saucy—they have no manners; they worship idols [totem poles?], and I saw one of their gods at the mouth of the river. There is no society here except the Camelites [Campbellites]. I shall return to the States next spring. Don't believe all that is said about Oregon, as many falsehoods are uttered respecting the country.

PETER H. BURNETT TO JAMES M. HUGHES AT LIBERTY, MISSOURI, "OREGON TERRITORY," MARCH, 1847[172]

My Dear Sir:

By the late emigrants I received your welcome letter, written last spring . . . .

The emigration of last year have all arrived with the exception of some five families now at Dr. Whitman's,[173] and about the same number at Fort Umqua, at which place they will perhaps remain until May, and then leave for the Wallamette valley. That emigration was not so large as the one of the previous year. The emigrants came in by two new routes, one across the Cascade mountains near the Columbia river, and the other a southern route entering the Wall[a]mette valley near the sources of that River, and crossing the head waters of the Sacramento in California, and the Umqua and Klamet rivers in Oregon. Mr. Barlow obtained from the Oregon Legislature a charter for the opening of a wagon road across the Cascade mountains to the Wallamette valley, and allow him to charge certain amounts of toll as a compensation for the labor incurred. This road was in readiness when the first portion of the emigrants arrived, and those who came the old accustomed route by Fort Baise [Boise], the Grand Round and the Blue mountains came through Barlow's road, with their wagons, teams, families and loose stock to the Wallamette Falls before the rainy season sets in. Some of these arrived as early as the 15th September, and the greater portion by the close of that month. Among others, Mr. [Joseph] Waldo, (brother of Dr. [David] Waldo of Independence, Mo.) reached the Wallamette Falls [Oregon City] in 4 months and nine days after quitting Independence. This road had been just opened, was exceedingly narrow, full of stumps and other obstructions, which makes it much the worst portion of the route from the U. S. to Oregon. It was a serious undertaking to open such a road among mountains, along dark and dismal vallies and through immense masses of timber, to which the tallest forest in the U. S., will not bear a comparison. This route is susceptible of such improvement as to become at least a practicable way; and Mr. Barlow expects to expend more labor on it during the coming summer. The time occupied in passing from the Dalles to Oregon City with wagons, is generally from ten to fifteen days. The great objection to this route is the scarcity of pasturage upon the way. The grass is only found in small quantities at different points; and where there are many teams to pass, those behind must necessarily suffer much. This road, however, must be of great benefit to emigrating parties; as their loose stock can be driven through in so short a period as not to suffer materially: I am well satisfied and have long been so that the safest and most practicable route, run[s] down the Columbia river. [Points out, at length, the advantages.]

The southern route was surveyed by Messrs. Jessee Applegate, Moses Harris and others, prompted no doubt by the most laudable motives; and cost them much labor and expense, and subjected them to much censure. These gentlemen left the Wallamette Settlements in the latter part of last summer, and reached Fort Hall after the larger portion of the late emigrants had passed. Those they met at that place agreed to try this new route with their wagons, teams and cattle. They continued the old route for the distance of about 40 miles this side of the Fort, when they turned to the left, fell upon Mary's river which they travelled down some three hundred miles over an excellent road. This route passes thro' a portion of California, crosses the head waters of the Sacramento, then falls upon the waters of the Klamet and Umqua rivers. I am unable to give you any very accurate inform- ation as to the ultimate practicability of this route, as the emigrants who travelled it, are not agreed in their opin- ions respecting it. Those who came that way certainly suffered very much, losing most of their cattle, and reach- ing the settlements in November and December, half starved and half naked. But the most calm and dispas- sionate men among them do not attribute all the hardships endured to the impracticable nature of the route itself. Much delay occurred in opening the way; and much time was lost in protecting the teams and stock from the depra- dations of the indians. These Indians are amongst the poorest and most degraded of the human race, and are generally thievish, and cowardly. They were not disposed to attack the emigrants themselves, but sought every op- portunity to destroy their stock, that they might obtain their carcasses, after the emigrants had past. It became necessary to keep the stock up every night, to save them from the Indian arrow. This as a matter of course occa- sioned delay, as it was necessary to stop during the day for the cattle to feed. From the best information I have been able to obtain, there appears to be no very serious obstruction in the way, until the road reaches the Umqua mountains dividing the waters of the Umqua and Klamet rivers. There is a defile passing through the mountains, cutting it to its very base, and opening a passage that might be made quite practicable for loaded wagons. The distance through this passage is about 18 miles, about 12 of which is quite a passable road, and the remaining 6 miles almost wholly impracticable in its present state: in this defile there is a pool of water about fifteen feet in diameter from which two small streams take their rise, one running into the Umqua, and the other into the Klamet river. In that po[r]tion of this defile called the "Kanyons," the road runs in the bed of one of these streams for the distance of 3 miles, and large loose rock and a long an[d] exceedingly narrow passage. The emigrants reached this point just as the fall rains set in, which raised these two streams and obstructed the passage to such an extent, that many oxen were left dead in the Kanyon, and many families were left without teams, and had it not been for friendly aid they received from the settlements in the upper Wallamette they must have perished. Had these emigrants reached this defile and passed through it, before the rainy season came on, they would have suffer[e]d much less. They were however some ten days too late.

That this route may become in a few years of great importance there can be no question; as it will afford a wagon way to California and the nearest route for emigrants from the U. S. who intend to settle in the Umqua and Klamet vallies. But at this time it is unsafe. The road requires much improvement; and there are no settlements from which supplies can be had in cases of emergency. The advantages of the old route at this time, are very obvious. There are no Indians upon this old route that are troublesome; it is more healthy, and passes Fort Basie and near to Dr. Whitman's Mission and Fort Walla Walla, and strikes the Columbia river a short distance above the dalles, passing by the Methodist Mission at the latter point. At all these places provisions and other supplies can be had, if required. That portion of the emigrants who came the old route to the dalles had more provisions than they needed, and many of them exchanged flour at the dalles for the same quan[t]ity at Oregon City. When the Govt shall extend its laws over our new Country (*And when will this be?*) and establish its Indian Agencies and its Military Posts, then the southern route may become of great importance. It is now well known that the vallies of the Umqua and Klamet (or Rogue) river, form one of the richest and loveliest portions of Oregon, but what is there extent, it is hard to say because not fully known. A company is now forming the object of which is to make a full exploration of that beautiful portion of our territory, during the ensuing summer. . . .

I neglected to state in the proper place that two of the late emigrants who came the southern route, were killed by the Indians. The first was a man whose name I do not now remember, but who was killed before the party reached the Kanyon. He is said to have been partially insane, verry indolent and careless. He had lain down by the way side and had fallen asleep. In this situation the wagons passed him, and the Indians no doubt found him. When he was missed in camp two men went back to search for him, and found his dead body pierced with six or seven arrows. He had evidently fled from the Indians when attacked, and had fallen some hundred yards from the point where he had laid himself down.[174] The other person was Mr. Newman [Newton], who was assassinated by two Indians in his tent late at night after he had passed through the defile. These Indians came to his camp in the evening, and pretending to be very friendly, asked leave to stay all night, this liberty was granted them, but Mr. Newman suspecting them of an intention to steal his fine American mare, determined to keep awake and watch their movements. Being, however, tired and sleepy, he found his task too hard; and while he slumbered the Indians fired upon him and gave him a mortal wound, of which he died the next day. They robbed the camp of many things and left, and have not since been seen. Of what tribe they were, is not certainly known. Some few others of the emigrants were wounded in different skirmishes with the Indians.

We have just passed thro' the most extraordinary winters ever seen in Oregon, within the memory of man [a severe winter, that is.] . . . At Nisqually 6,000 sheep perished out of 40,000 head. Large quantities of grain were fed away equal in value, perhaps to the stock lost. The late emigrants lost about one half of their cattle. Some nearly all they had. The cattle that have survived are in very poor condition; and as most of our teams consist of

oxen, our crops of wheat will be generally of late sow-
ing.[175] There will be some scarcity of grain for bread, and
perhaps some suffering amon[g] the late comers, but all
that can be done for the country in its present destitute
condition, will be most cheerfully performed by those who
have the means. . . .

PETER H. BURNETT

Since writing this I have made inquiry and find that
I was misinformed as to the number of sheep lost at
Nisqually. The company only lost about 150 at Nisqually
and Vancouver together. . . .

RICHARD R. HOWARD TO A FRIEND IN ILLINOIS,
"OREGON TERRITORY," APRIL 6, 1847[176]

We arrived safe in Oregon City on the 12th of September last.[177] We reached Fort Laramie in 42 days from
Independence; Fort Hall in 33 days more; the Dalles
in 37 days more; and Oregon City in 16 days more—
making in all 128 days. Our journey was two weeks
longer than necessary had we lost no time. We met with
no serious obstructions on our journey. We had to raise
the front of our wagon beds two or three inches in crossing
the Larimie Fork to keep the water out; sometimes we
had long drives to find a good place for camping, with
water and grass. [The writer gives a long detail of the
necessary outfit for the journey and cautions to be used
on the road—which we omit. *Illinois Journal*] No single
man should come to this country. One third of the men
in Oregon at this time are without wives. Nothing but
men of families are wanted here to till the soil, to make
this one of the greatest countries in the world. This country does not get so muddy as Illinois. There is no dust in
summer here. The good land in this country is more
extensive than I expected to find it. The hills are not so
high as represented. From the Cascade mountains to the
Pacific, the whole country can be cultivated. The natural
soil of the country, especially in the bottoms, is a black

loam, mixed with gravel and clay. We have good timber; but there appears to be a scarcity of good building rock. The small streams furnish us with trout the year round.

My wife to the old lady—Greeting; says she was never more satisfied with a move in her life before; that she is fast recovering her health; and she hopes you will come to Oregon, where you can enjoy what little time you have remaining in health.

The roads to Oregon are not as bad as represented. Hastings in his history speaks of the Falls of Columbia being 50 feet and roaring loud, making the earth tremble, &c. The falls are about like that of a mill-dam. Every thing in this country now is high, except molasses, sugar and salt; but when we raise our wheat crop to trade on, we will make them pay for their high charges. I think no place where a living is to be made out of the earth can be preferable to Oregon for that purpose—and let people say what they may—all agree that it is healthy. It is certainly the healthiest country in the world, disease is scarcely known here, except among the late emigrants, ninety-nine out of a hundred of them get well the first season. I have heard of only two deaths since I have been in Oregon; one of them was a man who came here diseased and in one year died; the other was a woman who it is said was near dead ten years before she came here.

RICHARD R. HOWARD

THE CALIFORNIA STAR, YERBA BUENA, JANUARY 9, 1847

One thousand five hundred emigrants from the United States have arrived in the California Valley within the last three months by the route over the mountains!

THE CALIFORNIA STAR, YERBA BUENA, JANUARY 16, 1847

EMIGRANTS IN THE MOUNTAINS.

It is probably not generally known to the people, that there is now in the California mountains in a most distressing situation, a party of emigrants from the United

States, who were prevented from crossing the mountains by an early heavy fall of snow. The party consists of about sixty persons, men, women and children. They were, almost entirely out of provisions, when they reached the foot of the mountain, and but for the timely succor afforded them by Capt. J. A. Sutter, one of the most humane and liberal men in California, they must have all perished in a few days. Captain Sutter as soon as he ascertained their situation, sent [by Charles T. Stanton] five mules loaded with provisions to them. A second party [under James Frazier Reed] was dispatched with provisions for them, but they found the mountain impassable, in consequence of the snow. We hope that our citizens will do something for the relief of these unfortunate people.

THE CALIFORNIA STAR, YERBA BUENA, JANUARY 30, 1847

CONDITION OF THE LATE EMIGRANTS

We would call the attention of the authorities of our government here, to this class of our citizens. They have come here without any previous correct knowledge of the situation of the country, expecting to find the greater part of the farming lands unappropriated, and that they would be able soon after their arrival, to get grants for such portions as they might select. In this they have been disappointed. They find the greater part of the country taken up by large grants of from five to twenty leagues. Many of them are too poor to buy, even at a very low price, and in order to get land, must go some distance beyond the present settlements where they will be exposed to all the dangers and difficulties incident to the frontiers of a new country, unless they will be permitted to occupy the mission lands, which are now the public property of the United States. We would therefore suggest to the authorities of our district, that written permission be given to the late emigrants to settle on the mission lands, and occupy the mission houses until they can make other permanent arrangements.

— — —

☞ We learn from persons recently from Oregon, that
there will be a large emigration from that country to
this next spring. They will start as soon as they can
cross the Cascade mountains. Many of these emigrants
never designed settling in Oregon, but merely went there
to remain until there should be a change in the affairs of
California. The permanent citizens in Oregon, are not
to be reconed we understand, among those who are dissatisfied.[178]

WILLIAM EDGINGTON TO THE REV. THOMAS ALLEN,
"LOWER PUEBLO, CALIFORNIA," JANUARY 24, 1847 [179]

Dear Sir,

I take the earliest opportunity of writing according to
promise, at the time of our parting. By the time we had
arrived at Fort Hall we were met by Mr. Applegate, who
recommended a new road to Oregon, by the way of
Mary's river, which we pursued 350 miles, to the point
where the road forks, the right hand leading to Oregon
and the left to California. We traveled 15 miles on the
fork leading to Oregon, where we found a written paper
informing us that it was two or three days journey to
grass and water, and we also observed mountains that
could not be crossed without much difficulty. These circumstances discouraged us so much that we concluded
to turn back to the forks, and pursue our way to California. Accordingly on the evening of the same day we
started and traveled back the same road 15 miles by 2
o'clock the next morning. We arrived in the neat valley
of the Sacrimento on the 20th of October, after a tedious
and tiresome journey. Four days previous however, to
our entering the valley we were met by a recruiting Ser-
geant, from whom we learned that California was in a
state of revolution and that the country had been taken
by the American authorities, and the American colors

raised, but that the Spaniards had retaken the Lower Pueblo and that his business was to enlist men under Col. Fremont, for the purpose of visiting the lower country, routing the enemy, and putting an end to the war. Accordingly Foster and I, together with many other emigrants enlisted for three months, at 25 dol. per month.[180] I immediately started on to join the Colonel, leaving my friends and their ox-wagons in the valley, promising them to return in time if possible to accompany them to Oregon. A boat afforded us a passage down the Sacrimento and across the bay to the Upper Pueblo [San Jose], where we found a sufficient number to make one company, and Hasting[s] among others whom we elected captain. The Col. by this time was at Monterey. In a few days we started for that place and when we arrived the Col. with all of his troops amounting to 420 men including about 40 Indians set out for the Lower Pueblo [Los Angeles]. We traveled very slow the most of our horses being tired and broken down by former bad usage. While on our way to the lower country we frequently saw small parties of the enemy, but at no time more than a hundred. They were all mounted on good horses and took good care not to come within gunshot of us. Their object seems to have been to ascertain our forces, and at the same time to be in readiness, to cut off any small party they might meet with, but we kept well together and gave them no chance. When we were within two days journey of our place of destination we learned that Com. Stockton had taken the town, with his marine[s]. But little fighting has been done and but few slain on either side. The enemy has now surrendered and the war appears to be at an end. I had no fighting yet and hope that no more fighting will be necessary.—Fremont's men were all armed with rifles and the Spaniards were evidently afraid to meet them although their numbers were superior to the Col's.

The Col. is now appointed Governor by commander Stockton until such time as the President may appoint

another, and this town is now the capitol. I am now about
700 miles from Sutter's Fort, and having had a good
chance to see the country and am not at all satisfied with
it. The accounts that you hear of it in the States are
greatly exaggerated. There is at least nine tenths of the
country mountainous and unfit for cultivation, and the
most of the mountains too barren to be valuable for grazing. Besides there is a great scarcity of water and timber
and what timber there is, is of a very inferior quality
consisting for the most part of scrubby oaks. There is no
timber that I have seen in the country since I have left
the California mountains that is suitable for rails. Pine,
fir and red wood may be obtained in those mountains,
and some others but is with great difficulty brought to
the settlements. There are some beautiful vallies the largest and most important of which is the Sacrimento. This
valley is remarkable for its great abundance of game consisting principally of elk, antelope, grizzly bear, and
black-tailed deer; and numerous herds of cattle may also
be seen scouring the plains as wild as the buffalo. The
Sacrimento river and its tributaries abounds in fish of an
excellent quality, the most plentiful of which are salmon
and trout.—Water fowls are also very numerous indeed
such as geese, ducks, cranes, pelicans, and sea gulls. In
all parts of this country where the raising of wheat has
been tried, it has succeeded remarkable well although the
ground has been poorly cultivated. With suitable culture
I believe that some of the land in this country would produce more abundant crops than what is generally raised
in the States. Corn can be raised but not to make very
good crops, because of the drought that prevails in the
summer season.

The [Santa Clara] valley south of the bay, generally
called the valley of the upper Puebla is the most beautiful and fertile portion of the country that I have seen—
the missions of St. Joseph and Santa Clara are situated
in this valley. I have travelled considerably over this valley with scouting parties for the purpose of preparing

horses for the service. I would be well pleased with this valley if there was any rail timber but there is none; the only dependence here as well as in other parts of the country is ditches instead of fences. The country lying between the two Pueblos 400 miles is exceedingly mountainous with but small vallies intervening, some of which have scarcely any entrance, scarcely any water except in the winter season. This town is situated about 30 miles from the seashore, and I have been down to the coast and seen considerable about this place and pronounce it an excellent farming country, if there was any timber even to burn. I have heard considerable of the valley of St. Wakeen [San Joaquin], but have not seen any part of it. It is said to be a fine section of country, and to have a great many wild horses. The vine flourishes and comes to great perfection through the whole extent of this country, and the vineyards look beautiful and produce very abundantly; there are also some very fine orchards of apple and pear trees, peach trees are said to do well, but I have not seen any of them. The houses both in country and town including the extensive, and in many respects magnificent buildings at the missions are constructed of sun-burnt brick called adobies, the Indians make the brick, build the houses, and do most of the labor that is performed in the country, and their services can be obtained for a trifling compensation * * *

I have heard from Warren Brown and David Allen whom I left sick at Bridger, they have both recovered their health and gone to Oregon, not knowing but those before them had also gone there.[181] On the road between Bridger and Fort Hall, there was a number of us taken sick, myself among others, and by the time we arrived at Fort Hall, there was 14 of us helpless all from our neighborhood.—There was no doctor in our company and our medicine had give out, and by the time we had got to Mary's river, Thomas Adams died and was buried, 22d August, we continued our journey untill the 27th when Isaac Allen also died. * * * By the time we arrived at the sink of Mary's river, we suffered another loss in the death of Betsy Allen consort of David Allen. The funeral rights of the dead were attended to in a decent manner. * * * We got all of our wagons safe into California. I have learned that the families of Squire [Elam] Brown and David Allen are at the mission of St. Clara south of the Bay.—The balance of the company with Joseph Child's [Chiles] are all together on the north side of the bay of St. Francisco. They were all in good health at the time I left there, but not satisfied with the country. I have now a prospect of obtaining my discharge in two or three weeks, when I shall go up the river probably aboard of a ship. I am not able to say whether we can get to Oregon next summer or not, but I wish you to write to both places, and I will write again the first chance I have to send a letter.—Give my best respects to all enquiring friends.

I remain yours,

WM. EDGINGTON

WILLIAM H. RUSSELL TO THE *Missouri Republican,* "CIUDAD DE LOS ANGELOS, OR CITY OF ANGELS, UPPER CALIFORNIA," JANUARY 26, 1847 [182]

After a long interruption of my correspondence, occasioned by the want of a conveyance, I avail myself of the opportunity of a courier about being sent home to write you a brief letter.

I resigned the command of the emigrating party at Fort Laramie, and, with only eight other persons, traded my wagons for pack-mules, and thus proceeded on our long journey, and finally reached Sutter's Fort, on the Sacramento, on the last day of August, when I beheld the glorious spectacle of the Stars and Stripes floating where, but a short time before, the Mexican flag and rule maintained undisputed sway.

I found Sutter's Fort garrisoned by a detachment of Col. Fremont's command, who, himself, with the balance of his little army, with a celerity that I believe no other person could equal, was traversing every portion of the territory, and subjecting it to the mild rule of our own government.

I remained but a short time at Sutter's, when I repaired to the mouth of the bay of San Francisco, to the most growing town in California, called Yerba Buena, where I found Commodore Stockton, in the United States frigate *Congress,* and several other United States vessels, portions of our squadron on the Pacific; and shortly after Col. Fremont arrived, preparatory to the entering on the duties of Civil Governor, a position assigned him by Commodore Stockton, in deference to the wishes of all who had witnessed his efficiency and gallantry in the field.

At this very juncture, however, an insurrection broke out in this portion of the country, and in this city, which has been the capital of Upper California; to suppress which Col. Fremont, whom I have attached myself to as a member of his staff, forthwith set out by sea, and after a calm of two weeks on the justly named Pacific, we landed at Monterey where we equipped ourselves, mounted our men, and after a long and tedious march of near two months, met the enemy near this place, who, without a regular fight, came in, capitulated, and the country is again at peace, and Col. Fremont is Governor, and, strange as it may seem, I am Secretary of State, and am now writing to you in the Government house of California, in a room of which I have my office.

While our command lay at Monterey, Charles Burrus, whom you recollect in St. Louis, and whom I found in this country, was sent out with a party to bring in a band of horses, and on returning was attacked by a party of Spaniards, and Burrus and a young Mr. Ames, also of St. Louis, who came out with me from the States, were both killed, and were buried in an old Catholic Mission, called St. John's.[183]

I cannot, in a short letter, give you the details of our

march from Monterey to this City of Angels, but it was replete with incidents, and throughout furnished me continued evidence of the gallantry, skillful maneuvering and noble bearing of our youthful commander. He is a scholar, an officer and a gentleman; and if not thrust aside by the envy and cruel malevolence of those whom his talents have supplanted, he is destined to occupy the proudest niche in the Temple of Fame.

We found Gen. Kearny here with instructions from the Secretary of War to conquer the country, and institute a Civil Government; but Com. Stockton, who was also here, maintained that the conquest had been made by him and Col. Fremont, and as an incident to it, the right of forming a Civil Government belonged to him, and that Gen. Kearny's orders were now obsolete, because the business for which he had come had been anticipated by others.

The Commodore therefore appointed, as before remarked, Col. Fremont as Governor, and myself as Secretary of State, and ordered the convocation of a Legislative Assembly, which is to meet on the 1st of March.

This is truly, in many respects, a fairy land. We are now luxuriating in oranges, grapes and pears—crops of the last year.

W. H. R.

The California Star, YERBA BUENA, FEBRUARY 6, 1847

PUBLIC MEETING.

It will be recollected that in a previous number of our paper, we called the attention of our citizens, to the situation of a company of unfortunate emigrants now in the California mountains. For the purpose of making their situation more fully known to the people, and of adopting measures for their relief, a public meeting was called by the Honorable Washington A. Bartlett, Alcalde of the Town on Wednesday evening last. The citizens generally attended, and in a very short time, the sum of eight hundred dollars was subscribed to purchase provisions, clothing, horses, and mules to bring the emigrants in. Committe[e]s were appointed to call on those who could not attend the meeting, and there is no doubt but that five or six hundred dollars more will be raised. This speaks well for Yerba Buena.

Californian, MONTEREY, FEBRUARY 13, 1847

By the arrival of the Brig *Francisca,* 3 days from Yerba Buena, Le Moine, Master, brings to us the heart rending news of the extreme suffering of a party of emigrants who were left on the other side of the California mountain, about 60 in all, nineteen of whom started to come into the valley. Seven, only have arrived, the remainder died, and the survivers were kept alive by eating the dead bodies. Among the survivers are two young girls.

A public meeting was held at Yerba Buena, and about eight hundred dollars raised for the relief of the sufferers who still remain in the mountains, Messrs [Frank] Ward and [C. C.] Smith kindly offered the use of their Launch, and a party, under direction of Pas'd Midshipman [Selim E.] Woodworth with the intention of disembarking at the foot of the mountain and then going on foot, with packs of provisions. It is to be hoped they will succeed in reaching them with sufficient provisions to get them in.

We have but few of the particulars of the hardships which they have suffered. Such a state of things will probably never again occur, from the fact, that the road is now better known, and the emigrants will hereafter start and travel so as to cross the mountain by the 1st of October. The party which are suffering so much, lost their work cattle on the salt planes, on *Hasting's cut off,* a rout which we hope no one will ever attempt again.

The California Star, YERBA BUENA, FEBRUARY 13, 1847

☞ A company of twenty men left here on Sunday last for the California mountains with provisions, clothing &c. for the suffering emigrants now there. The citizens of this place subscribed about fifteen hundred dollars for their relief, which was expended for such articles as the emigrants would be most likely to need.[184] —Mr [Caleb] Greenwood, an old mountaineer went with the company as pilot. If it is possible to cross the mountains they will get to the emigrants in time to save them.

— — —

DISTRESSING NEWS.

By Capt. J. A. Sutter's Launch which arrived here a few days since from Fort Sacramento—We received a letter from a friend at that place [George McKinstry, Jr.],[185] containing a most distressing account of the situation of the emigrants in the mountains, who were prevented from crossing them by the snow—and of a party of eleven who attempted to come into the valley on foot. The writer who is well qualified to judge, is of the opinion that the whole party might have reached the California valley before the first fall of snow, if the men had exerted themselves as they should have done. Nothing but a contrary and contentious disposition on the part of some of the men belonging to the party prevented them from getting in as soon as any of the first companies.

The following particulars we extract from the letter:—

The company is composed of twenty-three waggons, and is a part of Col. Russell's company, that left the rendezvous on Indian Creek near the Missouri line on the 13th day of May last. They arrived at Fort Bridger in good time, some two weeks earlier than the last company on the road. From that point they took the new road by the south end of the Great Salt Lake, which was then being marked out by some seventy-five waggons with Messrs. Hastings and Headspeth as pilots.[186] They followed on in the train until they were near the "Weber River canion," and within some 4 or 5 days travel of the leading waggons, when they stopped and sent on three men, (Messrs. Reed, Stanton and Pike) to the first company, (with which I was then travelling in company,) to request Mr. Hastings to go back and show them the pack trail from the Red Fork of Weber River to the Lake. Mr. H. went back and showed them the trail, and then returned to our company, all of which time we remained in camp, waiting for Mr. Hastings to show us the rout.[187] They then commenced making the new road over to the Lake on the pack trail, so as to avoid the Weber river canion, and Mr Reed and others who left the company, and came in for assistance, informed me that they were sixteen days making the road, as the men would not work one quarter of their time.[188] Had they gone on the road that we had made for them, they would have easily over-taken us before we reached the old road on Mary's river. They were then but some 4 or 5 days travel behind the first waggons; which were travelling slow, on account of being obliged to make an entire new rout for several hundred miles through heavy sage and over mountains, and delayed four days by the guides hunting out passes in the mountains;[189] and these waggons arrived at the settlement about the first of October. Had they gone around the old road, the north end of the great Salt Lake, they would have been in the first of September. After crossing the long drive of 75 miles without water or grass, and suffering much from loss of oxen, they sent on two men (M[ess]rs. Stanton and McCutcher [McCutchen].) They left the company recruiting on the second long drive of 35 miles, and came in to Capt. J. A. Sutter's Fort, and asked for assistance. Capt. Sutter in his usual prompt and generous manner, furnished them with 7 of his best mules and two of his favorite Indian baqueros, and all of the flour and beef that they wanted. Mr. C. S. [T.] Stanton, a young gentleman from Syracuse, New York, although he had no interest in the company, took charge

704 _Overland In 1846_

of the baqueros and provisions, and returned to the company.[190] Afterwards Mr. Reed came in almost exhausted from starvation; he was supplied with a still larger number of horses and mules and all the provisions he could take. He returned as far as the Bear river valley, and found the snow so deep, that he could not get to the company. He cached the provisions at that place and returned. Since that time (the middle of November,) we heard nothing of the company, until last week, when a messenger was sent down from Capt. Wm. Johnson's settlement, with the astounding information, that five women and two men had arrived at that point entirely naked, their feet frost bitten—and informed them that the company arrived within three miles of the small log cabin near Trucky's Lake on the east side of the mountains, and found the snow so deep that they could not travel, and fearing starvation, sixteen of the strongest, (11 males and 5 females,) agreed to start for the settlement on foot. Scantily clothed and provided with provisions they commenced that horrid journey over the mountains that Napoleon's fete on the Alps was childs play compared with it. After wandering about a number of days bewildered in the snow, their provisions gave out, and long hunger made it necessary to resort to that horrid recourse casting lots to see who should give up life, that their bodies might be used for food for the remainder. But at this time the weaker began to die which rendered it unnecessary to take life, and as they died the company went into camp and made meat of the dead bodies of their companions. After travelling thirty days, 7 out of the 16 arrived within 15 miles of Capt. Johnson's, the first house of the California settlements, and most singular to relate, all the females that started, 5 women came in safe, and but two of the men, and one of them was brought in on the back of an Indian.[191] Nine of the men died and seven of them were eaten by their companions.—The first person that died was Mr. C. S. Stanton, the young man who so generously returned to the company with Capt Sutter's

Baqueros and provisions; his body was left on the snow. The last two that died was Capt Sutter's two Indian baqueros and their bodies were used as food by the seven that came in. The company left behind, numbers sixty odd souls; ten men, the balance women and children. They are in camp about 100 miles from Johnson's, the first house after leaving the mountains, or 150 from fort Sacramento. Those who have come in say that Capt Sutter's seven mules were stolen by the Indians a few days after they reached the company, and that when they left, the company had provisions sufficient to last them until the middle of February. The party that came in, were at one time 36 hours in a snow storm without fire; they had but three quilts in the company. I could state several most horrid circumstances connected with this affair: such as one of the women being obliged to eat part of the body of her father and brother, another saw her husband's heart cooked &c.; which would be more suitable for a hangman's journal than the columns of a family newspaper. I have not had the satisfaction of seeing any one of the party that has arrived; but when I do, I will get more of the particulars and send them to you. As soon as we received the information we drew up the appeal of which I enclose you a copy, called a meeting in the armory of the Fort, explained the object of the meeting and solicited the names of all that would go. We were only able to raise seven here—they started this morning for Johnson's to join the party raised there. Capt. J. A. Sutter in his usual generous manner ordered his overseer to give this little brave band of men, all the provisions they could carry. They took as much beef, bread, and sugar, as they thought they could carry and started in good spirits on their long and perilous trip. Capt Kern the commander of the Sacramento District, will go up as far as Johnson's to-morrow to assist in starting the party, and may go as far as the Bear River Valley.[192]

[GEORGE MCKINSTRY] TO THE *California Star,*
NEW HELVETIA, FEBRUARY 13, 1847 [193]

Mr. E. P. Jones,

Dear Sir.—

An opportunity offering today to send to your town by Mr. [Peter] Lassen on his way down in a canoe, I write to inform you of the latest news from the mountains—Capt. E. M. Kern, commander of this district returned from Johnsons settlement on the 11th inst. after an absence of some ten days; he traveled on horse back and found the road very good both going and returning. On his arrival at that settlement he found the five women and two men that had succeeded in geting in from the unfortunate company now on the mountains, in much better health than could have been expect[e]d; in fact they were suffering merely from their feet being slightly injured by the frost. They are living with the families of Messrs. [Sebastian] Keyser and [Pierre] Sicard, and will come down to the Fort for protection as soon as they can walk. Capt. Kern succeeded in getting off the company that we raised here, by mounting them on horses belonging to Capt. J. A. Sutter. The men that returned from the mountains thought they could get to the company with but four days travel in the snow! (one of the two men [William H. Eddy] returned with the party,) but before Capt. Kern left Johnson's they had a heavy fall of snow on the mountains reaching within 15 miles of Johnsons house. They started in good spirits, and we are in hopes they will be able to reach them. Capt. K. would have accompanied the party as far as the Bear River Valley immediately at the mountains, but was not able to cross the Bear river at Johnson's with his horses as the raft and boat had been carried off by high water. I hope your citizens will do all in their power to assist the unfortunate party on the mountains. All the horrid reports that they have received, part of which I wrote you in my last were corroborated by those who were so fortunate as to get in.

The California Star, YERBA BUENA, MARCH 6, 1847

☞ We received a few days since, from our Sacramento correspondent, a letter containing the intelligence of an attempt by another party of twenty-four of the emigrants to cross the California mountains. They succeeded in reaching the top of the mountains, about the first of December, but they all perished in a severe snow storm, a few days after.

The same letter furnishes us with the names of those belonging to the first party who died from hunger, in attempting to cross the mountains, which are given below.

Patrick Dolan, Wm. Stanton, Wm. Fosdick, L. Murphey, Mr. Graves, Patrick Brin, two baqueros in the employment of J. A. Sutter, Esq., two New Mexicans, and two young men whose names are not recollected. The writer was not able to ascertain the names of any of the party of twenty-four.[194]

— — —

☞ In noticing the amount subscribed here, for the relief of the emigrants in the mountains, we neglected to state, that the officers, marines and sailors, belonging to the U. S. vessels of war then here, subscribed liberally.

The California Star, YERBA BUENA, MARCH 13, 1847

LATER FROM THE CALIFORNIA MOUNTAINS.

Fort Sacramento, March 5, 1847.

SIR—

Last night Mr. Aquila Glover, one of the noble men that went to the assistance of the suffering emigrants on the California mountains, arrived at this post with a letter from Lieut. Woodworth, U. S. N., and in compliance with his orders, I have thought proper with Capt. J. A. Sutter's consent to forward to you by couriers attached to this garrison, the information we have received, which must be interesting to every American. I send via Sonoma, as Capt. Sutter will detain his Launch here until Lieut. Woodworth returns from the mountains, as we will have no communication by water from Yerba Buena until that time. The following is a copy of the letter received from Lieut Woodworth:

                    Cache Creek, Feb. 28, 1847.
Mr. George McKinstry, Jr.
Sir:—

An opportunity offering to write by Mr. Glover, now in my camp and to leave for Fort Sacramento in the morning, I inform you that we reached this camp to-day at noon, it being the last point we can reach for grass— and to-morrow, Capt. Kern takes the camp back to a creek twelve miles from this place, where the grass is better for the animals, and will remain until I return to this camp with the people from the mountains. I start in the morning with four men and three mules packed with provisions.—I have cached here four hundred pounds of flour and shall carry about that quantity with me, also coffee and sugar. Mr. Glover will give you all the information about the first expedition, and I wish you to write to Capt. J. B. Hull commander of the northern district of California the information you receive from Mr. Glover, I shall not return until all the people are in camp. I shall then hasten down with them to the Fort as soon as they can travel.
                    Your's &c.
                    S. E. Woodworth
                    U. S. N.

Capt. E. Kern informed you of the men sent up from this place to the assistance of the sufferers when we were first informed of their situation. I will again give you a list of their names as I think they ought to be recorded in letters of gold: Aquila Glover, R. S. Montrey [Moutry], Daniel Rhodes, John Rhodes, Daniel Tucker, Joseph Sel, and Edward Copymier. Mr. Glover who was put in charge of this little brave band of men, returns to me his Journal, from which I extract as follows:—On the 13th of February, 1847, our party arrived at the Bear

River valley—14th remained in camp preparing packs and provisions; 15th, left Bear River valley, and travelled 15 miles and encamped on Yuba river; 16th travelled three miles and stopped to make snow shoes; 17th travelled five miles and camped on Yuba river—snow fifteen feet deep, dry and soft; 18th travelled eight miles and encamped the head of Yuba river; 19th travelled nine miles, crossed the summit of the California mountains and reached part of the suffering company about sun down, in camp near Truckey's Lake.[195] Mr. Glover informs me that he found them in a most deplorable condition, entirely beyond discription. Ten of their number had already died from starvation; and he thinks several others will die in camp, as they are too low to resusitate. The whole party had been living on bullock hides four weeks. On the morning of the 20th, the party went down to the camp of Geo. Donner eight miles below the first camp, and found them with but one hide left. They had come to the conclusion that when that was consumed to dig up the bodies of those who had died from starvation and use them as food. When the party arrived at the camp, they were obliged to guard the little stock of provision that they had carried over the mountains on their backs on foot, for the relief of the poor beings, as they were in such a starving condition, that they would have immediately used up the small store. They even stole the buckskin strings from their snow shoes and eat them. This little brave band of men, immediately left with twenty-one persons, principally women and children for the settlements. They left all the food they could spare with those (twenty nine in number) that they were obliged to leave behind; and promised them that they would immediately return to their assistance. They were successful in bringing all safe over the mountains. Four of the children they were obliged to carry on their backs—the balance walked. On their arrival at the Bear river valley, they met a small party with provisions, that Capt. Kerns of this fort had sent for their relief. The same day they met Mr. Reed with fifteen men on foot, packed with provisions, who, ere this, have reached the sufferers. Lieut. Woodworth was going ahead with a full force and will himself visit them in their mountain camp, and see that every person is brought out. Mr. Greenwood was three days behind Mr. Reed with the horses. Capt. Kern will remain in camp with the Indian soldiers to guard the provisions and horses and will send the sufferers down to this post as soon as possible, where they will be received by Capt. J. A. Sutter with all the hospitality for which he is so celebrated. And in the mean time Capt. Sutter will keep up a communication with Capt. Kern's camp, so as to be in readiness to assist him on all occasions. Mr. Glover informed me that the waggons belonging to the emigrants are buried some fifteen feet under the snow. He thinks that it will be some three weeks from this date, before Lieut. Woodworth can arrive at this fort. Mr. Glover left the party at Bear river valley on express, as I had written to him by the second party, of the death of one member of his family, and the severe illness of his wife.— The balance of the party will reach here in some four or five days. The weather is very fine, and we have no doubt but that Lieut. Woodworth will be able to bring all left on the mountains.

GEORGE MCKINSTRY.

To Capt. J. B. Hull

P. S. We have just learned that the party of Walla walla Indians that have been with Col. Fremont the past winter, arrived at their camp five miles from this fort last night. They have not yet reported themselves here.

The California Star, YERBA BUENA, MARCH 13, 1847

If we were to search the annals of human suffering for centuries past, we would not be able to find a more appalling account than is contained in the intelligence received within the last few days from the California mountains. Nearly half of those who were detained by the early fall of snow, have died from starvation; and the residue have been only snatched from the jaws of death by the indomitable courage and perseverance of a small band of brave men; who deserve the lasting gratitude of every citizen of California, for their noble conduct.

Some of the names of those who have been most active in rescuing the unfortunate emigrants are to be found in our paper to-day.

We would not allude to the causes which led to the dire misfortunes of this company of emigrants were it not for the belief that the publication of the various accounts which we have received might otherwise produce a wrong impression abroad in relation to the ability of companies starting at the proper season from Missouri, to reach the California valley before the mountains are rendered impassable by snow. All candid persons who have traveled the route, will agree with us that the trip over land from the frontier of Missouri to the Sacramento valley can be made by waggons in four months and a half, and allow sufficient time for the cattle to rest.—The company that we [Elbert P. Jones] traveled with, arrived at Fort Hall, fourteen hundred miles from the Missouri line, in less than ninety days, having laid by unnecessarily twenty-five days. We reached the California valley in sixty days from Fort Hall, distance seven hundred miles, having laid by at least twenty days unnecessarily,—making the time necessary to perform the whole journey a little less than four months. Messrs. Craig and Stanley, with two waggons, who started in the same company with us, on the first day of May last, arrived here in a few days less than four months. These facts are sufficient to show that but for a few contrary and evil disposed persons to be found in almost every company, all the emigrants using ordinary industry and care would be able to cross the mountains long before the first fall of snow. We understand that the misfortunes of the company in the mountains may be attributed to delays occasioned by that discription of persons. There are also many other causes of detention to the companies which a proper exertion on their part would remove.

The California Star, SAN FRANCISCO, MARCH 20, 1847 [196]

FROM OUR SACRAMENTO CORRESPONDENT.

Mr. E. P. Jones, Sir.—

I sent in great haste an express via Sonoma, and had no time then to write to you, of the result of the expedition sent out from this Fort for the relief of the emigrants on the California mountains. This little party of seven men, deserve great credit for their exertions.—They reached the sufferers on the 19th of February, in camp near Truckey's Lake, on the east side of the mountains, and left with twenty-one persons, principly women and children; they were successful in getting them all over the mountains; but three of them died on this side of the mountains, one of them from over eating.[197] Part of the company are now here under the care of Capt Sutter. I am told that the scene of distres[s] in their camp is indiscribable, fourteen had already died from starvation, and not more that [than] 12 or 15 of the thirty left, can be brought in, as they are too weak to walk. Lieut. Woodworth has gone to their assistance, but I am fearful from the appearance of the weather on the mountains the past four days, that they suffered much. It has been colder here than at any other time this season, and has been snowing incessantly on the mountains.

You will get the particulars from the express I sent to Capt. Hull, I write in great haste, as we have started the Launch, and the baquero is now waiting for the letters (which I send to your care) to overtake the launch by land.

[GEORGE McKINSTRY, JR.]

Californian, MONTEREY, MARCH 27, 1847

It is with feelings of the most lively gratification, that we are enabled to lay before our readers the information of the saving of nearly all of that unfortunate party of emigrants who were stopped by the snow on the California mountains, and of whom we recorded on the 13th ultimo, that nine had died of starvation out of a party of *sixteen,* who attempt[ed] to get through the snow to the settlements. Before the arrival of that sad news the Citizens, U. S. Officers and seamen at San Francisco, subscribed over $1500 to raise supplies for their releif, the citizens of Sonoma and Nappa also contributed over $400. Captain J. B. Hull Commanding the Northeren District sent Passed Mid'n S E. Woodworth U. S. N. in command of the party who were to carry over the supplies of provisions and clothing. He has Mr. Greenwood a celebrated old mountaineer (now 84 years old) for a pilot and Mr. Ried (whose wife and children were in the mountains) as assistant in Command. Mr. Woodworth met great difficulties at every step having had to warp up the Sacremento against the current for fifty miles, before he reached Sutters Fort, there he obtained the aid of that celebrated woodsman Jack Neal (the same person who performed the dashing feat of riding through the Clamet country in search of Colonel Fremont by which Capt. Gillespie's little party was saved from massacre last spring) and in four hours after Mr. Woodworth reached "Sutters Fort," his provisions were packed and they were off to the rescue—for further particulars see the following—

[*There follows George McKinstry's letter of March 5, 1847, omitting the postscript.*]

PETER QUIVVEY TO A FRIEND IN MISSOURI, "LOWER
PUEBLA," MARCH 24, 1847, CONDENSED IN THE
INDEPENDENCE *Western Expositor* [198]

The writer arrived at the first settlement in California on the 14th of October, after a very long and tiresome journey. Very soon after their arrival in California, hearing of the revolution, and that the American colors were raised, these emigrants enlisted as volunteers in a regiment formed under Col. Fremont, with the promise of twenty five dollars per month—sergeants thirty five. He speaks very favorably of the country over which he has passed, and says, that if he were now back in Missouri with his family, and with his present knowledge of the country, he would not hesitate to move there.

The charms of the country must be very great to counterbalance the difficulties which the emigrants encounter in getting there, and of which he gives some account in this letter. He went out with Moran & Boon [Josiah Morin and Alphonso Boone], who changed their minds on the route, and went to Oregon. Gov. Boggs reached California, about the same time Mr. Quivvey did, after much difficulty, having lost his cattle.

A party of emigrants, who went out, or started, with Col. Russell, suffered almost incredible hardships in the mountains last winter, having been prevented from crossing them by snow. This company was composed of twenty-three wagons and left Indian Creek on the 13th day of May 1846. About a month previous to the date of the letter, five women and two men arrived at Capt. Johnson's, the first house of California settlements, entirely naked, and their feet frost-bitten. They stated, that their company had arrived at Truckey's Lake, on the east side of the mountains, and found the snow so deep that they could not travel.

Fearing starvation, sixteen of the strongest [eleven males and five females] agreed to start for the settlements on foot. After wandering about a number of days, bewildered, their provisions gave out.—Long hunger made it necessary to cast lots to see who should be sacrificed, to make food for the rest, but at this time the weaker began to die, which rendered the taking of life unnecessary. As they died, the company went into camp and made meat of the dead bodies of their companions. Nine of the men died and seven were eaten. One of the men was carried to Johnson's on the back of an Indian.

From this statement, it would seem that the women endured the hardships better than the men, as none of them died. The company left behind numbered sixty souls, ten of them men, the others women and children. They were in camp about one hundred miles from Johnson's. Revolting as it may seem, it is stated that one of the women was obliged to eat part of the dead body of her father and brother, and another saw her husband's heart cooked! It ought to be a very fine country to justify an exposure to such suffering and horrors.[199]

Benjamin [Benoni] Hudspeth had been appointed Captain of a company in the California Battalion, with a salary of $120 per month.

The writer says that Gen. Kearney was then Governor and Commander-in-Chief of Upper and Lower California.

The California Star, SAN FRANCISCO, APRIL 3, 1847

The following report of Lt. S. E. Woodworth, U. S. Navy, who had command of the party of men sent to the relief of the emigrants in the mountains, exhibits the result of the labors of the expedition. He has accomplished more than could have been expected under the circumstances:[200]

To the Editor of the Star.

San Francisco, April 1st. 1847.

Sir.—

I have but this moment arrived in Capt. Sutter's launch from Fort Sacramento, after a passage of $2\frac{1}{2}$ days, and learning that your paper is about going to press, I hasten to drop you a few lines.

Mr. McKinstry has already informed you of the result of the last expedition, in which I brought in 17 of the sufferers. In my last report from the mountains, I stated that one of my men by the name of [Nicholas] "Clark" (one of the men left at the cabins by Mr. Reed) was lost in the snow storm, in which Mr. Reed and party suffered so severely. I am happy to state that he was rescued by the last party of 5 men, that I sent—he had succeeded in killing a bear and had subsisted upon the meat until the day before the timely aid arrived, and has come in safely as also 5 others from the Cabins; Likewise 11 of the 14 persons left by Mr. Reed on the road, viz: Mr. Brinn, wife and 5 children, and 3 children of Mr. Graves, one of which was an infant at the breast, and Mary Donner, a girl about 11 years of age; three of the latter children having been packed on the backs of [Howard] Oakley, [John] Stark and [Charles] Stone; the other 5, were 3 children of Mr. Geo. Donner, between the age of 1 and 4 year,—girls; John Baptiste a spanish boy in the employment of Mr. Donner, and Simon Murphy a boy of 6 years of age.[201]

The persons left on the road by Mr. Reed, were Brinn, wife and 5 children, Mrs. Graves and 4 children, Mary Donner and Isaac Donner. The day that Mr. Reed left them, the boy Isaac Donner died, and the same night Mrs. Graves and 1 of her children died; the remaining sufferers continued two days without food, but on the 3d day were obliged to resort to the only alternative,—that of eating the dead; they commenced on the two children, and when my party reached them, which was the 5th day, they were eating Mrs. Graves, they had already eaten the "breast, heart, liver and lungs" of Mrs Graves, when a timely supply of food and assistance reached them.— the night previous, Mary Donner fell in the fire and burned her foot so severely that amputation will be necessary in order to save life.

I have hastened down here, with some of the sufferers that required immediate medical attendance. Among them are two of my men, Henry Dann [Dunn] and Charles Cady, with feet badly frozen. I have brought Mary Donner and her brother down that they may obtain medical aid; the spanish boy John Baptiste and Howard Oakly came down with them as nurses.

When I left the mountains there were still remaining

at the cabins, Mr Kiesbury and Geo. Donner the only two men; Mrs Geo Donner, one child, and Mrs Murphy,—Mrs. Murphy, Mr Donner and the child could not survive many days when left, but Mrs Donner and Kiesbury could subsist upon the remaining bodies yet some ten days. The snow at the Cabins was going off rapidly; but in Bear Valley and on the Juba River it was yet 20 feet deep on the level.

When I arrived at Johnson's, on the 23d, I found a letter from Mr. McKinstry, stating that the bearer, J. Sel, as also D. [*i. e.,* Reasin P.] Tucker, John Rhodes and E. Caffemeyer, were willing to return to the Cabins, and endeavor to save the remaining few. I immediately organized another party consisting of John Rhodes, John Stark, E. Caffemeyer, John [*i. e.,* Joseph] Sel and Dan'l. Tucker, Mr. Foster and the son of Mrs. Greaves volunteering to return with them, and despatched them immediately, furnishing them horses, provisions, &c., and I hope ere this that they have succeeded in saving at least two of those remaining there; the other three, Geo. Donner, Mrs. Murphy and the child I do not think can be saved, even should they be alive, as it will be impossible to remove them, they being so very feeble, and otherwise ill. When I arrived at Fort Sacremento, I despatched Wm. Thompson to meet the party on their return, with a fresh supply of coffee, sugar, cocoa, &c.[202]

Since the 28th of February I have been twenty four days in the snow, I may say, without seeing land—have travelled over 140 miles on the snow, on foot, carrying a pack on my back,—have crossed Bear River Mountains four times,—have been twice over on Juba River, and can say that I never onjoyed better health, but have suffered a little from the cold, and rather hard fare. I herewith subjoin a schedule of the persons saved, and those that have perished since the original party first arrived at the foot of the California Mountains, and were overtaken by the snows.

The whole party consisted of 81 souls.

Started with Eddy & Foster, 16,—came in, 7
    "   "   Glover, - - - - - 21,   "   " 19
    "   "   Reed, - - - - - - 17,   "   "   3
Came in with myself, - - - - - - - - - - - - 16
                                            ——
                                    Total, 45.

Thus you will perceive, that through the instrumentality of the expedition fitted out for the relief of the sufferers, 38 souls have been rescued from inevitable death, and at least 2 others, making in all 40; and relief has been afforded to the whole number, 45 persons, Yet it has not been effected without great suffering and hardships by the men employed in this arduous duty. Mr. Reed has suffered much himself from frost and over-exertion, having carried one of his children over the snows on his back.

As I shall be obliged to return again to the "Fort." I will forward to you immediately upon the arrival of the party now out, the result of their labors.

In haste I must conclude very respectfully.

                          S. E. WOODWORTH,
                           P's. M'D. U. S. N.
Com'dg. Expedition to the California Mountains.[203]

The California Star, SAN FRANCISCO, APRIL 10, 1847

The following lines are from the journal of Mr. John Denton, one of the unfortunate emigrants who perished during the past winter in the California Mountains. He was found dead on the mountain, having made an effort, with a few others, to cross. His journal was taken from his pocket and brought in. It is said to contain many interesting items in relation to the route from Missouri to the California Mountains, and a graphic description of the sufferings of the unfortunate party, of which he was a member. The journal will probably in a few weeks be placed in our hands.[204]

Oh! after many Roving Years.
Oh! after many roving years,
How sweet it is to come
To the dwelling-place of early youth,
Our first and dearest home.
To turn away our wearied eyes,
From proud ambition's towers,
And wander in those summer fields,—
The scene of boyhood's hours.

But I am changed since last I gazed
On yonder tranquil scene,
And sat beneath the old witch-elm
That shades the village green;
And watched my boat upon the brook—
As it were a regal galley,
And sighed not for a joy on earth
Beyond the happy valley.

I wish I could recall once more
That bright and blissful joy,
And summon to my weary heart
The feelings of a boy.
But I look on scenes of past delight
Without my wonted pleasures,
As a miser on the bed of death
Looks coldly on his treasures.

The California Star, San Francisco, April 10, 1847

A more shocking scene cannot be imagined, than that witnessed by the party of men who went to the relief of the unfortunate emigrants in the California Mountains. The bones of those who had died and been devoured by the miserable ones that still survived, were lying around their tents and cabins. Bodies of men, women, and children, with half the flesh torn from them, lay on every side. A woman sat by the body of her husband, who had just died, cutting out his tongue; the heart she had already taken out, broiled, and eat! The daughter was seen eating the flesh of the father—the mother that of her children—children that of father and mother. The emaciated, wild, and ghastly appearance of the survivors, added to the horror of the scene. Language cannot describe the awful change that a few weeks of dire suffering had wrought in the minds of these wretched and pitiable beings. Those who but one month before would have shuddered and sickened at the thought of eating human flesh, or of killing their companions and relatives to preserve their own lives, now looked upon the opportunity by these acts afforded them of escaping the most dreadful of deaths, as a providential interference in their behalf.—Calculations were coldly made, as they sat gloomily around their gloomy camp fires, for the next and succeeding meals. Various expedients were devised to prevent the dreadful crime of murder, but they finally resolved to kill those who had the least claims to longer existence. Just at this moment however, as if by Divine interposition, some of them died, which afforded the rest temporary relief. Some sunk into the arms of death cursing God for their miserable fate, while the last whisperings of others were prayers and songs of praise to the Almighty.

After the first few deaths, but the one all absorbing thought of individual self-preservation prevailed. The fountains of natural affection were dried up. The cords that once vibrated with connubial, parental and filial affection were rent asunder, and each one seemed resolved without regard to the fate of others to escape from the impending calamity. Even the wild hostile mountain Indians, who once visited their camps, pitied them, and instead of pursuing the natural impulse of their hostile feelings to the whites, and destroying them as they could easily have done, divided their own scanty supply of food with them.

So changed had the emigrants become that when the

party sent out, arrived with food, some of them cast it aside and seemed to prefer the putrid human flesh that still remained. The day before the party arrived, one of the emigrants took a child of about four years of age in bed with him, and devoured the whole before morning; and the next day eat another about the same age before noon.

It is thought that several more of these unfortunate people might have been saved, but for their determination not to leave their property. Some of them who started in, loaded themselves with their money and other effects to such an extent, that they sunk under them and died on the road. According to the best accounts, forty-three died from starvation. They were principally from the neighborhood of Independence, Missouri.[205]

Californian, Monterey, April 24, 1847

THE FATE OF THE LAST EMIGRANTS, — We conversed freely with Mr. Woodworth and with some of the men who accompanied him to the Mountain for the relief of the suffering people who had been stoped in the snow, as well as with some of the persons who were rescued. It is a most horrid picture of human misery: such as has not been witnessed since the siege of Jerusalem. It could not be gratifying to our readers to detail all the horrers and sufferings of that unfortunate company, but one fact is to[o] remarkable to pass without particular notice.

It is said by Jewish historians, that parents subsisted upon the bodies of their children, in time of the siege by Titus: if true, it was so much like fiction or exaggeration, that it was with difficulty that we could bring the mind to bear upon such a thought! But in the case of the sufferers in the Mountains, mothers possessing portions of their dead companions, refused to divide it with their own children, while *alive,* and when the children died, actually devoured the bodies of their own offspring!

Truly the "mother may forget her sucking child."

It is our duty to sum up the facts, and show *why* this company was so late in crossing the Mountain.

Many of the persons belonging to this company, were among the first who started from the States, but one little trouble after another induced them to fall back, the companies behind gathering one or two at a time, of those who could not, or would not keep up with their own companies, so that this last company was formed mostly of the discontented and unfortunate of all the companies before them. Some of them lost their teams by the Indians, others, on the dry planes, all combined with a want of proper energy on the part of the people, threw them back to the first of November before they reached the mountain. The snow, last winter fell at least *one month earlier than usual,* and *two* months earlier than the year before, when we [Robert Semple, in Lansford W. Hastings' party] crossed on the 18th of *December,* found little or no snow, and good weather up to the 22d, when it commenced raining in the valley, and probably snowing on the mountain.

Persons starting from Missouri, can always reach the Sacramento valley before the first of November. The first waggons arrived early in September, last year.

The California Star, SAN FRANCISCO, MAY 22, 1847

[We publish below an interesting communication, together with a journal written by one of the late emigration, detained by the snows on the Sierra Nevada. Owing to its length, we have omitted several paragraphs of minor importance, nothing of a tendency to affect its interest, however. For these and other documents we are indebted to Mr. Geo. McKinstry Jr.]

[Publishers of Cal. Star.]

New Helvetia, April 29, 1847.

Gent.—

As the last member of the unfortunate emigrating company has arrived from the California Mountains, I have thought proper to send to you for publication in your valuable paper, the 'Star,' the name of every member of the company, those that have arrived in the valley, and those that died from fatigue and starvation. I also enclose a copy of a journal kept by one of the sufferers (now at this fort) during the past winter in that horrid mountain camp; the gentleman that kept the journal also furnished me with the list of names, and has taken great pains to make it correct. I copy his diary verbatim, and I think it will give the friends and public a correct idea of the manner that they spent the last winter on the frightful mountains.

By publishing on receipt of this, you will have ample time to send your mail here to be forwarded by the pack company that leaves for the States this Spring, as Mr. [William O.] Fallon, an old mountain man, who has just returned from the mountains, informs me that the mountains cannot be crossed with horses for some six weeks, as the snow is deeper than ever known before.[206] When this melancholy news reaches the United States, it must create great excitement, and hundreds will mourn the loss of relatives; and I presume emigrants from the United States would like copies of your paper containing a correct statement of the affair to send to their friends at home. When Lieut. Woodworth and myself were in your town, we informed you that a party had been sent to bring out the last of the sufferers, four in number, viz., Geo. Donner and wife, Mrs. Murphy and Mr. Kiesburg; the party went as far as the base of the mountain, and found the snow so deep they could not cross, and returned. Since that time, a party of seven men succeeded in getting to the camp; they found all dead excepting Mr. Kiesburg, who they brought, with some seven hundred pounds of specie and dry goods, to the valley. Mr. K. is now at the fort in a very emaciated state, having subsisted on human flesh alone some two months. The snow has melted from the valley where the company encamped during the winter, and presents an

awful spectacle; the ground is strewed with the skulls
and bones of the dead, and the carcasses of horses, mules,
and oxen that have been buried with snow the past winter. Out of eighty persons, thirty-six have died from
fatigue and hunger! The most melancholy death was that
of Mr. Charles T. Stanton, of Syracuse, N. Y., a merchant of that city. I became acquainted with him on the
road soon after leaving the States, and travelled with
him as far as Fort Laramie, at which place I left the
wagon company and packed through; I found him one
of the most kind hearted and gentlemanly men I ever
met with. As I stated in one of my former letters to you,
he left the company at the Great Salt Lake, travelling
with but one other man several hundred miles over mountains and deserts, and through hostile Indian tribes, he
reached this place about the first of October, and asked
the assistance of Capt. Sutter for the suffering company.
Capt. S. furnished him with seven mules loaded with
provisions, and two Indians, he immediately returned
alone to the company, and met them at the crossing of
Mary's river on Trucky's Lake. Had it not been for his
disinterested sympathy for those unfortunate beings, all
must have perished long before our first party sent from
this fort to their assistance reached them; the company
reached within three miles of the summit of the mountain,
and found the snow too deep to travel, and on the 31st
day of October forty six returned to Truckey's Lake,
and went into winter quarters; Mr. Stanton made several unsuccessful attempts to cross the mountains with
Capt. Sutter's Indians and mules, and on the 16th Dec.
he started in company with fifteen others on foot for the
valley; after traveling five days, Mr. S. became snow-
blind and did not reach camp at night, the next morning,
the company being short of provisions, and lost in the
snow, started without searching for their lost companion,
and he was left to die on the fathomless snow of the
Sierra Nevada. Before leaving the fort to return to the
assistance of the company, he left a vest in charge of

Capt. Sutter; since his death, we have found in one of
the pockets a small package directed to Capt. S., with
memoranda as follows: "Capt. Sutter will send the within, in the event of my death, to Sidney Stanton, Syracuse, N. Y." Enclosed was a diamond breast-pin, with a
note from his sister directed to him at Chicago, from
which I extract as follows: "Sidney has requested me to
do up your breast-pin and send to you, so you perceive
I have done it up in a piece of newspaper. * * * * May
God bless you my dear brother! A——— S———.''[207]

The only article on the piece of newspaper was the
following translation from the French. It does not appear from her letter that the paper was selected on account of the poetry, but as it appears to [be] peculiarly
appropriate to the occasion I enclose copy.

Translated from the French for the *True Sun*.

THE WITHERED FLOWER.
Oh! dying flow'r that droop'st alone,
    Erewhile the valley's pride,
Thy wither'd leaves, disordered strown,
    Rude winds sweep far and wide.

The scythe of Time, whose stroke we mourn,
    Our common doom shall bring;
From thee a faded leaf is torn,
    From us a joy takes wing.

As Life glides by; oh! who but feels
    Some sense, some charm decay?—
E'en ev'ry fleeting moment steals
    Some treasured dream away.

Some secret blight each hope destroys,
    Till at length we ask in grief,
If, than life's ephemeral joys
    The flowret's be more brief.

I immediately informed his brother of the melancholy event, and deeply sympathized with the family for the irreparable loss of an affectionate brother.

It is the opinion of the party just returned from the emigrant camp on the mountain, that it will be impossible to cross these mountains until the middle of June. The water is so high that Messrs. Craig and company, who advertised to rendezvous here previous to their departure for the U. States, have not been able to get here from Sonoma.[208] We despatched two couriers some few days since for San Francisco, via Sonoma, but they were obliged to return, as the road is impassable; the Sacremento, American Fork and other tributaries, are higher than they have been for some years. The Wheat crop looks very promising in this section of country, and from appearance will be much larger than any ever raised for previous years. Yours, &c.,

GEO. MCKINSTRY, JR.

[*There follows the text of the Patrick Breen diary, under the heading, "Copy of a Journal kept by a suffering Emigrant on the California Mountains, from Oct. 31st, 1846, to March 1st, 1847." Following the diary are these remarks*:]

The above mentioned ten men started for the valley with seventeen of the sufferers, they traveled 15 miles and a severe snow storm came on;—they left fourteen of the emigrants, the writer of the above journal and his family, and succeeded in getting in but three children. Lieut. Woodworth immediately went to their assistance, but before he reached them they had eaten three of their number, who had died from hunger, and fatigue; the remainder, Lieut. Woodworth's party brought in. On the 29th of April 1847, the last member of that party was brought to Capt. Sutters Fort: it is utterly impossible to give any description of the sufferings of the company.—Your readers can form some idea of them by perusing the above diary. Yours &c.

GEORGE MCKINSTRY JR.

NAMES OF THE LATE EMIGRATION FROM THE U. S., WHO
WERE PREVENTED BY THE SNOW FROM CROSSING
THE CALIFORNIA MOUNTAINS, OCT. 31ST, 1846.[209]

ARRIVED IN CALIFORNIA.

William Graves,
Sarah Fosdick,
Mary Graves,
Ellen [Eleanor] Graves,
Viney [Lavina] Graves,
Nancy Graves,
Jonathan Graves,
Elizabeth Graves,
Loithy [Elitha] Donner,
Lean [Leanna] Donner,
Francis [Frances] Donner,
Georgeana Donner,
Eliza Donner,
John [Trubode] Battiste,
Solomon Hook,
Geo. Donner, Jun.
Mary Donner,
Mrs. [Doris] Woolfinger,
Lewis Kiesburg,
Mrs [Philippine] Kiesburg,
William Foster,
Sarah Foster,

Simon Murphy,
Mary Murphy,
Harriet Pike,
Miomin [Naomi] Pike,
Wm. Eddy,
Patrick Breen,
Margaret Breen,
John Breen,
Edward Breen,
Patrick Breen, Jr.
Simon Breen,
James Breen,
Peter Breen,
Isabella Breen,
Eliza Williams,
James F. Reed,
Mrs. [Margret] Reed,
Virginia Reed,
Martha Reed,
James Reed,
Thomas Reed,
Noah James.
[Amanda McCutchen]

PERISHED IN THE MOUNTAINS.

C. T. Stanton,
Mr. [Franklin Ward]
  Graves,
Mrs. [Elizabeth] Graves,
Mr. J[ay]. Fosdick,
Franklin Graves [Jr.],
John Denton,
Geo. Donner, Sen.
Mrs. [Tamsen] Donner,

Bertha Kiesburg, (child)
Lewis Kiesburg,
Mrs. [Lavina] Murphy,
Lemuel Murphy,
George Foster,
Catherine Pike,
Ellen [Eleanor] Eddy,
Margurette [Margaret]
  Eddy,

Charles Berger,
Joseph Rhinehart,
Jacob Donner,
Betsey Donner,
Wm. Johnson [*i.e.,* Hook],
Isaac Donner,
Lewis Donner,
Samuel Donner,
Samuel Shoemaker,
James Smith,
Ba[y]lis Williams,

James Eddy,
Patrick Dolan,
Augustus Spitzer,
Milton [Milford] Elliot,
Lantron [Landrum]
    Murphy,
Mr. [William M.] Pike.
Antonio, [New Mexican]
Lewis, (Sutter's Indian)
Salvadore, do   do
[Harriet McCutchen]

The California Star, SAN FRANCISCO, MAY 22, 1847

CALIFORNIA EMIGRANTS. — The disastrous calamity which befel the emigration, the mortality and the dire sufferings of the miserable survivers, who have passed through an ordeal more terrific, than either fire or water—that of starvation, will create much sensation throughout the States whenever the tidings of this thrilling event become fully known. We have this day published a journal, which possesses great interest, and also, in another column, the names of both the survivers and the dead. But, notwithstanding the distress recorded in the diary, and the thrilling scenes heretofore published of that lamentable affair, we do not consider that one half is, or ever will appear in print, nor the *full* story of their sufferings ever be related. It does not exist in language, and imagination alone can supply the defect. The agony of mind, the dim hope of succor, succeeded by despair, frenzy, and the crushed reliance in relief, never appear on the cold pages of the journal, nor are the most sympathetic capable of pourtraying this, the anguish of the soul.—When the long night came down, and yet the driving snow heaped impenetrable drifts about them, the last little fuel is added to the miserable fire, and closing around it, they indulge in idle questioning, or surmising upon their approaching, and apparently inevitable fate, or resign themselves, in gloomy silence, to the tortures of thought.—Day after day passed, and the scanty supply of food rapidly diminishes,—hunger more and [more] keenly oppresses, and at length the last remaining hide is divided and devoured, then

> "You might see
> The longings of the cannibal arise,
> (Although they spoke not,) in their wolfish eyes!"

Their situation becomes known, and relief is extended to the survivers. Forty four arrived in safety at their travel's end,—lost in every thing that renders life desirable and blessed—helpless, emaciated and distressed, dependant on the sympathies of strangers for even their daily bread.

When this sad intelligence reaches the States, it will, we apprehend, occasion a considerable dimunition in the emigration to California for a few years to come; but we trust however it will be productive of a good result, in awakening the authorities of the Union to the actual necessity of another and a better road to this country, until which is effected, a yearly occurrence of similar mishaps may be expected, and emigration, at length, entirely ceases, for the difficulties and dangers are too appalling for even the bold and energetic emigrant to face, and he defers his "heart's wishes" in hopes of a better and more practicable route to California.

Oregon Spectator, MAY 13, 1847

IMMIGRANTS TO OREGON.—As this is possibly the last paper that will be published before the various parties returning to the States will have started, we deem it a duty to say a few words to the immigrants to this country, who will probably receive this paper in the valley of the Sweetwater, or on Platte river. We would advise the immigrants after recruiting upon Sweetwater to take Greenwood's "cut off" into Bear River valley, by doing which they will save a detour of several days journey through rocky ravines almost destitute of grass and water.

After resting several hours and filling their kegs at the
last water, which is called "Big Sandy," they had better
commence the "cut off" about four o'clock in the afternoon and they will reach the next water about noon of
the next day. Some forty miles this side of fort Hall,
they will strike what is termed the Southern Route into
the Willamette valley; they will exercise their pleasure
about taking this road, or the old one, after a plain nar-
ration of facts. The old road to the Dalles of the Columbia and across the Cascade Mountains is difficult, with
a scarcity of grass. Nevertheless the first wagons of the
last immigration which traveled it, reached this city on
the 13th day of September, at least two months earlier
than any previous immigration.

It was about the centre of the immigration last year
that turned into the new or Southern route to Oregon.
Much of the road had to be made and the difficulties and
detentions incident thereto were in a great measure the
occasion of the unfortunate results that followed. Of perhaps one hundred wagons that were on the road about
twenty succeeded in reaching the first settlement before
winter set in with such severity as to compel the immigrants to leave the remainder of their wagons, with much
valuable property, and push for the settlements in the
most expeditious manner possible. From personal knowledge, we know nothing of this road, it is said to be abundantly supplied with grass and water, yet it is but fair
to remark that there is a diversity of opinion existing in
the minds of those who have traveled it concerning its
advantages. Numerous fortuitous circumstances transpired last year to its prejudice. We have no hesitation in
saying that we believe there will ultimately be a Southern
road that will be traveled into the Willamette valley.[210]
Facts however, and the transpiration of events, with your
own judgment, we would say to the immigrants, must
determine you in the choice of routes. When you have
chosen, push steadily on and do not stop to wrangle or
dispute about it. Make the most of your time, without

taxing your teams beyond their strength or endeavoring
to be the first upon the road, for it has so happened that
the first in starting have been last in getting in. There
is plenty of excellent land in our Territory, so much of
it indeed that you need not *rush* yourselves into difficulties in order to obtain the first choice. Let harmony and
good feeling prevail among you, and with resolution and
perseverance we do not doubt but that you will overcome
all difficulties in your way, and safely arrive at the end
of your journey.

The Gazette, St. Joseph, August 27, 1847

SUPPOSED LOSS OF EMIGRANTS.

Mr. S. L. Campbell, late from Oregon,[211] has furnished
us the following list of persons supposed to have been
murdered by the Indians, on the southern route to Oregon. This company left St. Joseph under Capt. Smith,
and were joined at the north fork of Platte river by a
company of six wagons from Independence. They separated near Independence Rock, where the hindmost company took what is called the Southern route, and travelled
it some distance. About this time a portion of emigrants
becoming dissatisfied with the route, a council was held
whether to proceed onward or return. In the mean time
a paper was found signed by several persons in Oregon,
urging all the emigrants to take this route, as it was some
300 miles nearer, besides a much better road. Notwithstanding this several persons refused to travel the road
any further, and returned back.[212]

Those that attempted to go through have never been
heard of since, only by the Indians at the Dalls, who state
that a party of Oregon emigrants were killed on this
route. Mr Campbell was personally acquainted with a
number of persons in this company, a list of which follows:—Col. [Mathew D.] Richie and family of 11 persons, from Henderson co., Illinois; J. Starkes and family,
of 5 persons, from Henderson co., Ill. Mr. [Reasin P.]

Tucker and family of 7 persons, from Rock Island, Ill. Job and Jonathan Parr and families of 11 persons, from Lee co., Iowa. Mr. [Franklin Ward] Graves and family of 11 persons from Peoria, Ill. Mr. [John ?] McCracken and family of 5 persons, from Wapello co., Iowa. Wm. Daniels and family of 4 persons, from Jefferson, co. Iowa. Mr. Bothe and family of 6 persons, from Lee co., Iowa. John Lenox and family of 5 persons, from Indiana. Mr. [Isaac ?] Howell and family of 12 persons from Hannibal, and John Bowles from Galena, Ill.

From this, it will be seen that near one hundred persons have been murdered by the Indians or have perished for want of food, and all owing to the false representations of a few heartless speculators, who may wish to benefit themselves at the expense of several valuable lives. The emigrants inform us that these men have property in certain parts of Oregon, and by forcing the emigration to a particular point, they are benefited thereby. Emigrants cannot be too careful in taking new roads, unless experience has proven them to be practicable.

Californian, SAN FRANCISCO, MAY 17, 1848

SUPPOSED LOSS OF EMIGRANTS.—We find the following in a Boston paper, copied from the St. Joseph's *Herald* [*i.e., Gazette*]:

Mr. S. L. Campbell, late from Oregon, has furnished us the following list of persons supposed to have been murdered by the Indians on the southern route to Oregon:—Colonel Richie and family, of 11 persons, from Henderson county, Illinois; J. Starkes and family, of 5 persons, from Henderson county, Illinois; Mr. Tucker and family, of 5 persons, Rock Island, Illinois; Job and Jonathan Parr and families of 11 persons, from Lee county, Iowa; Mr. Graves and family of 11 persons, from Peora, Illinois; Mr McCracken and family of 5 persons from Wapel county, Iowa; William Daniels and family of 4 persons, from Jefferson county, Iowa; Mr Booth and family, of 6 persons, from Lee county, Iowa; John Lenox and family of 5 persons from Indiana; Mr Howell and family of 12 persons, from Hannibal, and John Bowles, from Galena, Illinois.[213]

For the information of the friends of the above named persons in the United States, we will state that we are personally acquainted with them, and that they have all safely arrived in California in due season, are doing well and are highly pleased with the country; with the exception of Mr. Graves and family, who attached themselves to Captain Reed's company to take a supposed "cut-off," and were caught in the snow of the California Mountains, in which himself and part of his family shared the fate of that unfortunate company.

The Shively Guide

ROUTE
AND
DISTANCES
TO
OREGON AND CALIFORNIA,
WITH A DESCRIPTION OF
WATERING-PLACES, CROSSINGS, DANGEROUS
INDIANS, &c. &c.
BY J. M. SHIVELY.
WASHINGTON, D.C.
WM. GREER, PRINTER
1846.

THE
ROAD TO OREGON AND CALIFORNIA,
ACROSS THE ROCKY MOUNTAINS.

When the emigrants start to the sun-down diggings of Oregon, they should not fancy that they are doing some great thing, and that they need military array, officers, non-commissioned officers, &c: all this is folly. They will quarrel, and try to enforce non-essential duties. till the company will divide and subdivide, the whole way to Oregon. When you start over these wide plains, let no one leave dependent on his best friend for any thing; for if you do, you will certainly have a blow-out before you get far. I would advise all young men who have no families to have nothing to do with the wagons nor stock. Buy two horses and two good mules in your own neighborhood; for if you depend upon getting animals on the frontier, you will have to pay very high for them; make your way to Independence with your provisions—such as cannot be obtained at Independence; here get pair-fleshes [parfleches] for your pack-mules, enough of flour and bacon to season it, to last you to Fort Hall; proceed to the Spanish encampment, twenty miles on the Santa Fe road, and swap your horses for Indian horses, and be not too particular; for the shabbiest Shawnee pony you can pick up will answer your purpose better than the finest horse you can take from the stable. Thus equipped, 25 or more, with a riding horse and pack-mule to change every day, the trip can be made in 70 or 80 days. Take with you plenty of horse-shoes and nails, a hammer and clincher, and keep your animals shod. If any

734

of your animals give out, leave them, for your time is of more value than all your horses; and be assured that soon as you arrive in the settlements you will find profitable employment. Go well armed, and never let your guns get out of order; and, to avoid accident, carry them without caps. Take no tents with you, nor any thing of weight that you can dispense with. It will be necessary to keep watch nearly all the way, particularly through the Pawnee country; that is, from the crossing of Big Blue to the crossing of South Platte. The Sioux will not likely molest you in any way; let your watches be divided so as to fall equally on each; but, should any one refuse to bear his part, the best mode of punishment is for some one to fill his place without grumbling. Should you discover danger from Indians, travel at the top of the speed of your animals, till you get through their territory, when you can stop and recruit your animals. You should take with you an iron pan, the handle so jointed as to fold up; a kind of knife, fork, and spoon, that all shut in one handle—such knives are common in all hardware stores. In addition to this, you will need a fire-proof iron kettle, to make tea, coffee, boil rice, make soup, &c.; a tin pan, quart cup and a butcher knife, will about complete your kitchen; delay no time to kill game, unless it comes in your way, which will frequently happen along the road from the time you strike the Platte till you reach Fort Hall. At the Kansas crossings you will find a ferry; if the Platte should be high, make a bull-boat, which is made in the following manner: procure two buffalo skins, sew them together water-tight; then get willow poles and make a frame; over which stretch your skins, and your boat is done. Should Green river be high, you will find plenty of dead cotton wood to make a raft: no other water courses will be in your way. Wagons and stock had better cross Snake river, on account of grass; those on horseback had better keep down on the south side.

Those who emigrate with families, and consequently, wagons, stock, etc., cannot expect to accomplish the journey in less than four months, under the most favorable circumstances; and, in order that they be prepared in the best possible manner, first buy a light strong wagon, made of the best seasoned materials; for, if the timbers be not well seasoned, your wagon will fall to pieces when you get to the dry, arid plains of the mountains; let the bed of your wagon be made of maple if you can get it, and let the side and end boards be one wide board, without cracks; let them so project the sides and ends of the bottom of the bed as to turn off the water from the bottom. Next, let your wagon sheet be either linen or Osnaburg, well oiled or painted, and fixed to fasten well down the sides; let the bed be straight, procure wooden boxes of half or three-quarter inch pine boards, of the same convenient height, and let them fit tight in the bed of your wagon. In these boxes place your provisions, clothing, ammunition, and whatever articles you choose to take along; close the boxes by hinges or otherwise, and on them is a comfortable place for women and children to ride through the day, secure from dust or rain, and a place to sleep at night for a small family. Take as much tea, coffee, sugar and spices as you please; but above all take plenty of flour and well cured side bacon to last you through if you can. Let each man and lad be provided with five or six hickory shirts, one or two pair of buckskin pantaloons, a buckskin coat or hunting shirt, two very wide brimmed hats, wide enough to keep the mouth from the sun. For the want of such hat thousands suffer nearly all the way to Oregon, with their lips ulcerated, caused by sunburn. Take enough of coarse shoes or boots to last you through —three or four pair a-piece will be sufficient—moccasins will not protect your feet against the large plains of prickly pear along the road. However much help your wives and daughters have been to you at home, they can do but little for you here—herding stock, through either dew, dust, or rain, breaking brush, swimming rivers, attacking grizzly bears or savage Indians, is all out of their line of business. All they can do, is to cook for camps, etceteras, &c.; nor need they have any wearing apparel, other than their ordinary clothing at home.

Thus equipped, let your team be light oxen from three to five years old,—and if you take horses for servitude along the road, trade for Indian horses in the Shawnee nation before you start over the plains; mules will serve you well, if you can get them.—Proceed on your way to the Spanish encampment, as before directed, and here your journey across the plains must commence. You should be ready to take up your march as early as the first of April; and if there is no grass, carry enough of feed for your animals to last you to the crossing of the Kanzas, which is 102 miles from Independence; here you will find the grass quite high. See before you start that you have forgotten nothing; and if you have much money, buy some Indian trade, such as small beads of different colors, cotton handkerchiefs, cheap red ribands, mocasin awls, &c.

All equipped, move on in companies of not less than twenty, nor more than fifty wagons together. You will leave this early, and travel in haste until you reach the Platte, for the reason that the district of country along the Kanzas has many creeks putting into it, which are swollen to very great depth, by the hardest rains I ever seen. Should you take the advice above, you will have passed over the districts of those tumbling floods before they commence. I will instance that the emigration of '43 arrived at a small stream, not more than a foot deep; they struck camp without crossing; it raised in the night, and they were there seventeen days before they could get across.

Keep your guns in good order, but never have caps on them unless you are going to shoot; when you come in from your hunt, be sure to take your cap off before you put your gun in the wagon. There are many graves along the road, occasioned by the accidental discharge of guns being put away with caps on; flint locks are always dangerous, and should never be taken along.—Forty miles from Independence, take the right hand road, which is the long road to Oregon—there is wood and water plenty,—so you can camp where you please. When you arrive at the crossings of the Kanzas, if it be past fording, there is a ferry there; or, if you choose, caulk and pitch some of your wagon beds, made as before described, and you have a ferry of your own. When you get across, it will be necessary to set a watch at night— and this watch should be kept up nearly the whole way—for where there are no Indians, a guard is necessary to keep the stock out of camp. You will find your cattle, horses and mules will often take fright at night, and run into camp with great fury; this is no particular sign of Indians, and is an occurrence you will often witness. Form a circle or square with your wagons at night, by running the tongue of each hinder wagon between the hind wheel and bed of the wagon before, alternately; chain them together, and you have a secure breast-work against attack by Indians, as well as a secure place to cook, sleep, &c.

Your road to the Platte passes along the north side of the Kanzas, some distance from the river, crossing many of its tributaries; 202 miles from the crossings of Kanzas—wood and water any where—you will come to the river Platte. There the whole face of nature begins to change; the earth in many places is crested with salt—the few springs you meet with are impregnated with mixed minerals—the pools are many of them poisonous—and the emigrants should be care-ful, and use only the water of the river; for I know of but two good springs from the head of Blue to the north spring branches of Sweet Water; one is at Scott's bluff on North Platte—the other the well known Willow Springs, between the crossings of North Platte and Sweet Water. You will have several camps to make along this river, without wood; but there is plenty of buffalo dung, which is a good substitute for wood. 184 miles will bring you to the forks; you keep up the South Fork 75 miles to the crossings—(plenty of buffalo and antelope)—if it is past fording, off with some of your best wagon beds, and in less than two hours you will have a very good ferry boat. When you are across the river, fill your kegs with water—for there is none fit to drink 'till you reach the North fork, a distance of 20 miles, 143 miles up North Platte to Fort Larima, up a valley similar to the South fork, (thousands of buffalo.) You are now through the Pawnee country, and must look out for the Sioux; and when you get to Larima, make as little delay as possible, for fear the Indians molest you.

You are now 640 miles from Independence, and it is discouraging to tell you that you have not yet travelled one-third of the long road to Oregon. Be off from Larima 12 miles to a spring at the foot of the Black Hills; about 4 days will take you through these dreary hills; and you again come to North Platte. Keep up the stream to the red butes, cross and fill your kegs,—for it is 20 miles to any water fit to drink,—fill your kegs again at the Willow Springs. 20 miles will bring you to the Independence rock on Sweet Water—830; here, a little to your right, is a great basin of Salaratus, white as snow; fill your bags with it—it is very good for use, and quite scarce in Oregon— up Sweet Water one hundred and two miles, where you leave it. Your next camp, seventeen miles, will be at a spring in the mountain pass, which runs towards the Pacific; fifteen miles brings you to Little Sandy. The road here turns down south, and the traveller must lose at least 100 miles by keeping it to Bridger's fort; here, on Sandy, let your animals rest a few days. Get on your horse and ride back on the road, far enough to get a view of the country westward. You will see a blue mountain in the distance, straight on your course; that mountain is on Bear river, near your track; take a pocket compass and a small party, and see if you can get through with the wagons. I was one of the company that made the road to Bridger's, and opposed it all I could. There is no use in going that way; they have no provisions, nor anything else that you want. Should you fail to find a route for wagons to Bear river, keep down Sandy along the wagon road, 65 miles, to Green river; cross it, as before instructed; keep down Green river 6 miles, and fill your kegs, and cross over to Ham's fork, 16 miles; up Ham and Black's fork, 38 miles, to Bridger; you are now 1059 miles from Independence; fill your kegs; it is 12 miles to Muddy, but the water is salt.

18 miles, another camp on Muddy.

16 miles, another camp on Muddy.

12 miles, a good spring at the foot of the mountain, 5 miles from Bear river.

5 miles brings you to Bear river; keep down Bear river 94 miles to the Soda Springs, (1221 miles,) where you must stop a day or two and enjoy the luxury of those exhilarating Springs. There are in the vicinity a great many of these springs; the best of all of them you will find at the foot of the mountain, one mile and a half from the camping ground on the river; it is situated one hundred yards from a lone cedar tree at the foot of the mountain. It is cool, resuscitating, and exceed- ingly delicious.

Leave the Soda Springs early in the morning, and when you go down the river about 4 miles, fill your kegs, as you cannot get to the water here, you leave the river. Six miles below, opposite the great Sheep mountain [Sheep Rock], you leave Bear river, from which it is 12 miles to a little branch of good water, but no wood; 6 miles farther to Portniff [Portneuf] creek, one of the tributaries of Snake river, from which it is 48 miles to Fort Hall (1278 miles.) Here you will have an opportunity of buying provisions, swapping cattle for horses, and will receive many acts of kindness from Captain [Richard] Grant, the superintendent of the Fort. Here you must hire an Indian to pilot you at the crossings of Snake river, it being dangerous if not perfectly understood.

Fort Hall is situated in a large fertile valley on Snake river; you will not travel far, however, 'till the gloom of desolation will spread around you, grass very scarce, water and wood plenty. 160 miles below Fort Hall, you will come to the Salmon Falls, where you will find a great many Indians fishing; you can buy the fish very cheap, but you need not lay in any supply, as you will have opportunities of trading for them the balance of your journey. Two days below, you come to the crossing where you must follow the instruction of your Indian guide; when you are across Snake river, all you will gain is good grass for your animals—there not being a sufficient quantity for a large band of stock on the south side, from the crossings of Snake river.

It is 70 miles to Bosie [Boise] river, where you will again get fine salmon,—(45 miles crossing Bosie river to Fort Bosie, 1574 miles)—on Snake river. Here you recross Snake river by ferry. All across, your first camp 12 miles to the Mallair [Malheur] river. Here I wish to remark that, when I left the settlement, a well known mountain man, Black Harris, in company with Dr. [Elijah] White, was about to start to look out a road across the Cascade mountain, by keeping up the Mallair and crossing over a depression in the mountain to the head waters of the Santyam [Santiam], the eastern branch of Wilhamet [Willamette]. If they have succeeded, they have shortened the road for the emigrant at least 300 miles. It would land him just where he wants to be, for the land north of the mouth of the Santyam is nearly all taken up. Another important benefit to be derived is, that there would be no Indians along this way to molest the emigrant; but if the road has not been opened, we must take the old track. And here let me put the emigrant on his guard—for, from this camp to the Dallis [Dalles], a distance of 320 miles, you will be surrounded with swarms of the most mischievous Indians that ever disgraced the human form. They are now hostile, and you must have your guns in good plight, and travel in large companies; keep them from your camps, one and all. Here for the first time, on the long road, you must set a rigid guard over your camp and stock. 130 miles brings you to the fertile valley of the Grand Round; water, wood, and an abundance of grass all the way. Here you may meet with some friendly Indians of the Skyuse tribe—but watch them close.

From the Grand Round, it is 70 miles to Dr. Whitman's Mission, over the blue mountain, which is not bad. This is a very fertile country, and the Indians raise a quantity of corn, wheat, peas, and the finest potatoes you have ever seen. They have thousands of horses, which are always very fat, they are a treacherous Indian, and retain an unbroken hatred for the white man. From Dr. Whitman's to Wala-wala is 25 miles—here you strike the Columbia, and many would do well to go the balance of the journey by water, were it not for the Indians. I would advise all to keep down the river by land to the Dallis mission, 120 miles; here you can repose yourself and family in comparative security. Here you take your wagons to pieces, and take all by water except your stock, which is driven across the Cascade mountain.

Fifty miles below the Dallis is the Cascade falls, on the Columbia; you here make a portage, and find a schooner ready to take you to the falls of Wilhamet. Fort Vancouver is 40 miles below the Cascades. It is a pleasant sight, after months of toil through the wilderness, to see the ships in the harbor, the carts, drays and hammers, and a general stir of business throughout the vicinity of the place. Should any of you be in need of provision or clothing, you can here obtain them. The chief factors of this place, Dr. John McLaughlin and James Douglass, are universally beloved, and well deserve the gratitude of all nations for their hospitable kindness to all whomsoever come under their notice, regardless of birth or country.

From Vancouver to the Wilhamet falls is 30 miles; here is a town [Oregon City] of considerable size, (500 inhabitants;) it is very expensive living here. Be off to the country, and take a fresh bag of flour and your family with you, and find a location to suit you—then go to work; a little labor will seed you a fine field of wheat, and this same land that you locate, in a few years will make you rich beyond doubt.

The country is not settled south of the Santyam. The farther you go south, the better the country is. There have been many projects for settling the rich valleys of the Unquair [Umpqua] and Clamet [Klamath], but none have been put into execution. This is unquestionably the most desirable part of the territory. With a soil scarcely surpassed, and a climate much milder than the Columbia, it offers but one barrier to the happiest abode of man; this barrier is the Indians who live on these rivers. It is thought that if a settlement would locate there, that could raise 100 well armed men with a small fort, would meet with success; such a settlement would be of great benefit to all the settlers in Oregon, as well as California; for, at present, none can pass without the loss of their stock and probable death to themselves.

But I did not set out to give a history of the country, nor its resources. The only design is, that you be fitted out in a proper manner, and have your pilot in your pocket. I have carefully warned the emigrant to fill his keg with water at all those places where it is requisite; and though there are many unforseen difficulties to beset you, be of good cheer—you will find a country in Oregon that will fill your desires, and repay you for all your toil. Lieut. Wilkes has given the only impartial account of the Oregon country that I have seen. I should recommend it to your perusal.

ROUTE TO CALIFORNIA.

The emigrant to California travels the same route to Oregon, from Independence to the river Casua [Raft River]. 60 miles below Fort Hall, keep up the Cesua three days, where cross over a southwest course three days to Goose creek—up Goose creek three days; thence a southwest course six days (distressing bad road,) to Mary's [Humboldt] river—down Mary's river 250 miles to its sink (a small lake.)

Along this river keep your guns in order, and sleep on your trail ropes, for the arrows of death are pointed at you from every Gulch, and without the strictest care you will lose your animals, if not your lives. This is the most sterile desert on the Continent of America, for a distance of 350 miles; not a tree nor shrub, except the hated sage and gresewood, can be seen. The water is all strongly tainted with mixed minerals, and hundreds of lakes in winter are now dry, and form a crest at bottom as white as snow. The water, before evaporated, is like lye—the white pearlash at bottom is of the same nature, and is used in California for making soap. Here you will see hundreds of Indians destitute of a particle of clothing, living on snails, crickets, worms, and grass, (where there are any.) They are the last link in the chain of human beings. They occupy the country from Mary's river to Snake river. They dig holes in the ground to shelter them from the storms of winter, and must lie in a partial torpid state 'till spring, when they leave their burrow, and wander over the wide plains of desolation, without the means of killing the few antelope that are thinly dispersed over their unparalleled barren country.

But to proceed, I left you at the sink of Mary's river,—take a due west course 50 miles to the foot of the Cascade [Sierra Nevada] mountains. This mountain is a smasher, being 2000 feet higher than the Rocky Mountains; you cannot expect to cross it without difficulty; and if you are as late as November, you will be much troubled with snow; and, as there is no trail which you will be able to follow, keep your course west as well as you can. When you cross over the division of the great mountain, you will be on one of the tributaries of the Sacrimento; follow it down to its mouth, and you will turn out your animals at Captain Sutter's Fort in California, and rest from the toil of your long journey. From the eastern foot of the Cascade mountains to the Fort, it is 110 miles.

The reader need not be disheartened by reading a description of the expansive desolation along the road; for in California, as in Oregon, the country along the sea is very fertile, and the plains produce an abundance of oats and clover spontaneously. Cattle and horses are so easily raised here, that they are only prized for their hides—consequently, they are diminishing. But we hope that when a few more of our citizens get settled there, they will put a stop to killing stock merely for their hides. Seek a good location for your farm, and stick to it. The Spaniards may molest you—but be firm, and soon the destiny of California will be governed by yourselves.

DISTANCE FROM INDEPENDENCE TO ASTORIA.

From Independence to the Crossings of Kanzas,	102	miles.
Crossings of Blue,	83	
Platte River,	119	
Crossings of South Platte,	163	
To North Fork,	20	
To Fort Larima,	153	640
From Larima to cross'g of North fork of the Platte,	140	
To Independence Rock on Sweet Water,	50	830
Fort Bridger,	229	
Bear River,	68	
Soda Springs,	94	
To Fort Hall,	57	1278
Salmon Falls,	160	
Crossings of Snake river,	22	
To crossings of Bosie river,	69	
Fort Bosie,	45	
Dr. Whitman's Mission,	190	
Fort Walawala,	25	
Dallis Mission,	120	
Cascade Falls, on the Columbia,	50	
Fort Vancouver,	41	
Astoria,	90	2117

☞ In preparation by the author a concise description of the Oregon and California Countries, climate, soil, natural productions, together with a map of the same.

Notes

HO! FOR CALIFORNIA AND OREGON

1. Reed Papers, Sutter's Fort Historical Monument Collection.

2. *The Gazette,* St. Joseph, January 23, 1846. William J. Martin had gone to Oregon in 1843, commander of the caravan during part of the journey. See Index for further information on his part in the 1846 emigration.

3. *Missouri Reporter,* St. Louis, March 9, 1846.

4. Andrew Jackson Grayson had a prominent role in the 1846 emigration, as in California afterward. More would be said of him here except that a biography by Lois E. Stone may be looked for at an early date.

5. Elizabethtown, from what is said here, was located on the west bank of the Missouri in what was technically Indian country. Outside the documents reprinted in the present work, I have seen no references to the place.

6. J. L. Parrish's diary of that portion of the 1844 emigration which set out from St. Joseph is printed in Oregon Pioneer Association, *Transactions,* 1888, pp. 82-122. Diaries of the 1845 emigration out of St. Joseph include those of Jesse Harritt, printed in *ibid* (39th Reunion, 1911, not printed till 1914), pp. 506-526, and Samuel Parker, MS., Oregon Historical Society.

7. "Mr. Clarke" sounds like a man with some Western experience, but I have no plausible suggestion as to his identity.

8. William Fowler was the son of William Fowler. The father was born in New York in 1799, removed to Illinois in 1818, to Oregon in 1843, and to California in 1846; he settled first in Sonoma but later moved to Calistoga, where he died in 1865. The son, born in New York, gave his age as 49, a miner, when he registered as a voter in Napa County in April, 1867; but when he again registered in November, 1871, gave his age as 55. He set out for California in the Bartleson party in 1841, but from Soda Springs went to Oregon instead. With his father and younger brother Henry, he came to California in 1844 in the Kelsey party, having married Rebecca Kelsey. After a divorce early in 1845, he went east in William H. Winter's party to bring out the rest of the family, consisting (Jacob Wright Harlan says) of "his mother, a half brother, and three sisters, one of whom

743

was a Mrs. Hargrave (wife of John Hargrave, who died and was buried [at the south end of Great Salt Lake], and her four small children. Also he had with him two brothers named Musgrave, one of whom was his stepfather." According to Harlan, during the crossing of the Salt Desert Fowler "lost his seven yoke of oxen. The man who was in charge of them went to sleep, and the cattle turned back and recrossed the desert—or perhaps died there. Thus he was left with his two wagons, and no teams to haul them. It was a hard case, as he had a large family with him. He had married my sister, Malinda, after we left Fort Bridger. . . . The rest of our company helped him with teams, and he managed to keep with us."

Obviously Bancroft is mistaken in conjecturing that the younger William Fowler might have been the Fowler killed immediately after the Bear Flag Rebellion. Fowler was living at Calistoga as late as 1879.

9. Reed Papers, Sutter's Fort Historical Monument Collection.

10. *The Gazette,* St. Joseph, March 13, 1846. For Stephen Cooper see Index.

11. The probability is that Stephen Cooper's "Capt. Craig"—here intimated to be coming from Iowa rather than from the Platte Purchase—is the same person called Gregg by Carriger and Riley Gragg by A. E. Garrison. See Index.

12. *Sangamo Journal,* Springfield, March 26, 1846. The notice was again printed in the issue of April 2.

13. These remarks about Congress are somewhat premature; on May 6 following Congress authorized the establishment of military posts along the road to Oregon and the organization of a regiment of Mounted Riflemen. Fort Kearny was established, and Fort Laramie purchased, pursuant to this authority — but in consequence of the Mexican War, not until some time elapsed.

14. The English travelers would be Francis Parkman's future trail companions, "Captain Bill" Chandler, his brother Jack, and one Romaine. See Volume I, Introduction; and see also Mason Wade, ed., *The Journals of Francis Parkman* (New York and London, 1947, 2 vols.), vol. 2, index. The Chandlers after separating from Parkman went on to Oregon and Hawaii, thence via the Isthmus to New York, where Parkman encountered them next year. For some of the rumors concerning the English party, see Bryant's journal on his arrival at Independence.

15. Putnam Papers, Oregon Historical Society.

16. Sutter's letter, dated New Helvetia, May 14, 1845, was printed in three installments in the St. Louis newspaper, *Anzeiger des Westens,* September 23, 25, 27, 1845. A translation of most of the letter may be found in the *Weekly Reveille,* March 23 and 31, 1846, reprinted from the *Daily;* this translation was copied in whole or in part by

a number of other papers, obviously including the Independence *Western Expositor.*

17. Edwin Bryant, after a visit from Webb at Independence three weeks later, had another tall tale respecting California to set down in his journal. A man who had lived in that favored country 250 years became tired of life and traveled into a foreign country, where he soon took sick and died. "In his will, however, he required his heir and executor, upon pain of disinheritance, to transport his remains to his own country and there entomb them. This requisition was faithfully complied with. His body was interred with great pomp and ceremony in his own cemetery, and prayers were rehearsed in all the churches for the rest of his soul. He was happy, it was supposed, in heaven, where, for a long series of years, he had prayed to be; and his heir was happy that he was there. But what a disappointment! Being brought back and interred in California soil, with the health-breathing California zephyrs rustling over his grave, the energies of life were immediately restored to his inanimate corpse! Herculean strength was imparted to his frame, and bursting the prison-walls of death, he appeared before his chapfallen heir reinvested with all the vigor and beauty of early manhood! He submitted to his fate and determined to live his appointed time. Stories similar to the foregoing, although absurd, and so intended to be, no doubt leave their impressions upon the minds of many, predisposed to rove in search of adventure and Eldorados."

18. For Selim Woodworth see Index; he was going via Oregon, not to Monterey direct.

19. This notice of Curry's forthcoming tour was well received by other newspapers; and the *Reveille* promoted the letters by "Laon" as one of the feast of good things to be expected by subscribers to its next volume.

20. So was noted the departure from Springfield of the Donner Party, George and Jacob Donner and James Frazier Reed each with three wagons.

21. *Weekly Reveille,* St. Louis, May 4, 1846.

22. Edwin Bryant's literary purpose in making the overland journey in 1846 was well-heralded before he left the frontier, during his stay in California, and after his return. No one has ever been disappointed in the result.

23. For those who crossed at Iowa Point, see Nicholas Carriger's diary in Volume I. This northerly point of departure, just below the future Nebraska-Kansas line, is referred to in some of the reports that follow as at the mouth of the Nishnabotna.

24. At the time this report was written, April 26, the main body of the Mormons had got as far across Iowa as Garden Grove, on the west bank of the Grand River, and in almost unremitting rain, making

little progress.

25. *Weekly Reveille,* St. Louis, May 11, 1846.

26. This report would seem to describe the Mormon company known as the Mississippi Saints. They reached Independence May 26 and moved on into the Plains next day; see John Brown's journal as quoted in Volume I, pp. 111-114. The whole record is printed in John Z. Brown, ed., *Autobiography of Pioneer John Brown* (Salt Lake City, 1941).

27. *Weekly Reveille,* St. Louis, May 25, 1846.

28. Stephen W. Kearny must have returned Russell a verbal answer, for his letterbook in the Missouri Historical Society contains no such report. That he did entertain some idea that the Mormons were crossing the Missouri in force is shown by Francis Parkman's various chronicles as cited in Volume I, p. 101.

29. Putnam Papers, Oregon Historical Society.

30. The mention of (T. H.) Jefferson by the *Western Expositor* is the only one known, apart from his *Emigrant's Guide.*

31. *Missouri Republican,* St. Louis, May 18, 1846. This letter was reprinted in the *New York Herald* ten days later; many of the items in this volume were widely republished.

32. *Weekly Reveille,* St. Louis, May 25, 1846. Compare Edwin Bryant's account of the organizational meeting Curry describes.

33. Putnam Papers, Oregon Historical Society.

34. Original letter in Henry E. Huntington Library.

35. Transcript in McGlashan Papers, Bancroft Library.

36. *Ibid.*

37. See Virgil Pringle's diary in Volume I.

38. The *Missouri Republican's* correspondent here uses "Nishnebotna" as synonymous with Iowa Point, and miscalls the Sacs "Sioux."

39. This train being organized at St. Joseph has come down in history as "Smith's company." Smith has conjecturally been identified as Fabritus W. Smith. For a fuller account, see Note 213.

THE PLAINS

40. No Mormon wagons as such crossed the Missouri at St. Joseph. Some Saints went west as individuals in 1846, taking the Hastings Cutoff and passing through the Valley of the Great Salt Lake a year before the Mormon Pioneers got there; Thomas Rhoads and his family are an example. But whether they passed through St. Joseph has not been established. The organized Mormon emigration to the north is described in Note 24 above. The Mississippi Saints, who would leave from Independence, had not got there yet.

41. *Weekly Reveille,* St. Louis, June 1, 1846.

42. *Liberty Tribune,* Liberty, Mo., May 30, 1846; reprinted from the Independence *Western Expositor.* The 1850 census for Polk

County, Oregon, includes in the family of Reason and Martha Hall two children, Reuben and William, aged 4, born "Rocky Mts."

43. *Missouri Republican,* St. Louis, May 28, 1846.

44. *Weekly Reveille,* St. Louis, June 1, 1846.

45. These emigrants would be the last component of "Smith's company." *The Gazette* did not publish the promised list.

46. The rumors about the Mormons continued to shake down toward reality. The advance companies reached the Missouri opposite Bellevue on June 13 but the necessary ferry was not completed until June 29. On the 27th the refugees from the Pawnee mission arrived (see Note 88.), and a company under Bishop George Miller contracted to haul in their effects from the Loup Fork. It was at first contemplated that Miller would go on to winter at Grand Island, but was persuaded by the Ponca Indians to winter at the mouth of the Niobrara instead. The main company under Brigham Young eventually settled into "winter quarters" north of present Omaha.

47. Apparently the *Republican's* correspondent is not here talking about the emigration Nicholas Carriger chronicles, which crossed the Missouri at Iowa Point. The emigration out of St. Joseph with which William J. Martin started soon split apart, as seen in Volume I, pp. 91-92. The only other distinct company that left St. Joseph was the one mentioned in Note 39.

48. Putnam Papers, Oregon Historical Society. This letter was postmarked in St. Joseph July 18.

49. P. D. Papin's party.

50. *Weekly Reveille,* St. Louis, July 27, 1846.

51. *New York Herald,* August 7, 1846.

52. Rice Dunbar's company, in which J. Quinn Thornton was traveling.

53. *Missouri Statesman,* Columbia, July 24, 1846.

54. Others of Russell's fellow travelers have been described elsewhere; here we may appropriately say something about West and Branham. Frederic Hall, *History of San Jose and Surroundings,* pp. 140-141, lists both among the 1846 arrivals, "Isaac Branham, wife, two sons, and two daughters. . . . Thomas West and four sons, (Thomas M., Francis T., Geo. R., and Wm. T.)." A sketch of Branham (*ibid.,* pp. 368-369) says he was born in Kentucky in 1803, at the age of 21 removed to "Calway county, Missouri," and prompted by ill health in his family, migrated to California in 1846, becoming a prominent and influential member of the San Jose community. An extended sketch in Horace S. Foote, *Pen Pictures from the Garden of the World or Santa Clara County, California* (Chicago, 1888), pp. 491-494, contains many more details on his life, mentioning that his children in 1846 ranged from 11 years of age to about 9 months, and saying that the overland journey was made "in two wagons drawn

by three yoke of oxen to each wagon, taking at the same time two horses and two cows, the latter furnishing milk all the way across the plains, and from which he afterward raised considerable stock in the Santa Clara Valley. The trip from Independence, Missouri, to the California State line, was made in six months and eleven days. . . . The trip was made without any unusual difficulties or hardships, there being but one fight with the Indians, that being on the Humboldt River near where the town of Elko now stands, which took place in the pursuit and recapture of cattle stolen by the Indians." Branham died November 3, 1887.

Less is known about the Wests, though the son William T. served in the California Battalion, the son George served in Captain Charles M. Weber's San Jose Company along with James Frazier Reed, John C. Buchanan, Carolan Mathers, and other familiar names. The record of Captain Joseph Aram's Santa Clara Company shows that "F. T." and "T." West served therein, along with George Harlan, A. A. Hecox, Otis Ashley, Elam Brown, G. D. Dickenson, and others. John S. Hittell, "Notes of California Pioneers," *Hutchings' California Magazine,* November, 1860, vol. 5, pp. 209-211, with Elam Brown's help listed some pioneers of 1846, after saying, "About fifty families were in that year's migration, of whom about three-fifths went to Santa Clara Valley, and the remainder to Sonoma and vicinity." Among those who came to Santa Clara, he lists first, "Mr. West, who has returned to the 'States,' wealthy."

55. The advance contingent of Joel Palmer's party, which rode on from Fort Laramie June 10.

56. *New York Tribune,* August 3, 1846, reprinted from the Lexington, Ky., *Reporter.* Edwin Bryant was born in 1805, in Massachusetts, but at the age of 11 migrated with his family to Kentucky. He studied medicine, but never practised, and only reluctantly served the overland emigration of 1846. Failing health is said to have persuaded him to throw up his job as one of the editors of the Louisville *Courier* and make the overland journey. After service with the California Battalion and as alcalde at San Francisco, Bryant returned east with Kearny in the summer of 1847. His book must have been written in large part before he got home, for a long excerpt recounting his crossing of the salt desert in the Russell party is reprinted in the *Sangamo Journal,* October 14, 1847, from the Louisville *Morning Courier.* *What I Saw in California* was published in New York a year later. Bryant returned to California in 1849 at the head of a company which took the Truckee route he had traveled in 1846 and 1847. He turned his attention to real estate speculation rather than to mining, and is said to have returned to Kentucky in 1853. Bryant died by his own hand in 1869.

57. *Sangamo Journal,* Springfield, July 23, 1846.

58. *Weekly Reveille,* St. Louis, July 20, 1846.

59. Wall's letter appears in the text, in part, under date of July 20.

60. Putnam Papers, Oregon Historical Society. The letter was postmarked in St. Joseph July 8.

61. Nothing afterward appeared in the *Oregon Spectator* to show that an express was sent to Fort Hall to rebut "the misrepresentations of L. W. Hastings"; and it would appear from subsequent references to Finley, Rynearson, and T'Vault that they themselves did not go. Yet there is evidence such an express was sent. *California Star* on February 27, 1847, under a head, "Public Meeting in Oregon," published the following:

"We notice in the Oregon Spectator of June the 25th, the proceedings of a public meeting held there a few days before, for the purpose of devising means of turning the emigrants then on their way across the mountains, to Oregon. Two committees were appointed, one to proceed immediately to meet the emigrants, and the other to take the written statements of persons, who pretended to know something about the soil and climate of California, and the condition of the people here. Some of the statements will be found below. They are erroneous in almost every particular; and seem to have been worded to suit the objects of the committee. A number of the papers containing them were circulated among the emigrants, but they had no effect upon them. There happened to be several persons among them who had been in California and knew the statements to be incorrect. Instead of having any influence upon the emigrants, we are confident that many who had previously determined to go to Oregon, came to this country.

"Since seeing the proceedings of the meeting alluded to, we have taken some pains to obtain information in relation to the agricultural capabilities of the country, and find that the average crops of wheat are from forty to one hundred bushels to the acre. Irish potatoes as good as can be produced in any part of the world are raised here in great abundance—all kinds of vegetables, and in fact every thing raised in other countries in the same latitude. The climate is mild and pure, and sickness of any kind, is rarely known in any part of the country, with the exception of a small district on the Sacramento river.

"As an evidence that the gentlemen whose names are signed to the certificates have become convinced themselves that they were incorrect in their notions of this country, they are all without a single exception, preparing to return here during the ensuing spring. This we learn from persons recently from Oregon. [See the next Note. Apparently only Keyes returned.]

"We have deemed it our duty to say this much, in regard to the meeting in Oregon and the certificates, to prevent them from having any improper influence abroad.

"The statements in reference to the designs of Capt Hastings, were probably made without any personal knowledge of his intentions. We can bear testimony to his impartial and honorable conduct concerning Oregon and California, when he met the emigrants. [Then follow the statements by Truman Bonney, "Jairus" Bonney, Abner Frazer, and Robert C. Keyes, dated Oregon City, June 17, 1846.]"

On April 22, 1847, Governor George Abernethy issued *To the Oregon Emigrants,* one of the earliest Oregon broadsides, printed at the *Spectator* office without the knowledge of the editor, George L. Curry. Some controversy resulted from this circular; see, *Oregon Spectator,* October 14, 1847, and *California Star,* December 4, 1847, but this later wooing of emigrants is mentioned only for its obvious relationship to the events of 1846.

62. Robert C. Keyes has heretofore appeared in this work as "Cad" or Cadden Keyes, brother of Margret (Keyes) Reed. He had left Springfield for Oregon in 1845 but changed his mind and accompanied William Brown Ide into California. The Reed Papers in the Sutter's Fort Historical Monument Collection include a letter to Reed from James W. Keyes, May 15, 1846, which says: "I this day rec^d a letter from Cad dated Monterey California 2nd March 1846 he wrote but little—he is working at his trade in Monterey—is making 13$ per week Clear—Says the climent is very good and that is all he can say for the Countrey he has not been to Oragon—Says he is going to Start there in April—When he explores oragon, he then intends to come home by the way of Cape Horn to Boston—Says nothing about Ide or the last Springs emigrants at all, does not say when he Reached Monterey or how he will very likely meet you on the way as you expected, for by reference again to his letter I see that he says if you come out to oregon this Spring he will in that case come home by water, otherwise I infer that he will come through by land...." (This letter was addressed: "Jas F. Reed Esqr Oregon Emegrant Independence Mo Care of James Mexey Esqr please forward." When Reed received the letter is not apparent.)

After the statement of June 17, 1846, printed in the text, R. C. Keyes is next heard from in a letter in the Reed Papers dated Oregon City, December 10, 1846:

"Dear Brother & Sister

"I again take my pen in hand to wright you that I am well at this time and hope that this letter may fine you all in good health. I am in Oregon I reach this place the 16 of Jun last after a trip of 40 Days and a Vary plesant trip [*word illegible*] with the exception of me loosing one Horse and pack crossing Sacrimento Mountin I lost everyting I had but the Shirt and pantilons that I had on me. that was the 4 day from Mr Lasons the Mountain is vary thick with

Brush and like the Old Horse got out of the trace and I couldnt find him, the things that I lost cost me $100 but I got hear in good health with milling woork [apparently the name of his mare] & one Maule & two others Horsis milling woork is aflected at this time with a sore leag and is very poore but I think that she will be well so as to come to California in the spring as I intend to come to sea you befor I go home. this is a good timbered and soiled Contry this of wich I wright is the valie of the willamet it is to much shut in from Ship navigation I want to go acrose the Columbia River to [?] in [?] May to look at pugts Sound and the Country around it this valie dont please me you can youse your pleasur to come and see it or not I would recomend you to leave your family thare if you dont like that Country till you looke at this for if you can git land thare I think thare will be large Company thar next Somer from hiar with packs and Wagons for they can go on to Appelgats Road within one Hundred Mils of P Lasons and that Houndred mils is a valie vary [? eazy?], so I am told, the folks are in the Mountains yet on Appelgates Road that is what is arrive of them. . . ."

A second letter addressed to Reed "Yerba Buana, San Francisco To the car of Jas G. Donleavy," is dated Oregon City, March 31, 1847. Acknowledging receipt on February 22 of Reed's letter of February 4 written just before Reed left Yerba Buena on the Second Donner Relief, he "was vary sorey to hear of yourr familes sufrings but I hop that God will protect them and you." He was then working for Governor Abernethy at his sawmill.

Keyes returned to California by land in the spring of 1847, and in consequence we find George McKinstry, under his pen-name Sacramento, writing from Fort Sacramento, July 13, 1847, a letter printed in the *California Star,* July 24, 1847: "On my way up [from San Francisco via Sonoma] I met the Oregon emigration, consisting of 80 odd souls on horseback, they inform me that the past season in Oregon has been very unfavorable for the farmer, and that there will be hardly wheat enough raised in that country for home consumption. In this party I found several that had left California for Oregon some year or two since, and had returned to live here perfectly satisfied; among others was a Mr. Keyes, who was induced to write and publish June 19, 1846, to induce emigrants for California to turn to Oregon, a letter, a copy of which you will find in your file No. 8., in which among other things he says, 'I have seen enough of Oregon to perceive that it is the best grazing country of the two, and for agriculture they wont compare,' he has returned to California — 'nuff sed.' . . ."

The Reed papers contain one other letter from R. C. Keyes, addressed to James Frazier Reed at San Jose from "Montry" August 28, 1847; this letter mentions that he has plenty of work. Robert C.

Keyes eventually made his home in San Jose, where the 1860 census finds him, aged 40, a farmer, born in Virginia.

63. See Volume I, pp. 70-71, Note 36, for the unsuccessful exploration referred to by the *Spectator*. The new group just setting out was Jesse Applegate's company of southern road-hunters.

64. This may be the appropriate point to bring out some of the history of the Barlow Road, as described in two articles by his daughter Mary, printed in Oregon Historical Society *Quarterly*, March, 1902, vol. 3, pp. 71-81, and September, 1925, vol. 26, pp. 209-224, with added details from Joel Palmer's narrative. Samuel Kimbrough Barlow was born in Nicholas County Kentucky January 24, 1792. He grew up opposed to slavery, though his father was a slaveholder, and settled in Indiana. He had lived for some time at Farmington, Illinois, before migrating to Oregon in 1845. He was one of those who set out from Independence in Presley Welch's company, captain of one of the divisions all the way to The Dalles. Being told of an Indian trail across the "insurmountable" Cascades, he went to see for himself, having already descried from a point in the Blue Mountains "a low sink in the Cascades just south of Mt. Hood." He came back to report prospects favorable. Soon after the little company of seven wagons left The Dalles, which Barlow's daughter says was on September 24, Joel Palmer arrived at that point, and Palmer induced another 23 wagons to attempt the route. However, the season was so far advanced that it seemed unnecessarily hazardous to get through before snowfall, and a number turned back.

According to Barlow's daughter, "In the party that finally came through were S. K. Barlow and wife, Albert Gaines, wife and three children, Jane Ellen Barlow, William Caplinger and wife, John M. Bacon, Gasner, Reuben Gant, who drove the first wagon over the road in 1846, William Berry and William Barlow and possibly others. J. L. (Dock) and James Barlow, Joel Palmer, W. G. Buffum and wife, and one other traveled the Indian trail [from which the wagon road had parted]." They had a difficult time and finally found it necessary to leave the wagons. William Berry stayed on through the winter to look after them, and the others, with considerable hardship, kept on to reach Oregon City. Soon after Barlow was given a charter for a toll-road, employed 40 men, and built a passable road. In 1848 Barlow donated his right, title, and interest to the Territorial government, and the road was then leased for some years, the lessees doing much collecting and little road-work, so that the Barlow Road deteriorated. Much later it again came into private hands, but in 1912 was deeded to the State of Oregon. Today the old road forms part of the scenic highway called the Mount Hood Loop Road. Barlow died at Camenah, near Oregon City, on July 14, 1867.

65. *Weekly Reveille*, St. Louis, August 10, 1846.

66. Respecting Elam Brown at Fort Laramie, see the Pringle diary, Note 34.

67. Fort Bernard is shown on Jefferson's map as "Rosseaux Fort," his conception of the name Richard or Reshaw. Jefferson depicts an "Old Fort" nearby; thus Curry says that the post was "almost reconstructed last year." This "Old Fort" had been erected in 1837 by Peter L. Sarpy, incident to the rivalry between North and South Platte traders. Sarpy gave up the post next year, and the site was not again utilized until the Richard brothers located here late in 1845. Francis Parkman, saying it was "built by Sapi," describes the fort as it existed in the summer of 1846, "log houses in the form of a square, facing inwards," only two sides yet built; he also records an impression of John Richard as "a little swarthy, black-eyed Frenchman." Richard had earlier been associated with Sibille & Adams, opposition traders on the Laramie, and his proclivity for bringing trading goods north from Taos, especially the potent "Taos lightning," made him thoroughly objectionable to the traders at Fort Laramie. A few weeks later he conducted the Mississippi Saints south to Pueblo, and it would appear that the opposition improved the opportunity to get rid of his fort, for 1847 emigrants recorded burnt ruins on the site. The name Fort Bernard was given in memory of the deceased Bernard Pratte, or in honor of Bernard Pratte the younger, a Richard backer.

68. Among the California emigrants of 1845 Sam Kinney acquired a reputation as a Texan with a yen to kill an Indian. After wintering at Sutter's, he had come east with Clyman and Hastings. He evidently was one of those who separated from Clyman at Independence Rock on June 22; Clyman was not yet this far along. Kinney may have been the objectionable character referred to in the McKinstry diary, Note 70, but if so, Bryant was in error in saying that he had resided in California four years—unless that was a piece of mendacity on Kinney's part.

69. The *Weekly Reveille,* August 17, 1846, printed a eulogy signed "B.," preceded as follows: "Died, at Fort Helvetia, (Capt. Sutter's,) Upper California, on the 8th of February [24th of January], 1846, in the 26th year of his age, WM. BROWN GILDEA, M. D., Dental Surgeon, late of St. Louis, Mo.

"He was born in Dauphin county, Pennsylvania, and became a resident of this city about eight years ago, when he entered upon the study of medicine and dental surgery under the instruction of his uncle, Dr. B. B. Brown. In the spring of 1843 he graduated at the St. Louis University. In May, 1845, he accompanied the emigrant expedition to California, with a view of practising medicine in that country. . . ."

Gildea's arrival at Sutter's is mentioned in the New Helvetia Diary on September 27, 1845. On January 16 the Diary noted, "Dr. Gildea is very sick," and on January 24, 1846, "Died *Dr* W. B. Gildea and was buried—the former about 3 o'clock A. M.—the latter about 4 P. M." On February 20, as also recorded in the New Helvetia Diary, Sutter as alcalde appointed L. W. Hastings administrator of Gildea's estate.

70. At first sight Curry is speaking of the Bear River which flows into Great Salt Lake, but his mention of the Arapahos makes it likely that he is talking of the Yampa River of northwestern Colorado, sometimes called Bear River by the trappers. Eastbound in June, Clyman had heard from the Ute Indians in Salt Lake Valley "that the snakes and whites ware at war and that the snakes had killed two white men." But that would seem to be another affair. Francis Parkman in his diary, after telling of his visit to "Richard's fort" on June 28, at which time he encountered the Russell or Boggs company, says, "News of two traders killed by Arapaho(e)s—one just going up told me, remarking that he was bound to meet the same fate." In his book Parkman declares that the information came from the trader Rouleau, in the following language: ". . . the Arapahoes have just killed two of us in the mountains. Old Bull Tail has come to tell us. They stabbed one behind his back, and shot the other with his own rifle." In the diary later, on July 23, Parkman tells of Rouleau's setting out with a companion, bound for the Rocky Mountains. "All the Inds. here try to dissuade them, saying that, since the death of Boot and May, the Arapahos have grown very audacious, having got over their first terror, and call the whites dogs, saying that none of them shall leave their country alive. They laugh at the government and the dragoons. (On August 6 Parkman made a similar diary note.) The trappers are resolved to go on." One of the dead men, in consequence of Parkman's rendition of his name as above, has been misidentified as the trapper William S. May, who died in Utah in 1855. The latter Parkman encountered at Fort Laramie; the other man, he makes clear, had been killed before he reached the fort.

71. The estimate of approximately 20 wagons for the 1844 California emigration is higher than the usual figure—13 according to Clyman; 11 according to Sutter's contemporary letter and Moses Schallenberger's recollection (see George R. Stewart, *The Opening of the California Trail*, p. 14). The estimate of 50 wagons for the 1845 emigration is in accord with Joel Palmer, who says 15 wagons were fitted out expressly for California, and 35 more were diverted from the Oregon emigration at Fort Hall through the persuasions of Old Greenwood and (George) McDougall. Two companies totaling 25 wagons are mentioned by William L. Todd, as quoted in Volume I, Introduction, but there was doubtless at least one company behind.

72. *Sangamo Journal*, Springfield, August 13, 1846, with the prefatory remark, "The following letter from an old neighbor has been

politely communicated to us for publication." George Donner's reference to the popularity of California sea shells among the Sioux is an interesting addition to trade lore.

73. *New York Herald,* August 31, 1846.

74. The prior letter, presumably written June 15 or 16, has not been found; it would have been deposited in the St. Joseph postoffice by J. B. Wall. Compare the McKinstry and Miller diaries, as also Bryant's journal, though all refer to a spring rather than to Twin Springs.

75. See the Carriger diary, Note 15.

76. Stanton is speaking of Rice Dunbar's company, which had separated from the Russell company on June 2; see the McKinstry diary, Note 40. J. Quinn Thornton says on June 17, "Our party unanimously determined to continue our route up the river in search of a new ford, instead of remaining until the companies before us [one of 29 wagons, another of 8] had crossed." They went about 20 miles that day, and on June 18 "resumed our journey in search of a ford, Mr. [Reason] Hall, however, affirming that it was 'to head the Nebraska.' At 10 o'clock A. M., we arrived at a place, where, upon examination, it was believed the receding of the waters would enable us to ford on the following day." On the 20th "The wagon beds were raised about ten inches, by putting blocks under them, for the purpose of rendering them in some measure water-proof. We at length commenced crossing the river, which was here about a mile and a half wide; but it was necessary to proceed diagonally, so that the actual distance across became two miles. All was finally conveyed over without any material accident. It became necessary to take some of the dogs into the wagons to prevent them from drowning." The company encamped upon "the west side," and next day in 20 miles reached the North Platte (seemingly above Ash Hollow, which Thornton does not mention). The attractions of the young ladies in Dunbar's company are manifest, for Thornton recorded a marriage on June 14 and two more on the 18th.

77. Clyman's company, with whom the Donners encamped at Fort Laramie on June 27.

78. Printed from a typescript copy in the Bancroft Library, reported to be an "Exact copy as it was given to Sibyl V. Mauerhan," and preserved in the Henry Tucker family. The Bancroft Library also has a dictation given by B. F. Kellogg in 1887, which notes that he was born in Franklin County, Illinois, in 1822 "and is one of California's earliest pioneers. . . . He crossed the plains in 1846, stopping in Wyoming where he took a contract to build Fort Larame. Explored the country towards the S. Platte and Arkansas Rivers. At one time his whole party were captured by the Indians on foot. The horses of his party were weak, and after a ride of twenty miles,

they were obliged to halt and surrender. They were robbed of nearly all they had except their guns, a little amunition and drafts, even the most of their clothing, and the shirts they wore.

"They then set out on foot but soon suffered so much from hunger that they shaved the hair from buffalo-skins and ate them for food. After a long perilous journey, they came across some black walnuts which they cracked and eat freely. They also laid in a store of the kernels for future use. Mr. K got sick from eating them and had to be left alone for three days, before relief came. When the party reached the settlements they could get plenty of money on their drafts, which the Indians had no use for. . . ."

This account seems a little confused, perhaps describing experiences earlier in the 1840's, possibly 1841—it is evident from the letter that Kellogg had set out in 1846 from the States. Corroborative information is found in Frank E. Kellogg, *The Ancestors and Descendants of Florentine Erwin Kellogg* (Santa Barbara, 1907), which relates that Florentine (born at Batavia, New York, January 1, 1816), and his younger brother, Benjamin Franklin Ephraim (born April 30, 1822) set out for California with Florentine's wife, Rebecca Jane Williams, and three children, Angeline, Philander, and Jane. Their outfit consisted of "a two-horse carriage, two wagons loaded with provisions, tools and household goods. . . five yoke of oxen, two yoke of cows, and three horses, two of which were exchanged for mules at Fort Bridger on the way. He and his family rode in the carriage, while he put the wagons in charge of his brother Frank, William Mc-Donnell and John Spitler." Florentine died at Goleta, California, October 1, 1889, Benjamin at Anaheim, California, December 16, 1890.

79. Philander Kellogg was born at Batavia June 17, 1810; his name occasionally occurs in fur trade records during the 1840's. According to the 1907 work cited in the preceding Note, he did not go on to California this year or ever, being accidentally killed by an Indian in 1848. Heinrich Lienhard, who speaks of the Kelloggs later, on the Hastings Cutoff, also tells of hiring Philander here, at the crossing of the North Platte (a good many more than 15 miles from Fort Laramie) to hunt buffalo, also mentioned in the present letter.

80. I have suggested in the text that "Eren Browns" may be an intended reference to Elam Brown, but it is possible that "Erens" refers instead to Joseph Aram, whose reminiscences cited in the Carriger diary, Note 36, mention Charles Imus as captain of his company. Adna A. Hecox's recollections of the same party are also cited in this Note. "Abentore" I have not identified.

81. What was this "company coming from Oregon"? The Genois company had passed by at least a week earlier, encountered by Bryant in the Black Hills on July 1.

82. *New York Herald,* October 25, 1846. Beaver (LaPrele) Creek was upwards of 80 miles west of Fort Laramie; in the original letter, Stanton may have written "Ninety."

83. Robert Ewing had originally set out in company with Edwin Bryant. See Note 247 for further comment.

84. A reference to the killing of Edward Trimble in Smith's company.

85. Dunbar's company, with its three marriages mentioned in Note 76. For J. Quinn Thornton's account of this reunion on June 30, see the McKinstry diary, Note 73; and see also the Reed diary, Note 16.

86. Evidently the Genois party, mentioned in Note 81; see Index.

87. More usually and less poetically called "the red hills." See the Taylor diary, Note 20, and the Reed diary, Note 14.

88. This Sioux attack on June 12, 1846, signalized the destruction of the Pawnee Mission on the Loup Fork of the Platte; the missionary mentioned here was Samuel Allis. See John Dunbar's letters dated Bellevue, June 30, 1846, and Savannah, October 12, 1846, printed in Kansas Historical Society, *Collections,* 1915-1918, vol. 14, pp. 683-689. A letter by Allis dated Bellevue, February 8, 1847, includes a paragraph: "The Pawnees have the summer past robed Emigrants going to Oregon & California, and I understand by the Pawnees and also from other courses [sources], that they have killed some two or three white men the past season." (*ibid.,* pp. 739-740).

89. See Notes 24 and 46.

90. It appears from George L. Curry's letter of June 12 that Papin left Fort John (Laramie) May 7, which approximately dates the arrival of Vasquez and Bridger. No more is heard of Bridger at this time, though he and Vasquez were on hand when James Frazier Reed wrote from their fort on July 31. When Parkman reached Fort Laramie on June 15 he mentioned "Vaskis" as among the traders and hunters then present. In his book Parkman explains the animosity of the Sioux toward the Snakes by saying that in 1845 the Sioux had sent ten warriors to the Snake country, "led by the son of a prominent Ogillallah chief called The Whirlwind. In passing over Laramie Plains they encountered a superior number of their enemies, were surrounded, and killed to a man. Having performed this exploit, the Snakes became alarmed, dreading the resentment of the Dakota; and they hastened to signify their wish for peace by sending the scalp of the dead partisan, with a small parcel of tobacco attached, to his tribesmen and relatives. They had employed old Vasquez, the trader, as their messenger, and the scalp was the same that hung in our room at the fort." The Sioux were inexorable; but nothing came of the "grand combination to chastise the Snakes." Vasquez' diplomatic mission would have been secondary to bringing down furs and hides,

and taking supplies back to Fort Bridger.

91. *Missouri Reporter,* St. Louis, July 11, 1846, reprinted from the Independence *Western Expositor* (of July 4).

92. These five men, only three of whom are named, had left Oregon in company with Joel Palmer. Apparently these are the ones who went ahead on June 10 when the others delayed at Fort Laramie to enable arriving emigrants to write home; it would seem that Palmer's group never did catch up. These five men made their way to Independence, the others to St. Joseph.

93. Compare John Brown's journal of the Mississippi Saints, quoted in Volume I, pp. 111-114. Only 19 wagons carried Mormons.

94. This report more correctly sums up the Mississippi Saints.

95. Here we first encounter "Smith's company" as such. The Graves family, the last to join the Donner Party, started from the frontier in this company. William C. Graves, "Crossing the Plains in '46," *Russian River Flag,* Healdsburg, Calif., April 26, 1877, recalled:

"On the twelfth of April, 1846, my father, Franklin Ward Graves, started with his family, consisting of my mother, and Sarah, Mary Ann, myself, Eleanor, Lavina, Nancy, Jonathan, Franklin and Elizabeth, the latter only about nine months old, from Marshall county, Illinois, to come to California. My oldest sister, Sarah, had been married to Jay Fosdick a few weeks before we started; he and a hired man by the name of John Snider completed our company from that place till we got to St. Joseph, Missouri, where we joined a large party, some bound for Oregon and some for California. This was about the 25th of May. We crossed the river, called a meeting and elected a Captain and other officers, such as we deemed necessary in crossing the great plains. . . . I did not know the exact number in the company at that time but there were about 85 wagons, and I think would average about five persons to the wagon; about half were women and children. . . . [We] got along smoothly till within about fifty miles of Scott's Bluffs; here we found some . . . Pawnee Indians, or they found us, and stole some of our cattle and killed two men; one of them, Wm. Trimble, left a wife and two or three children. She and some of her relatives turned back [a mistake], because they lost so many of their cattle, and we never heard any more of them.

"At Scott's Bluffs we met a party of Mormons [actually, Clyman's party], who had been in California and did not like it and were then returning to Illinois. We got to Fort Laramie on the third of July and stayed there till the fifth, celebrating the fourth by giving the Indians a few presents. From here on to Fort Bridger we did not pay much attention to company; my father's three wagons, Mr. Daniel's one and Mr. McCracken's one left the rest and pushed to the South Pass; there we left them, for they talked of going to Oregon and we were bound for California. With our three wagons we went on to Fort Bridger; here we heard of the Donner Party, some three days ahead of us [and went on to overtake the Donners on the new Hastings Cutoff]. . . ."

For further information, see Note 213.

96. As a curious sequel to this affair, the *Oregon Spectator* reported on August 19, 1847: "The most truly gratifying intelligence brought from the immigration is that Mr. Edward Trimble, who it was supposed had been killed by the Pawnees last year, while on his way to this country, is alive and well and coming in with the immigrants. It appears that he had been wounded only and was made prisoner of by the Indians. He succeeded after a period of confinement in effecting his escape, returned to the States and started again for Oregon last Spring, when the immigration set out. The joyful feelings of his family who have resided in this city since their arrival here may be imagined."

But the next issue of the *Spectator*, September 2, 1847, corrected this report: "It is with exceeding sorrow that we feel ourself called upon to contradict the statement in our last paper relative to the late Mr. Edward Tremble. The report of his being alive probably originated from the circumstance of a cousin of the family, of the name of Tremble, being upon the road to this country, who unfortunately died on Sweetwater. It is singular that a report so utterly unfounded in truth, should have gained such general circulation and belief."

97. Compare the condensed note in Parkman's diary for August 6, 1846: "Ind. Outrages: The Pawnees—their alarm—stopping Finch —alarm subsides—killed Bradley with an arrow in June—stopped Bissonette June 4th—tried to rob Turner—steal horses—whip an emigrant into camp. Told Rouville that they would rob and kill every white who passed through their lands. . . ."

98. No more is said of these returning members of Smith's company. Palmer's journal repeats essentially the information given here: Palmer's party separated from these emigrants on June 30.

99. *The Gazette*, St. Joseph, July 17, 1846. It would seem that Palmer's party consisted of 18 men on arrival at St. Joseph July 7, though Hiram Smith and three others, left behind at Fort Laramie, did not come up with the main party till June 21. In addition to Palmer, Smith, and J. B. Wall, Spencer Bulkley is named by Palmer as one of his fellow travelers (and is also mentioned in the *Sangamo Journal* of August 6, which prints a long interview with him and says he had brought in 840 letters from Oregon which he deposited in the St. Joseph post office. "Several young men who had been on a visit of exploration to Oregon, returned in company with Mr. B. They design to do 'a considerable quantity of courting between this time and next spring, and then return with their wives.' Mr. Bulkley is

decidedly of opinion that Oregon is no place for Bachelors.'').

NEW AND NEARER ROUTES

100. Putnam Papers, Oregon Historical Society.

101. It is singular that the Putnams should be thinking of the Umpqua Valley, not yet knowing of the pioneering through that country of the Applegate Cutoff, which would bring both brothers into the Valley by autumn. Charles settled in that area in 1849.

102. Putnam Papers, Oregon Historical Society.

103. John C. Buchanan set out from Kentucky with the Putnam brothers, John Bosworth, and W. B. Brown. The latter joined the Russell pack party at Fort Bernard. Thereafter, on July 6, Edwin Bryant tells of crossing the North Platte and finding "Capt. West's company of emigrants encamped for the day. Several of the emigrating parties have been encamped here, and have *jerked* buffalo meat. By invitation, Mr. John C. Buchanan, of Lexington, Ky., joined us at this place." Thus Buchanan accompanied the Russell party to Fort Bridger and on to Sutter's Fort. With Reed, he served in the San Jose Company captained by Charles W. Weber during November and December, and he afterward settled in San Francisco. W. F. Swasey, *The Early Days and Men of California* (Oakland, 1891), pp. 271-272, terms Buchanan "altogether a most worthy and honorable man," who "still resides in San Francisco, in reduced circumstances and feeble health."

104. *Missouri Republican,* St. Louis, September 11, 1846, printed in conjunction with the interview with Solomon Sublette reprinted herein.

105. *Weekly Reveille,* St. Louis, July 12, 1846; this is George L. Curry's last letter from the overland trail, though he expected to write from Fort Bridger and Fort Hall. Curry did not overtake Selim E. Woodworth, and arrived independently at Oregon City—on August 30, it is said.

106. The full names of all the company (excepting Captain Wells) are provided only by Curry. Wells separated from the pack party at Fort Bridger, and Curry and Holder went on from there to Oregon. Next year Holder returned overland.

107. The fiscal records for Fremont's Third Expedition indicate that Charles Taplin was paid off by Fremont on March 31, 1846, after a period of service as voyageur which began October 1, 1844. Reddick had not been on the Fremont payroll.

108. *New York Herald,* November 4, 1846.

109. The mountain man Kinney mentioned here must not be confused with Sam Kinney, the recent arrival from Sutter's mentioned by Curry at Fort Bernard on June 26.

110. Stanton may here be documenting the final emergence of the

Donner Party as such. Five wagons, including the three W. C. Graves says comprised the Graves family detachment, subsequently joined to make the whole number 23.

111. Lilburn W. Boggs was shot by an intending assassin at his home near Independence on May 6, 1842. It has always been supposed that Orrin Porter Rockwell, a hard case among the early Mormons, did the deed as an act of revenge for the expulsion of the Mormons from Missouri during Bogg's term as governor. Against all expectations, Boggs recovered, though he showed the effects of his wounds till his death in 1860. Rockwell was jailed, but eventually released for lack of evidence.

112. *New York Herald,* November 15, 1846.

113. The capture of Hastings at Independence Rock by the Sioux in 1842 was a celebrated incident, related in his *Emigrants' Guide.* He and A. L. Lovejoy remained behind, when their company went on, "with a view of spending a few hours, in examining its peculiar structure, as well as to observe the various names, there to be seen, of individuals who have passed that way; and at the same time, to inscribe our own names, with the number of our company, the date of our passing; and whatever else might occur to us, as being serviceable to those who might subsequently pass that way." They had barely finished when they were captured. The Sioux released them unharmed a couple of days later.

114. The Three Crossings of the Sweetwater. The company went on this day, July 15, where Jefferson notes the "First view of the Wind River Mountains." For the next few days, Stanton better describes the travels of the Donner Party than Reed's diary does.

115. McGlashan prints part of this paragraph and portions of the next two. The various companies were encamped on the 16th near Jefferson's campsite of the day before, below the point where the road left the Sweetwater at present Chimney Creek. J. Quinn Thornton in Dunbar's company tells of making only a brief journey on the 16th, halting at 10 A.M. "in an open plain, at a place where the Sweet Water is shut up between high, perpendicular walls of rock. This is, therefore, the head of the valley, which, commencing about one hundred and twenty miles below, with an average width of about five miles, and bounded on both sides by granite mountains, here terminates."

116. Fremont examined this canyon on his first expedition. On August 6, 1842, his Report tells of reaching the "entrance of a kanyon where the Sweet Water issues upon the more open valley we had passed over." As had fur traders earlier, Fremont rode up through this canyon, though noting that "The usual road [better suited to wagons] passes to the right of this place. . . ."

Reed's diary falls into confusion on the 16th and has only a brief entry on the 17th, "Came from the mountain 16 to last Crossing of Sweet water," so we appreciate Stanton's details all the more. Thornton writes on the 17th: "The little company with which I had been traveling having left camp, I remained until Ex-Gov. Boggs came up, about 10 o'clock, with some sixteen wagons, when I joined his company, and we ascended on our right to a high and somewhat broken prairie, or rather open country, upon which we encamped at 6 o'clock, at some distance from the river, near a small stream." Thornton also tells of nooning on the 18th at the last crossing of the Sweetwater, and going on to camp on Pacific Creek.

117. So we are left with a riddle: how was Stanton able to send this letter back to Fort Bridger from Bear River—by an Indian, a mountain man, an emigrant who turned back?

118. *Liberty Tribune*, Liberty, November 21, 1846. As reprinted in the St. Louis *Daily Union,* November 28, 1846, the name of the writer is rendered, an obvious misprint, "T. Popp Long." Asterisks, indicating elisions, are those of the *Tribune.* Long's letter is valuable on several counts, indicating that Hastings might not have got back to Fort Bridger from the last crossing of the Sweetwater until July 16, and that it was expected 40 wagons would set out with him on the Hastings Cutoff (the following day), which was what Edwin Bryant reported later.

Heinrich Lienhard's narrative, under date of September 25, 1846, tells of overtaking Long in the Forty Mile Desert between the Sink of the Humboldt and the Truckee, "two fine Americans with a small, light vehicle and two mules. They had been waiting some time for the arrival of emigrants who might help them get through the sandbank. Since we were the first to come along, they naturally approached us, and we gladly promised to help them if they would, in turn, hitch their mules to our wagons. . . . The older one was a man by the name of Lang, and he was a doctor; the younger was John Miner [Minter?], from Kentucky. . . . Lang and Miner had been at the Truckee River, and Lang told us something about it, but his stories about the Indians did not serve to put our fears to rest. According to his story, they had driven off much of the stock belonging to the emigrants who had gone on before, and they were always on the lookout to steal. He said that a man who was looking for his animals had bent down to take a drink when he noticed that three arrows struck the water very near his head. When he jumped up and left, he saw that he was being followed by three Indians all the way back until he approached his camp. It was Lang's opinion that the Indians in this area were the most dangerous of all on the whole journey, and that we should be prepared to receive them properly in case they dared to attack us. He had once gone to Santa Fe for his health, and thought that he knew the Indians. . . ." Lienhard last refers to the wagon belonging to "Dr. Lang and Miner," one of seven comprising the company in which he himself was traveling, on reaching the foot of the Sierra—October 3, by Lienhard's dating.

119. These provocative remarks, including the last report on Curry before his arrival in Oregon, arouse fruitless conjectures as to the authorship. Joe Walker, to whom the latter was entrusted, left about July 25 for Bent's Fort. Alexander Barclay at the Hardscrabble fort on the upper Arkansas noted on August 20 the arrival of "Tim Goodale and party & Cap Walker from Blacks fork." Two days later he recorded the departure of "Walker Goodale & party" for Pueblo. Walker was mentioned by Lieutenant Abert on August 26 at Bent's Fort, where he would have found facilities for sending in mail.

120. Clyman and Crosby (mentioned in the *New Era* story of the same date, the A. H. Crosby who accompanied Hastings to California the previous autumn) are the only ones in this party who are named. Sam Kinney, mentioned at Fort Bernard by Curry, may not have arrived yet. For others who had accompanied Clyman east, see Volume I, pp. 51-62.

121. As in Volume I, pp. 16-17, Joseph Chiles had gone out to California with the Bartleson party in 1841, and after returning to Missouri next year, set out a second time in 1843. Although Chiles accompanied P. B. Reading on the pack route to the Sacramento via Fort Boise and the Malheur River, he had entrusted his wagons to the guidance of Joe Walker. Walker got his detachment into California safely via Walkers Pass, but had to abandon the wagons. Edward M. Kern on December 21, 1845, noted passing near the lower end of Owens Lake "Child's cache, where, on account of his animals failing, he was obliged to bury the contents of his wagons, among which was a complete set of mill-irons."

122. Reprinted from the *Weekly Tribune,* New York, August 15, 1846.

123. This account of James Clyman's arrival in St. Louis is inaccurate in many respects, not getting his name right, and misquoting his journal, but it is reprinted to show the impact of Clyman's arrival on the frontier. Clyman's diaries, extracts of which are quoted in Volume I, pp. 42, 50-62, should be compared with this news story, not fully reprinted by Camp.

124. The *Republican* might better have said that a *report* to this effect was recorded in Clyman's diary on March 22.

125. This report concerning Hastings is most interesting, but how much of it reflects Clyman's own thinking? The *Republican's* correspondent was too hasty to learn from Clyman or his diary that after the latter originally separated from Hastings near Johnson's Ranch, he waited in the Sierra for him to catch up, and afterward traveled the Hastings Cutoff in company with him.

126. Possibly this was Spencer Bulkley of Palmer's party, with whom the *Journal* printed a long interview the following week, as remarked in Note 99. On August 13 the *Journal* printed extracts from a letter to his father by William L. Todd, "who went out with the emigrants to California, in the spring of 1845, dated on the 17th of April"; for a quotation from this letter, as reprinted in the New York *Tribune,* see the Taylor diary, Note 58.

127. *Daily Union,* St. Louis, December 22, 1846, reprinted from the *Weston Democrat:* "The following is an extract of a letter just received from Fort Hall, from a gentleman who left last spring with a company of many others for the Oregon Territory. It is worthy the attention of persons intending to emigrate thither." As the letter intimates, Daniel Toole was a member of the Harrison Linville company, which David Goff's letter of April 3, 1847, terms the first to have turned into the Applegate Road at Raft River, apparently on August 8, 1846. Tolbert Carter, in his recollections of the Applegate Cutoff in 1846, recalls "a man by the name of [Dan] Tool, of Missouri, a large, portly young man, and a very agreeable gentleman, and, by the way, a Methodist," who ate something like a quarter of an acre of salal berries, vines included, when told they were edible —this in the Calapooya Mountains. The Crowley family which gave name to Grave Creek is mentioned to have had "the aged Linville" as an in-law.

128. Putnam Papers, Oregon Historical Society. This letter by Charles is the last sent home by either of the brothers. Charles does not here intimate that he would join Applegate's party at Fort Hall. The letter was postmarked at Kansas, Mo., October 3.

129. Apparently Joel M. Ware caught up with the Mississippi Saints soon after leaving Independence, and accompanied them through the Pawnee country, the six wagons with which he traveled comprising the nervous Oregon contingent John Brown describes, see Volume I, p. 111; they had taken heart and gone on ahead after meeting some of the returning Oregonians. Clyman encountered "J. M. Wair" on July 1 just west of Ash Hollow, immediately after he separated from the Mississippi Saints. As seen later in the present volume, the *Oregon Spectator* of October 1 reports his arrival at Oregon City, having accompanied Jesse Applegate from Fort Hall. Ware is mentioned as having been present at the first claim-jumping meeting in Oregon City, May 27, 1847. Oregon Historical Society *Quarterly,* March, 1918, vol. 19, pp. 69-71, contains a biographical sketch of Joel Ware, a pioneer of Lane County, a native of Ohio who "died in the spring of 1901 aged seventy-one years." Perhaps this man was a son of the Joel Ware to be remembered as the last emigrant to leave the frontier for Oregon in 1846. (Putnam supplies the date: June 2.)

130. The original of this letter did not pass into the Coe Collection with Jesse's other letters to Lisbon Applegate; the text is derived from Maude Applegate Rucker, *The Oregon Trail and Some of Its Blazers* (New York, 1930), pp. 239-242. It will be noted that Jesse says he set out June 22; Lindsay Applegate's reminiscences would make the date June 20.

131. For the elder Grant, factor at Fort Hall from 1842 to 1851, see T. C. Elliott, "Richard ('Captain Johnny') Grant," *Oregon Historical Quarterly*, March, 1935, vol. 26, pp. 1-13; and Louis S. Grant, "Fort Hall under the Hudson's Bay Company, 1837-1856," *ibid.*, March, 1940, vol. 41, pp. 34-40. He was born at Montreal January 20, 1794, and died at Walla Walla June 21, 1862. Apparently Elliott had not seen this letter by Applegate, for respecting Grant's family he is able to say only: "Grant was married at Montreal in 1821 to Mary Ann Berland; she died there in 1834. Two sons by that marriage, Stanislas Richard and John F., remained in Montreal with their grandmother until her death in 1849, and then joined their father at Fort Hall. Stanislas brought with him a wife of French descent, who is said to have been of remarkable mental and physical ability, and one son, Joseph Richard. Another son, Louis Joseph, was born at Walla Walla in 1851, became a resident of California and died there. Stanislas Grant died and was buried at Soda Springs, Idaho, in 1854 or 1855. John F. Grant, the other son, after coming to Fort Hall, married into the Shoshone tribe, went into the livestock business with his father and later moved to Montana. He was well known near Deer Lodge, where he became a prominent rancher. Still another son, James Cuthbert Grant, born to Richard Grant while in the Indian country of Canada, joined the family at Fort Hall, afterward moved to Montana and was killed near Browning in a fight with Blackfeet Indians some years later."

Elliott did not know of the daughter, nor apparently of the eldest son. That this son was then at Fort Hall, if not definitely shown by the letter of introduction which follows, is strongly intimated. William J. J. Scott's letter of August 14 says, "I Sen this letter by Mr Grant," and Lindsay Applegate has a clear reference to the son, as seen in Note 133. How the younger Grant reached Missouri remains to be learned, but he was the bearer of a number of letters printed in the present work, postmarked at Kansas on October 3.

It is possible that one of young Grant's companions may be identified, for the *Sangamo Journal* dated October 22, 1846, contains a long account of a Springfield lecture the previous week by A. L. Davidson, "late of Iowa Territory, now of Oregon, . . . [who] left the Wallamette valley in June last, and arrived in the States some days since," having been 18 months in Oregon. This Davidson apparently cannot be identified with the A. F. Davidson referred to in Note 135.

Is it possible that he was one of those who carried the express to Fort Hall discussed in Note 61? The *Journal* depicts A. L. Davidson as scarcely 22 years of age. Apparently he was from Burlington, Iowa, for the *Sangamo Journal* of December 17, 24, and 31, 1846, prints a communication from him dated in that city, December 1, 1846, accompanying extracts from his journal, September 24 - October 11, 1845, describing travels in the Willamette Valley.

132. Applegate Papers, Coe Collection, Yale University Library. Lisbon was addressed at Keytesville, Chariton County, Missouri.

133. This waybill by Jesse Applegate I have found reprinted from the Independence *Western Expositor* in a number of papers, including the *Sangamo Journal,* October 29, 1846; in some sheets it is misdated September 10. The waybill Applegate promises in this letter for the guidance of the emigration of 1847 may not have been sent, but such a document was printed in the *Oregon Spectator,* April 6, 1848, as observed in the Pringle diary, Notes 63, 69, and 71. This waybill, except for an inadvertently omitted line, was reprinted by Georgia Willis Read and Ruth Gaines in *Gold Rush* (New York, 1944, 2 vols.), vol 2, pp. 1213-1217.

Jesse Applegate's list of those who comprised the exploring party accords generally with that of Lindsay Applegate, quoted in Volume I, p. 78, though with some variations in the spelling of names. The principal difference is that Henry Boggs as written here becomes Henry Boygus in Lindsay's list. Whether the name be Boggs or Boygus, Lindsay names him among the advance party of five men sent on to Fort Hall, and says strangely: "Before the party of five reached Fort Hall, one of them, young Boygus, hearing that a son of Capt. Grant, commander of Fort Hall, had recently started for Canada, via St. Louis, concluded to leave the party and, by forced marches, endeavor to overtake Grant, as he was anxious to return to his home in Missouri. Boygus was brave and determined, and expecting to meet immigrants occasionally, he set out alone on his hazardous undertaking. We never heard of him afterwards, and his fate has always remained a mystery. There was, perhaps, truth in the report current afterwards that his gun and horses were seen in the possession of an Indian at Fort Hall, and it is most likely that he was followed by Indians from the very moment he left his companions and slain, as many a poor fellow has been, while all alone upon the great plains."

When Jesse Applegate turned back from Fort Hall, he was accompanied by the British botanist Joseph Burke, who wrote Sir William Hooker on October 17 from Walla Walla: "Late on the evening of the 8th of August Mr Applegate from the Walla Amett settlement arrived [at Fort Hall]—He had discovered a South route from the Walla Amett valey to Ogdens river & then east to Fort Hall—He gave such a fine description of the country between the California line

& the Walla Amett valey that I felt most anxious to accompany him & his party on their return—The next day being sunday he allowed me this much to prepare for the journey—I packed a small quantity of paper, a quantity of such bags & forty days provisions—On the 11th we left the Fort—After following the Snake river about 45 miles we turned up the raft river, then striking over to the heads of Goose creek, then crossing [to] the hot spring valey, & from thence to Ogdens river. It was then the 17th of August—We were at that time about 200 miles from Fort Hall—We followed Ogdens river until the 26th of August—The river & California trail which we had been following, turns with a sharp bend to the S., a little inclining to E—& about 400 miles from Fort Hall—After leaving the river we passed over about 60 miles of most miserable volcanic region, with many boiling springs. With Mr Applegates party, & some young men from the waggons, which came to clear the coast where it was absolutely required—we numbered 24— On the 8th of Septr we entered the sacramento valey — after crossing the valey — about 20 miles, we crossed the Sacramento [Lost] river a short distance below [above?] the lake, which is divided from the clamet lakes by a narrow ridge— That evening we encamp[ed] by the [Lower] Clamet lake—On the 14th we entered the Rogue river or Shasty valey. . . . The next day we struck the rogue river. . . . On the 19th we entered the Umpqua Mountains—on the 20th we encamped on the Callipeua Mountains. . . . On the 26th we arrived at Mr Applegates farm in the Yam hills about 50 miles from Oregon city—Our horses were compleatly worn down, & ourselves much fatigued—By great attention to watching both day & night, we passed through the different tribes of Indians without any mishap which has seldom occured to a party before. . . ."

This Applegate chronicle may be closed by quoting another of Jesse's letters to Lisbon printed by Mrs. Rucker, dated Polk County, Oregon, Oct. 11, 1847: "Unfortunately for the present emigration the emigrants who travelled the Southern rout to Oregon did badly for want of energy and diligence in travelling they were caught by the rains which were of unusual severity, at the Umpqua mountain about 75 miles from the Willamette Valley being out of bread and much discouraged many of the families abandoned their wagons and much of their property and were packed into the settlements—the merchants at Oregon City, a chartered company which has a toll gate in the Cascade Mountains, and the major part of the old settlers, being interested in the profit arising from the old road down the Columbia — eagerly seized upon this circumstance to denounce the newly discovered rout, and of course the man who had found and recommended it. As our whole party with I think few if any exceptions undertook the hazardous duty of discovering a better road from the purest spirit of philanthropy having no pecuniary views whatever

—you may imagine our feelings when for our exertions for the general good instead of the thanks of our fellow citizens, we were assailed from all sides with abuse, and slanders the most injurious—By exercising my patience and summoning all my fortitude to my aid, I steadily maintained my position, and defended the *road* without noticing private slanders—in a series of articles signed Z. [See Volume I, pp. 69-77.] I reviewed the difficulties encountered by the several emigrations in reaching this country and closed by showing plainly the advantages of the southern rout over any heretofore known.

"Tho' fully convinced of the truth of any statements yet I made no effort to induce emigrants to travel the road—

"Your friend Mr. Burch with 25 wagons were all that we know of who travelled the new road [in 1847]—they have all arrived safely and are highly pleased with the road, a great reaction in the public mind must take place—as an even greater amount of suffering and loss is now taking place on the old road than usual—the result will be the permanent establishment of the southern road. . . ." (See Note 210.)

Although Applegate signed his articles in the *Oregon Spectator* only with the pen-name "Z," it was understood that he was the author, for Thornton, *op.cit.*, vol. 1, pp. 214-215, quotes from "Z's" description of the divide between the Umpqua and the Rogue as being Applegate's.

134. Original letter in de Coppet Collection, Princeton University Library. It would appear that Scott's company continued on to Oregon by the old route, and that their seven wagons are the seven mentioned by the *Oregon Spectator* of October 29 as coming in by the Barlow Road; see David Goff's letter of April 3, 1847, printed hereinafter. Scott's letter, like others earlier from Fort Hall, was carried to the States by Richard Grant, Jr., postmarked "Kansas Mo Oct 3."

135. What in this book I have termed the Genois party has been given its name by reason of this notice on the frontier. In Volume I, p. 65, it was suggested that one Hockerman (Abner Hackleman?) might have accompanied the party. Possibly there is a record of others among Genois' fellow travelers. In the Coe Collection at Yale is a group of 22 manuscript maps by A. F. Davidson, who went out to Oregon in 1845 and returned in 1846. These maps appear to cover the last five weeks of the journey, from June 26 or 27 to July 31 or August 1; they depict the trail from the upper Platte to St. Joseph. The journey is said to have taken 104 days, which would indicate that April 18 or 19 was the day of departure. The accuracy of the maps is attested on August 1-3, 1846, by four of Davidson's companions, S. Eikenburg, J. B. Holliday, J. A. Hunt, and Henry Williamson. Perhaps, then, as many of the 16 men Edwin Bryant claims to have

encountered on July 1 (a total now shrunk to 11) may be regarded as identified.

136. *Arkansas State Gazette,* Little Rock, September 7, 1846. This letter is the last direct report from Leavitt, but as appears from the following document, he started on from Santa Fe. News of hostilities between Mexico and the United States had not yet reached the New Mexican capital.

137. *Missouri Republican, St.* Louis, August 24, 1846.

138. Compare T. D. Bonner, *The Life and Adventures of James P. Beckwourth* (New York, 1856), pp. 474-475, which describes a California horse-stealing enterprise by Beckwourth and "five trusty Americans" as an incident of the war—of which Beckwourth could not have learned until long after he reached the Arkansas. Alexander Barclay, at the Hardscrabble fort, mentions on May 28 the arrival of "Beckworth, Waters, & party from Calafornia La Bonte Markhead &c. . . ." Waters and party left for Pueblo on the 30th, and the comings and goings of Waters and Beckwourth are mentioned by Barclay down to August 4. After the reference to Leavitt by Colburn and Waters in the present letter, however, the Arkansan vanishes from the record.

139. Solomon Sublette had gone to California in 1845 by the emigrant road, not as one of Fremont's party; the newspaper story would best have said that Solomon last heard of Fremont on the Sacramento. Charles Taplin had left Fremont's employ on March 31. As seen in the Taylor diary, Notes 33 and 34, Sublette had traveled from Pueblo de los Angeles to Fort Bridger in company with Joe Walker at least part of the way. Edwin Bryant, who encountered him in Russell's party on the Sweetwater July 11 (see Russell's and Curry's letters of that date), says that Sublette's three companions at that time were Taplin, Reddick, and one other, not named. "Mrssrs. Taplin and Reddick had been members of Captain Fremont's exploring party. They left California with a party with which they travelled as far as Fort Hall, and from thence have proceeded on by themselves, expecting, as I understood, to fall in at Fort Laramie with some party of traders bound to the frontier towns of Missouri. Mr. Reddick is a nephew of an old friend and neighbor of mine, Charles Carr, Esq., of Fayette county, Kentucky, and had been absent from his friends two years."

Bryant clearly should have said Fort Bridger, not Fort Hall, in the passage quoted above.

140. See William E. Taylor's diary for July 7-8. "Mr. Davis" remains to be identified; if he kept on to California, he would have captained the second company after that of Craig & Stanley, which presumably parted from him on the morning of July 8, leaving him with ten (or eleven) wagons.

141. Compare Wales B. Bonney's account, given to the *Western*

Expositor on reaching Independence September 30. Francis Parkman has some scattered references to the passage of Sublette and Bonney through the country. Thus in his diary for August 6, after detailing some Pawnee outrages, he says the Sioux were never so turbulent as this year: "Declare that if the emigrants continued to pass through, they would rob them and kill them if they resisted. Broke up the pots and pans of the emigrants who feasted them. Robbed Sublette and Reddick, and fired upon them. Robbed Bonny. Robbed a party of eight waggons at Independence Creek [*i.e.,* Independence Rock?], in July." For Sublette's further journey from Fort Laramie to the Mormon camp at Pueblo, and on past Bent's Fort, see Note 142. The *Republican's* account is defective in locating the Mississippi Saints near "Fort Bent" rather than at Pueblo. For a biographical sketch of Solomon, see John E. Sunder, "Solomon Perry Sublette: Mountain Man of the Forties," *New Mexico Historical Review,* January, 1961, vol. 36 pp. 49-61. Sunder follows the mistaken view of Doyce B. Nunis, Jr., "The Enigma of the Sublette Overland Party, 1845," *Pacific Historical Review,* November, 1959, vol. 28, pp. 331-349, in bringing Solomon east via Walker's Pass, the Humboldt, and Fort Hall.

142. Robert M. Ewing has appeared frequently in these pages since setting out for California in company with Edwin Bryant and R. T. Jacob; see Index, and in particular, the McKinstry diary, Note 71. Francis Parkman, who at St. Louis on April 25, had found Ewing an "impulsive, unobserving ardent Kentuckian, who lays open his character to everyone, and sees nothing of those about him," is speaking of him or his companion Hewitt when he says: "A young Kentuckian had come out to the mountains with Russell's party of California emigrants. One of his chief objects, as he gave out, was to kill an Indian; an exploit which he afterward succeeded in achieving, much to the jeopardy of ourselves and others who had to pass through the country of the dead Pawnee's enraged relatives. Having become disgusted with his emigrant associates, he left them, and had some time before set out with a party of companions for the head of the Arkansas. He left us a letter to say that he would wait until we arrived at Bent's Fort, and accompany us thence to the settlements. When, however, he came to the fort, he found there a party of about forty men about to make the homeward journey, and wisely preferred to avail himself of so strong an escort. Sublette and his companions also joined this company; so that on reaching Bent's Fort some six weeks after, we found ourselves deserted by our allies and thrown once more upon our own resources."

The Conn mentioned in the present newspaper account is no stranger to Western annals. Osborne Russell, who describes John Conn as Irish-born and given to speaking with a broad brogue, tells of a hunt with him in the Yellowstone country in the fall of 1837, when he was no more than a green campkeeper. (Coincidentally, another companion of Osborne Russell on that hunt, John Greenberry, who had come to the mountains as a Wyeth engage in the spring of 1834, is mentioned as a guide for the William H. Russell company as far as the Kansas River, at least.) Conn's experiences after his greenness wore off have gone unrecorded. Ewing's account places him on Big Timber Creek (*i.e.,* Lodgepole Creek?) in 1843, and the Navaho experiences might have come after that date. Alexander Barclay mentions him at the Hardscrabble Fort on June 1, 1846, then evidently on his way north to Fort Bernard with Bill New and others.

143. At Hardscrabble Barclay noted on July 18 the arrival of "Ewing Huett Brown La Roque from North fork." Captain Benjamin D. Moore had reached Bent's Fort on July 22, after an unsuccessful effort to overtake the Santa Fe traders who had set out from Missouri before the news of war arrived.

144. See Note 139 respecting this April 3 separation from Fremont. It would appear from this account that Taplin did not reach Independence till after Solomon Sublette returned to St. Louis, but more likely there is some error in the September 11 date.

145. The same story, as printed in the St. Louis *Daily New Era,* October 8, 1846, says the emigrants separated at Independence Rock on the 12th rather than the 15th of July, and that fits the facts much better. Bonney has appeared and reappeared frequently in our pages, and now he speaks for himself, first in this report of his arrival from Oregon, and second through some biographical sketches of later years. The most extensive of these, *A History and Biographical Cyclopaedia of Butler County, Ohio. . . .* (Cincinnati, 1882), p. 530, relates:

"Wales B. Bonney is a native of Charlestown, New Hampshire, where he was born June 26, 1799. His father, West Bonney, finds a line of family descent from Thomas Bonney, who was born in Dover, England, in 1604, and who came from Sandwich, in Kent, England, in the ship Hercules in 1634 or 1635, and who located in Duxbury, Massachusetts. The mother's maiden name was Lydia Reed, she also being of Welsh-English parentage. In early life the boy Wales, in addition to the advantages offered by the common schools of the day, spent nearly a year in Dartmouth College. In 1816, in company with his parents and an only brother, he came into Ohio, the family settling on a farm one mile northwest of the village of Oxford. He soon after entered Miami University as a student, boarding with his parents and taking his hand at the work of the farm nights and mornings, riding to and from school on horseback. He continued at the university until the following year, remaining at home afterwards until about twenty-one years of age, when in the spring of 1820 he made a trip to his native state, making the entire distance on horseback. There he spent the Summer, and in the Fall returned as far as Chautauqua County, New York, where he engaged in teaching school until the next Spring, when he took up his residence for several years at Rochester and Brighton in the same State, and while there formed the acquaintance of and married Miss Lucinda Abbey, whose family were of Massachusetts origin. This was in January 1829. Two years thereafter Mr. Bonney, with his family, returned to the home of his parents in Oxford, and there they spent the Winter. The next Spring Mr. and Mrs. Bonney emigrated to Texas, landing from a schooner from New Orleans at Brazoria, near the mouth of the Brazos River, then an insignificant collection of low shanties and huts. Their intention had been to make that province their future home, but after living there some months they decided to retrace their steps to their Oxford home, and reached that place late in the Fall following, having lost one of their little children while absent.

"But the spirit of unrest was upon the subject of our sketch, and in the Spring of 1845, accompanied by two other young men by the names of Buell and Worstell, he started for an overland trip to Oregon, a hazardous adventure in those days. Joining another party at Independence, the company were five months on the way before they reached Dalles on the Columbia River, their place of destination. Arriving there the earlier part of October most of the party made this their home the ensuing Winter. But Mr. Bonney was not yet content. He did not discern his desired fortune in the immediate future. So the following Spring, with no company save a couple of horses, one for the saddle and the other to carry his clothings and provisions, a couple of guns, and a bold spirit, he set out for a return to the States. When crossing the plains he fell in with some Indian scouts in advance of a roving tribe, who took from him his horses, pack of provisions, and one gun. The traveler, however, managed to save one gun and a sack containing a large packet of letters which had been intrusted to his care by comrades and others in the West for loved ones at home. He pursued his lonely way on foot for some three days when he was overtaken by a party of returning Californians, with whom he kept company to the States, and reached home early in the Fall of 1846. He soon after settled in the village of Oxford, which place has since been his residence. Here he has many years been honored by his fellow-citizens in repeated elections to the office of justice of the peace, the delicate and responsible duties of which he has performed with uniform acceptance to the people. Here a family of eleven children has been born to him, of whom a daughter, Julia, and four sons, Franklin, Oregon, Robert and Edward, are now living, the sons all being engaged in trade in Louisville, Kentucky, the daughter residing with the parents."

Another sketch, in *Centennial History of Butler County, Ohio* (n.p., 1905), p. 959, says in part: "In 1830 he removed to Texas and the next fall he returned to Oxford where he resided until 1845 and then emigrated to Oregon. The following spring he started with two horses and a wagon on the return trip from Oregon to Oxford. . . . He died June 10, 1887, age seventy-nine years, eleven months and fourteen days. . . ."

Apart from their immediate contribution to the history of Wales B. Bonney and the annals of 1845-1846, these biographical notes suggest how much information respecting Oregon, California, and the West is interred in county histories, awaiting the day when some scholar or team of scholars embark upon a project of indexing U. S. local histories for Western content.

THE NEW LAND: OREGON AND CALIFORNIA

146. See Note 129. Ware evidently brought the news of "Wm. Tremble's" death.

147. Here is the sole indication that Farnham may have come to California in Leavitt's party. Perhaps instead he voyaged around the Horn with the New York Regiment, arriving in 1847.

148. Rather remarkably, the *Californian* accurately forecasts where the Mormons would settle a year later. The Mississippi Saints in 1846 did not get west of Fort Laramie.

149. See William E. Taylor's diary, Note 2; John W. Ladd apparently was the "Mr Lad" who set out from Missouri with John Craig and Larkin Stanley, the first to enter California with wagons this year. George Gary's diary, as printed in Oregon Historical Society *Quarterly*, September, 1923, vol. 24, pp. 323-328, provides some interesting details on the incoming emigration by the Barlow Road. On August 26: "A few of this year's emigrants arrive today. They bring the report that there is war between Mexico and the United States." On the 28th: "This day we receive a letter from Rev. A. Adams . . . brought over the mountains by Lieu. Woodward of U. S. Navy, who has been sent by the government at home with dispatches for the commodore of the navy in the Pacific ocean. I suppose now the American armed vessel 'Shark' will leave this river soon as possible, and take these dispatches to the proper officer." (The *Shark* was wrecked while crossing the Columbia bar September 10.) On September 13, the day of Ladd's arrival: "The emigrants with wagons over the mountains; a few of them reach the suburbs of this city this day." Next day: "More emigrants with wagons arrive. They left Missouri in May and are now here. From the best information I can gather, they have had a very successful journey and are coming in, not only in very good season, but also with some supplies of provisions still on hand." On September 23: "The emigrants occasionally pass along.

Report says about half of them have gone on a new route, so as to come into the upper part of the Williamette valley; a very great relief to our mission at the Dalls." And on October 15: "We are having very fine and warm weather. The emigrants who came by the Dalls are mostly in." For additional comments by Marcus Whitman, see Note 173.

150. The weather took a severe turn for the worse just as this issue of the *Spectator* appeared; see the Pringle diary, Note 89.

151. Presumably John J. Scott and his companions; see Notes 134 and 156.

152. These casualties reported by George L. Curry among the emigrants merit further explanation. Sarah Hunt Steeves, *Book of Remembrance of Marion County, Oregon, Pioneers, 1840-1860* (Portland, 1927), pp. 88-89, publishes a biographical sketch of Henry Smith, an 1846 pioneer by the Applegate route in association with "John Long, Underwood, James Smith, Campbell, Lorenzo Byrd and others, with their families." After the rains set in, "the sun came out one day and James Smith, a brother of Henry, who, with his large family, was of their party, looked up and jokingly remarked, 'Boys, you better take a look at the sun; maybe it will be the last time you see it,' and in ten minutes he was a dead man, having succumbed to a heart attack." (See also Thornton's account in Note 160.) James may have been born in Virginia or in Missouri; Henry was born in Tennessee while the family was migrating in 1818.

David Tanner, the second of Curry's casualties, is evidently the unnamed emigrant, "partially insane, verry indolent and careless," referred to in Peter H. Burnett's letter of March, 1847 (see Note 174). Tolbert Carter also recalled his death, saying that when the emigrants left Lost River they got an early start in order to reach Lower Klamath Lake, there being no water between. "Arriving late and preparing to place guard, and in calling the roll, it was found that there was a man missing. The lateness of the hour prevented any investigation that night; but next morning a party went back, and found the missing man, stripped and dead. He was a man 50 years of age, and had been walking and driving cattle. He probably became weary and stopped to rest and perhaps fell asleep. The Indians stealthily approached him and shot him with arrows. We buried him alone on the desert, to remain till the final summons for all to appear."

The third death, that of one Sallie or Sallee from Callaway County, Missouri, is the best known, yet paradoxically his first name is nowhere given; and the proper way to spell his last name is not known. He was fatally wounded on the Humboldt, and therefore not by Klamath Indians. Edwin Bryant remarks: "The company of Capt. West on Mary's river had a difficulty and a fight with a large party of Digger Indians. In this encounter a Mr. Sallee lost his life from a wound by a poisoned arrow. Mr. Lippincott was wounded in the knee, but he recovered." J. Quinn Thornton, *op. cit.,* vol. 1, p. 171, also remarks the death of "Sallee" in one of the forward companies in consequence of an otherwise slight wound by a poisoned arrow.

Perhaps A. J. Grayson best tells the story. A collection of his papers in the Bancroft Library includes several different versions of a letter written from San Francisco to his brother-in-law, Isaiah Garrett, on February 22, 1847. Grayson says he left Fort Bridger on July 26, having taken Joe Walker's advice not to attempt the Hastings Cutoff. "After proceeding down Mary's R. nearly to the Sink, where it disappears entirely, we met with a new species of trouble. The Indians here stole a number of our cattle and shot a good many with arrows poisoned which they left.

"Our company was quite small at that time and could only muster a few fighting men. About ten of us, however, followed them. We soon came up with the main body of them at their own village where they numbered upward of 300 fighting men and all arrayed for battle, whooping and yelling all kinds of defiance. Though their numbers were much stronger than ours, we had no idea of backing out; they had raised the tomahawk against us, notwithstanding our kind treatment of them when they came about our camp. We advanced upon them with the determination to teach them a lesson. Four of our men were mounted and the balance on foot; we charged upon them as fast as we were able but before we got within rifle shot they all disappeared behind the rocks, like so many squirrels into their holes. We still advanced upon them until within a few paces of where they were hit when they charged upon us with all the fury of savages. We met them, however, with steady aim, and every shot killed an Indian. They fell back in the rocks again and continued to pour their arrows at us faster than the hail from the clouds. We fought them from behind rocks all day shooting them through the head whenever we could catch one peeping over the rocks, until we finally routed them after killing 18 of their number. We also recovered the most of our cattle. We lost one on our side—one man killed, 3 badly wounded and others slightly. One horse was also killed. I had the honor that day of leading the company.

"Next day we proceeded slowly on our journey uninterrupted until we arrived at the Sink of St. Mary's river where we again had nearly all our cattle stolen from [us]. We followed them next morning but recovered only a few, which were so badly shot with arrows as to be rendered entirely of no service to us. I lost half my team and some of us were rendered almost helpless in the way of traveling, and the most difficult part of the road was yet to be encountered...."

In 1902 Frances Grayson Crane added from memory: "Sometimes

things of a serious nature have a ludicrous side, as was the case in our party. We did not think of any danger. A Mr. —— (I'll not mention name for the sake of surviving friends) buckled on his armor, pistol and knife in belt; and shouldered his rifle. He was the most formidable looking one of the whole party. He soon returned, said, 'I did not think it safe for the women and children to be without some man about the camp.' I'll explain right here; our *fighting* men were between us and the Indians, we were in no danger.

"Mr Salley left home an invalid, in a few weeks became a strong, robust man—then to meet with such a death, by the poisoned arrow of an Indian—The saddest funeral I have ever witnessed was that of Mr Salley. We buried him in the middle of the road, during the night, next morning our wagons were driven over the spot, so that his remains should not be disturbed and robbed by the Indians. . . ."

It is evident, from the Jefferson map and other sources, that this battle with the Paiutes occurred north of present Winnemucca, before reaching the point where the Applegate Cutoff separated from the California Trail. The declining Sallee was carried on by his friends and buried as remarked in the Mathers diary, Note 58.

In another account, Grayson says that involved in this affair were a company of "five or six wagons, bound for Oregon"; and among those wounded in the ensuing battle was "Mr Whitelsy Captain of the Oregon party." (Thornton gives the latter's name as Whately in his book, but in his 1878 address to the Oregon Pioneer Association corrects the name to Whitley, "the same one who was killed at Dallas [Oregon] about three years ago.") No doubt this was Samuel Whitley, recorded in Marion County, Oregon, by the 1850 census, a Virginian then aged 60.

According to Jacob Wright Harlan, who came along after "Salley" was buried, "a board sticking by the side of the trail" warned that Indians were hostile and gave information that "on the previous day Governor Boggs' party had a severe fight with the Indians; that one man named Salley was killed in the fight, and Ben Lippincott badly wounded; that they had killed about forty Indians; that the savages fought with poisoned arrows, tipped with the venom of the rattlesnake; that many Indians had concentrated at this point to steal stock, and murder emigrants, and that they had buried Salley in the road, and run the wagons over the grave to conceal it. Notwithstanding these precautions, a few rods past this notice we found poor Salley's body. The savages had found the grave, dug him up, scalped him, and mutilated his body in a cruel manner."

153. Moses ("Black") Harris, one of the most celebrated of the mountain men, a South Carolinan, had come to Oregon as an emigrant guide in 1844. During 1845 he participated in several road-

hunting expeditions, and in 1846 was one of Jesse Applegate's party. He went east in 1847 and died of cholera in 1849 when about to leave for California. For a biographical sketch, see Dale L. Morgan and Eleanor T. Harris, eds., *The Rocky Mountain Journals of William Marshall Anderson.* This letter shows that he was well educated and articulate.

154. Harris leaves out of consideration the Siskiyou Mountains, not to mention lesser obstacles. But he may have shared in the misconception that the Applegate party had reached the head of the Sacramento River, from which point as he supposed a railroad could be constructed with little difficulty.

155. Campbell and Van Bebber are occasionally mentioned in Thornton's journal; for references to some of the others, see the Index.

156. Probably the Iowa company in which William J. J. Scott traveled; see Note 134.

157. George L. Curry had become editor of the bi-weekly *Spectator* with the issue of October 1, 1846.

158. *Oregon Spectator,* December 10, 1846.

159. J. Quinn Thornton has become a familiar name in these pages, and now we should get acquainted with him as an individual. According to a manuscript Autobiography written for H. H. Bancroft in 1879-1880, he was born near Point Pleasant, Mason County, (West) Virginia on August 24, 1810, but in infancy moved with his family to Champaign County, Ohio. In 1835 he began to practice law at Palmyra, Missouri, and on February 8, 1838, he married Mrs. Nancy M. Logue, who accompanied him to Oregon in 1846. Opposition to slavery led him to remove to Quincy, Illinois, in April, 1841. He resided there until he set out for Oregon five years later, his poor health and that of his wife a primary consideration in making the journey. Soon after reaching the Willamette Valley, on February 9, 1847, Thornton was appointed by Governor Abernethy judge of the supreme court of the provisional government. That fall he started off to the States to lobby for a territorial government. He voyaged to San Francisco, where in November and December he interviewed survivors of the Donner disaster, and from where he was given passage to Boston in the U. S. sloop-of-war *Portsmouth.* Arriving in Boston May 5, he went on to Washington, where he was an effective lobbyist. He contributed letters to the New York *Tribune* over the pen-name Achilles de Harley, and also improved his time by writing his two-volume *Oregon and California in 1848,* published at New York early in 1849. Thornton returned to Oregon City in May, 1849, and was long active as a lawyer and legislator, though reduced in circumstances in his latter years. At different times he lived at Oregon City, Albany, and Portland, but from 1871 until his death on

February 5, 1888, made his home in Salem.

More is said in Notes 160 and 167 concerning Thornton's acrimonious part in the controversies over the Applegate Cutoff. Here, in connection with his arrival in the settlements, we shall note only that George Gary at Oregon City wrote in his diary on December 29: "We are visited by Mrs. Thornton, who came the new route; she has lately arrived; gives a most distressed account of the latter part of their journey; their company turned off of the old route at Fort Hall, and the story of their sufferings is almost incredible; women waded for miles in water from two to four feet deep; and for weeks day and night had not a dry thread in any of their garments; nearly all their cattle perished for want of grass and water; they were assured by Mr. Applegate who persuaded them to take the new route that they would be in to the Williamette valley by the middle of September, and here is, near the last of December, and but a part of them have yet arrived." Gary favorably noticed Mrs. Thornton in subsequent diary entries, and on February 3 wrote: "Mr. and Mrs. Thornton dine with us. The lady has been in the city a few weeks. The man reached this place last evening; he is a lawyer; appears as though he would be a good inhabitant in this distant land. He is a professor of religion." (From then on, Gary was a Thornton man.)

160. *Oregon Spectator,* March 4, 1847. With this communication J. Quinn Thornton opens the bombardment of Jesse Applegate he would continue scarcely unabated till his death. Thornton was resolved that the disasters upon the Applegate Cutoff must be somebody's fault, not his own; he made Applegate the scapegoat. What he began in this letter Thornton followed up in his vituperative book. Necessarily, this will be a long Note, but we should summarize Thornton's primary narrative.

Thornton says he passed Fort Hall on August 7 and camped that night 8 miles west of the fort. He and his companions elected to recruit their stock on the 8th, and on the forenoon of that day Applegate came into camp. Thornton declares that he was immediately suspicious of the man, but Ex-Governor Boggs "to the fullest extent, confided in the statements of Applegate," so Thornton says he allowed himself to be persuaded. At this time, influenced by Clyman at Fort Laramie, Boggs was bound for Oregon, and would have gone on by the Old Oregon Trail except for the advent of Applegate.

Thornton resumed the journey on August 9. On the 12th he notes that "Mr. John Newton left our company in the morning," driving forward to unite with one ahead. On the 13th "Mr. Roby [Rupert] died . . . in the company led by Mr. Dickinson. . . . He was a young man from Independence, Missouri, whose parents had united with him in the opinion that a residence in Oregon or California might restore him to health. . . . His brother, Dr. Rupert . . . had accompanied him some distance into the great prairie wilderness, for the purpose of observing whether he would probably endure the fatigues and hardships of the journey." Consumption was the cause of death. Thornton also says this day: "Wm. Kirquendall and Charles Putnam left our company in the morning, to go forward with others, led by Captain Applegate, to mark and open the new road."

On the 14th Thornton camped near (James) Campbell's company, in which traveled a very sick man, Hicklin, with his wife and two children, also ill. "They had for a driver a worthless fellow, who, becoming angry with Mrs. Hicklin, because of her desiring him to bring a bucket of water from the spring, left them in their helpless condition, and was employed by Mr. Crump, who traveled in our company. I have been informed that an individual in Mr. Campbell's company proposed to drive the team for $1 per day, but that Mr. Hicklin, refusing to pay so much, was abandoned. Subsequently, the company led by Mr. Dickinson came up, and finding the family in that helpless condition, and in a country filled with treacherous savages, furnished a driver. It is likewise probable, that Mr. Hicklin contracted to pay an agreed sum for the services of the man furnished."

On the 15th "Messrs. Nealey, Burns, Perkins, and young Kirquendall, left us in the morning, and we were thus reduced to seven wagons." Thornton reached Goose Creek on the 16th, traveled up it the next two days, then made more southerly for "Ogden's River." At noon on the 21st "we passed the grave of Mr. Burns, who died at 3 o'clock, A. M., and was buried at 10 o'clock, A.M. He left a wife and three children." Thornton went on to camp "in the Hot Spring Valley" at 2 P.M. And here, in Thousand Springs Valley, since he lost his subsequent diary on the Applegate Cutoff, Thornton's journal becomes a more general narrative. At the forks of the road, he says, they were surprised to meet Major Goff. "Ex-Gov. Boggs, in a letter to me, dated '*Sonoma, Upper California, April* 20, 1847,' speaking of the time when we arrived at the forks of the road, says, 'I do not recollect the day of the month we separated at the forks of the road' (Applegate's cut-off), 'but to the best of my recollection it was after the middle of September, or about the middle'." Thornton also mentions a journal kept by "Mr. Charles James Stewart, who entered upon the Applegate cut-off September 6th, that is, about ten days before I did." Thornton quotes further from Boggs's letter: "From the best of my judgment, we must have traveled 400 miles on Ogden's River. I know that I was so much disheartened with the length of the road on Ogden's River, before we reached the Forks, that I lost all confidence in Applegate's judgment of distances; and concluded, if he had made as great an error of judgment in the residue of the route, that we should not be able to reach the settlements before winter set in, and that we should in all probability perish. These considerations determined me to take the route to California."

Thornton goes on to say that as his company entered upon the Black Rock Desert "we saw a dense cloud of dust rolling up in the distance behind. This we believed to be raised either by a large body of hostile Indians, or by the company of Messrs. Brown and Allen, whom we knew to be not far behind us. . . . I have since been in California, where I saw Mr. [Elam] Brown, who informed me that they entered upon this cut-off, and sent forward one of their company forty-five miles, on horseback, and that they were met by him after the wagons had traveled thirty miles, without finding water, as they had been told. Their messenger stated, upon meeting them, that he had been fifteen miles farther forward, without finding water. It was finally deemed hazardous to rely any longer upon the word of this untrustworthy guide [Applegate]. They therefore turned about, and made a hasty retreat to Ogden's River, where they remained for a brief period to recruit their cattle, after which they proceeded to California."

Companions of Thornton at this stage of the journey were Crump and David Butterfield. At an unspecified place, most likely Surprise Valley, "we came up with Messrs. Hall, Croizen, and Whately. Whately was suffering much from a wound received in a battle with the Indians on Ogden's River. In addition to these, our company now consisted of Messrs. Caldwell, Crump, Baker, Butterfield, Bosworth, Morin, Putnam, Newton, Lovelin, Boone, and Dodd, who was with Morin, and [William] Stokes [whom Thornton had hired as an ox-driver], and also with myself." They remained here recruiting two or three days, then continued on "over a country that was generally very barren, until we arrived at the Sacramento Valley [*i.e.,* Lost River], where my wagon was dashed in pieces upon an exceedingly rough and dangerous road. Here I cast aside some more of my property. I succeeded in making an arrangement with Mr. David Butterfield, for the use of one of his wagons, he having one that was nearly empty." He tells of going around "a lake which was said to be the Tlamath, although it is certain that none of our party knew it," crossing with much difficulty a ridge beyond, then going on to cross "a mountain usually known as the Siskia Mountain." Newton and Townsend are mentioned as now in company, and Josiah Morin presently overtaken. David Goff at this time was serving as pilot.

Thornton resumes daily entries on October 11, when he reached "the western side of the Siskia Mountains." He had had to abandon his wagon the previous day, his oxen having given out. On the 12th he says: "Mr. Hall agreed to carry my provisions for two-fifths of my bread stuff, and some articles of clothing. Josiah Morin contracted to carry the remainder of my clothing in one of his wagons, in consideration of my giving him the exclusive ownership of [two oxen], and their yoke and chain, and the use, into the settlements, of all the other oxen that still survived, and were fit for service. I gave to Major Goff, a medicine-chest, a set of cut-glass bottles filled with medicine for the journey, a cast-steel spade which I had carried up to this time, for the purpose of working road where necessary, and a number of other articles, as a compensation for returning with me to the place where I had left the wagon. Having been one of the instruments used by Applegate in misleading the emigrants, it was his duty to have rendered me assistance without compensation. But the conduct of some of these road-hunters has given them an infamous notoriety, which has its parallel in the character of a class of outlaws and banditti, who during many years infested the Florida reefs, where they often contrived so to mislead vessels, as to wreck them; when, without scruple or ceremony, they, under various pretenses, would commence their work of pillage." (This is one of the more beneficent comments Thornton makes on the roadhunters.)

Thornton tells of going forward on the 13th, then jumps to the 18th, when "We met Messrs. Brown, Allen, and Jones, and some two or three other persons. The two first had come out to the wilderness for the purpose of meeting their friends in the company of Messrs. Brown and Allen. . . . The two first named gentlemen who met us were the sons of those emigrants." Thornton then remarks approvingly on John Jones, as quoted in Holt journal, Note 2.

On the 19th, says Thornton, "Messrs. Brown and Allen succeeded in inducing some of our party to return upon our back trail for the purpose of meeting their friends and relatives. It will be remembered, that at that time, we did not know any thing certainly of them." The others went on, "accompanied by Labin Morin, and a son of Goffs," crossing the Rogue River in the forenoon. On the 20th the company recruited; and if we can believe Thornton, they went on next day heaping imprecations upon Applegate's head, for the first rain drops began to fall, "and soon after, the long dreaded rainy season commenced." (He thus seems to be advancing the rains by a full week.) On the 26th, by his reckoning, "Messrs. Brown and Allen, and party, returned to us, informing us that they had proceeded as far as the Siskia Mountains, without learning any thing of the fate of their friends. I succeeded in hiring Mr. Allen to carry into the settlements a traveling bag filled with clothing, which would probably, otherwise, have fallen into the possession of one who hung about the camp, and seemed to hold himself in readiness to appropriate any property he could lay his hands on." Thornton pictures October 27 as dawning cold and rainy, and the journey next day to "the foot of the Umpqua Mountains" made through rain and mud. All this is seriously faulty in view of the known weather history, but Thornton

may correctly date as October 29 the attempted crossing of the
Umpqua Mountains. Josiah Morin, he says, had to abandon his large
wagons on November 1. Skipping events till November 4, Thornton
declares that he and his wife that day undertook the passage of the
Umpqua canyon. "We passed household and kitchen furniture, beds
and bedding, books, carpets, cooking utensils, dead cattle, broken
wagons, and wagons not broken, but, nevertheless, abandoned. . . .
Upon approaching near the entrance of the close canyon, we came to
where many most miserable, forlorn, haggard, and destitute-looking
emigrants were encamped. Some of the men looked as angry and
fierce as tigers, under the influence of their justly excited indignation
and wrath against him who had thus jeopardized the lives of their
families. Some of the men appeared to be stupefied by their misfortunes. One of them, a Mr. Smith, had lost every thing, and he
appeared to be overwhelmed. His wife had on a coarse and tattered
calico-dress. She was thinly clad, and the covering for her head was
an old sun-bonnet. Her child was not in a better condition, while
that of her husband was, perhaps, even more pitiable. They had not
a cent of money; though had it been otherwise, it would not have purchased food, for there was none to be sold. In addition to this, they
were so weak, in consequence of want of food, that it was believed
they would scarcely live through this journey. I remonstrated with
this hapless fellow traveler, persuading him that it would be better
for him, and his wife, to perish in the cold snow of the canyon, than
to await a more miserable death by starvation at that place. He
seemed to see at once the folly of remaining there. . . . immediately
took up his child, and about a pound of food, and desired his afflicted
and almost helpless companion to follow him."

Thornton adds, telling the tale of the death of James Smith mentioned in Note 152, "A relative of his . . . had been standing at that
place a few days before, counseling with some of the party, as to the
means of escaping their present danger. As he was thus anxiously
deliberating, death summoned him away, and he fell dead in a moment,
leaving a poor widow with seven helpless and almost starving children. . . . A Mr. Brisbane had also died here, and I was informed
that a child had died at this place. . . ."

The Thorntons went on, finally emerging from the "narrow gorge"
to come upon "the tent of the Rev. Mr. Cornwall," who had lost his
oxen and "was in no condition to afford us any shelter under his tent.
It was literally filled with others as helpless and distressed as ourselves. But the privilege of standing at his fire, was, in itself, a
favor that made us feel grateful; and its warmth, when contrasted
with the cold and suffering occasioned by the waters of the disastrous
canyon, made us, for the time, comparatively happy." On the 5th,
Thornton declares, they resumed their journey, wading Canon Creek

39 times, and about noon "arrived at the place of general encampment," on the left bank of the Umpqua River. "Here I found the wrecks of all the companies who had been induced to enter upon a road along which our wagons were lying in scattered fragments, upon the side of the hills, from the tops of the mountains, and along the rocky glens, and the almost impassable canyons, which marked this disastrous cut-off. Some of the emigrants had lost their wagons; some of their teams; some half they possessed; and some every thing. Here were men who had a wagon, but wanted a team; there, others who had a team, but no wagon. Mr. Humphrey was the only man who, so far as I have since been able to learn, got to this point with a whole wagon and a complete team. All looked lean, thin, pale, and hungry as wolves. The children were crying for food; and all appeared distressed and dejected."

Not yet out of provisions, though on short rations, the Thorntons went forward. He tells of a relief expedition sent out by Applegate, but only to heap fresh imprecations upon the man's head; among others, William Kirquendall and Asa Williams arrived with this relief, apparently on November 14. Kirquendall turned back toward the settlements with them on the 15th. From a mountain summit Thornton saw "persons upon the plain below, approaching from the direction of the camp. Upon inquiring of Mr. Kirquendall who they were, he informed me that they were Mr. and Mrs. Newton, and Sutton Burns, who were probably endeavoring to come up with us, in order that they might accompany us into the settlement. We continued traveling until about sunset, when we encamped. Mr. Newton, I have been informed, continued traveling until after dark, for the purpose of overtaking us." Thornton suggests that it was the next day Newton was killed by three Umpqua Indians, as mentioned in the Holt journal, Note 4. Thornton's version is that Newton "was met late in the afternoon by three Umpqua Indians, one of whom spoke English, and informed him that he would do well to encamp at the place at which he then was, there not being water and grass as they affirmed at a convenient distance ahead. They asked for food, and it was given to them. After which they asked for three loads of powder and ball, and stated that they would bring in a deer. It was given to them, and all by them put into one gun as one load. Mr. Newton finally suspecting that harm was designed, desired them to go away; but this they refused to do. He sat near the door of the tent to watch them, but being at length overcome with sleep, he was shot. He immediately rose, and sprang into his tent for his gun, when one of the savages, seizing an ax, inflicted a blow which nearly severed one of his legs. The tent was then robbed, and the articles placed upon an American mare, owned by Mr. Newton, after which they fled."

For the rest, Thornton merely says that on November 18 "just seven months from the time of entering upon our journey, we entered the head of the Wilhamette Valley. . . . On Tuesday, the 25th of the same month, we arrived at the house of Mr. Lewis, where a little milk and butter having been added to our now rapidly increasing luxuries, we regarded ourselves as having renewed cause to be grateful." On the 29th he reached "Forest Grove, which is the name bestowed by me upon a 'claim' in Polk county, then possessed by Mr. William Allen. . . . To this gentleman I paid a sum for boarding with him during two weeks. We greatly needed rest, and regular and healthy food. And at this place we were very much improved in health and strength. We were comparatively cheerful and happy also, for although we had lost upon our journey nearly every thing that we had owned, yet we did not permit the recollection of these losses to unfit us for the discharge of new duties, or the enjoyment of comforts that were now at hand. . . ."

161. Compare Thomas Holt's journal of the Applegate Relief, reprinted in Volume I.

162. Here Thornton equates the front-runners by the Barlow Road with the last to pass Raft River before Jesse Applegate came by. We may infer from William E. Taylor's diary that the vanguard of the Oregon emigration reached or went on from Raft River about July 27, and that these were the wagons which arrived across the Cascades on September 13.

163. As Thornton afterward learned and set forth in his book (see Note 160), the company of Brown and Allen veered off to California. James Savage also went to California in the Boggs company, as Thornton remarks a little farther along; Jacob Wright Harlan says his wife died during the crossing of the Forty Mile Desert to the Truckee.

164. A letter from Boggs to Thornton is quoted in Note 160 above; William M. Boggs, in an 1886 statement dictated for H. H. Bancroft (MS., Bancroft Library, C-D 269), tells of starting out upon the Black Rock Desert. "After going a ways my father not liking the looks of the camp he got the men to turn round & come back. We went into the California route with 3 wagons & followed along until we overtook the Company at the sink of the Humboldt. Just before we got there I found a man's feet sticking out of a grave—the Indians had killed him." (This is another reference to the killing of "Sally from Missouri." Young Boggs says that "every company that came along had to rebury him as the Indians kept digging him up.")

165. In the University of Oregon Library is "A Historical Sketch of the Family of Rev. J. A. Cornwall in Arkansas and on the Plains to Oregon," written by Joseph H. Cornwall in 1900, which I have been enabled to examine through the courtesy of Mr. Martin S.

Schmitt. Josephus Adamson Cornwall was born in Franklin County, Georgia, February 18, 1788, removed as a child to Kentucky, and grew up to enter the ministry of the Cumberland Presbyterian Church. In 1828 he married Nancy Hardin, and with her settled in Arkansas. In 1846 the family departed for Oregon via Independence, their little company consisting, so J. H. Cornwall says, of "Father, forty-eight years old, Mother, thirty-five, sister Elisabeth, sixteen, myself thirteen, Narcissa nine, George seven, and Laura nearly two years old; and three young men whose names were Lorenzo Byrd, Richard Chrisman and a Mr. Jones, who was an excellent young man. Father had hired him to drive one of our ox-teams to Independence, Mo." (Young Jones turned back soon after leaving Independence.) At Independence they were joined by "Cousin Israel Stoley." According to this account, the Cornwalls did not overtake the Russell company until after crossing the Kansas River. With Thornton, they joined the Rice Dunbar train west of the Big Blue. They were persuaded by Jesse Applegate at Fort Hall to take the new cutoff, and Joseph H. Cornwall winds up the tale as follows:

"Leaving Rogue River, we passed through a hilly, barren region and about the first week in October we reached the famous Umpqua Canyon. The teams were poor and jaded with the long, weary travel. Many of the people, especially the old and sick needed rest. We camped a day there before any of our company entered the canyon. That day Father prospected the road in advance, and said that it was desperately bad: A great deal of it very miry and badly worked up by the advance train which had but recently passed over it. Father took Lorenzo Byrd from driving the loose stock to help with the wagons. He killed and distributed a beef among the masses with the request that they would drive his loose stock with theirs.

"After a day's rest we entered the canyon with our wagons and teams. The rest of the company decided to stay in camp another day. We started but on that miserable road we made little progress. When camping time came we estimated our day's travel at three miles. In the afternoon, however, the face of the sky was overcast with dark, portentous clouds, and sad for us it began to rain. Before night [October 28?] our poor stock were drenched with the rain and had nothing to eat, except a little browsing. Next morning we attempted to advance, but our road soon entered and followed directly in the channel of the creek which drained the canyon. That cold mountain water soon chilled our poor oxen and several of them fell down and died. We found it necessary as soon as we reached a little opening in the canyon to camp there. There we remained several days, during which time we lost a good American horse and all of our oxen, except three head. One yoke of oxen disappeared in the yoke and we never got a trace of them.

"The day after we started the rest of our company broke camp and followed after us. They made one day's journey, then their teams gave out and most of the oxen died. What a terrible predicament that left us all in, still so far from the settlements and left without means to transport our baggage. The misfortune fell with crushing force on some of the company. Two old men died on the spot; but most of the people rallied their energies, and resolved to take their way on foot to the Willamette valley. We remained at our camp until most of our company had passed by us on the march; and a forlorn procession they made. Many women and children on foot, and some women as well as men with heavy packs on their backs.

"In the meantime Father had been entirely through the canyon, ten or twelve miles distant and returned to our camp. Having cashed two trunks full of books and sent forward our tent and some bedding by Mr. Byrd and Mr. Chrisman, we prepared to join the forlorn procession moving on toward the Willamette. Mother, yet weak from her mountain fever, was placed on Jude, our fine saddle mule, with little sister Laura, the babe, in her lap. As we had to cross the cold mountain stream Father often led Sister Narcissa and Brother George. Sister Elisabeth and I were old enough and strong enough to keep step in the march on foot. And in that plight we passed through the canyon. A short distance from the exit from it, we overtook quite a number of our company. They were in camp resting and making the best possible preparation for finishing the journey. The grass was becoming good from the recent rains and that was a boon for our remaining live stock. While we were there Father made arrangements with Mr. Campbell and by joining teams, they brought his two ox wagons out of the canyon. And he gave one of them for help to haul the other, as by that arrangement he was able to save his library and transport the rest of our baggage. He also brought out the family carriage with his mules. The other wagons of our company were all destroyed by Indians.

"After resting a few days, Mr. Campbell's family and ours and some others, as best they could, went on leisurely, until we reached the vicinity of Oakland in the Umpqua valley. There we met some men with a small supply of provisions from the Willamette and some of us decided to winter there . . . .

"Before we reached our winter camp near [present] Oakland . . . Cousin Israel Stoley rejoined us and decided to remain with us for the winter. He was then nearly twenty-one years of age and being one of the best hunters in our train was a desirable companion. Father was anxious to save his wagons and a fine library which he brought with him. Therefore, he considered it absolutely necessary to wait for better weather and better roads, before resuming our journey. But we could have neither until winter was over. Another thing that caused us to stop there was that we had reached the district in which a tribe of Umpqua Indians lived that was friendly toward the whites. That friendship was cemented by Father presenting their chief with some presents that greatly pleased him . . . . The question how to obtain food for the winter was an important one for us then. Our only supply of flour was eighty pounds sent by a friend from the Willamette. That friend was Mr. Middleton Simpson . . . . The supply of flour and bacon with which we left Missouri was exhausted, when we were at the canyon; and we were learning to do without them. Father purchased a fine beef driven from the Willamette and slaughtered it at camp. We, also, milked two or three cows, and the above mentioned flour, beef and milk were our only known supply of provisions for the winter, except the venison, which our hunters might secure and a little camas, a wild tuber, which we could purchase, at times, from the Indians. Fortunately wild deer were then abundant in the Umpqua hills, and our hunters kept us well supplied with venison while we staid there. Of course, we regretted the lack of home comforts; but especially the want of bread, bacon, sugar and coffee.

"During the winter Stoley and two others from our camp visited the Hudson Bay fort, far down the Umpqua River, where each was supplied with a bushel of wheat or peas, according to choice; and a few handfuls of salt, nothing more being obtainable from there.

"With gratitude I record that our health was good throughout the time that we tarried there. Father having brought a cross cut saw and a frow with him and there being excellent cedar timber near our camp, we went to work in early winter to build a cabin. About Christmas it was completed, with excellent cedar shakes for the roof, and excellent cedar puncheons for the floor and a comfortable chimney. After that time we were well housed for the rest of our stay there. One cold spell struck us and lasted a week or ten days; but after that the weather was good and spring came early.

"With the return of spring came warm days, fine grass and the woods were vocal with the hooting of grouse. Then we became anxious to leave camp and finish our journey to the Willamette.

"Father had sent word by some of our company the previous fall that we would need aid to reach the settlements, and three men [Joseph Hess, Josiah Nelson, and Clark Rogers], whose names I record with gratitude, came to us and brought us to the settlements in Chehalem Valley, Yamhill County, Oregon, where we found a home among kind friends and neighbors.

"We left our camp in Umpqua Valley, on the tenth of April, 1847; which was just a year after we had left our old home in Arkansas and started to Oregon . . . ."

166. The recipient of this letter may have been Lazarus Van Beb-

ber; but compare Curry's remarks in the *Spectator*, November 26, 1846, to which reference is made here.

167. *Oregon Spectator*, April 29, 1847. This bitter letter would seem to have been written in David Goff's name by his son-in-law, James W. Nesmith, since Goff reputedly was unable to read or write—a point Thornton himself made in a reply of May 4 published in the *Spectator* for May 13, 1847. That reply is not here reprinted because it deals mostly with personalities and sheds little light on the history of the emigration.

Here we see the origins of one of the celebrated incidents of Oregon history—and of Oregon printing history. Once more George Gary's diary is the source. On May 13 Gary noted, "Mr. and Mrs. Thornton came to spend a few days with us while Mr. Abernethy moves, &c &c." On the 21st: "Mr. Cornwell, a Cumberland Presbyterian minister, visits us; he came in on the southern route. The history of this route is painful." On June 2: "We are having a circumstance about or attending us quite new to us. Mr. and Mrs. Thornton are stopping with us a few weeks; he has said and written (for the Spectator) such things about the southern or Applegate route as has provoked the road hunters so that his life is threatened and he is somewhat busy preparing to resist any attacks. A Bowie knife and a six shooting revolving pistol are among his habiliments. We are not in the community of New York or the eastern states. Our community is made up to a considerable degree of southern and western people, whose differences of opinion and insults of character are easily and readily settled with the Bowie or pistol. This rage against Judge Thornton is wholly uncalled for only as the truth goads, stings and wounds these road hunters even unto madness. While they had the suffering emigrants on their new route, who generally suffered the loss of all of their property and some of them the loss of health and of life, it was all very well. But now, to be told of their deceptions, or more properly to give the public an account of it, so that others may not be led into similar sufferings and losses, is an offense which subjects a man to a threatened loss of his life. I hope the emigrants in future may be kept from the tender mercies of these road hunters."

On June 7: "This is an important day, it being the first Monday in June, it is, therefore, the day for election throughout the territory. It is also the appointed time for holding the Supreme Court for the territory. It is, moreover, an important day as it is said Judge Nismith is in the city to get revenge on J. Q. Thornton, judge of the Supreme Court, for what he has published in the Spectator concerning the southern or Applegate route into which quite a proportion of the immigrants of last year were persuaded greatly, very greatly to their injury. Nismith, who has been judge when the timber was scarce, is now here for the sake of hunters—their champion and bully;

to whip or kill Judge Thornton for the trouble springing out of the developments made by said Judge Thornton. The Judge being a true courageous southerner is abundantly armed and is attending to his affairs as a citizen and Judge; intending either to kill Nismith or be killed by him provided said Nismith shows anything menacing in his manners towards him. Nismith will have a trial between his bragging and clamorous honor and his fears of personal danger. I am satisfied Judge Thornton will run any risk rather than retract. So here we are, not knowing what an hour or a minute may bring forth . . . .

"The day has passed without bloodshed between our road hunter champions and Judge Thornton. Nismith sent a challenge for a duel, it is supposed, but Judge Thornton refused to receive any communication from him or have any conference with him; and the mighty bustle has ended (I suppose) in a scurrilous hand bill issued by the said Nismith and posted up in sundry places, filled with low and villifying epithets concerning the judge. Is this the mouse the mountain has brought forth? When I was a boy, if I remember right, I heard it said, 'A barking dog seldom bites.' "

A copy of the handbill Gary mentions is owned by the Oregon Historical Society, a remarkable affair:

"TO THE WORLD!! J. Quinn Thornton, Having resorted to low, cowardly and dishonorable means, for the purpose of injuring my character and standing, and having refused honorable satisfaction, which I have demanded; I avail myself of this opportunity of publishing him to the world as a reclaimless liar, an infamous scoundrel, a blackhearted villain, an arrant coward, a worthless vagabond, and an imported miscreant; a disgrace to the profession and a dishonor to his country

OREGON CITY, JUNE 7, 1847.   JAMES W. NESMITH."

Gary left shortly after for the States, his successor having reached the mission field, so his interesting reporting ends. Feeling about Thornton continued to smolder, and later in the fall was primarily responsible for the ouster of George L. Curry as editor of the *Spectator*. It should be added that in publishing Goff's letter in the *Spectator* of April 29, Curry remarked: "We regret exceedingly that we were obliged, on the score of strict justice and impartiality, to admit such a violently personal article into our columns . . . . The merits of the difference between Judge Thornton and himself, we do not presume to adjudge, and we can only say that we have no disposition to allow the columns of the Spectator to be used merely for the purpose of personal controversy and invective. Had we imagined what end Judge Thornton's article would have tended, we certainly should have hesitated in publishing it. Although the liberty of the press is vitally important, it is liable to great abuse, and we would not knowingly lend ourself to any perversion of its true and legitimate objects."

168. Thornton's reply in the *Spectator* of May 13 specifically rebutted these remarks.

169. Since Goff and Harris were members of the advance section of the Applegate company, this is useful information. Although Meadows Vanderpool ended up in Oregon, the mention of him here shows that California was his original destination; Goff's subsequent remarks shed a good deal of light on the history of the Applegate road.

170. Thornton has nothing to say of such an incident in his book, which seems to have omitted various episodes which do not present him in a wholly favorable light. As may be seen in Note 160, he got some hard words for Goff into his book.

171. *Illinois Journal,* Springfield, November 11, 1847, with a note that Hezekiah Packingham was "formerly of Putnam County, in this State."

172. *Weekly Tribune,* Liberty, August 21, 1847. Peter H. Burnett had gone out to Oregon with the emigration of 1843. He migrated to California during the Gold Rush and became that State's first governor in 1850.

173. Marcus Whitman, in letters to David Greene, printed in Archer B. and Dorothy Printup Hulbert, eds., *Marcus Whitman Crusader, Part Three* (Colorado Springs and Denver, 1941), pp. 183-184, 193-194, mentions the emigration passing Waiilatpu without specifically naming those who wintered at the mission station. On September 8 he commented, "Most of the Immigrants are now passed . . . A new road has been taken by those most in the rear who were met by a party from the Willamette. The party met them soon after leaving Fort Hall and took them in the direction of California and so on to the head waters of the Willamette. This season has been one of great prosperity to the Immigrants they being much earlier than formerly. Thus far no calls have been made upon me for provisions. A waggon route is now open through the Cascade Mountains to the Willamette Valley . . . . As the Immigrants have not called on me this year for any supplies, I shall have no means to meet the small bill I have made at Vancouver therefore I shall need to draw upon the Board . . . ." On November 3 he wrote, in connection with the new route: "I have recently been informed by a gentleman who passed that way that it bids fair to be a good route and that it passes through the country of Klamath and Umpqua and head waters of the Willamette all of which are the countries calling for speedy settlement. This route will doubtless greatly facilitate the settlement of the country and will at the same time take the Immigration away from our vicinity. This completes two distinct waggon routes to the Willamette Valley. After I wrote you a party came

this way and as is usual with the last of the parties some among [them] were in very needy circumstances, their teams being very much reduced and quite unfit to proceed. A number also were sick and stoped to winter with us. Six families and some young men remain. The families do not expect to go on untill they can pass the Cascade Mountains in June. I shall try to employ them to the advantage of the Mission, and the Indians so as to give them a living, but not to call for funds from the Board. I wish much to have the Indians aided in fencing and ploughing their land . . . . Three of the families are at the saw mill where I have been obliged to attend some of the sick . . . ."

Later, writing from Fort Vancouver on April 1, 1847 (*ibid.,* pp. 216-217), Whitman added: "The last only of the Immigration of last fall came to my house. No provisions were required by those who were able to pass on to the end of the journey. Of those who stoped four were very sick. Two or three must have died in all probability if they had not stoped & obtained Medical aid & rest. Three births have occurred also among those that stoped; The expectation of that event caused them to stop with us for the winter. In all six families besides eight young men wintered with us. The disaster was great again last year to those who left the track which I made for them in 1843 as it has been in every attempt to improve it . . . ."

174. Presumably David Tanner; see Note 152.

175. Burnett reports in Oregon the same devastating winter made famous in California by the Donner tragedy.

176. *Illinois Journal,* Springfield, November 11, 1847, with a headnote: "We copy the following letter from the 'Rough and Ready' newspaper, published at Charleston, in this State. It is from a man who emigrated from Shelby County in 1846."

177. Howard was one of the earliest emigrants to arrive by the Barlow Road; see Note 149.

178. The larger-than-expected emigration to Oregon in 1846 is here summed up correctly by the *Star.*

179. *The Gazette,* St. Joseph, Missouri, July 23, 1847, printed by courtesy of "the Rev. Thomas Allen." William Edgington was born in Kentucky in 1816, removed to Platte County, Missouri, in 1840, and according to a biographical sketch in *History of Napa and Lake Counties, California* (San Francisco, 1881), pp. 454-464, set out for California April 28, 1846, and reached the Sacramento Valley October 22. After being mustered out of the California Battalion in March, 1847, he made his way to Chiles Valley, Napa County, and eventually settled there. On November 8, 1848, he married Theresa A. Grigsby, who bore him nine children. He died at Napa, January 12, 1885.

180. Edgington and Overton H. Foster were recruited by William

O. Fallon at Bear Creek, on or about October 20, 1846. They served in Company C of the California Battalion with some 23 others including John Minter, Samuel Truit, Heinrich Lienhard, and three of Lienhard's fellow "German boys."

181. Here Edgington gives us valuable further sidelights on the history of Elam Brown's party. The biographical sketch of Elam Brown printed in San Jose *Pioneer,* January 26, 1878, says that at Fort Bridger he "had to leave his son Warren who had been sick for 20 days with typhoid fever. George March and Wm. Scott were kind enough to remain with young Warren and accompany him afterwards to Oregon. This separation was a sore trial to both father and son, while the train was compelled to go on. It proved to [be] the best course for both parties in the end. Warren left the Fort a month after his father, and was so weak when he started that he had to be helped on his horse for the first two hundred miles on his way to Oregon which country he reached that fall. When the train reached Fort Hall they met a company of road hunters from Oregon, who informed them that they had found a new and better route to that Territory than the old one, in which they might avoid crossing the Columbia and Snake rivers. The road hunters traveled faster, and went along back ahead of the emigrant train, but promised the latter that they would leave a sign at the forks of the road . . . . The train found this sign stating that it was 15 miles to the next water, and at the latter place they would get further information; but when they reached there they found no water to do any good, and a note stating that the next watering place was 22 miles, and from there 28 miles to where they would find both grass and water. They now became so disheartened, believing that their wearied teams could never travel 65 miles without water, and fearing that they might miss the water again, they returned to the forks of the road, and pressed on for California, having buried four heads of families of the company from the time they left the Humboldt Wells. It was so sickly in the train that they had to hire drivers for some of their teams from other teams, and some of the women had to drive their own teams . . . . There was very little improvement in the health of the company until they reached the Truckee river, where the sick began to improve rapidly from drinking the pure water . . . ." Like other emigrants, Brown thought afterward the Donners were only "four days behind" when they reached the Sierra Nevada. Much more of interest in this account must be passed over for lack of space.

182. *Missouri Republican,* St. Louis, May 17, 1847.

183. Russell thus briefly refers to the battle of Natividad on the Salinas plains, November 16, 1846. The two men killed, Charles D. Burrass and Hiram Ames (for whom see the McKinstry diary, Notes 10 and 76) were buried at Mission San Juan Bautista. Edward C.

Kemble's three accounts, the first printed in the *California Star,* August 21, 1847, the others in the Sacramento *Daily Union,* November 23, 1869, and November 18, 1871, are reprinted with a map by Fred B. Rogers in *A Kemble Reader* (San Francisco, 1963).

184. Thus is remarked the departure of James Frazier Reed with what became known as the Second Donner Relief. A specimen of the feeling for companion emigrants is a letter from James G. T. Dunleavy to George McKinstry (McKinstry Papers, Bancroft Library)

San Francisco, Feb. 6th, 1847

"Geo. McKinstry Jnr Esqr

"Sir yours of the first Inst Came to hand, on last evening at 9 oClock, and since that time unto this moment, now 10 OClock this morning, we have had no time to write, Eat, Drink, or Sleep—our time has been employed in makeing the best preperation for the relief of our suffering Countarymen, and women, now in the Mountains Oh! *God,* It is Shocking to here of their Suffering—May he that *Thunders* when he pleases, and holds the storms, in his hand *O* may *he* save *them* from perishing in the wilderness—Leut Woodworth wil tel you all about our action in this place in reference to this matter

"Captains Sutter and Kern—together with yourself, and your Alcalde, have done in this case what must ever entitle you to the thanks of your fellow citizens, and countary men—I asure you it is vewed here in the proper light may the dred *Soviron* of the Universe re ward you all I Refer you to Leut Wooworth for all the particulars in the matter—

"The 4 Blank petitions forwarde by you will be attended to as soon as we get this mountain Expedition started you may asure those Gentle men that I will atend to it immediately for them

"Your other Deeds are all redy for you in the hands of the Collector

"My love to Capt Sutter and Kern—to dayes paper will give all the news which is of pleasing importance

in the greatest haste I remain
Yours Affectionately
J. G. T. Dunleavey"

185. Although McKinstry is not immediately identified as the writer of this letter, the authorship is quickly apparent, and confirmed by Philip V. R. Stanton's letter quoted in the Introduction to the present volume.

186. McKinstry's figure of 23 wagons as comprising the Donner Party has been very generally relied upon, though Charles T. Stanton's letter of July 12 indicated that the Donner company then comprised only 18 wagons, and W. C. Graves says his family had no

more than three. (See Notes 95 and 110.) McKinstry's total of "some seventy-five waggons" as comprising the advance company with Hastings and Hudspeth is less than certain; see the Mathers diary, Note 18.

187. The Mathers diary shows this statement to be incorrect; some of the advance company, like Heinrich Lienhard, recruited at Twenty Wells while Hastings went back on the trail with Reed, but others moved on to Skull Valley.

188. The men of the Donner Party may not have worked as energetically as they would have, if gifted with the foresight, but they started on "Reed's route" August 11 and emerged into Salt Lake Valley on August 22, just twelve days later. Reed was always very sensitive to charges that the plight of the Donner Party resulted from the decision to cut this new road across the mountains, and he may have displayed a thin skin as early as the conversation McKinstry records. In 1847 William Clayton observed that the emigrants of 1846 "must have spent a great deal of time cutting a road through the thickly set timber and heavy brush wood," and after repeating the comment in the *Star* he observed, "it has taken us over three days after the road is made although a great many hours have been spent in improving it."

189. Compare the Mathers diary. The only day the Harlan-Young train may plausibly have remained in camp for McKinstry's stated reason was September 4. Other stop-overs may have had the primary purpose of recruiting before or after long drives. McKinstry may have been ahead of Mathers, but that is doubtful, once the Salt Desert was confronted in Skull Valley.

190. Compare the Reed narratives in Volume I.

191. Here we have the earliest chronicle of the Snowshoe Party, consisting of Charles T. Stanton, Sutter's two Indians, Luis and Salvador, Antonio, the New Mexican herder, Patrick R. Dolan, Franklin Ward Graves, his daughter Sarah and her husband, Jay Fosdick, the boy Lemuel Murphy, William H. Eddy, William M. Foster and his wife Sarah (Murphy), Harriet (Murphy) Pike, Mary Graves, and Amanda McCutchen, fifteen in all. "Dutch Charley" Berger and young Bill Murphy started but had to turn back, lacking snowshoes. All the women came through; all the men save Eddy and Foster died on the journey.

192. It is ever thus; Edward M. Kern, who had little to do with the First Donner Relief, other than passing on the payroll, gets his name in the papers, while those who actually undertook the rescue in McKinstry's letter are an anonymous "seven."

193. *California Star*, February 27, 1847, "From our Sacramento Correspondent."

194. There was no such "party of twenty-four." The misunder-

standing evidently was based upon the fact, as recorded in Breen's diary, that a party of 22 attempted to cross the Sierra on November 21, returning unsuccessful though without casualties two days later.

195. What McKinstry extracts as from "Glover's" journal seems rather to come from the diary kept by M. D. Ritchie and R. P. Tucker, printed in Volume I.

196. *California Star,* March 20, 1847, "From our Sacramento Correspondent."

197. William Hook, a Donner step-child, was the victim of his uncontrollable hunger. The others who died were John Denton and Ada Keseberg; see Index.

198. Reprinted in *The Gazette,* St. Joseph, July 30, 1847, with mention that the writer "went out last year with a company of emigrants to California." Peter Quivvey was born in New York in 1799, and after living in Kentucky and Indiana, settled in Missouri in 1839. After coming to California in 1846 he settled at San Jose as a farmer and stock-raiser. As recorded in Frederic Hall, *History of San Jose and Surroundings* (San Francisco, 1871) p. 376, he died January 28, 1869.

199. This account of the Donner tragedy would seem to have derived from McKinstry's communication to the *California Star* of February 13, 1847.

200. *California Star,* April 3, 1847, with a head note: "The following report of Lt. S. E. Woodworth, U. S. Navy, who had command of the party of men sent to the relief of the emigrants in the mountains, exhibits the result of the labors of the expedition. He has accomplished more than could have been expected under the circumstances." As against this view, historians are now disposed to think that Woodworth did too little and claimed too much.

201. Woodworth is here describing the Third Donner Relief, for which it is difficult to see that he deserves much credit.

202. See Volume I, p. 358, for this unsuccessful effort to reach Donner Lake between the Third and Fourth Reliefs. William Thompson, mentioned here, also figures in Edward M. Kern's accounts in the "Fort Sutter Papers." He was credited with 59 days' service at $3 per day, and also allowed $50 "For bringing out F. Donough," a total of $227, "Entered Feb 10 at Sonoma up to April 9th 1847."

203. Selim E. Woodworth appears in Frank Soule, John H. Gihon, and James Nisbet, *The Annals of San Francisco* . . . (New York, 1855), pp. 794-798. Born November 27, 1815, he was the second son of Samuel Woodworth, who wrote "The Old Oaken Bucket." After reaching Oregon with his dispatches, Woodworth remained in Oregon till the following winter, then came down the coast to Yerba Buena just before news of the beleaguered emigrants arrived. "Our

hero immediately volunteered to take command of a party," and by this account one would infer that Woodworth personally rescued the snowbound, starved emigrants. He continued active in California public life but re-entered the Navy during the Civil War, attaining the rank of commodore. Resigning in 1867, he returned to San Francisco, where he died four years later.

204. If it is true that Denton kept a journal, what happened to it is unknown. Little more is known of him than Thornton's remark, at the time he carved a headstone for Sarah Keyes' grave, at the crossing of the Big Blue, that Denton was "an Englishman from Sheffield." A man of the same name was in Oregon with Nathaniel Wyeth between 1834 and 1836, but the literature of 1846 has no hint that the English John Denton had ever been in the West; he had lived for some time in the Springfield area before taking the trail in 1846.

It will be seen that the *Star* does not specifically say that Denton composed these lines while waiting in the snow for death to come, an idea that has had a strong emotional appeal, from J. Quinn Thornton's time to the present. Thornton revised the poem, but he did not alter its character; for instance, he gives as the last four lines: "But now on scenes of past delight / I look, and feel no pleasure, / As misers on the bed of death / Gaze coldly on their treasure."

205. On the contrary, few of the Donner Party came from the neighborhood of Independence, Missouri.

206. For William O. Fallon and his journal of the Fourth Donner Relief, see Volume I, pp. 360-366. The New Helvetia Diary, which after a considerable lapse was resumed on May 20, 1847, has an unexplained entry on May 29, "O Fallen arrived back again from the Mountains." Where he had gone and for what purpose we are left to conjecture. Not until after his return, on June 2, did John Craig and Miles Goodyear set out for the East.

207. Sidney Stanton and his sister Almena sadly recalled this breast-pin in writing to C. F. McGlashan in 1879, and as seen in the Introduction to the present volume, Philip V. R. Stanton in February, 1848, acknowledged receiving the "vest and pin" from McKinstry in November, 1847.

208. For John Craig, see Volume I, pp. 119, 140-142.

209. This casualty list was reprinted in the St. Louis *Weekly Reveille*, August 30, 1847, and from that source in many other papers. Compare with the list in Volume I, pp. 366-368.

210. As a sequel to these remarks, see Jesse Applegate's letter to his brother Lisbon, October 11, 1847, quoted in Note 133. The *Oregon Spectator*, October 14, 1847, contains a letter from Applegate dated 12 days earlier, announcing the arrival of Capt. L. Scott and party by the southern route, a company of 25 wagons. This ar-

rival was viewed as a vindication of the route. Levi Scott's own letter, October 25, 1847, is printed in the *Spectator* for November 11. Finally, on November 25, the *Spectator* printed the following:

"MORE IMMIGRANTS. — By the subjoined letter it will be seen that another company of immigrants have arrived in the valley by the Southern route — making a surprisingly short trip — having left the States the 22d of last June. 'The almost impassable *Kanyon*' is certainly being redeemed.

"Polk County, Oregon,
"Nov. 16th, 1847.

"Dear Sir — I have the pleasure to announce to you the safe arrival by the Southern route of a fourth company of immigrants of 20 or more wagons. This party left St. Joseph on the 22d June and being in the rearward of so large an immigration fared but badly until they took the S. route. — Finding on it abundance of food, their teams rapidly recruited and upon their arrival here were in fine condition. From the best information I can get they have made the most saving trip that has ever yet been made from Fort Hall, having lost but *four* animals on the road (which were stolen by Indians.) — The party kept up no guard, and it is remarkable they lost no more; a woman was wounded in the arm by an arrow. So terrible had the *kanyon* been described to them that they were expecting daily to arrive at it until they came into the settlements, and declare there is no *kanyon* on the road. They brought with them 80 sheep. [This letter may have been written by Jesse Applegate.] "Here are some interesting particulars relative to the arrival of the last companies on the Southern route, received too late for insertion in our last paper.

"A company of 16 wagons, under the direction of Mr. Gordon, left the forks of the road on the 27th day of August, bound for California. They met the party of Com. Stockton, who advised them to keep the Southern route to Oregon, until they arrived at the Sacramento river, and by descending it they would avoid the Siera Nevada. They followed his advice, but after *laying by one week* at that river [*i. e.*, at Lost River] examining the country, they concluded it would be safer to follow the road to Oregon. While lying at the Sacramento a party of 11 wagons passed them on their way to Oregon (the party of Mr. Davis,) they did not overtake this party, but they arrived in the Willamette valley on *the morning of the 25th of October*, being two days less than two months on the road including all stoppages and lying a whole week in one camp. The small party starting in behind and getting through before them have made the trip much sooner."

Thus, from 1847, the Applegate Cutoff was permanently established as a road to Oregon. Peter Lassen, in 1848, undertook to

guide a small company into California from the States, following
the Applegate Road as far west as Goose Lake, and from that venture came the Lassen Cutoff traveled next year by so many gold-
seekers.

211. Marcus Whitman wrote David Greene from Waiilatpu on
May 19, 1847: "Two young men from Chester, Mass. are now here
who came out last year, and are now returning in order to come back
with their Father and family if possible next year. Their names are
William B. and Samuel Campbel . . . ."

212. Although this account of Smith's company is somewhat confused, especially about taking a "Southern route" from Independence Rock, it tells us where Joel M. Ware's six wagons from Independence overtook the company. Smith's train may well have begun
to break apart west of Fort Laramie; see the remarks by W. C.
Graves in Note 95.

213. Fabritus Smith is regarded as possibly the Captain Smith
of the tail-end St. Joseph company. This identification rests primarily on Bancroft's mention of him as an 1846 emigrant, the only
recorded Smith among the year's Oregon contingent. However, he
would seem to have been rather young to have been captain of a
large company. The 1850 census for Marion County, Oregon, lists
him as a New Yorker, aged 30.

In his statement written for C. F. McGlashan in 1879 (McGlashan
Papers, Bancroft Library), George W. Tucker recalled that his family started for Oregon in 1846 from Rock Island County, Illinois:
"when we reached the Missouri River at St Joseph we were informed
that a Company was collecting a bout 4 miles above for the purpose
of crosing the plains to Oregon & California—we went up the river
and crst over & found a large Company. On the 23rd of May we
Started on our long Journey—all bound for Oregon except the Graves
family which afterwards became members of the Doner party—we
all traveld together till we Came to Fort briger where the California
and oregon Roads forked—there we Seperated we takeing the oregon
road via Fort Hall—and the Graves family the California road, Via
Salt Lake . . . ." At Fort Hall, Tucker says, "we took a copy of a
guide that a man by the name of Aplegate had left . . . . and went
according to it till we got to the turning point on the Humbold
River." There they decided to take the California Road—"the day
that we wer laying by some 2 or 3 Companys of the California Emigrants past us—that at fort Briger was 3 weeks ahead of us we
had went round by fort Hall some 150 miles farther and Struck the
Humboldt before they did—but I supose at that time the Doner
Company was some 75 or 100 miles behind us—from there we traveld
mixed up more or less with the California Companys till we reached
the Sink of Humboldt—a few days before we reached the Sink one

of Our Company an old man by the name John Bowles from Galena
Illinoise left us to go through to Sutters fort to get provisions and
meet us as far back as he Could for we wer getting short of Provsins
[Jacob Wright Harlan performed a similar mission for the Harlan
train] at the Sink we lay by a day or so to rest our teams before
Starting on the Humboldt desert while laying there the Most of the
other Companes left us we then traveled alone from there to Truckey
I think about 20 or 25 wagons—in all In going up Truckey from
where we first Struck the river to truckey Lake—we Crost the river
27 times—but before we left truckey Stanton & McCutchen of the
Doner party past us on hoseback going through to Sutters fort for
Provisions—when we reached Truckey Lake we wer nearly out of
provisions had been on Short allowence for some time and our teams
were so faged out that we Could not make more than from 3 to 5
miles pr day. the day after we Crost the Summet of the Sieras we
met Old Johney Boles with Some 2 or 3 hundred lbs Flour and a
large Spanish ox which was very fat—we butchered the ox that evening & divided him up among the different families in a few days
we reached Bear Valley which is on the head of Bear River about 30
miles from the Summit of the Siereas here we lay by Several days
for the purpose of recruting our Cattle while laying there Stanton
of the Donner Company past us going back to meet his Company he
had been through to Sutters fort Captan Sutter had furnished him
with eight or ten mules and horses and loaded him with provisions
and gave him two of his best Indian Vacaros to assist him—and told
him to hury back to his Company

"that Same day J. F. Reed of the Donner party also past us. Said
they wer short of provisions and he was going in to get more suplies
but we afterwards learned that he had got into a difficulty with John
Snyder one of his Company and Killed him and was leaveing to
escape the indignation of his Company—Stanton went on and met
the Donner Company somewhere on Truckey and the day after we
left Bear Valley it Comenced raining which I think was about the
18th [28th or 29th?] of October the next day we could See the Snow
on the Mountains behind us. we knew the Donner Company would
have trouble—the road got very muddy and we got entirely out of
provisions. before we got through—the day before we reached the
Valley or the first settlement—we met McCutchen [and Reed, not
mentioned by Tucker in this context] who had Came out with Stanton he also had 6 or 8 horses and mules packed with Flour and
dried beaf with 2 men to assist him—going back to meet his Company—he gave us some bread and dried beaf we had then been entirely out of anything to eat for 2 days—but that evening we reached
Johnsons Ranch . . . ."

Index

Abentore, 581, 756
Abernethy, George, 63, 598, 668, 750-1, 777, 788
Abert, James, 45, 373, 381, 763
Acres, Burlington, 145
Adams, A., 773
Adams, David, 753
Adams, Thomas, 697
Aguira, —, 534
Aird, —, 643
Alcove Spring, 209, 404
Alder Creek, 350, 357-8
Alderman, Albert L., 394
Allen, —, 397, 781
Allen, Betsy, 698
Allen, David (several so named), 397, 673-4, 677, 697-8, 780, 784
Allen, Isaac, 697
Allen, Thomas, 390, 694, 791
Allen, Wm., 784
Allis, Samuel, 220-1, 757
American Falls, 32, 127, 179
American Fur Co., 91
American River, 236, 273, 324, 726
Ames, Hiram, 201, 204-5, 214-5, 401, 410, 413, 422, 510, 699, 792
Anderson, Wm. Marshall, 431
Antelope Island, 45, 48
Antonio, Donner herdsman, 294, 367, 449, 728, 794
Applegate, Betsy, 635-6
Applegate, Jesse, 90, 128, 179, 190, 373-4, 386, 392-3, 465-6, 633, 662, 665, 667, 672-5, 680-1, 687, 694, 752, 764, 766-8, 777-9, 781, 785, 798; *letters by*, 69, 634-8, 765-8, 796-7; *articles signed "Z,"* 69-77, 768; *waybills*, 393, 638, 768
Applegate, Lindsay, 393, 635-8,

765-6; *reminiscences of 1846,* 77-87
Applegate, Lisbon, 69, 634-7, 765-7, 797
Applegate Cutoff, 65, 69-88, 90, 100, 116, 128, 160, 162, 179-198, 233, 272, 392-9, 471, 571-2, 634, 636-8, 662-84, 686-90, 694, 729-32, 751, 760, 764, 766-8, 774, 779-84, 790, 792, 797-8
Applegate Relief, 189-198, 669-76, 679-84, 767
Aram, Joseph, 385, 748, 756
Arkansas, 26, 40, 459, 472-4, 509, 642, 644-5, 660, 760, 785, 787
Arkansas River, 44, 47, 62, 113-5, 459, 479, 488, 528, 645, 653, 755, 763, 769, 770
Armijo, Antonio, 288, 446
Armijo, Manuel, 511, 644, 649
Ash Creek, 153, 370
Ash Hollow, 69, 67, 107, 111-2, 125, 132, 213, 370, 383, 391, 409, 426, 572, 578, 651-2, 755, 764; "Hotel," 213, 391
Ashley, Otis, 224-5, 228, 415, 748
Ashley, Sallie M. (Mathers), 224-5
Ashley, Sarah E., 224
Astoria, 742
Aull, —, 510
Auvaux (Loutre) River, 163
Avery, J. C., 397

Bacon, John M., 752
Bailey, W. J., 464
Baker, John, 194-7, 398, 780
Baldroach, J. B., 191
Bale ("Bail"), Edward, 120
Bancroft, H. H., 30, 143, 199-200, 307-8, 325, 398, 459, 744,

Weinberg, James, 326

Weir; *see* Ware

Welch, Presley, 752

Wells, Capt., 201, 215, 280, 412-3, 443, 611, 760

West, Capt. F., 408, 558, 617, 747-8, 760, 774

West, George R., 747-8

West, Thomas, 747-8

West, Thomas, 747-8

West, Wm. T., 747-8

Weston, Mo., 64, 224, 499, 501, 535, 540, 549, 625

Westport, Mo., 21, 44, 102-4, 110, 116, 210, 493, 495, 510

Wheeler, J., 163

Wheeler, L., 523, 525-6, 565, 608

Whirlwind Valley, 423

White, Mr., 168

White, Elijah, 16, 32, 170-1, 739

Whitley (Whately, Whitelsy), Samuel, 680, 776, 780

Whitman, Marcus, 599-600, 686, 774, 790, 798; Massacre, 162; Mission, *see* Waiilatpu

Whitton's Springs, 45

Wickliffe, Mr., 497

Wilkes, Lt., 605, 741

Wilkes, Duke, 602

Willaker, Mr. T., 602

Willamette Falls, 740; *see* Oregon City

Willamette River and Valley, 48, 64, 69-7, 88, 92, 187-8, 190-3, 196-8, 277, 490, 493, 569, 571, 634-7, 665, 674, 681, 683, 685-6, 869, 729, 739, 751, 766-7, 774, 784, 790, 797

Williams, Asa, 783

Williams, Baylis, 250-1, 281, 304, 313, 368, 446, 728

Williams, Eliza, 250, 255, 284-8, 315-7, 368, 446, 451, 456, 727

Williams, Joseph, 430-1

Williamson, Henry, 768

"Willow Creek," 258

Willow Spring, 57, 126, 154, 200, 259, 371, 612, 639, 647, 649, 737-8

Wills, Capt.; *see* Wells

Wilson, —, 602

Wilson & Clark, 241

Wilson, Isaac, 145

Wilson, John M., 96

Wilson, John S., 516

Wimmer, Peter L., 401-2, 420

Wind River, Wyo., 371

Wind River Mountains, 31, 126, 176, 227, 241, 617-8, 761

Winter, Wm. H., 18, 20-1, 374, 743

Winter Quarters, 747

Wolf River, 124, 369

Wolfinger, —, 314, 367

Wolfinger, Doris, 367, 451, 727

Wolfskill, William, 147-8

Wood, —, 670

Woodbury, D. P., 381

Woodworth, Selim E., 98-9, 102-3, 106, 213, 293, 295,-6, 299-301. 305, 330, 334, 336, 338, 341-3, 347, 352-4, 409, 448, 453-4, 500, 514-5, 610, 646, 656-7, 701, 707-8, 710, 712-3, 721, 723, 726, 745, 765, 773, 793, 795-6; *letters,* 708, 715-8

Wright, —, 104

Wyeth, Nathaniel, 771, 796

Yamhill Valley, 685, 767

Yampa River, 754

Yaulwager, Louis, 534

Yerba Buena, 27, 36-7, 47, 120-1, 138, 288, 324, 338, 677, 692-3, 699-702, 707, 710, 751, 795; *see* San Francisco

Young, Brigham, 111, 113, 267

Young, Ella (Pringle), 160

Young, Samuel C., 214, 409, 417, 794

Yount, George, 148, 303, 342, 446

Yuba (Juba) River, 147, 294, 297, 299-301, 305, 332, 336-7, 343, 345, 347, 353, 355, 365, 377, 425, 709, 717

L'Envoi: Errata

I take leave of this book in parting with the index, and I am assured that readers will find it a happy hunting ground for large and small mistakes, all of which reflect upon my intelligence and industry. I invite hunters to share their bag with me, and by way of opening the season, call attention to the following:

p. 26, Note 7. For "Poughskeepsie" read "Poughkeepsie"; and for "1922" read "1932."

p. 54, last paragraph. For "Hastings conducted" read "the wagons Hastings conducted passed down the canyons of the Weber."

p. 57, line 5. For "south" read "north."

p. 90, Note 41. For "Thomas" read "John."

p. 107, line 3. For "site" read "sight."

p. 289. The bracketed date "[August]" is insufficient correction for "20th of September;" compare Reed's diary.

p. 377, Note 59. For "Coldstream Creek" read "Coldstream Valley."

p. 378, Note 60. The location of Mule Springs is carelessly stated; refer to p. 452, Note 3, for better information.

p. 401, Note 10. For "December" read "November."

p. 413, Note 76. For "the following month" read "later in the month."

p. 447, Note 10. For "Whig interests" read "published in the Whig interest."

p. 448, Note 116. Reed participated not in the Natividad campaign of mid-November, 1846, but in the Santa Clara campaign of early January, 1847. (It will be seen that in this book I have been decisively defeated by Natividad.)

p. 774, Note 151. For "John" read "William J."

Trouble with names may be observed here and there. Thus proper spellings are: (p. 104) Deslauriers; (p. 105) Keithly; (p. 106) P. D. Papin; (p. 350) Rhoads; (p. 391) Robidoux; (p. 397) Rickreall [in the second name]; (p. 399) Gary; (p. 401) Boggs's and Ames's; (p. 410) Buckelew; (p. 453) Moutrey; (p. 471) Quivvey; (p. 760) Charles M. Weber; (p. 794) Burger.

Here and there words have crept into or out of the text with no harm done. I am charmed with one typographical error; on p. 408, Note 52, "ruddy" was originally "muddy." After further reflection, I feel that I should have followed Marcus Whitman rather than Peter H. Burnett, and on p. 116 indicated that the families who wintered at Waiilatpu in 1846-1847 numbered six, not five.

DLM